# THE

## Faith of Our Fathers

# THE

# Faith of Our Fathers

AN ANTHOLOGY

EXPRESSING THE ASPIRATIONS OF THE

AMERICAN COMMON MAN

1790–1860

———◄•►———

EDITED BY

# IRVING MARK

AND

# EUGENE L. SCHWAAB

# OCTAGON BOOKS

A DIVISION OF FARRAR, STRAUS AND GIROUX

New York   1976

## OCTAGON BOOKS

A DIVISION OF FARRAR, STRAUS & GIROUX, INC.

19 Union Square West

New York, N.Y. 10003


Library of Congress Cataloging in Publication Data

Mark, Irving, 1908-          ed.
        The faith of our fathers.

        Reprint of the ed. published by Knopf, New York.
        1.   United   States—Politics   and   government—1789-1815—
        Sources. 2. United States—Politics and government—1815-1861
        —Sources.   I. Schwaab, Eugene Lincoln, 1909-        II. Title.

[E302.1.M37   1976]                    323.4′01′0973                    76-13498
ISBN 0-374-95286-8

# PREFACE

———————◆▶—————————

THIS BOOK is an anthology expressing the democratic aspirations
of the American common man. The "faith of our fathers" is presented through writings, speeches, resolutions, and petitions that
exemplify the ideals of political, social, and economic betterment
of the American plain people. These expressions represent much
that is good in the American way of life.

Today, more than ever before, Americans invoke their democratic heritage for guidance in political action. Even those whose
practices identify them with intolerance and bigotry claim the
sanction of American tradition. Since this tradition is inadequately
understood by many, this volume may serve to clarify its meaning.
These statements from the American past should cast light upon
the present period of deepening doubt and confusion, and they
should serve as well to hearten the friends and confound the enemies of the people today.

The materials in this anthology show the democratic character
of our Revolutionary heritage. They depict the struggles of ordinary men and women to fulfill the promise of the Declaration of
Independence. The sources encompass the period 1790–1860, when
these strivings molded the American pattern into a definite form.

Some may suggest that the American faith ought to be described
by more selections in praise of our achievements. But those who
enjoy democratic rights usually take them for granted, rather than
passionately expound them. Clearly, the democratic faith is a tradition of struggle and not of self-congratulation. It is affirmed
best by those who strove towards its fulfillment, for they of necessity advanced the now forgotten arguments that won rights now
enjoyed.

This anthology is concerned with those who were of or close to the common people, rather than those who spoke for them from high places. The ideas of men like Jefferson, Jackson, and Lincoln, whose inspiring words epitomize the hopes of the common man, are well known. But little noted have been the words of Sojourner Truth, David Brown, Robert Walker, and the multitudes of carpenters, mechanics, farmers, and other toiling people. Nevertheless, from such ordinary people and their less renowned leaders does the program of a great leader in large measure stem. It is their voices that have moved statesmen to present the demands of the people in legislatures and constitutional conventions.

Statements by the plain people have not been recorded as abundantly as those of men of eminence. We have therefore often had to look from the plain people to their lesser leaders, such as George Hay, Norton S. Townshend, Dr. Smith A. Boughton, Dorothea Dix, and Rev. David Rice—men and women of some education, many of them ministers, lawyers, legislators, and teachers. Indeed, the democratic faith was often expressed by the merest handful of nonconformists standing at bay or pleading for their visions to unheeding men. Perhaps these rebels and reformers have served to answer the "where to?" and the "what next?". To these voices of, and spokesmen for, the many, this anthology is devoted.

Because of the integrated character of the democratic viewpoint, the same individuals were often found championing nearly all phases of the quest for freedom. The temptation to cite them repeatedly was great but had to be resisted in order to give as many as possible a hearing that anthologists have often confined to the few. An anthology that traces the contour can never claim to be the mountain itself. Nor is this one presented as the only or best sketch possible. The problem of choice always plagues the anthologist. Although many readers may have in mind more appropriate selections, we hope these will be found to fulfill their purpose—to express the democratic aspirations of the American common man.

Subject synopses and editorial and biographical notes are included, but the sources speak for themselves. Their vitality transcends any inadequacies of presentation. They themselves contribute most to the clarification of the concepts discussed in these volumes. They are the grass roots of the American heritage.

Since some of these selections may be of interest to the professional scholar, we have reproduced them exactly as they appear in the earliest text we could generally secure, except for a few minor changes indicated in square brackets and ellipses dictated by rigorous space limitations. Moreover, even inconsistencies in style and spelling have been faithfully recorded, except in some few cases where distortion of meaning or extreme awkwardness would result. The reader will find that this procedure, without impairing readability, transmits an authentic flavor to the collection. The date in the descriptive title indicates when the work first appeared.

We wish to express our gratitude for the many courtesies and suggestions extended by library staffs, research directors and executive secretaries of various organizations, and professional colleagues, but the sole responsibility for this work is ours. We record our thanks for the encouragement and suggestions rendered by those who have read all or substantial parts of the manuscript in various stages of preparation: Dean Harry A. Carman, Professors Arthur C. Cole, Merle Curti, Ralph H. Gabriel, and Allan Nevins. Professor Leo Henkin and Murray Young of Brooklyn College, Samuel M. Greenstone, Murray Rogofsky, and Zachary A. Serwer, as well as student assistants, have helped in the many details of readying the final draft.

IRVING MARK
*Brooklyn College*

EUGENE L. SCHWAAB
*Newton Center, Massachusetts*

# CONTENTS

# VI: COMMUNITY HUMANENESS 163

# VII: FREE PUBLIC EDUCATION 193

## VIII: PEACE AMONG NATIONS 225

# X: SHARE THE LAND 287

## XI: RIGHT TO EARN A LIVING 325

## XII: EQUITABLE RETURN FOR, WORK DONE 353

C: JACKSONIAN DEMOCRACY, 1824–40

D: DEMOCRACY AT STAKE, 1841–60

# THE

## *Faith of Our Fathers*

WE HOLD THESE TRUTHS to be self-evident, that all men are created equal, that they are endowed by their Creator with certain unalienable Rights, that among these are Life, Liberty and the pursuit of Happiness. That to secure these rights, Governments are instituted among Men, deriving their just powers from the consent of the governed, That whenever any Form of Government becomes destructive of these ends, it is the Right of the People to alter or to abolish it, and to institute new Government, laying its foundation on such principles and organizing its powers in such form, as to them shall seem most likely to effect their Safety and Happiness.

—— THE UNANIMOUS DECLARATION OF THE THIRTEEN UNITED STATES OF AMERICA, JULY 4, 1776 *

* P. L. Ford (ed.): *The Writings of Thomas Jefferson*, 10 v. (New York: 1892–9), II, 50.

# CHAPTER ONE

## CIVIL RIGHTS

———◆———

*He then said that another distinction had been set up, that this law was not to restrain the freedom, but the licentiousness of speech. This, he observed, was an epithet which might be applied to any attempt to restrain usurpation. Men find no difficulty in pronouncing opinions to be both false and licentious, which differ from their own. That this same distinction (if it was just) would empower Congress to regulate religion, the freedom of which is secured by the same article which secures the freedom of speech. . . .*
———JOHN TAYLOR: *On the Alien and Sedition Laws,*
Virginia House of Delegates, December 13, 1798

*All, too, will bear in mind this sacred principle, that though the will of the majority is in all cases to prevail, that will to be rightful must be reasonable; that the minority possess their equal rights, which equal law must protect, and to violate would be oppression. . . . If there be any among us who would wish to dissolve this Union or to change its republican form, let them stand undisturbed as monuments of the safety with which error of opinion may be tolerated where reason is left free to combat it.*
———THOMAS JEFFERSON: *First Inaugural Address,*
March 4, 1801

Sources of the quotations on the preceding page:

JOHN TAYLOR: *Virginia Report of 1799–1800, Touching the Alien and Sedition Laws* . . . (Richmond, Va.: 1850), 26.

THOMAS JEFFERSON: James D. Richardson: *A Compilation of Messages and Papers of the Presidents, 1789–1897*, 10 v. (Washington, D. C.: 1898–9), I, 322.

THE conception of civil liberties as the rights to think, speak, and assemble freely and to vote and hold office is deeply rooted in the American heritage. As means to an end these rights have been sought in every quest for political, social, and economic betterment; demand for them lay in part behind the Pilgrim and Puritan flight from Anglican intolerance and in Roger Williams's search for "soul liberty." Regarded as ends in themselves, civil liberties have been sought as essential to human dignity and self-expression.

The struggle of the American people to attain civil liberty had important colonial beginnings. One of the early historic battles was fought by John Zenger, a New York publisher who lent the columns of his *Weekly Journal* in November 1734 to an attack on Governor Cosby. Zenger was brought to trial for printing "seditious libels," and after two prominent attorneys were disbarred for participating in his defense, an eighty year old Philadelphia lawyer, Andrew Hamilton, took the case. Boldly pleading "truth" as the defense over the court's denial that he could so plead, Hamilton appealed to the jury, painting his case as "the Cause of Liberty . . . [the liberty of] opposing arbitrary Power . . . by speaking and writing Truth." * In defiance of the court's directed verdict, the jury returned one of "not guilty," thus establishing the precedent that a jury and not a judge should determine whether statements were libelous.

Recognizing the importance of civil liberties, the Revolutionary Fathers wrote a bill of rights into most state constitutions and into

* A Brief Narrative of the Case and Tryal of John Peter Zenger, Printer of the New-York Weekly Journal (Boston: 1738), 44.

the Federal Constitution as well. The property requirement for the franchise was reduced somewhat in five states; personal property was made acceptable in several more. All taxpayers were allowed to vote for the Pennsylvania legislators and for the North Carolina representatives. Universal male suffrage was written into the Vermont constitution of 1777.* Religious tests for citizenship, however, survived in a few states until the Civil War; in many states such tests were required for office-holding during the same period; and in a few, thereafter.

The first crucial test of free speech under the Constitution came with the Federalist attempts to suppress Jeffersonian opposition by means of the Alien and Sedition Laws. These curbs on any speech or writing showing "intent to defame" the President or Congress, or to bring them "into contempt or disrepute," brought widespread resistance similar to that expressed in Woodford County, Kentucky, or by General John Armstrong, George Hay, and David Brown (1, 2, 3, and Chapter Two, 1). The inviolable right of the individual to his opinions and beliefs was maintained by John Taylor of Caroline and George Nicholas in support of Virginia's rejection of the Sedition Law. Such popular protests prompted the Virginia and Kentucky Resolutions, which used arguments drawn from the pens of Madison and Jefferson to prove these laws unconstitutional.

Since the franchise arrangements of the Revolutionary era were still recent, there was little popular pressure for further change during the Federalist period. Nevertheless, there was some progress: in 1792, Delaware gave up the requirement that all voters be landed-property owners and gave the suffrage to all who paid taxes to a certain amount; and in this same decade Georgia and New Hampshire eliminated even the second qualification.

During the Jeffersonian period the administration was well disposed towards preserving free speech and widening the franchise. Jefferson's tolerance of "error of opinion" prevented any significant violation of free speech. Jefferson practiced the precepts voiced in his First Inaugural Address by getting Congress not to reenact the Alien and Sedition Laws and by giving wide latitude to the activities of the Essex Junto and other secessionists. Furthermore, the Republicans lent encouragement to the extension of franchise.

* Vermont was not admitted as a state until 1791.

Thus, although the pressures reflected in the *Virginia Argus,* July 31, 1801 (4), failed in Virginia, those represented by John Cramer's plea (5) gave the vote in New York to all taxpayers in 1821 and to all white men in 1826. Connecticut and Massachusetts took the first step in 1818 and 1821 respectively; Maryland and South Carolina took the second in 1810. By the 1830's the people rather than the legislatures had won the right to select electors. Moreover, in the face of pressure from the Jackson men congressional caucus nomination of presidential candidates had yielded to nomination in party convention.

The Jacksonian era was a time for popular stirrings. The small farmer, mechanic, and worker were on the march. George Bancroft's *July Fourth Oration* of 1826 voiced the democratic faith in people echoed in 1829 in the summons of *The Cause of the People* "to choose representatives from among their own body." Nurtured by the Workingman parties of Philadelphia, New York, and Boston, the Eastern seedbeds of democracy sprouted. By the end of the thirties their influence conditioned Democratic party politics and prepared the way for Loco Focoism, the expression of radicalism among the New York Democrats. Moreover, more states adopted white male suffrage—New York in 1826, Tennessee in 1834, and Mississippi in 1832. Although Virginia was stirred by arguments such as those advanced in the Memorial of the Non-Freeholders of Richmond (6), victory did not come to the non-freeholders until 1850.

Although the Nation under Jackson tried hard not to face the slave question, this issue threatened the tradition of free speech. The South was passing from apology for the "necessary evil" to resentment of all criticism of the "positive blessing." Fear stifled the right of petition in Congress; suppression of free speech drove John Quincy Adams and others to its defense even for abolitionists. From the murder of Reverend Elijah P. Lovejoy, despite his cry for protection of the law (7), from the burning of Pennsylvania Hall, which followed Lewis C. Gunn's appeal for free speech (8), and from other such incidents, thinking men of the North gradually learned their liberties, too, were threatened.

Grave dangers confronted free speech in the two decades preceding the Civil War. The proslavery South took the offensive. Nativist and anti-Catholic intolerance subverted the democratic heritage (see Chapters Four and Nine). Conservatives frowned upon the projects for social betterment that flourished in these decades—the communistic utopias at New Harmony and elsewhere, farmers' dreams of homesteads, and factory workers' militant trade unions. Opposition to these stirrings made necessary constant watchfulness to keep open the lanes of thought. In such spirit the *Social Revolutionist,* a radical Ohio periodical, proclaimed in January 1856: "We believe it the right of all to utter any candid thought, however heretical, unpopular or revolutionary." *

Progress was made towards a universal franchise. Universal white male suffrage was won in New Jersey in 1844, in Louisiana and Connecticut in 1845, in Virginia in 1850, and in Ohio in 1851. By 1860, arguments such as those reflected in George S. Camp's *Democracy* (9) had won the day in all states but Delaware, Massachusetts, North Carolina, Pennsylvania, and Rhode Island. In the meantime, women's quest for equality with men in suffrage, in legal status, and in the professions received vivid formulation in the Declaration of Sentiments at Seneca Falls in 1848 (10), Sojourner Truth's homely arguments at the Akron convention (12), Dr. Harriot Hunt's protest (13) against tax payments, and the Protest by Henry Blackwell and Lucy Stone (14). Ridicule and abuse, ruthless discrimination and physical violence, often greeted these efforts. Part of the difficulty can be perceived from Susan B. Anthony's testy defense of bloomers. She remarked that she found it impossible to obtain a man's attention to her talk when he was completely occupied with gazing at her ankles. By the time of the Civil War, a few women had made a successful breach in the professions; but many decades were to pass before there was real progress in the fight for women's rights.

The third issue of the battle for universal suffrage was the ballot for the free Negro. At the Ohio Constitutional Convention in 1850–1, Norton S. Townshend (11) saw no reason why democracy should "not [be] like christianity, comprehensive enough to embrace the whole family of man." But his was a lone cry and gained support only after the Civil War. By 1890 only six of the

* *The Social Revolutionist; A Medium for Free Discussion of General Principles and Practical Measures, Pertaining to Human Progress and General Well-Being,* I (1856), no. 1, p. 4.

thirty-four states permitted the Negro to qualify as a voter. Here indeed was an unvanquished frontier. Even today, the Negro insistently, but often vainly, still clamors for equal status.

---

## 1.

RESOLUTIONS ON THE ALIEN AND SEDITION ACTS FROM WOODFORD
COUNTY, KENTUCKY *
[1798]

*Ostensibly aimed at "dangerous" aliens and at editors guilty of "false and malicious" writings against the Government or of bringing its officials "into contempt or disrepute," the Alien and Sedition Acts in effect threatened Jeffersonian editors with heavy penalties. Resolutions such as these from Woodford County, Kentucky, which led to the adoption of the Virginia and Kentucky Resolutions, defended free speech and press and denounced the war policy of the Federalists against revolutionary France. The reproduction of these resolutions in a Vermont periodical indicates how widespread was the public reaction.*

1. RESOLVED, That we will, at the hazard of our lives and fortunes, support the Constitution and Independence of the United States. That being deeply impressed with the apprehensions that our Liberties are in danger, it becomes the primary duty of every good citizen to guard, as a faithful centinel, his constitutional rights, and to repel all violation of them, from whatever quarter offered.

2. *Resolved,* That the acts passed during the present session of Congress, respecting *Aliens,* and for the punishment of *Sedition,* are direct violations of the Constitution, and outrages against our most valuable rights—That to speak, write, and censure freely, are privileges of which a freeman cannot divest himself, much less be abridged in them by others: That for the servants of the people

* *The Scourge of Aristocracy, and Repository of Important Political Truths* (Fairhaven, Vermont: 1798), 132–5.

to tell those who created them, that they shall not, at their peril, examine into the conduct of, nor censure those servants for the abuse of power commited to them, is tyranny more insufferable than Asiatic: That the freedom of speech, the liberty of the press, trial by jury, and self-defence, are among the inseparable rights of Freemen: no one of which can be abridged, or taken away, without sinking and debasing him into the condition of a slave.

3. Resolved, That we deplore, as one of the most unfortunate events that could befall us, a war with the French Republic. . . .

4. Resolved, That we deprecate as an event of all others the most impolitic and humiliating, an alliance with Great Britain. . . .

5. Resolved, That we will, to the utmost of our ability, comply with any congressional demands for the purpose of repelling invasion and resisting attempts against our liberty and independence, from what quarter soever offered; but that we consider all maritime offensive operations as destructive and impolitic, tending only to accumulate the public debt, and give additional strength and influence to the dangerous and exhorbitant powers lately committed to the executive department.

6. *Resolved,* That fulsome and adulatory addresses to agents and servants of our own creating, are slavish, and anti-republican.

That it is prostrating the majesty and dignity of the people, puffing up those servants with false pride and vanity; filling them with ambition; and fixing their minds with stronger desires for increase of power and influence, to which men in office are always ready without any encouragement, to grasp at. That altho' flattery and adulation may be fit offerings for prostrate slaves to render at the altar of their tyrant Masters, yet, to true republican patriots the honor of serving their country, and a conscious and faithful discharge of those duties, is the only genuine and lasting honor they ought to expect or can receive.

7. *Resolved,* that the foregoing resolutions be published in the Kentucky Gazette and Herald, and such other newspapers as will please to give them a place, and that copies hereof be transmited to our Representative to be laid before the legislature and President of the United States.

JOHN TANNER, *Chairman.*
HERMAN BOWMAN, *Clerk.*

2.

John Armstrong:
ON THE ALIEN AND SEDITION LAWS *
[1798]

*Born in Pennsylvania, General John Armstrong (1758–1843)
was the son of a general and served in the Revolutionary
War. Although he was at first a Federalist, he became a supporter of the Jeffersonian party and played an outstanding
part in the struggle in New York against the Alien and Sedition laws. In this address he argued that the vague and comprehensive restraints under the Sedition Law tended to subvert
the Constitution.*

To the SEDITION LAW our objections are still stronger than to
the alien law; because the abuses to which it is liable, are equally
vicious in their character, and more general in their operation.
The former [i.e. the Alien Law] assails the *few*, the latter [i.e.
the Sedition] attacks the *many*. The former is directed at *foreigners;* the latter is levelled at *ourselves*. The former tyrannizes over
men, who in general have been born and bred under *oppression*.
But it is the superlative wickedness of the latter, to convert freemen into slaves.

By this law the citizens of these states are prohibited, under
the severest penalties, from expressing even their *disapprobation*
of any part of the conduct of the President, or of either house of
Congress, *through the medium of the press;* and whatever has in
the smallest degree a tendency to bring either into *disrepute* is
liable to be *punished* by fine and *imprisonment*. What stronger,
what more precise definition of slavery can be given than this?
That we can state no belief, that we can hazard no opinion, that
has even a *tendency* to lessen the public estimation of a public
servant.

The genius of this law pervades all its details, the crime is so
defined, that we know not when we become guilty of it; for in the
wide range of political opinion, how many things may be innocently said, how many even usefully suggested, which may be so

* John Armstrong: *To the Senate and Representatives of the United States*
(Poughkeepsie, N. Y.: 1798), 1–2.

construed as to incur these penalties? With a jury of partisans, warmed by zeal, and heated by contention, selected by an officer in the appointment of the President, and holding that appointment during the pleasure of the president, what opinion can be safe? To question the integrity, to doubt the wisdom, to assert or even to insinuate the ignorance of a chief magistrate, leads directly to ruin; and yet it will scarcely be deemed *impossible* that a president may be a profligate man or vicious magistrate; that he may be weak in intellect, or wanting in information; but, under the operation of this law, the most enlightened nation upon earth, must not only bear these imperfections with patience, they must also conceal them with care; to hint them to a neighbour, exposes you to *fine;* to breathe them to a brother subjects you to *imprisonment.*

A law thus alarming and despotic; thus new to the creed, and offensive to the feelings of a free people, cannot be bottomed on a constitution we love and admire. In this conclusion we feel ourselves warranted no less by the *spirit* than the *letter* of that instrument. . . .

To accomplish these [purposes set forth in the Preamble], it became necessary to enjoin certain duties, and to prohibit certain acts. Among these *prohibited acts* is the exercise of that very power we complain of, *"Congress shall make no law abridging the freedom of speech or of the press."* A prohibition more express can scarcely be devised; and yet, extraordinary as it may appear, there is a portion of the national legislature who have contended that the law in question does not infringe this prohibition. The argument most relied upon in defence of their construction, may be thus concisely stated: "The constitution indeed prohibits the passing of any law which shall abridge the freedom of speech and of the press. But the law in question does not abridge the *freedom* of either, it but prevents their *licentiousness.*" The fact however is, that this defence turns, not on a logical distinction, not on a clear and well marked difference, but on a mere quibble. It supposes that liberty and licentiousness are two things totally different; whereas they are the same thing under different modifications and degrees. . . .

3.

*George Hay:*
### AN ESSAY ON THE LIBERTY OF THE PRESS *
[1799]

*George Hay (1765–1830) was born in Virginia, son of an innkeeper. He became a lawyer and was prominent in the prosecution of Aaron Burr for treason. A staunch Jeffersonian, he was an able writer and a persistent critic of Federalist policy. In this selection Hay demonstrates the indivisibility of the concept of "freedom" and contends that the Sedition Act violated the freedom of the press guaranteed in the First Amendment.*

This argument may be summed up in a few words. The word "freedom" has a meaning. It is either absolute, that is, exempt from all law, or it is qualified, that is regulated by law. If it be exempt from the control of law, the Sedition Bill which controls the "freedom" of the press, is unconstitutional. But if it be regulated by law, the amendment which declares that Congress shall make no law to abridge the freedom of the press, which freedom however may be regulated by law, is the grossest absurdity, that ever was conceived by the human mind.

That by the words "freedom of the press" is meant a total exemption of the press from legislative control, will further appear, from the following cases, in which it is manifest, that the word freedom is used with this signification and no other.

It is obvious in itself, and it is admitted by all men, that freedom of speech, means the power uncontrolled by law, of speaking either truth or falsehood at the discretion of the individual, provided no other individual be injured. This power is, as yet, in its full extent in the United States. A man may say every thing which his passion can suggest, he may employ all his time and all his talents, if he is wicked enough to do so, in speaking against the government matters that are false, scandalous, and malicious, but he is admitted by the majority of Congress to be sheltered by the

---

* George Hay: *An Essay on the Liberty of the Press, Respectfully Inscribed to the Republican Printers throughout the United States, by Hortensius* (Philadelphia: 1799), 37–42.

article in question, which forbids a law abridging the freedom of speech. If then freedom of speech means, in the construction of the constitution, the privilege of speaking any thing without control, the words freedom of the press, which form a part of the same sentence, mean the privilege of printing any thing without control.

Happily for mankind, the word "freedom" begins now to be applied to religion also. In the United States it is applied in its fullest force, and religious freedom is completely understood to mean the power uncontrolled by law of professing and publishing any opinions on religious topics, which any individual may choose to profess or publish, and of supporting those opinions by any statements he may think proper to make. The fool may not only say in his heart, there is no God, but he may announce if he pleases his atheism to the world. He may endeavor to corrupt mankind, not only by opinions that are erroneous, but by facts which are false. Still however he will be safe, because he lives in a country where religious freedom is established. If then freedom of religion, will not permit a man to be punished, for publishing any opinions on religious topics, and supporting those opinions by false facts, surely freedom of the press, which is the medium of all publications, will not permit a man to be punished, for publishing any opinion on any subject, and supporting it by any opinion whatever.

4.

To the Citizens of Richmond, Not Freeholders *
[July 29, 1801]

*The struggle for extending the franchise to all Virginia freemen had its early champions in Nathaniel Bacon, Jr., Thomas Jefferson, and James Madison. The cudgels were picked up again shortly after 1800 by William Munford, a state senator, and by the writer of this letter in the* Virginia Argus. *Recurring attacks on the property qualification for voting cropped up in the* Virginia Enquirer *and resounded in the debates at William and Mary College. Defeat of similar strivings in the Virginia legislature intensified the pressure*

* *Virginia Argus* (Richmond: July 31, 1801).

*that finally led to the Constitutional Convention of 1829–30 (see 6). The much sought reform, however, did not take place until 1850.*

I HAVE often wondered that the citizens of Richmond should so long have been silent on the mode of election for the representative of that city: when I say "the citizens of Richmond," I mean that part of them, who, by the present regulations, are precluded from the right of suffrage; the numerous and respectable body of mechanics, and those of the mercantile body, who are not landholders. . . . Too long has it been, that they, who, by their industry and activity, have been increasing the wealth of the city and adding to its weight in the community, have been shut out from the right of suffrage, whilst they are taxed, not singly for the purposes of the corporation, but to the general revenue. It is a principle of democratic republicanism, that no man shall be subject to taxation but by his own assent; that he shall not be bound to contribute to the public aid but by his own concurrence, expressed thro' his representative. It is a principle acknowledged even in the British government in *theory*, tho' lost in *practice*. It should be *our* aim to preserve it in *fact* and in *action*. . . .

Recurring to the declaration of rights, I would ask, does not the native citizen, who has been reared among you, who has spent his youthful days in the regular acquirement of a trade by which he is to earn the bread of independence, who is in the exercise of that trade upon the spot, who has taken to his bosom, from amongst your daughters, a partner to share his felicities and participate [in] that independence which his industry will ensure him, give "sufficient evidence of permanent, common interest with, and attachment to the community"? Does not the adventurous mechanic, who, with his all, accompanied by his family, leaves his native European home, seeks your peaceful shores, and turns himself with steady industry to the pursuits of the occupation in which he has been bred, give sufficient "evidence of permanent common interest with, and attachment to the community"? And, if so, why should we be told that the qualifications of electors cannot be altered? . . . Will it be said, I ask, that this is not sufficient evidence of permanent attachment, because the one or the other of these, the native citizen, or he who seeks to be naturalized, has not purchased LAND amongst you? How many of your most useful and hardy citizens, those who, in fact, would, in the hour of danger, stand the brunt of your battles, are there, whose whole little capital, that which was absolutely necessary to set them out in business, it would take to purchase a small parcel of land: how very many whose pursuits and avocations require that this little capital should be in constant, uninterrupted motion! And because this useful mechanic cannot put his foot on a particular spot of earth, and say "thou art mine," whilst he is rendering every service to his country which industry, virtue, activity and economy can render, whilst that country is continually drawing upon his personal capital, by taxation, whilst he is standing in the front of the battle, and bullets whistle by his ears, he shall be told, "You have no right to interfere in the government; we will tax you as we please, and you shall not gainsay it; you shall have no voice in public debate; you shall have no choice in the mode of fixing the public burthen, you shall submit to *all* the laws, but you shall not, like us *landholders,* have the solace of feeling that you have a participation in the enaction of them"! Is this republican representation? Is it republican virtue or justice?

. . . Residence, citizenship, usefulness in the community, are, in truth, the only qualifications which ought to be required. Independent men, whether poor or rich, should always have a voice in democratic governments; I mean those who are citizens, and have abjured all other allegiance than to the society in which they live. . . . The most useful members of a city, those in whom much the larger portion of industry, economy & activity are to be found are the mechanical and mercantile, and you, citizens of Richmond, of this description, though you are not landholders, make a proper representation to the assembly, and it will not be in vain; remind them that you are subject to taxation, to be called to the field; let it be brought to their recollection that you and your property contribute to the public stock and wealth, and they will feel it a duty to admit you to the rights of freemen; and, though power, exclusive power, be the darling of man, yet the liberal minded of your fellow citizens who *are* the possessors of freeholds, will rejoice that you have obtained your proper footing; they will not grudge to their laborious and worthy fellow citizen and brother mechanic this participation of privilege. Justice de-

mands that this modification should take place; if representation
be reducible to rule, you are entitled to claim it, for, let it be confined to *personal* qualification, who can better claim it? Can the
enervated sluggard, living on his landed income and surrounded
by his slaves, compare with you, active and hardy citizens, when
most he may be wanted? Let it be *wealth,* otherwise money, the
sinews of government, as it has been termed, that is to be represented: take the aggregate, and, in every populous and mercantile
town, it will be found that the interests which I now advocate are
fourfold, speaking at the least, the landed. Thus, if it be *property*
that is to be represented, and not *persons,* you ought to be placed
upon higher ground; if it be *persons* and not property, your mode
of life, your active employments say to the priviledged elector,
"Shame on ye: ye lie in your bed; ye loll at your ease; you render
no service to your country, no useful calling occupies your time;
but you are the owner of a beggarly bit of soil, and you make laws
for me, by which I must be bound, though I execrate them."

*July 29, 1801.*                                              A CITIZEN.

## 5.

### John Cramer:
#### PLEA FOR EXTENSION OF THE FRANCHISE *
[September 24, 1821]

*John Cramer (1779–1870) was born in New York of German
descent. He practiced law and as a Democrat held various
legislative offices, including two terms in the United States
Congress. This speech, delivered in the New York Constitutional Convention of 1821, argued against property qualifications, stressing the priority of human rights over property
rights. It prompted Martin Van Buren, also a delegate, to
ask: "Is that not a little too Democratic?" Although the
Convention extended the suffrage, it retained a taxpayer
qualification. Five years later, however, Cramer's position was
fully vindicated when a referendum rejected even this limitation.*

* New York Constitutional Convention of 1821: *Reports of the Proceedings and Debates* (Albany, N.Y.: 1821), 238–9.

. . . I have heard much on this subject for several years past, and so far as I have been able to judge, there is but one sentiment among the intelligent and virtuous, which is "grant universal suffrage to all, except those excluded by crime, and abolish the distinction, in regard to electors which now prevails, because of one man's possessing more of the soil than another." . . .

But it has been said, that the landed interest of this state, bears more than its equal proportion of the burthens of taxation. This, sir, I deny. All property, real and personal, is equally taxed, and bears its just proportion of the public burthens; but, sir, is not life and liberty dearer than property, and common to all, and entitled to equal protection? No, sir. That gentlemen appeared to be impressed with the idea, that the *turf* is of all things the most sacred, and that for its security, you must have thirty-two grave turf senators from the soil, in that *Sanctum Sanctorum,* the senate chamber, and then all your rights will be safe. No matter whether they possess intelligence, if they are selected by your rich landholders, all is well.—But it is alledged [*sic*] by gentlemen, who have spoken on that side of the house, that the poor are a degraded class of beings, have no will of their own, and would not exercise this high prerogative with independence and sound discretion if entrusted with it, and, therefore, it would be unwise to trust them with ballots.—This, sir, is unfounded: for more integrity and more patriotism are generally found in the labouring class of the community than in the higher orders. These are the men, who add to the substantial wealth of the nation, in peace. These are the men, who constitute your defence in war. Of such men, consisted your militia, when they met and drove the enemy at Plattsburgh, Sacket's Harbour, Queenston, and Erie; for you found not the rich landholder or speculator in your ranks; and are we told, that these men, because they have no property, are not to be trusted at the ballot boxes! . . . They could, without apprehension, be permitted to handle their muskets, bayonets, powder and balls; but, say the gentlemen, it will not answer to trust them with tickets at the ballot box. I would admonish gentlemen of this committee, to reflect, who they are about to exclude from the right of suffrage, if the amendment under consideration should prevail.—They will exclude your honest industrious mechanics, and many farmers, for many there are, who do not own the soil which they till. And what for? Because your farmers wish it? No, sir, they wish no such thing; they wish to see the men who have defended their soil, participate equally with them in the election of their rulers. Nay, now you exclude most of the hoary headed patriots, who achieved your independence, to whom we are indebted for the very ground we stand upon, and for the liberties we enjoy. But for the toil and sufferings of these men, we should not now be here debating as to forms of government. No, sir, the legitimates would soon have disposed of all this business. And why are these men to be excluded? Not because they are not virtuous, not because they are not meritorious; but, sir, because they are poor and dependant, and can have no will of their own, and will vote as the man who feeds them and clothes them may direct, as one of the honourable gentlemen has remarked. I know of no men in this country, who are not dependant. The rich man is as much dependant upon the poor man for his labour, as the poor man is upon the rich for his wages. I know of no men, who are more dependant upon others for their bread and raiment, than the judges of your supreme court are upon the legislature, and who will pretend that this destroys their independence, or makes them subservient to the views of the legislature? Let us not, sir, disgrace ourselves in the eyes of the world, by expressing such degrading opinions of our fellow citizens. Let us grant universal suffrage, for after all, it is upon the virtue and intelligence of the people that the stability of your government must rest. Let us not brand this constitution with any odious distinctions as to property, and let it not be said of us as has been truly said of most republics, that we have been ungrateful to our best benefactors.

## 6.

### The Memorial of the Non-Freeholders of Richmond, Virginia *
### [1829]

*The Constitutional Convention of 1829 at Richmond was attended by ex-Presidents Madison and Monroe and Chief Justice Marshall, who presented the Richmond memorial with-*

* Virginia, Constitutional Convention, 1829–1830: *Proceedings and Debates of Virginia State Convention of 1829–1830* (Richmond, Va.: 1830), 25–8.

*out approving of it. Similar demands for universal white
male suffrage came from Fairfax County and from western
counties like Shenandoah. Although the final result embodied a small concession to leaseholders and taxpayers, property tests remained. In 1842 the call for another constitutional convention went unheeded; not until 1850 did a
convention meet and belatedly establish white manhood suffrage.*

THE MEMORIAL OF THE NON-FREEHOLDERS OF THE CITY OF RICH-
MOND, RESPECTFULLY ADDRESSED TO THE CONVENTION, NOW AS-
SEMBLED TO DELIBERATE ON AMENDMENTS TO THE CONSTITUTION:

Your memorialists, as their designation imports, belong to that
class of citizens, who, not having the good fortune to possess a
certain portion of land, are, for that cause only, debarred from the
enjoyment of the right of suffrage. Experience has but too clearly
evinced, what, indeed, reason had always foretold, by how frail a
tenure they hold every other right, who are denied this, the highest
prerogative of freemen. The want of it has afforded both the pretext and the means of excluding the entire class, to which your
memorialists belong, from all participation in the recent election of
the body, they now respectfully address. Comprising a very large
part, probably a majority of male citizens of mature age, they have
been passed by, like aliens or slaves, as if destitute of interest, or
unworthy of a voice, in measures involving their future political
destiny: whilst the freeholders, sole possessors, under the existing
Constitution, of the elective franchise, have upon the strength of
that possession alone, asserted and maintained in themselves, the
exclusive power of new-modelling the fundamental laws of the
State: in other words, have seized upon the sovereign authority.

. . . To ascribe to a landed possession, moral or intellectual endowments, would truly be regarded as ludicrous, were it not for
the gravity with which the proposition is maintained. And still
more for the grave consequences flowing from it. Such possession
no more proves him who has it, wiser or better, than it proves him
taller or stronger, than him who has it not. That cannot be a fit
criterion for the exercise of any right, the possession of which does
not indicate the existence, nor the want of it the absence, of any
essential qualification.

But this criterion, it is strenuously insisted, though not perfect, is yet the best human wisdom can devise. It affords the strongest, if not the only evidence of the requisite qualifications; more particularly of what are absolutely essential, "permanent common interest with, and attachment to, the community." Those who cannot furnish this evidence, are therefore deservedly excluded.

Your memorialists do not design to institute a comparison; they fear none that cannot be fairly made between the privileged and the proscribed classes. They may be permitted, however, without disrespect, to remark, that of the latter, not a few possess land: many, though not proprietors, are yet cultivators of the soil: others are engaged in avocations of a different nature, often as useful, pre-supposing no less integrity, requiring as much intelligence, and as fixed a residence, as agricultural pursuits. Virtue, intelligence, are not among the products of the soil. Attachment to property, often a sordid sentiment, is not to be confounded with the sacred flame of patriotism. The love of country, like that of parents and offspring, is engrafted in our nature. It exists in all climates, among all classes, under every possible form of Government. Riches oftener impair it than poverty. Who has it not is a monster. . . .

. . . In the hour of danger, they have drawn no invidious distinctions between the sons of Virginia. The muster rolls have undergone no scrutiny, no comparison with the land books, with a view to expunge those who have been struck from the ranks of freemen. If the landless citizens have been ignominiously driven from the polls, in time of peace, they have at least been generously summoned, in war, to the battlefield. Nor have they disobeyed the summons, or, less profusely than others, poured out their blood in the defence of that country which is asked to disown them. Will it be said they owe allegiance to the Government that gives them protection? Be it so: and if they acknowledge the obligation; if privileges are really extended to them in defence of which they may reasonably be required to shed their blood, have they not motives, irresistible motives, of attachment to the community? Have they not an interest, a deep interest, in perpetuating the blessings they enjoy, and a right, consequently, to guard those blessings, not from foreign aggression merely, but from domestic encroachment? . . .

If we are sincerely republican, we must give our confidence to the principles we profess. We have been taught by our fathers, that all power is vested in, and derived from, the people; not the freeholders: that the majority of the community, in whom abides the physical force, have also the political right of creating and remoulding at will, their civil institutions. Nor can this right be any where more safely deposited. The generality of mankind, doubtless, desire to become owners of property: left free to reap the fruit of their labours, they will seek to acquire it honestly. It can never be their interest to overburthen, or render precarious, what they themselves desire to enjoy in peace. But should they ever prove as base as the argument supposes, force alone; arms, not votes, could effect their designs; and when that shall be attempted, what virtue is there in Constitutional restrictions, in mere wax and paper, to withstand it. To deny to the great body of the people all share in the Government; on suspicion that they may deprive others of their property, to rob them, in advance of their rights; to look to a privileged order as the fountain and depository of all power; is to depart from the fundamental maxims, to destroy the chief beauty, the characteristic feature, indeed, of Republican Government.

## 7.

### *Rev. Elijah P. Lovejoy:*
### TO MY FELLOW CITIZENS *
### [November 5, 1835]

*Elijah P. Lovejoy (1802–37), a native of Maine, moved to Missouri where he taught school, edited a newspaper,* The Observer, *and became a Presbyterian minister. In this paper he thundered against slavery, intemperance, and "popery." When a mob forced his publishers to disclaim abolitionism, Lovejoy disavowed his publishers' policy in this open letter, which appeared in* The Observer, *and declared his determination never to surrender freedom of speech. Persistent mob hostility forced his removal to Alton, Illinois, where his*

* Joseph C. Lovejoy and Owen Lovejoy: *Memoir of the Rev. Elijah P. Lovejoy* (New York: 1836), 144–5, 153–4.

*conversion from gradual to immediate emancipation marked him as a militant abolitionist and caused his press to be destroyed three times. When he and his friends, seeking to protect a fourth press, sallied forth against a mob to prevent the burning of the building, he was murdered. His cry, "Have I not a right to claim the protection of the laws?," swept throughout the North, deeply stirring thoughtful men.*

See the danger, and the natural and inevitable result to which the first step here will lead. To-day a public meeting declares that you shall not discuss the subject of Slavery, in any of its bearings, civil or religious. Right or wrong, the press must be silent. To-morrow, another meeting decides that it is against the peace of society, that the principles of Popery shall be discussed, and the edict goes forth to muzzle the press. The next day, it is in a similar manner, declared that not a word must be said against distilleries, dram shops, or drunkenness. And so on to the end of the chapter. The truth is, my fellow-citizens, if you give ground a single inch, there is no stopping place. I deem it, therefore, my duty to take my stand upon the Constitution. Here is firm ground—I feel it to be such. And I do most respectfully, yet decidedly, declare to you my fixed determination to maintain this ground. We have slaves, it is true, but *I* am not one. I am a citizen of these United States, a citizen of Missouri, free-born; and having never forfeited the inestimable privileges attached to such a condition, I cannot consent to surrender them. But while I maintain them, I hope to do it with all that meekness and humility that become a Christian, and especially a Christian minister. I am ready, not to fight, but to suffer, and if need be, to die for them. . . .

I *do*, therefore, as an American citizen, and Christian patriot, and in the name of Liberty, and Law, and RELIGION, solemnly PROTEST against all these attempts, howsoever or by whomsoever made, to frown down the liberty of the press, and forbid the free expression of opinion. Under a deep sense of my obligations to my country, the church, and my God, I declare it to be my fixed purpose to submit to no such dictation. *And I am prepared to abide the consequences.* I have appealed to the constitution and laws of my country; if they fail to protect me, I APPEAL TO GOD, and with Him I cheerfully rest my cause.

Fellow-citizens, they told me that if I returned to the city, from my late absence, you would surely lay violent hands upon me, and many of my friends besought me not to come. I disregarded their advice, because I plainly saw, or thought I saw, that the Lord would have me come. And up to this moment that conviction of duty has continued to strengthen, until now I have not a shadow of doubt that I did right. I have appeared openly among you, in your streets and market-places, and now I openly and publicly throw myself into your hands. I can die at my post, but I cannot desert it.

———————————

8.

*Lewis C. Gunn:*
ADDRESS ON RIGHT OF FREE DISCUSSION *
[May 16, 1838]

*Lewis C. Gunn (1813–92), the son of a pastor of the Bloomingdale Dutch Reformed Church, was born in New York of Scotch and Scotch-Irish ancestry. When he had to give up preparation for the ministry because of a throat affliction, he entered the printing business in Philadelphia and became an active antislavery leader. In this address, delivered in Pennsylvania Hall, which a mob burned to the ground the next day, Gunn pleaded for free speech at a meeting attended by William Lloyd Garrison, Angelina Grimké-Weld, and other prominent antislavery leaders. In 1841, illness caused him to go West and he finally settled in California, where he prospected, practiced medicine, and maintained an interest in the Sonora Herald, while continuing his activity in the "Sons of Temperance" and the antislavery movement.*

To a foreigner it may seem strange that in this boasted land of liberty it is necessary to speak on the right of free discussion. Accustomed to hear our vauntings of freedom of speech and of

———

* *History of Pennsylvania Hall, Which Was Destroyed by a Mob, May 17, 1838* (Philadelphia: 1838), 62–5.

the press, of mind and of conscience, this is the last subject which
he would expect to hear argued anywhere in the United States,
much less in the state of Penn, and in this city of brotherly love.
But, strange as it may seem, the churches and public halls of
Philadelphia are closed against the advocates of human rights;
and, I believe, there is not a building in this city, except the one
in which we are now assembled, large enough to accommodate
such a meeting as this, which could have been obtained for the
advocacy even of that most valuable of all rights—the right of free
discussion. The fact can be no longer concealed, that in this land
this right is not enjoyed. There are two and a half millions of slaves
who are never allowed to speak in their own behalf, or tell the
world freely the story of their wrongs. There are also half a million
of so called free people of color, who are permitted to speak with
but little more liberty than the slaves. Nor is this all. Even those
who stand up in behalf of the down-trodden colored man, however
white their skins may be, are slandered, persecuted, mobbed,
hunted from city to city, imprisoned, and, as in the case of the
lamented Lovejoy, put to death! It is unnecessary here to refer
to Amos Dresser, who, for exercising the privilege of a freeman,
and acting in behalf of freedom, was publicly whipped in the
streets of Nashville. I need not speak of another devoted friend
of the oppressed, whose face I see in this assembly, who, some
years ago, was immured in a Baltimore prison, and has since been
led like a criminal to a jail in Boston, for no other crime than publishing what his conscience and his judgment told him was the
truth. Nor need I give a detailed account of the many mobs which
have disgraced our country within the last three or four years—
mobs collected together and infuriated, because some independent
minds and warm hearts had undertaken to canvass the sublime
merits of slavery and the dangers "of emancipation." . . . What,
I ask, do these things prove? Do they not clearly show that we do
not enjoy the right of free discussion? We may speak without reserve, it is true, on the subject of banks, and on many other political
and moral questions; but when slavery is selected as the theme,
when it is proposed to discuss the inalienability of human rights,
then, forsooth, our lips must be locked and our thoughts imprisoned. Our *right* here is assailed, and it is a stab at the *right* to
speak on any and every other subject. What do we mean by the

*right* of free discussion? Is it merely the privilege of "saying what the prevailing voice of the brotherhood will allow?" . . . Then our boasted right is not a right, but only a privilege—a privilege depending on the "voice of the brotherhood," who one day may will for us to speak, and the next for us to be dumb,—or this week may command our silence, and the next crowd in throngs to give a listening ear to our discussions. Depending on circumstances, and yet a right? Why, it is a contradiction in terms. If it is depending on circumstances, then it does not inherently belong to us—we have derived no right from our Creator. A privilege is a privilege, and not a right. Now freedom of speech we spurn as a privilege; we demand it as our own, and we shall exercise it, too, in the face of all the mobs which may array themselves in threatening attitude before us. Our right to speak freely the dictates of our minds and consciences is derived from our Creator, and we have no permission to surrender it ourselves, nor has any other man the permission to wrest it from us. Thus you see that abridging our freedom of speech on the subject of slavery, is tantamount to saying that freedom of speech on all subjects is not our *right*, but that we must depend for it upon "the voice of the brotherhood;"—that voice determining on what subjects we may speak, what kind of thoughts we may utter, and the language in which they must be clothed. Here, then, on the question of slavery the battle must be fought. . . . For this reason alone it is, that so many, since Lovejoy's murder, have taken a decided stand in favor of the abolitionists, although opposed to them in sentiment on the subject of slavery. They have seen the right of free discussion assailed and trampled under foot; and they have discernment enough to perceive that, although silence is now required only on *one* subject, the *right*, in all its length and breadth, is thereby completely destroyed. . . . Those who now remonstrate with the public touching the sin and evils of intemperance, may soon be silenced. The cause of peace may lose its advocates. Nay, subjects now regarded as of vital importance, may upon a fluctuation in the minds and feelings of "the brotherhood," be locked up in the tomb of thought until the day of the final resurrection. I repeat it, we must stand by the right where it is first assailed. And let those who now hesitate, or who take their stand in favor of checking free discussion *on the subject of slavery*, keep before their minds the consequences that may, and probably will, ensue. . . .

Why should men prevent the exercise of this right? It will merely develope the truth and place it in bold relief before the eyes of all. And is there in this house, or in this city, or in this land, a man who fears the truth? If so, you may depend upon it, he is *conscious* of error in his politics, morals, or religion. Such an one, and only such, has reason to be afraid. *Free discussion elicits the truth.*

9.

*George Sidney Camp:*
DEMOCRACY *
[1841]

*This work was offered by Harper and Brothers as an elucida-tion of democratic theory. They included it as part of the Family Library because of its importance and "absence of partisanship." It seems to have remained in print for a con-siderable period, appearing in the Harper trade lists as late as 1902.*

All should have an equal voice in the public deliberations of the state, however unequal in point of circumstances, since human rights, by virtue of which alone we are entitled to vote at all, are the attributes of the man, not of his circumstances. Should the right to vote, the characteristic and the highest prerogative of a freeman, be at the mercy of a casualty? I am rich to-day, worth my hundred thousands; but my wealth consists in stock and mer-chandise; it may be in storehouses, it may be upon the ocean; I have been unable to effect an insurance, or there is some con-cealed legal defect in my policy; the fire or the storms devour my wealth in an hour: am I the less competent to vote? Have I less of the capacity of a moral and intelligent being? Am I the less a good citizen? Is it not enough that I have been deprived of my for-tune—must I be disfranchised by community?

* George Sidney Camp: *Democracy* (New York: 1841), 145–6.

My having a greater or less amount of property does not alter my rights. Property is merely the subject on which rights are exercised; its amount does not alter rights themselves. If it were otherwise, every one of us would be in some degree subject to some wealthier neighbour, and, if the representation of property were consistently carried out, the affairs of every community, instead of being governed by the majority of rational and intelligent beings, would be governed by a preponderance of houses, lands, stocks, plate, jewellery, merchandise, and money. It is not true that one man has more at stake in the commonwealth than another. We all have our rights, and no man has anything more. If we look at the subject philosophically, and consider how much superior man is by nature to what he is by external condition, how much superior his real attributes are to what he acquires from the accidents of fortune, we shall then view the distinctions of rank and wealth in their true comparative insignificance, and make as little difference on these accounts with the political as with the moral man.

10.

DECLARATION OF SENTIMENTS AT THE SENECA FALLS CONVENTION *<br>[July 19–20, 1848]

*In the 1840's the rebellion of women forecast by Abigail Adams began brewing. Led by Mrs. Lucretia Mott and Mrs. Elizabeth C. Stanton, a women's rights convention met at Seneca Falls in 1848, where this "Declaration," drawing inspiration from the Declaration of Independence, was presented by Mrs. Stanton. A series of twelve resolutions followed and were passed unanimously except for the ninth on elective franchise, which was bitterly contested, though finally accepted by a small majority. When the storm of ridicule broke, however, many subsequently withdrew their signatures from the Declaration. This convention was the prelude to many others.*

* E. C. Stanton, S. B. Anthony, and M. J. Gage: *History of Woman Suffrage*, 3 v. (Rochester, N.Y.: 1887), I, 70–1.

When, in the course of human events, it becomes necessary for one portion of the family of man to assume among the people of the earth a position different from that which they have hitherto occupied, but one to which the laws of nature and of nature's God entitle them, a decent respect to the opinions of mankind requires that they should declare the causes that impel them to such a course.

We hold these truths to be self-evident: that all men and women are created equal; . . . [The deletion is substantially identical with the corresponding passages of the Declaration of Independence.]

The history of mankind is a history of repeated injuries and usurpations on the part of man toward woman, having in direct object the establishment of an absolute tyranny over her. To prove this, let facts be submitted to a candid world.

He has never permitted her to exercise her inalienable right to the elective franchise.

He has compelled her to submit to laws, in the formation of which she had no voice.

He has withheld from her rights which are given to the most ignorant and degraded men—both natives and foreigners.

Having deprived her of this first right of a citizen, the elective franchise, thereby leaving her without representation in the halls of legislation, he has oppressed her on all sides.

He has made her, if married, in the eye of the law, civilly dead.

He has taken from her all right in property, even to the wages she earns.

He has made her, morally, an irresponsible being, as she can commit many crimes with impunity, provided they be done in the presence of her husband. In the covenant of marriage, she is compelled to promise obedience to her husband, He becoming, to all intents and purposes, her master—the law giving him power to deprive her of her liberty, and to administer chastisement.

He has so framed the laws of divorce, as to what shall be the proper causes, and in case of separation, to whom the guardianship of the children shall be given, as to be wholly regardless of the happiness of women—the law, in all cases, going upon a false supposition of the supremacy of man, and giving all power into his hands.

After depriving her of all rights as a married woman, if single, and the owner of property, he has taxed her to support a government which recognizes her only when her property can be made profitable to it.

He has monopolized nearly all the profitable employments, and from those she is permitted to follow, she receives but a scanty remuneration. He closes against her all the avenues to wealth and distinction which he considers most honorable to himself. As a teacher of theology, medicine, or law, she is not known.

He has denied her the facilities for obtaining a thorough education, all colleges being closed against her.

He allows her in Church, as well as State, but a subordinate position, claiming Apostolic authority for her exclusion from the ministry, and, with some exceptions, from any public participation in the affairs of the Church.

He has created a false public sentiment by giving to the world a different code of morals for men and women, by which moral delinquencies which exclude women from society, are not only tolerated, but deemed of little account in man.

He has usurped the prerogative of Jehovah himself, claiming it as his right to assign for her a sphere of action, when that belongs to her conscience and to her God.

He has endeavored, in every way that he could, to destroy her confidence in her own powers, to lessen her self-respect, and to make her willing to lead a dependent and abject life.

Now, in view of this entire disfranchisement of one-half the people of this country, their social and religious degradation—in view of the unjust laws above mentioned, and because women do feel themselves aggrieved, oppressed, and fraudulently deprived of their most sacred rights, we insist that they have immediate admission to all the rights and privileges which belong to them as citizens of the United States.

In entering upon the great work before us, we anticipate no small amount of misconception, misrepresentation, and ridicule; but we shall use every instrumentality within our power to effect our object. We shall employ agents, circulate tracts, petition the State and National legislatures, and endeavor to enlist the pulpit and the press in our behalf. We hope this Convention will be followed by a series of Conventions embracing every part of the country.

## 11.

### Norton S. Townshend:
### SPEECH ON NEGRO SUFFRAGE *
### [February 8, 1851]

*Norton S. Townshend (1815–95), born in England, was brought to Ohio in 1830. Here he did farm work, snatching time to read widely in his father's library. After teaching school and studying medicine in New York, he returned to Ohio and became active in the temperance and antislavery movements. In 1848, while in the Ohio Legislature, he championed the repeal of laws that excluded Negroes from common schools and prohibited them from testifying against whites in court. At the Constitutional Convention in 1850, he made the appeal that follows for extending the franchise to Negroes, and a solitary speech in favor of women suffrage, both of which pleas the convention rejected. Later Townshend served as congressman and state senator. After the Civil War he taught agriculture in the Midwest, and he also served as trustee of the State Institution for the Training of Imbeciles.*

To attempt to govern men without seeking their consent is usurpation and tyranny, whether in Ohio or in Austria. There is a portion of the people of this State who have the same right to stand upon this part of God's earth, and to breathe this free air, that you or I have, and yet you seek to impose a government upon them without consulting them. I can only say that they are under no obligation to obey your laws or to submit to your authority. You burthen them with taxation without representation, and thus inflict upon them the identical wrong for which the thirteen United Colonies threw off the yoke of the mother country. To establish

* Ohio Constitutional Convention 1850–51: *Debates and Proceedings*, 2 v. (Columbus, Ohio: 1851), II, 550–1.

a government over them, not based on their consent; to subject them to laws they have had no voice in framing; to tax them while you deny them representation is clearly and manifestly unjust; and I might stop here without urging any further objections to the Report, for with governments there should be really but one enquiry, what is just?

Another objection I have to this limitation of the right of suffrage, I believe it is *anti-democratic*. I desire to speak on this point with becoming modesty, for I am but a young man, while I see around me many whose hair has grown gray in the study of democratic principles. One of these gentlemen has said with Jefferson that democracy consists in doing "equal and exact justice to all men," another gentleman has said that democracy concedes to others all it demands for itself, and demands for itself all it concedes to others. If the restriction of the elective franchise is tested by either of these rules it will be found anti-democratic. To justify the practice the report recommends, Jefferson's rule should be amended so as to read "equal and exact justice to all *white* men— or to all men *except negroes*." If I understand genuine democracy it is neither more nor less than the golden rule of christianity applied to politics, or to our civil relations—that is doing unto others as we would have others to do unto us, and I see no reason why democracy is not like christianity, comprehensive enough to embrace the whole family of man. . . . I believe it to be our duty here to erect a civil platform upon which the foot of every person in the State may stand and on exactly the same level. I have not intentionally given in this body, one vote, nor do I intend to give one vote, to place any man, or set of men, above the common level. I will vote for no franchise, if by that is meant a something which makes one man free to do what may not be done by others. I will vote for no privilege, if by that is meant a private law for the benefit of the few over the many. . . . I will not give the benefit of holy rood to any hoary abuse, but right the wrong wherever given. But sir, the same sense of justice, which will not permit me to place another man's foot higher than my own, will also prevent me from consenting to place any man a hair's breadth below the common level. If the government of Ohio is to be in the hands of a privileged class, whether that class be large or small it will be an aristocracy, a form of government for which I have no partiality; this government ought to be democratic—a government shared by all, for the good of all. Let us then have no limitations of suffrage—for who does not know that all such limitations are anti-democratic?

### 12.

*Sojourner Truth:*
AT THE WOMEN'S RIGHTS CONVENTION, AKRON, OHIO *
[May 29, 1851]

*Sojourner Truth (c. 1797–1883) was an abolitionist who had been born a slave. Although illiterate, this tall gaunt character of deeply mystic nature was remarkably effective at meetings such as the Akron convention, where the women in their demand for equal rights were being strongly opposed by the clergymen. Her presence there had been the occasion for vainly whispered enjoinders that the chairman keep her from speaking lest Negro rights be mixed with the convention's purposes. In the hush that fell over the noisy audience as she rose, she spoke her mind briefly, devastatingly, and to the point.*

Wall, chilern, whar dar is so much racket dar must be somethin' out o' kilter. I tink dat 'twixt de niggers of de Souf and de womin at de Norf, all talkin' bout rights, de white men will be in a fix pretty soon. But what's all dis here talkin' bout?

Dat man ober dar say dat womin needs to be helped into carriages and lifted ober ditches, and to hab de best place everywhar. Nobody eber helps me into carriages, or ober mud-puddles, or gibs me any best place! And a'n't I a woman? Look at my arm! I have ploughed, and planted and gathered into barns, and no man could head me! And a'n't I a woman? I could work as much and eat as much as a man—when I could get it—and bear de lash as well! And a'n't I a woman? I have borne thirteen chilern, and seen 'em mos' all sold off to slavery, and when I cried out with my mother's grief, none but Jesus heard me! And a'n't I a woman?

---

* E. C. Stanton, S. B. Anthony, and M. J. Gage: *History of Woman Suffrage*, 3 v. (Rochester, N.Y.: 1887), I, 116.

Den dey talks 'bout dis ting in de head; what dis dey call it? ('Intellect,' whispered some one near.) Dat's it, honey. What dat got to do wid womin's rights or nigger's rights? If my cup won't hold but a pint, and yourn holds a quart, wouldn't ye be mean not to let me have my little half-measure full?

Den dat little man in black dar, he say women can't have as much rights as men, 'cause Christ wan't a woman! Whar did your Christ come from? Whar did your Christ come from? From God and a woman! Man had nothin' to do wid Him!

If de fust woman God ever made was strong enough to turn de world upside down all alone, dese women togedder (and she glanced her eye over the platform) ought to be able to turn it back, and get it right side up again! And now dey is asking to do it, de men better let 'em.

## 13.

### *Harriot K. Hunt:*
### PROTEST AGAINST TAXATION WITHOUT REPRESENTATION *
### [October 18, 1852]

*Harriot K. Hunt (1805–75), born in Massachusetts, was early convinced that women should have some useful occupation. She at first became a teacher, but in 1835 she turned to medicine, hydrotherapy, and psychotherapy with great success. She became well known as a temperance reformer, phrenologist, antitobacconist, abolitionist, and, above all, a suffragette. The "Protest against Taxation" was written in 1852 and appeared in her* Glances and Glimpses *(1856), where she explained that she came to write this letter as she contemplated a feeble-minded Irish boy invested with rights that were denied her.*

Harriot K. Hunt, physician, a native and permanent resident of the City of Boston, and for many years a tax payer therein, in making payment of her city taxes for the coming year, begs leave

* H. H. Robinson: *Massachusetts in the Women's Suffrage Movement* (Boston: 1881), 215–17.

to protest against the injustice and inequality of levying taxes upon women, and at the same time refusing them any voice or vote in the imposition and expenditure of the same. The only classes of male persons required to pay taxes and not at the same time allowed the privilege of voting, are aliens and minors. The objection in the case of aliens, is, their supposed want of interest in our institutions, and knowledge of them. The objection in case of minors, is, the want of sufficient understanding. These objections certainly cannot apply to women, natives of the city, all whose property and interests are here, and who have accumulated by their own sagacity and industry the very property on which they are taxed. But this is not all; the alien by going through the forms of naturalization, the minor on coming of age, obtain the right of voting, and so long as they continue to pay a mere poll-tax of a dollar and a half, they may continue to exercise it, though so ignorant as not to be able to *sign* their names, or *read* the very votes they put into the ballot boxes. Even drunkards, felons, idiots, or lunatics of *men,* may still enjoy that right of voting, to which no woman—however large the amount of taxes she pays, however respectable her character or useful her life—can ever attain. Wherein, your remonstrant would inquire, is the justice, equality, or wisdom of this?

That the rights and interests of the female part of the community are sometimes forgotten or disregarded in consequence of their deprivation of political rights, is strikingly evinced, as appears to your remonstrant, in the organization and administration of the city public schools. Though there are open in this State and neighborhood a great multitude of colleges and professional schools, for the education of boys and young men, yet the city has very properly provided two high schols of its own, one Latin, the other English, at which the *male graduates* of the grammar schools may pursue their education still further at the public expense, and why is not a like provision made for the girls? Why is the public provision for *their* education stopped short, just as they have attained the age best fitted for progress, and the preliminary knowledge necessary to facilitate it, thus giving the advantage of superior culture to *sex,* not to mind? The fact that our colleges and professional schools are closed against females, of which your remonstrant has had personal and painful experience—having been in the year 1847, after twelve years of medical practice in Boston, refused permission to attend the lectures of Harvard Medical College—that fact would seem to furnish an additional reason why the city should provide at its own expense those means of superior education, which, by supplying our girls with occupation and objects of interest, would not only save them from lives of frivolity and emptiness, but which might open the way to many useful and lucrative pursuits, and so raise them above that *degrading dependence,* so fruitful a source of female misery.

Reserving a more full exposition of the subject to future occasions, your remonstrant in paying her tax for the current year, begs leave to *protest* against the injustice and inequalities above pointed out.

This is respectfully submitted,

HARRIOT K. HUNT,

Boston, October 18, 1852.                            *32 Green Street.*

14.

*Henry B. Blackwell and Lucy Stone:*
PROTEST *
[May 1, 1855]

*Lucy Stone (1818–93), born on a New England farm, devoted her life to improving woman's status. Working her way, she finally got to Oberlin College, where she joined the peace and antislavery groups. She declined to write the commencement oration upon learning that it would be read by a man. While lecturing for women's rights and for the American Anti-Slavery Society, she was mobbed, hit with books, and on occasion drenched with cold water. She married the abolitionist Henry B. Blackwell (1825–1909), English-born brother of the famous sister physicians. But first both signed this "Protest." The idea was Henry Blackwell's, and he wrote the final draft with some suggestions from his wife and their friends. His wife used the name Mrs. Lucy Stone, thus be-*

* E. C. Stanton, S. B. Anthony, and M. J. Gage: *History of Woman Suffrage,* 3 v. (Rochester: 1887), I, 260–1.

*coming the first married American woman to retain her
maiden name. Nor was her happy marriage clouded when she
permitted her household goods, even her baby's cradle, to be
sold for the taxes she refused to pay because she was not
represented in the government.*

While acknowledging our mutual affection by publicly assuming the relationship of husband and wife, yet in justice to ourselves and a great principle, we deem it a duty to declare that this act on our part implies no sanction of, nor promise of voluntary obedience to such of the present laws of marriage, as refuse to recognize the wife as an independent, rational being, while they confer upon the husband an injurious and unnatural superiority, investing him with legal powers which no honorable man would exercise, and which no man should possess. We protest especially against the laws which give to the husband:

1. The custody of the wife's person.

2. The exclusive control and guardianship of their children.

3. The sole ownership of her personal, and use of her real estate, unless previously settled upon her, or placed in the hands of trustees, as in the case of minors, lunatics, and idiots.

4. The absolute right to the product of her industry.

5. Also against the laws which give to the widower so much larger and more permanent an interest in the property of his deceased wife, than they give to the widow in that of the deceased husband.

6. Finally, against the whole system by which "the legal existence of the wife is suspended during marriage," so that in most States, she neither has a legal part in the choice of her residence, nor can she make a will, nor sue or be sued in her own name, nor inherit property.

We believe that personal independence and equal human rights can never be forfeited, except for crime; that marriage should be an equal and permanent partnership, and so recognized by law; that until it is so recognized, married partners should provide against the radical injustice of present laws, by every means in their power.

We believe that where domestic difficulties arise, no appeal should be made to legal tribunals under existing laws, but that all difficulties should be submitted to the equitable adjustment of arbitrators mutually chosen.

Thus reverencing law, we enter our protest against rules and customs which are unworthy of the name, since they violate justice, the essence of law.

*Worcester Spy,* 1855.                          HENRY B. BLACKWELL,
                                                 LUCY STONE.

# CHAPTER TWO

# RIGHT TO ALTER THE
# EXISTING GOVERNMENT

———◆———

*. . . Any people anywhere, being inclined and having the power, have the* right *to rise up and shake off the existing government, and form a new one that suits them better. This is a most valuable, a most sacred right—a right which, we hope and believe, is to liberate the world. Nor is this right confined to cases in which the whole people of an existing government may choose to exercise it.*

———ABRAHAM LINCOLN: *In the House of Representatives, January 12, 1848*

*All men recognize the right of revolution; that is, the right to refuse allegiance to, and to resist, the government, when its tyranny or its inefficiency are great and unendurable. But almost all say that such is not the case now. But such was the case, they think, in the Revolution of '75. . . . In other words, when a sixth of the population of a nation which has undertaken to be the refuge of liberty are slaves, and a whole country is unjustly overrun and conquered by a foreign army, and subjected to military law, I think that it is not too soon for honest men to rebel and revolutionize.*

———HENRY DAVID THOREAU: *Civil Disobedience,*
1849

Sources of the quotations on the preceding page:

ABRAHAM LINCOLN: *Congressional Globe*, 30th Cong., 1 sess., 1847–8, Appendix, p. 94.

HENRY DAVID THOREAU: Bernard Smith: *The Democratic Spirit* (New York: 1943, 2nd ed.), 317.

THE conception that government is founded on the free consent of the people and that when it no longer represents that consent, the people have a right to alter or overthrow it is firmly rooted in the American past. This political thesis was expressed in Jonathan Mayhew's *Discourse* on the "duty to resist," and Abraham Lincoln's First Inaugural Address. The right of revolution was practiced, too, by Americans in early times. In the seventeenth century, men with knives, staves, and rifles stood with Nathaniel Bacon, Jr., in Virginia, or with Jacob Leisler in New York, and battled for their rights; so, too, did the Paxton Boys of Pennsylvania, the New York antirenters, and the Carolina Regulators in the decade before the American Revolution. In affirming the right "to alter or to abolish" an oppressive form of government, Jefferson expressed what was in the minds and hearts of many of his countrymen.

The vision of the American Revolution stirred men in their ceaseless quest for self-improvement. In 1786, soon after the American Revolution, Daniel Shays led his embattled farmers through the Berkshire hills and, within eight years thereafter, western Pennsylvania was ablaze with the Whisky Rebellion. Men from Ulster gathered in the mountains near Mingo Creek and Parkinson's Ferry and covenanted never to pay "Hamilton's whisky tax." This was no luxury tax; for whisky provided the only practical means of transporting surplus grain over the mountains. Masked nightriders spread terror and roughly handled a federal marshal and some excisemen. At the instigation of David Bradford and Harmon Husband, mass meetings were called. The protesting farmers appointed a committee of safety and even called out the militia. Sober voices dissuaded them from a declaration of independence. Meanwhile the militia of four states, summoned by President Washington on Hamilton's urgent plea, put up a great show of force before which the rebellion collapsed. Some of the same smoldering resistance was reflected in David Brown's harangues against the Federalist Alien and Sedition Acts (1).

Those sympathetic to the South American, Greek, and French Revolutions invariably invoked the American Revolution as a glorious precedent. In this spirit, in 1817, Hezekiah Niles justified the Latin American uprisings (2). William Miller saw in the Greek Revolution that "the spirit of '76 is still abroad" (3). Robert Walker told the New York workers in November 1830 that the French were a spark "burst into a flame." (5).

During the Jacksonian period, democratic movements and ideas grew in strength. Thomas Skidmore (4) asked how the poor could avert their poverty, which was sharpened by machine production. His answer was: an "equal division of all this property among the citizens." Let the people seize the factories and recover their "rights" against those who, through control of property, command "the liberty and the happiness" of the citizens. Similarly, Seth Luther warned the rich that the poor were "determined to be gulled no longer," exclaiming that the Declaration of Independence "has gone forth like a flaming fire" (6). He threatened that "the people will yet rouse from their long slumber of a thousand years, and hurl their chains at their oppressors."

In Rhode Island in 1842, Thomas W. Dorr led a popular movement against the freehold suffrage provision of the state constitution, which disfranchised more than half the adult male population (7). A popular convention summoned by malcontents drafted a "People's Constitution." Despite efforts to head them off with concessions, they organized a new government based upon the "sovereignty of the people," and elected Dorr as Governor. The insurgent government prepared to defend itself. But a show of force by Governor Samuel King, on the assurance of President John Tyler's military aid, caused it to give way. The rebels' position was subsequently vindicated, however, by a new constitution that, with some minor restrictions, provided for manhood suffrage.

A similar spirit of revolt inspired the antirent agitation that swept New York in 1839–46. It sprang from the resentment of the small farmers in the up-Hudson counties against the "durable" leasehold system, under which the great landlords collected yearly rent *in perpetuo* and exacted a quarter or one third of the sale price of a leasehold. Farmers banded together and refused to pay rents. Their opposition caused Governor William H. Seward to call out the militia in 1839 to end the "Helderberg War." But soon thereafter the hills of Columbia and Delaware counties resounded to the tin horns that summoned men garbed as Indians to resist with tar and feathers and even arms the law-enforcing sheriffs and deputies. Governor Silas Wright retaliated with stern suppression and arrest of the leaders. "And let it be transmitted to posterity that a free people dared to rise and vindicate their rights instead of basely crouching to a monied aristocracy who would rob them of their dearest gift of heaven," wrote their imprisoned leader Dr. Smith A. Boughton to Thomas Devyr, the land reformer (8). The shooting of Deputy Sheriff Steele in August, 1845, led Governor Wright to proclaim Delaware County in a state of insurrection. The violent resistance was crushed; but the program of the antirenters was achieved. The New York Constitution of 1846 prohibited feudal tenures, and a court decision declared all "quarter sales" illegal.

In its extreme form the struggle against slavery and the fugitive slave law evoked deep-seated protest and even revolt (Chapter Five). William Lloyd Garrison, Wendell Phillips, and John Brown advocated secession from, and in Brown's case even rebellion against, a government that sanctioned "man-stealing." "We are a rebellious nation," said Theodore Parker. "Our whole history is treason; our blood was attainted before we were born; our creeds are infidelity to the mother church; our constitution, treason to our fatherland. What of that? Though all the governors in the world bid us commit treason against man, and set the example, let us never submit." Henry David Thoreau reflected this spirit in preferring jail to paying taxes to a state that supported slavery.*

What is significant in these various "lost" causes is that they drew inspiration from the American Revolutionary heritage. Fur-

---

* Quoted in Henry Steele Commager: "Who Is Loyal to America?" *Harper's Magazine* (September, 1947), 196.

thermore, most of them were not truly "lost" in the light of subsequent accommodations in law and institutions.

---

1.

*David Brown:*
SEDITIOUS WRITINGS *
[October 1, 14, and 22, 1798]

*David Brown (c. 1750–?), a "laboring man" who had been
a Revolutionary soldier, traveled through New England lecturing against the policies of the Federalists. Found guilty of
violating the Sedition Law in Dedham, Massachusetts, he remained in jail for two years, despite two petitions to President John Adams for clemency, until President Thomas Jefferson, recognizing the political character of his case, granted
him a pardon.*

What a sad dilemma do we find! For our own Constitution
(meaning the constitution of the United States) † has not been
formed by ten or twelve years and the history of ages has not produced so great a declention [*sic*] of administration and so great
tyranny in so short a period; for there is not an instance wherein
the property of the Union is concerned but what the leaders of
Government have ingroid (meaning ingrossed) the whole to themselves, and five hundred out of the union of five million receive all
the benefit of public property and live upon the ruins of the rest
of the community. Yet we (meaning the people of the United
States) sit still and see our fellow Citizens coming into a state
of abject slavery and do nothing to retrieve ourselves. . . . I shall
endeavor to shew in some instances wherein the leaders of the

---

* From a MS indictment of David Brown, June 1799, in the Archives of
the Federal Circuit Court in Boston.

† Parenthetical remarks have been rendered as they appear in the manuscript indictment.

Government have cheated the Union in the funding system in the first place. The session, before they passed the act to make the final settlement notes good, they (meaning the Congress) knew it would pass the next session, and in the intermedium of time they put their runners throughout the Continent and bought them up for two shillings and two and sixpence on the pound and then made the full nominal sum good in their own hands. . . .

What right has legislators or any other body of people to sell all the property of a community to themselves and a few individuals of the community without receiving a special power from the people to identify the property, and then if they are limited to a certain price they have no right to sell the property without they can obtain it which has been the case with Congress. . . .

They have no other pretense then that they are a sovereign body and have a sovereign right to do wrong or that the Community have no share in their own property. The case has been with Congress in the sales to Judge Simms of all that tract of land across the Ohio between the two Miami's, three millions of acres of which the six hundredth part of the community had no knowledge. . . .

The truth is they (meaning Congress) have sold the land (meaning the public unappropriated land of the United States) by fraud and without any power derived from the people to justify them in their conduct. . . .

Here is the one thousand out of the five millions that receive all the benefit of public property and all the rest no share in it. But now if they want to settle their sons they must give $10.00 instead of 10¢ to those gentlemen that the legislature have made rich and made themselves rich also. Indeed all our administration is as fast approaching the Lord and commons as possible, that a few men should possess the whole country and the rest be tenants to the others. . . .

By this we may easily see the fraudulent transactions of our government, like the subjects of Julius Caesar we must bow down and worship our Leaders as the God of Jupiter and Mars. And then look at the pension list the exorbitant salarys of our nabobs and you will find the name of liberty and equality are like a sounding brass and a tinkling symbal. . . .

This is not all for the history of ages hath not produced a set of leaders that hath so fraudulently taken the property of the Union from them without receiving any power from the people to justify them in their conduct. . . .

Dear and beloved fellow citizens of North America, Government and the people are so opposite that they have eternally been at war with each other. The government speaks in contrary terms with nature, with all the natural rights of the people, while the language of nature and the people is "live nature with all the natural rights of the people." . . . See Joel Barlow * first of his part second to speak in plain words or use the only language which the moral nature of the case will justify. The real occupation of government is to plunder or to steal as will best answer their purposes, while the business of the people is to secrete their property by fraud or give it peaceable up as the others demand it and thus in consequence of being driven to this necessity they become miserable through idleness to avoid the mortification of laboring for them they hate and detest. . . .

The language of government is reverence the Constitution, let the constitution be ever so corruptly administered, if it takes all their property with lives to support it, for the sake of one hundred out of the Union of five millions by teaching that a few men were destined by God to govern in Church and State and that the rest were made for the express purpose to see how miserable he could make them both in things of time and futurity? See Barlow * page 7. . . . Now fellow Citizens there is no door open for us to retrieve ourselves as it respects property. But never if we will annihilate reason and impose upon ourselves and choose to be treated like pack horses and mules. . . .

There always has been an eternal struggle between the laboring part of the community and those lazy rascals that invented every means that the Devil, has put into their heads, to destroy the laboring part of the Community and those that we have chose to act as public servants, act more like the enthusiastic ravings of mad men than the servants of the people and are determined to carry their own measures by the point of the bayonet. . . . Seven-eighths of the people are opposed to the measures of tyrants (meaning the

* The references are to Joel Barlow: *Advice to the Privileged Orders In the Several States of Europe,* . . . *Part II* (New York: 1794). Ed. note.

government of the United States) to enslave them; and Congress need not flatter themselves that they can carry their measures, for I never knew a government supported long after the confidence of people was lost, for the people are the government. . . . Notwithstanding all the petitions and remonstrances to Congress they take no notice of it and if they (meaning the people of the United States) do not get a redress of their grievances by petitioning for it, they will finally break out like the burning mountain of Etna, and will have an unconditional redress of their grievances.

## 2.

### Hezekiah Niles:
### EDITORIAL ON REBELLION *
### [March 15, 1817]

*Hezekiah Niles (1777–1839) was born in Pennsylvania of Quaker parentage. As editor of the* Baltimore Evening Post *and later of* Niles' Weekly Register, *which acquired a circulation of 10,000, he espoused the "American System" of internal improvements and protection. Although a Whig on the bank issue, he opposed slavery and sought to develop the heritage of the American Revolution.*

A writer at *Madrid,* speaking of certain reports that had prevailed there as to the United States being about to declare war against Spain, and lend their assistance to the colonies struggling for independence, observes, after some compliments on our condition,—"THE UNITED STATES WILL NOT ESPOUSE THE CAUSE OF REBELLION," &c.

Whether it is politic for us, in the present unsettled state of the world, to be the first to disturb its *dreadful* calm, portenting storms more destructive, perhaps, than any we have yet witnessed, by attempting to gain that redress of Spain for wrongs committed by her, by the argument of arms, which has been refused, in the most pitiful and prevaricating manner, to honest negociation—is not the

* *Niles' Weekly Register* (March 15, 1817), XII, 34–5.

question that presents itself at this time; but we may profitably offer some remarks upon the principle of the sentence just quoted.

"The United States will not espouse the cause of rebellion?" What is *"rebellion?"* A resistance of "divine right of kings" to govern the people! What caused these states to unite? A resistance of the *right* of the king to bind them in all cases whatsoever, or, a *rebellion.* Yet *they,* who have themselves profited so much by it —who have thereby given themselves a name and rank among the nations of the earth—who, in their childhood have performed deeds of highest renown, and, by their resistance of "legal authority," have arrived at a state of unrivalled prosperity and glory, marching rapidly to the fullness of strength and power, "will not espouse the cause of rebellion" (so called), the grand source of their own happiness and fame—will be unwilling that other countries, by like means, may reach the same state of liberty, safety and independence—will rather have the friendship of a thing like *Ferdinand,* than obtain the gratitude of a world of freemen!—Verily, the writer must have supposed that we had already forgotten our own origin; or meant to libel us by believing us capable of condemning the generation just passed; which, with *Washington* at its head, "rebelled" against the king. The case of South America, in relation to Spain, is precisely that which the present United States had in relation to Great-Britain, in what the world [*because it succeeded*] now calls our "revolution;" except, indeed, that where *we* had one just cause for complaint *they* have a hundred—and, perhaps, a thousand.

But as to "rebellion"—what is it? Is not *Ferdinand,* himself, as well a rebel to his king and his *father,* as to common sense and common justice? And shall he, or his friends, who by intrigue or force, divested the father of the throne of Spain, charge the transatlantic colonies with "rebellion" against *himself?* We wish the knavery of monarchy to become a thing to be hooted at by every one, and ask again, if a "divine right" can be abrogated by a human act—what change of circumstances amongst men can alter the decrees of ALMIGHTY GOD?—and yet on this is established the foundation of every throne in Europe, that of the "illustrious house of Brunswick" not excepted—for this house obtained it through force in "rebellion;" which *uncourtly* phrase, however, is changed for that of a "glorious revolution."

3.

### William W. Miller:
### AN ADDRESS FOR THE BENEFIT OF THE GREEKS *
[January 13, 1824]

*William W. Miller (1797–1825) of New Jersey was trained in the law. After practicing in Morristown, he moved to Newark, where he became renowned as an orator of uncommon ability, even though he lived to be only twenty-eight. This speech was remembered for more than a generation.*

It is truly said, that this is an age of wonders. The American revolution is an august era, not only in the history of this country, but in the history of man. The contest of '76 was not the mere effort of sturdy and overgrown colonies to emancipate themselves from the parent country. . . . It was a contest for PRINCIPLES. The heroes of the revolution asserted, "that all men are created equal—that government derive their just powers from the consent of the governed, and whenever any government becomes destructive of the end of its formation (the preservation of the inalienable rights of man,) it is the *right* of the people to alter or abolish it." For the truth of these principles, they appeal to the God of battles. . . . The spirit of '76 is still abroad in the earth. Its power was felt in the throes and convulsions of revolutionary France; was seen in the fragments of the Bourbon throne; . . . That same spirit, has recently moved along the Andes and liberty—liberty was the shout —and liberty was the result. It has been felt in Spain: and let not Ferdinand dream that he is safe from its power. It will write against him, on the wall of his palace—*mene, mene, tekel, upharsin.* All Europe has felt, now feels, its power, in that low and rumbling sound, in that slight but fearful tremor of the earth, which precedes the general quake—the bursting of the volcano. . . .

The blow shall be struck! The stupor of Greece is broken. Behold! there are the symptoms of returning life; they resolve—they

---

* William W. Miller: *An Address for the Benefit of the Greeks Delivered in Trinity Church, Newark, on Tuesday Evening, January 13, 1824* (Newark, N.J.: 1824), 11–13, 21–3.

rise—they burst their fetters—and in the mountains between Thessaly and Phocis, is again heard the cry of LIBERTY OR DEATH. Echo seems delighted to hear her ancient burden, and liberty or death! —Liberty or death!—is reiterated and reiterated, until all Greece is in arms and the tyrant's defied.

. . . Suffer me now to appeal to you as freemen. As men, the Greeks have strong claims on our sympathy—as freemen, stronger. They are contending for civil liberty. Anterior to the American revolution, liberty was regarded as the genius of disorder, the watchword of faction, the cant of the hypocrite, or the dream of the enthusiast. Our fathers asserted that it was the richest blessing of social man, his inalienable birthright, a *practical principle;* and to prove it they instituted a bold and sublime experiment, and the result was—my country. . . . To prevent the effect of this great truth on their subjects, the tyrants of Europe assembled in solemn congress, and have at length proclaimed to the world as the result of their consultation, "that no people have a right to change or improve their form of government, without the consent of their royal master." Is it so? Then these United States are not of *right* free and independent. Upon this principle, you perceive, that *we* and the *Holy Alliance* are directly at issue; and, mark me—it is an issue that must be tried. . . . Shall we remain cold and silent spectators of these movements against the rights of man? Shall we say nothing against a principle of slavery, extensive enough to reach even us? Is this a time for apathy and indifference, when the demon of oppression is abroad in the earth, grinding the nations, and casting a glance of envy and hatred towards our own hemisphere, an appeal is now made to us to speak and act in favor of liberty. Let us rejoice that we have an opportunity to manifest to the world, that the spirit of '76 is not extinct—that we still regard "a day, an hour of virtuous liberty, as worth a whole eternity of bondage." Let us send to the countrymen of Themistocles and Phocion, a cheering of gratulation. Let us bid them go on—go on— until triumphant hosannas shall resound in the dome of St. Sophia. Yes, from this place—from Jersey—from this battleground of American freedom, let a voice go forth that will speak of *death* to tyrants, and of *good will* to the oppressed of every land.

4.

## Thomas Skidmore:
### THE RIGHTS OF MAN TO PROPERTY *
### [1829]

*Thomas Skidmore (?–1832) was a radical mechanic who led a faction in the New York Workingman's Party in the late 1820's. An elaborator of Langdon Byllesby's ideas (Chapter Ten, 6), he believed in the equal right of every man and woman, Negro and white, to acquire property, education, and other privileges. He wanted to abolish all inheritances, debts, and monopolies, and to redistribute property. He also advocated a ten-hour day. He was almost elected to the New York Assembly, but then lost his following in a factional split with Frances Wright. She denounced his "agrarianism" and he, her "guardian schools," which he contended were destructive of the family. The Rights of Man to Property! was his only literary contribution, apart from his daily paper, the* Friend of Equal Rights.

#### PLAN

Let a new State-Convention be assembled. Let it prepare a new Constitution, and let that Constitution, after having been adopted by the people, decree an abolition of all debts; both at home and abroad, between citizen and citizen; and between citizen and foreigner. Let it renounce all property belonging to our citizens, without the State. Let it claim all property within the State, both real and personal, of whatever kind it may be, with the exception of that belonging to resident aliens, and with the further exception of so much personal property, as may be in the possession of transient owners, not being citizens. Let it order an equal division of all this property among the citizens, of and over the age of maturity, in manner yet to be directed. Let it order all transfers or removals of property, except so much as may belong to transient owners, to cease, until the division is accomplished. . . .

---

* Thomas Skidmore: *The Rights of Man to Property! Being a Proposition to Make It Equal Among the Adults of the Present Generation; and to Provide for Its Equal Transmission to Every Age of Maturity* (New York: 1829), 137–8, 382–8.

Under the present unequal distribution of property, where labor is the sole resource the poor have, by which to maintain their existence, degraded as it is, by the slavery in which they are plunged, it is not wonderful that they have been found to be opposed to the introduction of improvements. Fruitless and unavailing as such opposition is, it is yet less unreasonable than at first sight it may appear to be. It is true, that one consequence of such improvement, as we have already shown, is, that a poor man even, may obtain 4,800 times as much as he could obtain without it: yet, it may be asked, may he not be an ultimate loser? May not improvement extend to such a degree, that there will be no demand for his labor? Or if it does not reach this point, will it not approach so near it, as to make him an extreme sufferer? Let it not be forgotten, that while on the one hand, labor-saving machinery is advancing in its march to perfection, with rapid strides, and diminishing demand for labor; so on the other, are the numbers of the poor, among whom this demand is to be shared, augmenting in a fearful ratio. It will be said, perhaps, that by reducing price, the direct and certain consequence of improvements, (otherwise they do not deserve the name,) consumption is augmented; and, therefore, the demand is increased. This is true only in a limited degree; for, as these improvements supersede, sooner or later, in a great measure, all demand for the labor of the poor; it dries up their resources faster than it multiplies them; this, *in the end,* diminishes, rather than increases the demand; and the consequence is, that as inventions, any more than revolutions, never go backwards, are never given up, when their benefits are once tasted; that the whole laboring population must perish, as it were, in a sort of self-destruction, like useless beings on the earth, where, it would seem, they have no right to appear; or that they must avert such a calamity, by the best means in their power.

That they cannot destroy the existence, and even increase of labor-saving machines and processes, is evident from this; that every one of those whose feelings are enlisted against their inutility to them, on account of their destroying demand for their labor, whenever he has occasion, purchases, because they come cheaper, the very productions afforded by the agents which he so much deprecates. Of what use, then, is it, for a laboring man to cry out against improvements, when he goes and buys a coat, for example, or rather the materials of it, at a low price, which these very improvements have made? It is *reward* that keeps these improvements in existence; and it is not a volley of hard words and abuse that will do them any injury. If, then, the poor themselves contribute, and as they do, by an unavoidable necessity, to the support of that which threatens their own destruction, what hope have they to escape? It is not the rich, certainly, that *will; even if it were right that they should;* and, we see the poor *cannot* forego the advantages, individually speaking, of these inventions; how then, are they to avert so great a calamity?

The Steam-Engine is not injurious to the poor, when they can have the benefit of it; and this, on supposition, being *always* the case, instead of being looked upon, as a curse, would be hailed as a blessing. If, then, it is seen that the Steam-Engine, for example, is likely to greatly impoverish, or destroy the poor, what *have* they to do, but TO LAY HOLD OF IT, AND MAKE IT THEIR OWN? LET THEM APPROPRIATE ALSO, in the same way, THE COTTON FACTORIES, THE WOOLEN FACTORIES, THE IRON FOUNDERIES, THE ROLLING MILLS, HOUSES, CHURCHES, SHIPS, GOODS, STEAM-BOATS, FIELDS OF AGRICULTURE, &c. &c. &c. in manner as proposed in this work, AND AS IS THEIR RIGHT; and they will never have occasion any more to consider that as an evil which never deserved that character; which, on the contrary, is all that is good among men; and of which, we cannot, under these new circumstances, have too much. It is an equal division of property that MAKES ALL RIGHT, and an equal transmission of it to posterity, KEEPS IT SO.

. . . Take away from the possessors of the world their dividends, their rents, their profits; in one word, that which they receive for the *use* of it, and which belongs, freely belongs, to one as much as another; and what would become of the present miserable condition of the human race? It would be annihilated for ever [*sic*]. But these dividends, these rents, these profits, these prices paid for the *use* of the world, or of the world's materials, will never cease to be paid, till the *possession* of these materials is made equal, or substantially equal, among all men; till there shall be no lenders, no borrowers; no landlords, no tenants; no masters, no journeymen; no Wealth, no Want.

I approach, then, the close of this Work. I hasten to commit it to the hands, the heads and the hearts of those for whose benefit it is written. It is to them that I look, for the *power* necessary, to bring the system it recommends into existence. If they shall think I have so far understood myself, and the subject I have undertaken to discuss, as to have perceived, and marked out the path that leads them to the enjoyment of their rights, their interests and their happiness, IT WILL BE FOR THOSE WHO ARE SUFFERING THE EVILS, of which I have endeavored to point out the causes and the remedies, TO LEAD THE WAY. Those who are enjoying the sweets of the labor of others, will have no hearts to feel for the misery which the present system occasions. And the first throe of pain, which they *will* feel, will be that of *alarm,* that they are soon to be ordered to riot on the toils of others no more for ever! But those who *suffer,* will feel no cause of alarm. The very intensity of their sufferings, since now they understand their origin and cure, will add double vigor to their exertions to recover their rights. But let them understand, that much is to be done, to accomplish this recovery. IT IS TO BE THE RESULT OF THE COMBINED EXERTIONS, OF GREAT NUMBERS OF MEN. These, by no means, *now* understand their true situation; but when they do, they will be ready and willing to do what belongs to their happiness. If, then, there be truth; if there be reason; if there be force of argument, in the work which I thus commit to the hands of those for whose benefit it is written; let them read; let it be read; let it be conversed about, in the hearing of those whose *interest* it is, to hear whatever of truth, of reason, and argument it may contain; and as *often,* too, as there may be opportunity. Let them awake to a *knowledge* of their rights, and how they may be obtained, and they will not be slow (since it will *then* be so easy) to reclaim them.

Let the poor and middling classes understand that their oppressions come from the overgrown wealth that exists among them, on the one hand, and from entire destitution on the other; and that as this overgrown wealth is continually augmenting its possessions, in a rapid ratio, the public sufferings are continually augmenting also; and must continue to augment, until the equal and unalienable rights of the people shall order otherwise. Let the parent reflect, if he be now a man of toil, that his children must be, ninety-nine cases in a hundred, slaves, *and worse,* to some rich proprietor; and that there is no alternative, but the change proposed. Let him not cheat himself with empty pretensions; for, *he who commands the property of a State, or even an inordinate portion of it,* HAS THE LIBERTY AND THE HAPPINESS OF ITS CITIZENS IN HIS OWN KEEPING. And if there be some dozen, or fifty, or five hundred of these large proprietors, they are neither more nor less than so many additional keepers. He who can feed me, or starve me; give me employment, or bid me wander about in idleness; is my master; and it is the utmost folly for me to boast of being any thing but a slave.

In fine, let the people awake to their rights; let them understand in what they consist; let them see the course they must pursue to obtain them; let them follow up that course, by informing each as many as he can, his fellow citizens, of the truth which this Work contains; let all co-operate, in the early and effectual accomplishment of the objects it recommends, and these objects will easily and speedily be achieved, and none will have labored in vain.

## 5.

### *Robert Walker:*
### ADDRESS AT THE WORKING MEN'S DINNER *
### [November 26, 1830]

*The revolt of the French people in 1830 against Charles X was hailed with great sympathy and enthusiasm by the people of America, particularly because Lafayette was one of its leaders. In New York City a great celebration, organized by a "Committee of Mechanics and Working Men" of which Robert Walker was chairman, was opened on November 26 by a gigantic and colorful parade attended by many notables and joined by all the trade unions of the city. At one of the public dinners—the "Working Men's Dinner"—Robert Walker, who referred to himself as an "uneducated" "mechanic from youth," made this speech.*

* M. Moses: *Full Annals of the Revolution in France 1830 to Which Is Added A Full Account of the Celebration of Said Revolution in the City of New-York on the 25th November 1830* (New York: 1830), second pagination, pp. 108–10, 113–14.

To accomplish and hasten on this glorious work [i.e. the diffusion of knowledge], government must be changed or renovated. Too long has *might* usurped the place of right. Too long have the *rights* and the *interests* of the *many*, been sacrificed at the shrine of the *usurped* interests of the few: Too long have mankind been deceived by the cant of the interested, that they are unqualified to govern themselves. But little more than half a century ago, the idea of man's capability of self-government was considered Eutopian [*sic*] and visionary—as principles suited only for the minds and the pens of Historians, Poets and Philosophers: but to reduce them to practice, by putting them in active operation, was considered as "the wildest dream that ever entered the brain of a *visionary fanatic*," who was considered better fitted for the inmate of some madhouse, than to be allowed to roam at large in society, propagating his "disorganizing and dangerous principles!"

But thanks! immortal thanks! to the bold, daring and devoted spirits of a Jefferson, a Washington, a Franklin, an Adams, and a Paine, with the whole host of noble worthies, who placed in bold relief, and in practical operation, the "Equal Rights of man, and his capability for self-government." Yes, fellow citizens, the American Revolution was one of the greatest and most glorious events which the annals of the world can boast of. Its consummation marks a new and important era in the history of man. Till that period, mankind were but the dupes and the playthings of the triple unholy alliance of kings, nobles, and priests; who, in whatever else they might disagree, agreed in ruling and fleecing the people for their own selfish purposes. Yes, they displayed great unanimity in considering the producing and useful classes of society, but as "hewers of wood and drawers of water;" or, as Jefferson has it, as "born with saddles on their backs, for them to ride booted and spurred;" as merely brought into being for their special use, and to be their humble dependents and slaves!

Fellow Citizens—Your Fathers' Declaration of 4th July, 1776, burst these despotic chains asunder, and boldy proclaimed to an astonished world, "the unalienable and equal rights of man to self-government." Yes, and your patriot fathers boldly drew the sword to seal with their blood the rights they had dared to proclaim and to establish.

The lesson which the heroes of your revolution practically

taught the haughty aristocracy of Britain, stood, in the political wilderness, as a pillar of fire to light the way of the oppressed of every clime to the hallowed temple of liberty. Your fathers' noble daring stood as a bright beacon to degraded man, and successfully established the maxim, "That a nation to be freed need but will it." . . .

Is it, fellow citizens, in accordance with either the letter or the spirit of our constitution, for our Legislature to endow colleges for the children of the rich, and only establish paltry common schools for the children of the poor?

Is it in keeping with the Declaration of Independence, to proclaim "equal rights" the birthright of every American citizen, and yet charter monopolies for the benefit of the few, at the expense of the rights and the interests of the many?

Is it consistent with republicanism to keep up an antiquated, complicated, and expensive system of civil law, which emanated from aristocratic Britain, but which is at war with the rights and the interests of republican American?

Is it in unison with our constitution, with the improvements of man, or the intelligence of the age, to punish poverty as a crime, and brand with a stigma the unfortunate but honest debtor?

Think not, fellow-citizens, I wish to urge you to overthrow our constitution, as based on the declaration of independence; far from it: those evils I have hinted at are but excrescences fastened by the interested on our glorious constitution, and which require but the caustic of reform, efficiently applied, to remove them from the glorious edifice they contaminate and deface.

Move on, then, mechanics and working men, in your glorious career of mental independence, with republican education for your polar star, union and firmness your sheet-anchor, and the day is not far distant which shall crown your noble efforts with victory; and your country shall stand redeemed from the poison of fashion, and the canker-worm of party; and in their place shall spring up the tree of genuine republicanism, yielding the choice fruits of real equality of rights. Then man shall be judged by his actions, and not by his professions; by his usefulness to society, as an industrious citizen, and not by the texture of the garb which covers him.

6.

*Seth Luther:*

AN ADDRESS ON THE ORIGIN AND PROGRESS OF AVARICE *
[January 30, 1834]

*Seth Luther (c. 1800–46) was born in Rhode Island. Al-*
*though a carpenter with little formal education, he became a*
*popular labor reformer and lecturer, traveling down the Ohio*
*and throughout New England, where he attacked the abuses*
*of the factory system in speeches such as this. As secretary*
*of the Central Trades Convention in 1834, he toured the*
*country denouncing political and religious as well as eco-*
*nomic oppression, particularly the treatment of the poor. He*
*was active in the Ten-Hour movement and practically drafted*
*the Boston Circular (Chapter Eleven, 5).*

Our country has become the political pole-star of the world. The
oppressed of every nation, kingdom, and tongue, wherever our
glorious star-spangled banner has floated on the breeze, are looking to it as the political 'LIGHT OF THE WORLD.' Our institutions, imperfect as some of them are, are exciting the envy and
hatred of the 'principalities and powers' of the old world. Em-
perors and kings, and dukes, and lords, gnash their teeth upon us.
The Declaration of Independence, that immortal document, from
the pen of the illustrious Jefferson, has gone forth like a flaming
fire. It has carried terror and dismay into the hearts of tyrants. . . .
That paper has carried rays of light into the dark places of cruelty.
I would rather prefer to be the author of that document, than to
be the emperor of the whole planetary system, were each planet
as thickly inhabited as the ball on which we live; for this reason:
the principles there displayed '*in characters of living flame*,' will
one day emancipate the world. The people will yet rouse from
their long slumber of a thousand years, and hurl their chains at
their oppressors. . . .
     The flame of liberty, like the pent up fires of a volcano, has

* Seth Luther: *An Address on the Origin and Progress of Avarice, and Its*
*Deleterious Effects on Human Happiness,* . . . *Delivered before the Union As-*
*sociation of Working Men, in the Town Hall, Charlestown, Mass., January 30,*
*1834* (Boston: 1834), 6–9.

broken forth, and threatens to overwhelm thrones and dominions and principalities and powers, in one wide-spread ruin and desolation.

The people are inquiring into the divine right of their oppressions: the time seems to be passing away, when the fiat of Kings should involve the happiness or misery of the countless millions of our race. . . .

In England the haughty dukes, lords and prelates have recently had the alternative laid before them, either to have their palaces and castles burnt to the ground, and the ashes scattered to the four winds of heaven, or surrender their ill-gotten power into the hands of *'the people,'* its only safe depository.

The people, in order to convince their oppressors that they were in earnest, demolished a few of their splendid abodes of luxury, thereby sternly saying, *'If you will not do as you ought, we will do as we please, your divine right to the contrary notwithstanding.'*

Previous to the passage of the Reform Bill, the divine-right party said, through Blackwood's Magazine, that *'to grant reform to the people because they wanted it, was a destructive and dangerous principle.'* But the people convinced their oppressors that to *deny* reform when the people *demanded* it, was still more destructive and dangerous. When the *tories* saw their splendid palaces enveloped in *crackling flames,* they became convinced that it was no longer tenable ground, to withhold right from its owners; and they submitted to *'the people,'* as in duty bound.

The French nation have also risen in their strength, and trampled on the *'divine right'* of Charles Tenth to shackle the press. They drove him from the throne which he had disgraced by his tyranny, and from the land he endeavored to ruin and destroy by the 'GRACE OF GOD,' on which he blasphemously based his divine right to be a tyrant and govern the French Nation without their consent. If that nation gained nothing else by the *'three days'* revolution, they shook the foundation of every throne in Europe. The Revolution in England, under the name of reform, was one of the consequences which immediately followed the French Revolution of July.

Poland, too, long suffering under the galling chain of the bloodthirsty, savage Russian, has also poured out the life of her best and most patriotic sons in purple streams, as a sacrifice to the cause of liberty. But, alas! she has failed, once and again, and 'order,' to use the language of despotism 'order is restored at Warsaw'—'order' such as tyrants love. . . .

But all is not yet lost. The wild cry of horror and dismay bursting from the murdered women and children shall not be unremembered. The *blood,* the *tears,* the *anguish* and the *toil* of Poland shall not be forgotten. . . .

These attempts at throwing off oppression, have become more and more frequent since the American Revolution; and the more the principles on which that revolution was founded are disseminated, the more frequent will be the attempts to imitate, the most important political event the world ever witnessed. The Declaration of the Independence of the United States will one day be the declaration of the Independence of the whole world, *if we remain faithful to the trust,* placed in our hands by those who suffered so much in our behalf, in gaining the grand charter of our liberties.

7.

*Thomas W. Dorr:*

SPEECH BEFORE THE CONSTITUTIONAL ASSEMBLY
OF RHODE ISLAND *

[May 3, 1842]

*Thomas Wilson Dorr (1805–54) was born in Rhode Island, the son of a prosperous manufacturer. Elected to the Rhode Island Assembly in 1834, he actively worked to displace the old charter under which a real-property test barred almost half the male population from the franchise. In 1840 he and his followers held a convention and adopted a constitution overwhelmingly approved by a majority of the qualified voters, but rejected by a convention called by the legal government. When the reformers elected an entire state ticket with Dorr at its head, martial law was declared and a reward offered for the capture of Dorr and his supporters. Dorr surrendered and was sentenced to solitary confinement for*

* *People's Democratic Guide* (June, 1842) I, 238–9.

*treason. Public opinion forced his release in 1845 and even-tually the restoration of his civil rights. A third Constitution finally provided for the universal suffrage demanded in this speech.*

That the sovereignty of this country resides in the people, is an axiom in the American system of government, too late to be called in question. By the theory of other governments, the sov-ereign power is vested in the head of the State, or shared with him by the Legislature. The sovereignty of the country from which we derive our origin, and I may add, many of our opinions upon political subjects, inconsistent with our present condition, is in the King and Parliament; and any attempt on the part of the people to change the government of that country, would be deemed an insurrection. There all reform must proceed from the government itself; which calls no conventions of the people, and recognizes no such remedy for political grievances. In this coun-try the case is totally the reverse. When the revolution severed the ties of allegiance, which bound colonies to the parent country, the sovereign power passed from its former possessors, not to the General Government, which was the creation of the States, nor to the State Governments, nor to a portion of the people, but to the whole people of the States, in whom it has ever since re-mained. This is the doctrine of our fathers, and of the early days of the republic, and should be sacredly guarded as the only safe foundation of our political fabric. The idea that government is in any proper sense the source of power in this country is of foreign origin, and at war with the letter and spirit of our institutions.

The moment we admit the principle, that no change in gov-ernment can take place without permission of the existing authori-ties, we revert to the worn-out theory of the monarchies of Europe; and whether we are the subjects of the Czar of Russia, or of the monarch of Great Britain, or of a landed oligarchy, the difference to us is only in degree, and we have lost the reality, though we may retain the forms of a Democratic Republic. If the people of Rhode Island are wrong in the course they have pursued, they will never-theless have conferred one benefit upon their countrymen by the agitation of this question, in dissipating the notion that the people are the sovereigns of the country, and in consigning to the department of rhetorical declamation those solemn declarations of 1776, which are repeated in so many of the State Constitutions, and which are so clearly and confidently asserted by the most eminent jurists and statesmen of our country.

If time permitted, I should take great satisfaction in laying before you the most abundant evidence, that these are the well recognized principles of our republican system; and are not to be regarded as revolutionary.

The Declaration of American Independence asserts that governments derive their just powers from the consent of the governed; and that it is the right of the people, meaning the whole people, the governed, to alter or abolish their government whenever they deem it expedient, and to institute new government, laying its foundation on such principles, and organizing its powers in such form, as to them shall seem most likely to effect their safety and happiness. This Declaration was expressly adopted by the General Assembly of this State in July, 1776.

The Constitutions of many of the States, while they contain specific provisions for the mode of their amendment, set forth, in the strongest terms, the right of the people to change them as they may deem expedient. Any other construction would render a portion of the declarations of rights in these Constitutions entirely nugatory.

The Convention which framed the Constitution of the United States, acted as the Representatives of the sovereignty of the people of the States, without regard to the limitation attempted to be imposed by the Congress of the Confederation. That the whole people, by an explicit and authentic act—the great body of society, have a right to make and alter their Constitutions of government, we find ours is a principle which has been laid down by the fathers of the Constitution, and the ablest expounders of our political institutions—by Washington, Hamilton and Madison. The strong opinions of Jefferson on this point are too well known to need a particular repetition.

## 8.

### Smith A. Boughton:
### TO THOMAS A. DEVYR FROM PRISON *
### [June 25, 1845]

*Smith A. Boughton (1810–88), of French Huguenot descent, was born on a New York leasehold farm. While a medical student at Middlebury, Connecticut, he led a student protest against enforced religious tenets. In 1837 he joined the Patriots' War in Canada. Returning poor and broken in health, he soon developed a flourishing medical practice in Rensselaer County. Touched by the plight of the farmers who lived under the semifeudal "leases" of the Van Rensselaer family, he headed the antirent movement in the 1840's under the name "Big Thunder." Eventually he was convicted of "robbing" a sheriff of papers and was sentenced to life imprisonment by a vindictive judge. From his prison cell Dr. Boughton sent out this letter to Thomas A. Devyr, the fiery Irish land reformer who had been active in the New York struggle. In 1847, Boughton was pardoned and his political rights restored by Governor John Young, who had been elected by the antirent vote. The Constitution of 1846 upheld his views by prohibiting further feudal leases.*

*From a Hudson Jail, Columbia County, June 25, 1845*

DEAR SIR——

Once more through the will and pleasure of an All-wise Providence, I have an opportunity to communicate to you, . . . all the horrors and sufferings by which I am surrounded, and daily endure. My health is extremely bad, . . . I am raked with pain. Night and day the air of the prison is so bad that even our enemies who visit us declare that they could not endure it for one week. And when night comes the air of our cells is so close, that I many times think we shall all be suffocated, there being no plan for ventilation. Of this we have often complained; but get no relief. The reply is—"Let the d——d Anti-Renters die, for they have caused us trouble enough already!" But very few of our friends are permitted to see us to administer any consolation or comfort. And all

* Reprinted in *Young America* (New York: July 19, 1845).

the outbreaks committed by men who act with the mistaken notion that there is no other way than an appeal to arms, are immediately visited on us the instigators and cause; and I verily believe that we shall be charged with the commission of every crime in this country.

. . . It is cheering in the gloom of my imprisonment that my friends have not forsaken me. And may God grant that I may still live to repay them for all the efforts they have made in my behalf. Although broken down in health, my spirits are buoyed up with the fond anticipation that all our efforts are not in vain, and that I shall live to meet you all, who contribute in the glorious work of emancipating an unjustly wronged and insulted people for a state of slavery and landridden tyranny which would be a disgrace to modern Russia. And let it be transmitted to posterity that a free people dared to rise and vindicate their rights instead of basely crouching to a monied aristocracy who would rob them of the dearest gift of heaven. The anticipation of that happy day has pierced the gloomy walls of my prison and made my fellow sufferers clank their chains for joy. The health of my fellow sufferers is declining apace, but their spirits are still unsubdued. How long a free people will suffer this kind of martyrdom, God only knows.

The farmers of this County ask for nothing but what is consistent and right. The most substantial of the yeomenry deprecate and deplore the outrages that have been committed in this community, as much as any friend or well-wisher of the cause of Equal Rights, would. But a brave and free people cannot bear everything. They are willing to meet their landlords on the ground of equal rights and have the long and perplexing question of Title investigated. But all overtures of this kind have been treated with insult and disdain and accompanied with this threat: "We have the power to crush you and will do it." May God in his goodness bring about that happy state of things that every one may sit under the vine and fig tree of his own planting is the constant prayer of

*Your unfortunate friend,*

SMITH A. BOUGHTON

# CHAPTER THREE

## FRATERNAL AID TO THE COMMON MEN OF OTHER NATIONS

A *particular* people, *whatever extension we give to the mean-ing of the word, whether it means a parish or an empire, is every where a physical and moral agent, whose interests are analagous and reciprocal with those of another people of a like description, who inhabit a neighbouring territory. Each of them has a real interest in the prosperity of the other; because prosperity creates certain relative superfluities, which, being exchanged between the parties, supply their relative wants.*

> ———JOEL BARLOW: *On Certain Political Measures,*
> December 20, 1799

*The mention of Greece fills the mind with the most exalted sentiments and arouses in our bosoms the best feelings of which our nature is susceptible. . . . A strong hope is en-tertained that these people will recover their independence and resume their equal station among the nations of the earth.*

> ———JAMES MONROE: *Sixth Annual Message,*
> December 3, 1822

Sources of the quotations on the preceding page:

JOEL BARLOW: Joel Barlow: *To His Fellow Citizens of the United States. Letter II. On Certain Political Measures Proposed to Their Consideration* (Paris: 1799), 5–6.

JAMES MONROE: James D. Richardson: *A Compilation of Messages and Papers of the Presidents, 1789–1897*, 10 v. (Washington, D. C.: 1898–9), II, 193.

---

AMERICA has a rich heritage of sympathy for the democratic struggles of all mankind. Even though American pioneers were of necessity preoccupied with the immediate problem of subduing a wilderness, nevertheless foreign policy and international relations deeply interested them. As stable communities were established on the Atlantic frontier and spread inland, foreign news followed and occupied a large portion of local American newspaper space.

Interest in foreign affairs did not stop with mere knowledge. Over and over again Americans have expressed deep sympathy for the revolutionary struggles of the people of other lands. During the French, Latin American, Greek, and other revolutions, few July Fourth celebrations passed without popular toasts linking these to the American Revolutionary traditions. Spokesmen for the new republics were widely acclaimed when they arrived on these shores. Money was raised at mass demonstrations at historic Revolutionary shrines like Faneuil Hall. Some men went abroad personally to aid those battling for freedom. Even the American expansionist concept of "manifest destiny" has been tinctured with republican zeal to bring liberty and democratic virtue to all mankind.

During the first years of the Republic the French Revolution was the touchstone of American politics. The Federalists feared and detested it, especially after the excesses of its later phases, for they saw in it vindication of their fears of popular misrule. But the Republicans supported the French Revolution, and it aroused widespread popular enthusiasm in America. The Democratic-Republican Societies (2) hailed it as an upheaval for freedom and liberty. The Virginia legislature unanimously acclaimed the National Assembly of France (1). Passionate July Fourth celebrations and street carnivals paid tribute to the Revolution and the French minister plenipotentiary, Citizen Genêt. Popular anger flamed in burning effigies and burst forth in rock-throwing demonstrations when the Federalists defended the Jay Treaty with its seeming surrender to British terms. There was widespread demand that the United States aid the French Revolutionaries in their war with England and great resentment against Washington's policy of neutrality.

Latin America flared with revolutions in 1816, when Ferdinand VII demanded unconditional submission to Bourbon power. Revolutionary leaders like José de San Martin, Bernardo O'Higgins, and Simon Bolivar spread the flames to La Plata, Chile, and Venezuela. These leaders, seeking recognition for the three Republics, found warm response in the United States. Henry Clay orated on the "glorious spectacle of eighteen millions of people struggling to burst their chains and be free." * Henry Marie Brackenridge, secretary of a commission to study South American conditions (3), was a strong supporter, and many editorials in *Niles' Register* (Chapter Two, 2) firmly espoused the cause. The demands for immediate recognition were denied by the sympathetic but cautious President James Monroe, whose advisors wished to avoid the risk of war with Spain and the Holy Alliance. In 1822, however, the United States formally recognized these republics, and Columbia and Mexico as well. In 1823, partly to shelter them against the interference of European powers, we proclaimed the Monroe Doctrine.

The Greek Revolution of the twenties aroused general popular enthusiasm. The pulpits resounded with laudatory speeches (Chapter Two, 3), and President Monroe expressed sympathy in his annual message of 1822. The South Carolina legislature petitioned Congress to acknowledge Greek independence, and Albert Gallatin even proposed lending a fleet to the embattled Greeks. Many frontier hamlets bore the names of Greek martyrs; many schoolboys reluctantly endured large doses of Greek grammar for the cause. Samuel Gridley Howe went off to battle for

---

* *Annals of Congress*, 15th Cong., 1 sess., Vol. II, 1817–8, p. 1478. For a warmly sympathetic pamphlet by an anonymous writer, see below (4).

Greek freedom. A New York gentleman offered to provide the Greeks with "five hundred men, six feet high, with sinewy arms and case hardened constitutions, bold spirits and daring adventurers, who would travel upon a bushel of corn and a gallon of whiskey per man from the extreme part of the world to Constantinople." * Only John Quincy Adams's opposition to interference in Europe, a policy that he worked into the Monroe Doctrine, restrained the President from sending a mission to Athens.

The Revolutions of 1830 and 1848 evoked a warm response in America. A huge demonstration was held in New York City in November, 1830 (Chapter Two, 5). With the news of 1848, a "Young America" group burgeoned within the Democratic party, a group dedicated in part to enlisting young America's aid for democratic movements abroad. When Hungary fell, the legislatures of New York, Ohio, and Indiana called for action. Lewis Cass introduced a resolution supported by most western Senators, but not carried, to suspend diplomatic relations with Austria. In December, 1851, Louis Kossuth, the exiled Hungarian patriot, was brought to America on an American battleship assigned to that task. As a guest of the Nation he was banqueted by Congress. Ovations signalized his triumphal tour through the country, and prairie states renamed their counties in honor of the Hungarian revolt. Unfortunately more was expended in celebration than in contributions to this cause. But the warmth of America attracted many who fled Europe's bleak aftermath of 1848.

Among the many motives that underlay expansionist enthusiasm for the annexation of Texas and Oregon was a crusading zeal to spread republican government. The July Fourth oration of George Holley in 1839 (5) rapturously expressed the feeling "that the eyes of the whole enlightened portion of the human race are now turned" to America. In similar vein, Caleb Atwater the educator warned: "Extinguish the lamp of freedom in our country, and all the lights of liberty now burning in Europe may also be immediately extinguished in that continent." (6) The *Western Review* proudly boasted that we, "the most enterprising people on God's footstool," were "sending democracy throughout the

* From John Bassett Moore as quoted in S. Fiske Kimball: *Domestic Architecture of the American Colonies and of the Early Republic* (New York: 1922), 183–4.

world." (7) In Congress, the voice of William Allen of Ohio called for reoccupation of Oregon and passionately contrasted the British and American roles: "The one having the old decaying system of hereditary power, with its abuses, to defend—the other, the new and onward system of elective authority, with its freedom to protect." * Behind this fervor were, of course, many mixed motives, not the least of which was the hunger for land. But, like the enthusiasm for democratic revolutions, this desire to spread the American form of government into new territory indicates the importance Americans attached to democratic institutions.

---

### 1.

### A Vɪʀɢɪɴɪᴀ Aᴅᴅʀᴇѕѕ ᴛᴏ ᴛʜᴇ Nᴀᴛɪᴏɴᴀʟ Aѕѕᴇᴍʙʟʏ ᴏꜰ Fʀᴀɴᴄᴇ †
### [1791]

*Characteristic of the widespread sympathy for the French Revolution was this "Address to the National Assembly of France," unanimously agreed to in the Virginia legislature. These sentiments were not shared by the Federalists, particularly after the Revolution moved on to its "Jacobin" phase in 1793. But even then the common folk were generally enthusiastic supporters of the French Revolution.*

We, the representatives of the people of Virginia, long sympathising with the national assembly of France, in their glorious struggle for liberty, avail ourselves of the earliest opportunity, to present, with all the sincerity of fraternal affection, our warmest congratulations on the establishment of your new constitution—a constitution in which every masculine feature is portrayed that could strongly mark it as the legitimate offspring of liberty. Indeed, from such an illustrious band of patriots and philosophers,

* *Congressional Globe,* 29th Cong., 1 sess., Appendix, p. 839.
† "Address to the National Assembly of France, Unanimously Agreed to by the Legislature of Virginia," reprinted in *The American Museum,* XII (1792), App. II, pp. 12–13.

we anticipated nothing less, preserving, as you have done, with undiminished purity, through so many successive ages, that noble spirit of your ancestors, which often bade defiance to the ancient conquerors of the world. . . .

We venerate the wisdom that suggested—we admire the boldness that commenced—we applaud the manly firmness that pursued—we are pleased with the humanity and politic forbearance that insured—and we love the virtue that achieved the enterprise. Long may you enjoy the inestimable blessing which this combination of enviable attributes has secured to you: and may your example be imitated, not only by the rest of Europe, but by every enslaved nation upon the face of the globe—till despotism, with all its host of enemies to human happiness and improvement, is entirely chased away.

## 2.

### RESOLUTION OF THE DEMOCRATIC SOCIETY OF NEW YORK *
### [May 1794]

*The Democratic Society of New York was one of over forty popular societies organized between 1793 and 1800. Significantly, the first of these, the "German Republican Society" of Philadelphia, observed that "solitary opinions have little weight with men whose views are unfair, but the voice of the many strikes them with awe." Like the Sons of Liberty, the Democratic societies were generally drawn from the "lower orders." As devotees of republican government, they espoused popular education, free speech, press and assembly, and militia companies as checks against antidemocratic tendencies. Characteristically, this resolution expresses sympathy for the French Revolutionists.*

Yes, fellow citizens, we take a pleasure in avowing thus publicly to you, that we are lovers of the French nation, that we esteem their cause as our own, and that we are the enemies, the avowed enemies, of him or those who dare to infringe upon the holy law of LIBERTY, the sacred RIGHTS OF MAN, by declaring, that

* *New York Journal and Patriotic Register* (New York: May 31, 1794).

we ought to be strictly neutral, either in thought or speech, between a nation fighting for the dearest, the undeniable, the invaluable Rights of Human Nature, and another nation or nations wickedly, but hitherto (we thank God) vainly, endeavoring to oppose her in such a virtuous, such a glorious struggle.

If this is the language of treason, if this is the language of faction and sedition, come forward, ye votaries of opposite principles, ye stoical apathists, who can set [sic] with folded arms, with sullen silence, with unmoved composure, while the house of your next neighbor, your former benefactor, YOUR ONLY REAL FRIEND, is on fire, without affording even one single solitary bucket of water, to aid in quenching the raging, the wide spreading flame; ye secret abettors of tyranny and despotism, ye hermaphroditical politicians, come forward, we call upon you, bring us by legal means, if such you can contrive, to the bar of justice, and punish us for these our open, our avowed principles, from which no earthly consideration shall ever tempt us to recede. . . .

We would not be understood to mean, that every man who opposes our societies, is an enemy to this country, or even an aristocrat in his heart; but we most firmly believe, that he who is an enemy to the French revolution, cannot be a firm republican; and, therefore, though he may be a good citizen in every other respect, ought not to be entrusted with the guidance of any part of the machine of government. . . .

JAMES NICHOLSON *and*
TUNIS WORTMAN.

3.

*Henry Marie Brackenridge:*
SOUTH AMERICA *
[1817]

*Henry Marie Brackenridge (1786–1871) was born in Pittsburgh. Through his father, Henry Hugh Brackenridge, he acquired a love of reading, a wide range of interests, and a lib-*

* H. M. Brackenridge: *South America, a Letter on the Present State of That Country, to James Monroe, President of the United States* (Washington, D.C.: 1817), 14–16, 44–5, 46.

*eral political philosophy. Trained as a jurist, he practiced law
in St. Louis, New Orleans, and Baltimore. In this pamphlet
South America he early urged an American foreign policy
similar to the Monroe Doctrine. After serving as secretary
of a commission to study the political situation in South
America, he returned to Baltimore, where he supported the
bill designed to admit Jews to public office.*

There is nothing which tends so much to check the sympathy
we should be disposed to give the Southern Americans, in their
present interesting struggle, as the prevailing idea that they are
totally unfit for self-government; a character which we bestow,
without discrimination, to all, although there is by no means a
uniformity in the moral state of the different colonies. This is a
topic of which their enemies have availed themselves, unfortunately, with great success. They are represented without distinction or discrimination, as in a state of extreme ignorance and
debasement, (a state by the by, which ought to cover the Spaniard
with shame) without any kind of information, and without morals,
lazy, inconstant, worthless, and at the same time violent, jealous,
and cruel, composed of heterogenious [*sic*] casts, likely to be split
into separate factions, and if left to themselves, to be engaged in
the most bloody civil wars. In fact no pains have been spared to
represent them in the most hateful and disgusting colors, and
there are many of us who now take it for granted that they are
the most despicable of the human race. Let us for a moment inquire by whom is this indiscriminate character bestowed? It is
given either by their bitterest enemies or by those who are unacquainted with them, or whose opportunities have enabled to
see them only in the most unfavorable light.—Persons who have
never seen a Southern American are in the habit of condemning
them all by the wholesale, as stupid, depraved, and worthless.
Notwithstanding all this, if we consult the enlightened travellers,
who have visited those countries, we will find that they all concur
in bearing testimony of their native intelligence, and of the number of well informed, and well educated people they found there.
But is it for us to repeat or believe such slanders? We should recol-
lect the character which until lately, was charitably given to us
throughout Europe, and we should hesitate before we condemn

a people whom we have had no opportunity of correctly estimating. Until the American revolution, it was a fashionable opinion, extremely agreeable to European vanity, that we degenerated in the new world, and if not continually renewed by European intelligence, would be in danger of losing the faculty of reason. How long since this slander has been refuted? There are places where it is believed even now; yet the enlightened who knew that the true dignity of human character does not depend upon climate or soil, but on the liberty and freedom of government, as necessary as the sun and air to plants, foretold to what we should be, when left to ourselves. . . . Our enemies in Europe, are still in the habit, in spite of the proofs we have given, both in peace and war, of representing us as degenerate, at least as incapable of anything great. These things we know to be the slander of malevolence and envy, repeated by ignorance and prejudice; may we not in charity suppose that all we have heard of the Southern Americans is not true? . . .

Although the sentiment in favor of the Patriots, through the United States, is almost universal, and seems to become each day more earnest, yet there are a few who pretend to advocate a cold indifference, and even speak of the Patriots in the same terms that our enemies, during our revolutionary war, used to speak of us. The Patriots are called rebels, insurgents, and we are gravely advised to hold them in contempt. I would ask how long is it since we have got up a little in the world, that we should thus look down upon our poor relations? Can we bestow epithets upon these men, without, at the same time, casting the severest reproach upon ourselves? No—they are now, as we once were, nobly contending against oppressors or invaders, in a cause sanctified by justice, in a cause more just than ours—for where we had *one* reason to complain, they had *ten thousand.** This cold blooded indifference, to the fate of our fellow men, is unworthy of us. We sympathised with the Spaniards, when lawlessly invaded by France, we sympathised with Russia, we now sympathise with France, and have we no feeling for our brethren of the South?—Those who inculcate this

---

* Here Brackenridge includes a lengthy footnote in which he argues the right of the colonies to declare themselves independent of Spain, stating that there never was an act more easily supported and that nothing but lawless force was on the side of Spain. (Ed. note.)

apathy, tell us that since we are happy and contented, we ought to be indifferent to all the rest of the human race! If this sentiment is really serious, and not a mere concealment of enmity to the Patriots, it is despicable, it is unworthy of any one who wears the form of man. According to these, a wise nation ought to stifle all the finer feelings of human nature, it ought to have *no* charity but for itself; base selfishness should be every thing; and generosity, patriotism, liberty, independence, empty and ridiculous words. . . . It does not follow that because these sentiments are indulged, we must become Quixotic, and involve ourselves in war, on account of mere religious or political opinions. I am no advocate of French fraternization, but I am not therefore to condemn every generous feeling that glows in the bosoms of those who wish well to the patriot cause. I would wish to see our conquests, the conquests of reason and benevolence, and not of arms. There is nothing to forbid our feeling a generous sympathy with the Patriots of South America; a contemptuous indifference on our part, would be regarded by them as reproachful to our national character, and would lay the foundation of lasting hatred.

4.

## An Appeal in Behalf of the Independent South American Provinces [*]
### [1818]

*This pamphlet voices ideas similar to those advanced by Hugh M. Brackenridge, Hezekiah Niles, and Henry Clay. It claims sympathy for Latin American states not only on commercial grounds but also on the basis of the American Revolutionary heritage and of the aid received by Revolutionary America from sympathetic foreigners.*

Whoever as a politician can turn from these views with indifference, must be either insensible to, or ignorant of the best interests

[*] Anonymous: *Appeal to the Government and People of the United States in Behalf of the Independent South American Provinces* (New York: 1818), 27, 28–31.

of our country. But whoever as a man—as an American, can view the struggle of these people without feeling his bosom glow with all the sympathies of the philanthropist and the republican, is undeserving the title of an American—is unworthy the blessings of liberty. On the great question which this revolution presents to our government and people, we need no additional information.— Our judgment is grounded on events notorious to all the world. Much and important valuable intelligence as we shall undoubtedly receive from the commissioners lately returned from South America—it is altogether a mistaken idea to suppose that they can add any thing to the data on which the grand question depends. The great revolutions which have taken place, and are now taking place there, disclose facts sufficient to regulate our course. It cannot, therefore, by any means be thought premature to discuss this subject before the observations of the commissioners are laid before the public. The enthusiasm manifested in the cause of South American liberty and independence, by those attached to the mission, and by the officers of the Congress, leave little doubt however of the nature of the information we may expect from the commissioners themselves.

. . . If there be any relic of that spirit which once animated our countrymen still left among us;—if we are not absolutely impervious to all considerations of our own interests—as well as the voice of a people challenging from us only the same good offices we experienced from foreign powers under the pressure of suffering in the same cause,—we cannot hesitate—we cannot delay.—A sanguinary war—a war of extermination—if successful, to be succeeded by a peace of oppression scarcely less cruel, demands of us an energetic and prompt interference.

A commerce—that in the event of the triumph of independence and liberty, would soon rival that of either of the Indies, invites us to the alliance.

A people, who have evinced a more than Roman fortitude in the cause of liberty, claim our assistance and protection in the same glorious cause which eventuated in our country's independence and prosperity.—Her toiling and bleeding patriots have long cast an eye of hope, and extended a hand of supplication towards us— relying with confidence on the sympathy and succour of the only republic to which they can have recourse. . . . To the humanity and generosity of a free, powerful, and enlightened people—to their regard for their own interests—we confidently commit the guardianship of the liberty and independence of these infant republics—these sister empires.

FINIS

5.

*George Holley:*
AN ORATION DELIVERED ON THE FOURTH OF JULY *
[1839]

*George Holley was educated at West Point. He moved from Connecticut to Illinois, where in 1837 he published and edited the* Ninawa Gazette. *Through his paper, which flourished until 1841, he acquired a considerable literary reputation.*

And on the barren rock of Plymouth they kindled the first pale beacon-fire of liberty—a fire whose spreading flame burned up through a revolution that was destined to change all the political theories and politics of ages past; and which, at this moment consumes not, but warms into delightful and glorious existence the inhabitants of an empire extending from the Atlantic to the Pacific; from near the tropic to the arctic circle; and which illuminates and cheers onward the whole civilized world!

And it is neither boasting nor vanity to say, that the eyes of the whole enlightened portion of the human race are now turned, with anxious solicitude, to the progress of our experiment in self-government. . . . And if, with all our past experience, and all our present knowledge; if with the searching light of the Gospel streaming upon and illuminating our way, revealing the path of duty and making it so plain that the wayfaring man need not err therein; . . . if we become dead to the thrilling memories of the past, and the glorious fruitions of the future and prove a patricidal people; the bitterness of regret, remorse and shame; the greater

* George Holley: *An Oration Delivered on the Fourth of July 1839, at Peru, La Salle County, Illinois* (Chicago: 1839), 6–7, 11–12.

bitterness of a world's taunts and a world's scorn; the superlative bitterness of anarchy or despotism will be the just retribution of our more than folly—our fool-hardy madness. There is no other world for another Columbus to discover and unless the wheels of time can be stayed in their tracks, . . . there can be no possible combination of circumstances, no possible series of events, that shall be so favorable to the formation of a pure representative democracy, as those circumstances which were combined, and those events which did transpire, to consummate the establishment of our Government. Freedom, driven from all the old states, sought in this virgin world her last asylum, her noblest, fairest, final home. And here she hath scattered with lavish hand her choicest gifts, her richest blessings; here she hath established her altars and reared her fanes, and accursed forever be the sacrilegious hand that would mutilate or rend asunder either of the twenty-six columns that support her hallowed dome!

The discovery and colonization of the American continent, the commencement, progress and termination of the American revolution, the achievement of American freedom, with the new, inestimable and innumerable blessings resulting from that freedom to the whole human race, are not merely the epochs of a single nation, or a single century; they form one of the sublime eras of a world. And if we of the present generation but appreciate our situation as the inheritors of that freedom, as its guardians and protectors, as the instruments through whom it is to be transmitted, not mutilated and abridged, but enlarged and adorned, to future times, we cannot but be impressed with the momentous responsibility devolved upon us. . . .

But if our people remain true to themselves, to their constitution, their laws and their institutions, by what standard shall we attempt to measure our country's future glory. . . . I will not mar, by minute details, those reflections upon it which must suggest themselves to every enlightened mind, but will only add, that if some enthusiastic artist should attempt to give you an emblematical sketch of America's future glory, he would represent to you a colossal statue, standing with one foot upon the Atlantic, the other upon the Pacific ocean, with one hand receiving the furry wealth of the frigid zone, with the other gathering in the varied riches of tropical climes. Before that statue he should place the tree of liberty, its roots deep and firmly stricken into the earth, its foliaged branches overspreading, but not shading, the whole of America's vast empire, blooming in perennial beauty, its fruits and flowers offered to all without money and without price. Leaning against that tree, he would picture to you the benignant spirit of a tolerant and evangelizing religion, respected and revered by every member of the wide community, and their free will offerings strewn in lavish abundance at his feet. . . .

And everywhere through the wide landscape, he would show you the cheerful countenances of free and happy beings, giving life and vigor to the scene; and, from the highest summit of her loftiest mountain, he would represent to you, in gigantic proportions, the *Banner of Freedom*—THE AMERICAN FLAG—streaming to the freewinds in triumph and in glory, waving in splendor over time's (best), noblest empire; and, in the enthusiasm of the moment, perchance his overwrought imagination would whisper to him that there that banner should continue to wave, until the contents of the seventh vial shall be poured over the world; and when the thrilling fiat shall go forth, that time shall be no longer, and the heavens and the earth shall be rolled together as a scroll, that then that flag shall be, not the emblem of a (fallen) nation, but the winding-sheet of a departed world!

## 6.

### *Caleb Atwater:*
### AN ESSAY ON EDUCATION *
### [1841]

*Caleb Atwater (1778–1867) was born in Massachusetts of New England ancestry. He kept a school for young women in New York City while studying for the Presbyterian ministry, which he forsook for the bar. Settling in Ohio in 1815, he was elected to the lower house of the state legislature in 1821, where he served as chairman of the committee on school lands. He later headed a state board to formulate a*

* Caleb Atwater: *An Essay on Education* (Cincinnati, Ohio: 1841), vi–vii, 12–13, 122–3.

*system of education. He wrote one of the first histories of Ohio in 1838, but this essay on education has been characterized as his best writing. He lived and died a poor man, too deeply concerned with human welfare to amass personal wealth.*

Our free form of government, our vast domain, our means of instruction, our benevolent institutions, our pure religion, our love of liberty, the example of our ancestors and the high aspirations of their posterity; our distance from the old world, our soil, climate and productions, and the energy and sleepless enterprise of the American people; seem to promise the world that this nation is to be the greatest and most powerful one on earth. To its vast numbers, wealth and physical power, may its moral power be as vast, benevolent and good. . . .

Our object in this essay is, to bring all good men back into the arena, to take their places in the ranks of the common people, and do their duty and never despair of the Republic; but, by their precepts, example and influence, save this generation from destruction, and raise up a wiser one, to govern this country, and hand down all other valuable institutions from age to age forever. To this object, universal education is the only remedy, in a country governed by the whole people. On the very brink of political and moral ruin, as a free people, once moral, patriotic and quite too confiding, all hearts are imperiously called on to unite in the common cause for the common safety. . . . The histories of all former, free nations are but so many flaming torches which light us through the mouldering tombs of freedom. Shall we basely surrender our birthright? Have we paid the debt which we owe to our ancestors? Is our debt to our posterity paid? What will they say of us if we neglect our duty to them? Loaded with chains and bowed down in slavery, will they not curse us for our neglect, our pusillanimous neglect of our duty to ourselves, to them, to our country and our God? Can freedom long dwell where ignorance and vice prevail? . . .

Extinguish the lamp of freedom in our country, and all the lights of liberty now burning in Europe may also be immediately extinguished on that continent.

Could such an education as we advocate be extended to every

citizen of this republic, should a war ever occur between us and all the monarchs in the world, what an army should we be able to send into the field! What navies of ours would cover the seas! And these armies and navies would fight our battles, and defend our liberties, and hand down to our posterity such renown and glory, as the history of no other people records. At the bar, in the halls of legislation, in the pulpit, in the professor's chair, and in the popular assembly, what bursts of eloquence would convince the judgment, vivify and move along with them the human passions and the human heart! . . . Made up, as we are in the West, of the youthful vigor of the world, all thrown into one mass, living under such a free form of government, and occupying as we do, so large a portion of the very best part of our globe, it is not enough for us to boast of what we have already done, though it by far exceeds all that any other people ever achieved in any similar period of time, as that during which we have lived in the West. But, we repeat it over and over again, that the richest portion of our estate lies in the intellect of our people. Shall this portion of our inheritance become a paradise, or remain a waste? Let us all arise, clear, and cultivate this vast field, and fence it; surrounding it with a durable, strong wall, high as heaven; so that we may forthwith begin to reap an abundant crop of moral healthfulness and social happiness. Our vast region would morally resemble a tropical one, producing fruits and flowers at the same time on every tree. Looking down the long vista of future ages, on the millions, and millions of millions of human beings, who will yet dwell in this vast Western Valley, from age to age for ever! Who can estimate the vast amount of physical, mental, and moral evil to be prevented; and the vast amount of positive physical, mental, and moral happiness to be conferred by education on the myriads of human beings who are to come after us? Who can compensate us for neglecting, even for a day, to do our duty towards the rising generation? Let us all arise NOW, and lay a foundation broad, deep, and high, building on it the means of instruction, which shall eventually, like a crucible, melt down the whole mass of our citizens into one lump of liquid, living, active, moving virtue and intelligence. Finally, [*sic*]

Fathers and mothers, brothers and sisters, relatives, friends and neighbors, ministers of religion, doctors of law and doctors of medicine, professional teachers, rulers and ruled, and every man and woman in all the land—arise, and go forth, aiding us in the high and holy work of education: Save our free form of government from destruction, and immortal souls from ruin: rouse into activity every power of your bodies and every faculty of your souls, and apply them vigorously in your endeavors to diffuse knowledge, and increase the physical, mental, social, and political happiness of mankind.

## 7.

### *The Western Review:*
### THE OREGON QUESTION *
### [April, 1846]

*This April issue was the only one to appear. Launched by Charles Creighton Hazewell and G. R. Hazewell, its prospectus promised: "The articles . . . will to some extent be of a political character in which the principles and measures of the Democracy of the United States will be discussed in a more extended and elaborate manner than can be entered upon by the newspaper press. It will be the aim of the publishers, to make it acceptable, by its uncompromising advocacy of the Democratic party, and the aid which it can be made to afford, in the great and important work of exposing the aristocratic and monopolistic tendencies of Modern Whiggism."*

View it how you may, it resolves itself, at last, into a contest between the two great principles which are now agitating the world—the principle of *Progress*, and the principle of *Conservatism*. Shall *Democracy*, or shall *Aristocracy*, be the governing principle of the world? that is the question which must be decided by the settlement of the rival claims to Oregon. It is not a question as to the relative merits of Aristocracy or Democracy— whether the one or the other is the more favorable to humanity, the most likely, by its triumph, to add to the happiness of mankind. The existence of the two principles, on a large scale, and on

* *Western Review* (Columbus, Ohio: April, 1846), 186–8.

the same continent, is impossible. The life of the one, is the death
of the other. There can be no middle course—no compromise—no
halting the one principle on a certain parallel of latitude, to look
the other in the face, and blows not follow. When they meet,
they must contend for supremacy, from the workings of immutable laws. The *American Democracy* are impelled, by an
overbearing necessity, to combat and put down, or themselves
perish, every principle conflicting with that by which they are
animated; just as the monarchs of Europe, on the breaking out
of the French Revolution, were compelled to war against it, and
to seek the suppression of its doctrines, through the destruction
of its disciples and adherents. They knew that the triumph of the
revolutionary party, would be their ruin—that the establishment
of a republican government in France, would subvert every
throne in Europe, sooner or later. France is the heart of Europe,
and its political throbbings were sure to agitate the entire European system—to effect the overthrow of principalities and powers, and establish popular sovereignty, if those throbbings were
in favor of liberty and equality. . . . We are the depositories of
the *democratic principle;* and a stern and jealous principle it is,
which will admit of no divided empire. It claims for itself this
continent, as a rallying ground, from which to move the world;
and it will not tolerate the existence of any other political principle in its neighborhood, for the simple reason, that should it
do so, it would aid in its own destruction. It is this fact, which
gives to the Oregon question its immense importance—which
makes it the most momentous dispute in which we have ever
been engaged with a foreign power, and that power, the leader
of the world's conservative party—the nation which, with its gold
and steel, beat down the hosts of freedom, though led by the
mightiest genius which twenty centuries have produced. All other
matters sink into insignificance, when compared with this; and
it is not to be wondered at, that, in the eyes of hundreds of thousands of our countrymen, it leads to the obscuration of many
questions of internal policy of the first magnitude. It stirs up all
those feelings which are so deeply seated in the American heart,
—patriotism, the love of glory, attachment to freedom, a desire of
territorial aggrandizement, the spirit of enterprize, political propagandism, and that ardent wish which every man must have felt

at some period of his life, to make his country the first in the world—the sun of the system of nations.

It is often said, that the American people are not propagandists —that they do not seek to force their opinions upon other nations, and aim not at the overthrow of governments based upon principles different from those which animate their own. We are not propagandists, in the sense that the term is generally used. We have never declared, through Congress, as the French did through their National Convention, that we are ready to give aid and assistance to all who are struggling for freedom. Were Congress to issue any decree of the kind, its members would be afforded speedy opportunities of manifesting their sincerity on some very different and more appropriate stage. There is no necessity for our issuing any such declaration, because we are doing the same thing in another way—we are sending democracy throughout the world, 'conquering and to conquer,' without making any parade about the matter. Look at our progress, and admit the truth of what we say. Fifty years since, we were among the feeblest of nations—the flying fish of the world, preyed upon by the monsters of both sea and air—by England and by France. We rarely entered into the calculations of the powers of the old world, and our territorial increase was not to them a matter of much alarm. How different now the position occupied by us! Step by step have we advanced, amid the din of European wars and the turmoil of European politics, until the idea of controlling the whole continent, is what every village voter discusses, as something by no means wonderful. Louisiana, Florida, and Texas, have been acquired; and now we propose to assume rule over the *whole of Oregon,* and the Californias are soon to fall into our hands. Beyond these, we say only this, that that man must be dull of comprehension, who cannot see that the probabilities of a large portion of the Mexican republic being annexed to us, within fifteen years, are much greater than were those which existed fifteen years ago, that Texas would now form an integral portion of the Union. Now, what is all this, but propagandism? Are not all these advances, so many triumphs of our peculiar principles? Do we not, by thus incorporating new countries into the republic, give weight to those views of policy, upon the triumph of which depends our existence as one people? And when our title to Oregon shall have been maintained, as well as asserted—when the Californias shall have been acquired—when the northern provinces of Mexico shall have been 're-annexed' to Texas, through being admitted to the great North American confederacy; when all these things shall have been accomplished, what nation on earth will be sufficiently powerful to outweigh us? What despotism, or aristocracy, will be so vigorous as to be able to stand up against the moral and political example which we shall then exhibit to the world—the example of a nation of some eighty millions of the most enterprising people on God's footstool, and occupying a territory so fertile, so varied in its climate, its productions, its elements of greatness, and the means of education? Are we not, then, propagandists, and of a description most appalling to the advocates and supporters of adverse theories and contrary practice in life and government? Why, we are more to be feared, than would be a million of Frenchmen thrown loose upon Europe, shouting 'En avant!' singing Ca ira! and the Marsellaise, and resolute to follow the tri-color—that true fiery cross—wherever the most daring of its disciples might choose to carry it, in the wildness of their zeal and the fervor of their enthusiasm.

Much as the governments of the old world must dread our progress to vast territorial dominion, because thereby is strengthened principles whose supremacy is incompatible with their own existence, we do not see that they can have any right to complain, and as little to interfere to stop our onward march. We are only doing what they have done from the earliest period of their history, though we are not guilty of those gross violations of the rights of others, or of the acts of monstrous cruelty, which have marked their career.

# CHAPTER FOUR

# ALL MEN ARE
# CREATED EQUAL

———◆◆———

*In the full enjoyment of the gifts of Heaven, and the fruits
of superior industry, economy and virtue, every man is
equally entitled to protection by the law; but when the laws
undertake to add to these natural and just advantages artificial distinction, to grant titles, gratuities, and exclusive
privileges, to make the rich richer and the potent more powerful, the humbler members of society—the farmers, mechanics, and laborers—who have neither the time nor the
means of securing like favors to themselves, have a right to
complain of the injustice of their Government.*

——ANDREW JACKSON: *Bank Veto Message,*
*July 10, 1832*

*Every good man should protest against a caste founded on
outward prosperity, because it exalts the outward above the
inward, the material above the spiritual; because it springs
from and cherishes a contemptible pride in superficial and
transitory distinctions; because it alienates man from his
brother, breaks the tie of common humanity, and breeds
jealousy, scorn, and mutual ill-will. Can this be needed to
social order?*

——WILLIAM ELLERY CHANNING: *On Elevation
of Laboring Classes, 1840.*

Sources of the quotations on the preceding page:

ANDREW JACKSON: James D. Richardson: *A Compilation of Messages and Papers of the Presidents, 1789–1897,* 10 v. (Washington, D. C.: 1898–9), II, 590.

WILLIAM ELLERY CHANNING: Bernard Smith: *The Democratic Spirit* (New York: 1943, 2nd ed.), 249.

———◄◆►———

THE belief in social equality has been indelibly stamped upon the American past. Our colonial forebears experienced it in the social fluidity that brought ex-indentured servants to the Virginia House of Burgesses. They saw it nourished by land abundance, frontier conditions, and the spirit of independence of the earliest settlers—conditions that subverted the proprietary attempts to establish feudalism in colonial Maryland and the Carolinas. The American Revolution completed in America the destruction of monarchism and feudal hereditary privilege.

But if the old dragons were slain, special privilege kept marching on. Each epoch had its own forms. Before the Civil War it was the aristocracy, in part established in the colonial period, of large landholders, slaveholders, and merchant-bankers. After the Civil War it was the railroads; and today, it is the monopolies and trusts. At all times the common people of America have vigorously opposed entrenched privilege. They have resisted being crushed to the bottom of the social heap.

In the preliminary skirmishes over titles of officeholders, keen-minded Senator William Maclay from western Pennsylvania reflected the republican conviction that the Federalists "wished for the loaves and fishes of government . . . the creation of a new monarchy in America . . . to form niches for themselves in the temple of royalty." * The power of the "rich and well-born" seemed to bring with it a corresponding contempt for "the mob" and a detestation of the French Revolution. Spokesmen for the common people, however, deplored the power of great wealth (1), which might found a new nobility. They hailed the social

* Edgar S. Maclay (ed.): *Journal of William Maclay United States Senator from Pennsylvania 1789–1791* (New York: 1890), 12.

egalitarianism of the French Revolution and showed their contempt for the "new nobility" of America (2). As Jeffersonian
Democrats they accepted a social responsibility to help the
fallen (3) and to receive the stranger from distant shores with
kindness (4). Jefferson's own faith in social equality is reaffirmed
in his very last letter, June 24, 1826, where he wrote:

> . . . The mass of mankind has not been born with saddles
> on their backs, nor a favored few booted and spurred, ready
> to ride them legitimately by the grace of God.*

The Jacksonian policy bore the stamp of the Jeffersonian tradition. But it was infused with a strong antimonopolist and pro-
labor leaven (5). The measure of man was his usefulness to
society, rather than his birth. The inequalities in society could be
staved off if inequalities in wealth, especially in monopolies,
could be withstood (6, 7). The blanket of equality covered the
alien as well as the native American (8). The heady brew of social equality was deeply drunk by debt-ridden farmers and mechanics. They stood at Armaggedon with President Jackson and
battled for the Lord against the Bank of the United States. For
the coming of Jacksonian democracy meant, according to Frederick Jackson Turner "that a new, aggressive, expansive democracy, emphasizing human rights and individualism as against the
old established order which emphasized vested rights and corporate action, had come into control." †

With the advance of industrialism the quest for social equality
remained on the whole a struggle against the "tyranny of wealth."
"The great and fruitful source of crime and misery on earth,"
thundered the fiery Irish-born Michael Walsh in a speech at Tammany Hall in 1841, "is the *inequality of society*—the abject dependence of honest, willing industry upon idle and dishonest
capitalists." (9) But a new and powerful ferment was also at

---

* Thomas Jefferson to Roger C. Weightman, June 24, 1826, in P. L. Ford
(ed.): *The Writings of Thomas Jefferson*, 10 v. (New York: 1892–9), X,
391–2.
   † F. J. Turner: *The United States 1830–1850: The Nation and Its Sections* (New York: 1935), 30. Reprinted by permission of Henry Holt and
Company, Inc.

work. Margaret Fuller's cry (10) that "there is but one law for all souls. . . ." came from a new chapter—the women's rights crusade. The cry was to ring out even more insistently for the Negro (Chapter Five). Men dreamed of a better world of brotherhood and equality—a New Harmony, or a "Palestine of Redeemed Labor." (11) It was the season of Utopian Socialism in America, of Owenite colonies and Fourier phalanxes. And each expressed in its own way that all men were created equal.

---

## 1.

### George Logan:
### FIVE LETTERS ADDRESSED TO THE YEOMANRY *
[1792]

*George Logan (1753–1821) was born in Pennsylvania. Quaker son of a wealthy merchant. He studied medicine abroad but turned to farming upon his return to America. A personal friend of Jefferson, he was elected to the Pennsylvania legislature. When war threatened in 1798, he went to France as a private citizen to intercede with the government for peaceful relations. Although he attained great success, Congress was greatly annoyed at his "interference" and passed the so-called "Logan Act," forbidding a private citizen from undertaking diplomatic negotiations without official sanction.*

There are two kinds of inequality, the one personal, that of talent and virtue, the source of whatever is excellent and admirable in society—the other that of fortune, which must exist, because property alone can stimulate to labor; and labor, if it were not necessary to the existence, would be indispensible to the happiness of man: But though it be necessary, yet in its excess it is the great malady of civil society. The accumulation of that power which is conferred by wealth in the hands of the few is the

* George Logan: *Five Letters Addressed to the Yeomanry of the United States* (Philadelphia: 1792), 11–12, 21.

perpetual source of oppression and neglect of the mass of mankind. The power of the wealthy is farther concentrated by their tendency to combination, from which, number, dispersion, indigence and ignorance, equally preclude the poor. The wealthy are formed into bodies by their professions, their different degrees of oppulence, [*sic*] called ranks, their knowledge, and their small numbers:—They necessarily, in all countries, administer Government, for they alone have skill and leisure for its functions. Thus circumstanced, nothing can be more evident than their inevitable preponderance in the political scale. *The preference of partial to general interests, is, however, the greatest of all public evils:* It should, therefore, have been the object of all laws to repress this malady, but it has been their perpetual tendency to aggravate it. Not content with the inevitable inequality of fortune, they have superadded to it honorary and political distinctions. Not content with the inevitable tendency of the wealthy to combine, they have embodied them in classes. They have fortified these conspiracies against the general interest, which they ought to have resisted, though they could not disarm. Laws, it is said, cannot equalize men,—No—But ought they for that reason to aggravate the inequality which they cannot cure? Laws cannot inspire unmixed patriotism—But ought they for that reason to foment that *corporation spirit* which is its most fatal enemy? All professional combinations, said Mr. Burke, in one of his late speeches in Parliament, are dangerous in a free state. Arguing on the same principle, the National Assembly of France have proceeded further: They have conceived that the laws ought to *create* no inequality or combination, to recognize all only in their capacities as citizens, and to offer no assistance to the natural preponderance of partial over general interests.

It is not the distinctions of titles which constitutes an aristocracy: it is the principle of partial association. The American Aristocrats have failed in their attempt to establish titles of distinctions by law; yet the destructive principles of aristocracy are too prevalent amongst us, and ought to be watched with the most jealous eye. . . .

. . . A chain does not derive its strength and utility from being composed of a few heavy links, and the remainder weak and ill conditioned, but from every link being as much as possible of equal power. The same takes place in civil society; a state is rendered more respectable and powerful by the prosperity of all its citizens, than by the overgrown wealth of the few.

2.

## PLAN FOR A NOBILITY IN THE UNITED STATES *
### [1798]

*This satirical "plan" expresses the popular feeling of the day against monarchism and aristocratic privilege. The common man bitterly hated the speculators, who, with the help of a Federalist dominated Congress, were making personal fortunes out of the sale of the public domain.*

WHEREAS a king and nobility are ardently desired, by a few of the good people of the United States; and the said friends of aristocracy and rank, are daily more and more disgusted with that old-fashioned, republican equality, which, to the noble-minded, is the worst slavery: And whereas the aimers at so happy a change in the government of our country, are, and have been, much at a loss touching the ways and means of providing a set of men, of sufficient wealth, merit, and splendour, to form an hereditary and titled order; the following plan, for that purpose, is humbly offered to public consideration, by a citizen who has employed his thoughts on that all-important subject, and dares flatter himself, that his plan, if adopted, will, in providing as many noble lords as may be wanted, for this, at present, poor plebian country, be productive of many other and great benefits to the same.

THE PLAN.

Let a list be made of all the speculators, as well in as out of the government, who have been prudent enough to enrich themselves in the sum of 150,000 dollars at the least— It is then proposed,

* "Plan for a Nobility in the United States" in *The American Museum* (1798), 96–8.

1ST. That to each speculator, having not less than 150,000 dollars, nor more than 200,000, there shall be added (either by free grant from the treasury, or by some governmental douceur equal thereto) as much as will make up 300,000.

2D. To each speculator, having not less than 200,000, nor more than 300,000, to be added, in like way, as much as will make up 450,000.

3D. To each speculator, having not less than 300,000, nor more than 450,000, as much as will make up 600,000.

4TH. To each speculator, having not less than 450,000, nor more than 600,000, as much as will make up 800,000.

5TH. To each speculator, having A MILLION and upwards, nothing to be added.

The said estates to be entailed in the mail [*sic*] line, pursuant to the right of primogeniture; and the interest accruing thereon, to be made sure to the said speculators and their heirs forever, by perpetual taxes, unalterably appropriated, and quarterly payable to their use.

The noble speculators of the lowest rank or grade, to be styled, "The order of the Leech." Their title to be, "Their Fullnesses." Their arms, "A leech, clinging to the bowels of an old soldier." The motto, "The blood of the brave, the reward of the knave."

The noble speculators of the next rank, to be styled, "The order of Modern Justice." The title, "Their Rapacities." The arms, "A pair of scales, balancing 2s6 with 20s. The motto, "Cheating no felony."

The noble speculators of the next rank, to be styled, "The order of the Virtuous League." The title, "Their Hucksterships." The arms, "A member of c[o]ng[res]s, in the hand of fellowship with a broker—in the mouth of the former, a label, 'I'll bellow for contracts and morality'—in the mouth of the latter, a label, "And I'll be buying up the FINALS." The motto, "Public faith, private fraud."

The noble speculators of the next rank, to be styled, "The order of Assumption;" or, if thought more suitable, "The order of the Golden Fleece." The title, "Their Pirateships." The arms, "Three packetboats (their flag—a sheep, and its keeper, assisted by a stranger, in the act of sheering it) under full sail for the modern Colchis (*Charleston*); and a number of expresses in full speed, in different directions." The motto, "The many made for the few."

The noble speculators of the highest rank, to be styled, "The order of Scrip." The title, "Their Influences." The arms, "A Janus, fitting on a pile of certificates; Modesty under one foot—Fidelity under the other; one face towards the bank—the other toward c[o]ng[res]s; in one hand the federal constitution, blotted and torn—in the other, a copy of the British statute, incorporating the bank of England." A double motto, "Public debts, private blessings (and underneath) Corruption, the true oil for the political machine."

Manifold and great will be the advantages incidental to this, so generous a plan.

1st. As it will stimulate diligence and ingenuity, by so great a reward to citizens who have so exercised these virtues, as to possess themselves of the wealth of the country at the least possible expense.

2d. As it will encourage liberty of conscience, by confering honours and revenues on the men who have nobly dared to shake off its yoke.

3d. As it will improve morality, by recommending a latitude in dealings, which our narrow-minded forefathers never dreamt of.

4th. As it will increase the artificial energy of the government, by combining avarice with ambition in the administration thereof; so as to strengthen the motives and the means of a powerful set of men, to resist and keep down the insolent, republican spirit of the people. For a standing order of nobility, thus twisted into the government, will be more to be relied on, than any standing army whatever, of mere plebeians, as is evinced in the case of the French revolution; that detestable subversion of the noble prerogatives of the few, in favour of the vulgar rights of the many.

5th. As it will fasten the better, the blessings of an irredeemable debt. For, as the taxes, for the debt, will keep the people obedient and sober, the nobility, mounted on the debt, will perpetuate the taxes on the people; and so perpetuate both these blessings.

This idea, of founding a nobility on a funded debt, is perfectly an original invention; and, being no less ingenious than important, the author hopes to be rewarded with a special act of grace, admitting him to rank in the "Order of Modern Justice," if no higher. If not so rewarded, he hereby gives notice, that he insists on his right to a patent.

If the invention take with the public, as it deserves. he intends to complete the idea, by funding a king on the funded nobility; and shall then expect an advancement to the "Order of Scrip."

ARCHIMEDES.

### 3.

*William Wirt:*
## ESSAY IN BEHALF OF THE POOR *
[1804]

*William Wirt (1772–1834) was born in Maryland, son of Swiss-German tavern keepers. Probably aided by a few friends, he wrote anonymous articles for the* Virginia Argus *and this series of essays entitled* The Rainbow, *which shows a deep concern for the fate of mankind. He was prosecutor in the trial of Aaron Burr, a Delegate to the Virginia House of Delegates, and Attorney General under Madison. In 1832 he received the Anti-Mason nomination for the presidency.*

It is not for me to draw before your imagination the weeping form of Charity, surrounded by her disconsolate family, who, with uplifted hands and broken voice, petition you for a scanty relief. I choose rather to bring before you the venerable figure of JUSTICE, bearing aloft the indestructible balance, in which are weighed the most comprehensive measures of nations, and the minutest actions of individuals. . . . May I, venerable Divinity! expect to escape thy disapprobation, while for a moment, I assume thy attributes; while I dare to expound thy holy nature, and employ thy principles for the use of those who most want thy aid: of the heartbroken, the ignorant, and the poor.

No man in society stands alone. There is not an individual, who has not drawn out and fastened his lines of connection to innumerable others, by which like the divergent rays of a spider's

* *The Rainbow* (Richmond, Va.: 1804), first series, 66–8.

web, he communicates and receives ten thousand sensations. There is not an individual, whose talents, temper and employment, have not a certain influence upon the happiness of others. The very meanest and lowest of mankind have their circles to fill up; a family to felicitate or disturb, some little friendships to cultivate, or some petty resentments to revenge. But if we wish to see the extent and attenuation of this influence completely unfolded, we must seek it in the history of those extraordinary characters, "who have filled a vast space in the eye of mankind." . . .

This influence may be various in different individuals; and yet it is equally clear, that there is one only way, in which this influence can be *best* exerted. The capacities of any thing can receive but one direction, that is productive of the greatest possible happiness. Apply it to a different purpose, and you pervert its proper tendency; you so far injure the welfare of society. Would any prudent man consent to "hew blocks with a Razor?" Should a man, whose endowments are rare, admirable and extensive, whose wisdom might enlighten the ignorance of his countrymen, and "scatter plenty o'er a smiling land," should such a man be doomed to languish under the labours of the oar, or perish amid the damps of a mine? Could any one approve of the destination of capacities even less useful in degree, to purposes even less improper in their tendency? I ask whether such a perversion could be considered as moral? May I not then be permitted to say, that no man's influence can be regarded as perfectly moral, that is not exerted to produce the greatest possible happiness, with which he is sufficiently acquainted; and that his actions only become so, when they tend to that object? . . .

Adverse situations have exposed many individuals to 'the stings and arrows of fortune.' The want of industry, the want of prudence, unexpected misfortunes or unjust persecution, have heaped upon their heads disease, poverty and disconsolation. Many have been disabled in the battles of their country: And many an unhappy female, who has wandered from the path of propriety has enlisted the agonies of want under the banners of infamy. Shall these misfortunes pass by without the necessary relief? And yet these abodes of misery will frequently contain more unfortunate objects, who have even a greater claim upon our justice. Let us enter their houses. You will observe their chil-

dren with tattered garments and pallid countenances. Converse
with them, and perhaps you may find the spirit of useful curiosity
slumbering, or their minds awake only to young debauchery and
cunning prudence. When a deformed child was born among the
ancient Spartans, it was their barbarous policy to expose it to an
early death. 'Tis true that civilized society does not murder the
children of the wretched, yet how often does she subject them
to imbecility and disease, by frequent abstinence, & insufficient
support! . . . Civilized society, 'tis true, does not turn the children of the wretched into brutes, yet how often do they wear the
form of man, divested of all pretensions to the dignity of his nature! And yet let the capacities of these unfortunate children be
impartially analysed. Will not their frames be found as complicated and subtile, as those of the rich? Are not their senses as
susceptible of impression? Can they not see and hear, and smell,
and taste & touch as delicately? Is their memory imperfect? Cannot they compare, reflect and reason? Has no individual on whom
"Fortune frowned unfeeling at his birth," ascended afterwards to
the heights of distinction and science? . . . When we accompany Gray to this melancholy receptacle of the dead, and when
like him we meditate over the mouldering ruins of the poor; what
is it that gives a more thrilling sensation to the soul, than the
comparison which our imagination is so prone to indulge, of what
these humble inhabitants of the hamlet formerly were, with what
they were once capable of becoming? . . . Even then we fanci-
fully retrace the incidents of each one's life, and conceive how
much of fortune and fame their native genius might have enabled them to attain, had a more fortunate star shone upon their
birth.

We have thus a simple picture of the intellectual condition of
the poor; of mind struggling in its very birth for the means of
unfolding its finest energies. For these lamentable misfortunes
we have found also an adequate cure. Would society cultivate
these capacities; would she exert a maternal affection for their
support and improvement, she would scarcely fail to raise them
up into useful and respectable children. But should she suffer
them to protract a miserable existence, surrounded as they too
often are by thoughtless debauchery and wild intoxication, stimulated by poverty and degraded by contempt, what security can

she have that she will not hereafter find in them an active nuisance calculated to interrupt her order, and disturb her repose?

Compare now this complicated chain of consequences with those which may be expected to arise from the different destinations that were imagined to be given to the supernumerary fund of society; compare the subsistence, the cloathing [*sic*], and the information of the poor, with the injurious superfluities of the rich; and to which side, let me ask, may not the greatest happiness be expected to fall! It is now that justice weighs them in her golden balance, and pronounces her impartial decree: *Let Society fulfill the Claims of the Poor.*

### 4.

#### ESSAY ON NATURALIZATION *
#### [1816]

*The generous spirit of hospitality towards immigrants is firmly implanted in this essay. The anonymous author is evidently aware of the attacks of the Kentucky legislature and George Nicholas against the harsh features of the Alien and Naturalization Acts in 1798.*

There is no rational person but must condemn the doctrine of unalienable allegiance, and admit the propriety of naturalization. There is no one in the least acquainted with the history or nature of man who does not know that expatriation and naturalization have ever been his practice, whether, in the simple state of the untutored Indian, and wandering Tartar, or in the civilized one of the European and republican American. Emigration seems almost necessary to man for the preservation of his intellect, and the constitutional strength of his frame. Besides the obvious direct arguments which may be brought in support of this principle, nature, throughout her works, furnishes us with a strong analogy. In all her extensive operations we see a constant mutation, succession, and revolution. Every thing is constantly undergoing some change, and these changes are the causes of con-

* *Essay on Naturalization* (Washington, D.C.: 1816), 117–18, 123–5.

tinuance; a degeneracy of one part produces a regeneration of another; and the continual mutations and motions of the various parts of our globe, and the constant revolution of the whole, is what preserves our planet in its vigour and in its beauty. Shall man then be the only object which is not the subject, and has not the privilege of constant change? While other animals are confined, like vegetation, to particular spots within separate parallels of climate, man alone, the universal heir, ranges at large, and finds his food and raiment in every zone. . . . Thus every where we perceive constant changes and similar appearances in the operations of nature, and the whole globe, throughout all its parts, moving in the majestic unity of the grand principle which the divinity ordained.

When once the congress of the United States, giving way to the flagitious and contaminating policy of despotic monarchies, will so forget itself as to legislate on any other basis than that of nature and reason, we may be certain there is some canker corroding the vitality of their liberty. . . . Beware, then, Americans, of the indications of any system, however specious its pretexts, which will be founded on any other basis than the broad ground of rational principle. Young as the United States are, as a nation, their legislation was for a time, disgraced by two laws which had the merit of copying and exceeding the enactments of the most jealous and despotic governments.

One * of these laws, professed indeed not to intermeddle with the rights of citizens, but only to hamper and controul [*sic*] the "foreigner." But this law once passed led the way to another, a suitable companion, which trammeled the citizen with clauses of constructive sedition. The celebrated resolutions of the legislature of independent Kentucky, in 1798, observing on these laws,

---

* The manly and intelligent Mr. Nicholas, of Kentucky, in a letter to a friend in Virginia, speaking of the alien law, thus well observes upon it. . . . "But, if the policy of party extended its views still further, and from a knowledge of the existing convulsions in Europe, and the causes which have produced them, wished to put it in the power of the president, to discourage and prevent all who are engaged there in struggles for liberty, from emigrating to America, if they are unsuccessful at home; at the same time that the door was left open, to receive all the abettors of tyranny, if they failed in their present contests: this act may, in its operations go a great way towards contaminating and destroying those republican principles which now exist in America, and which are the only real support of our present constitution." [Note in the original.]

acutely remarked. . . . "the friendless alien has, indeed, been selected as the safest subject of a first experiment; but the citizen
will soon follow, or rather has already followed; for, already has
a sedition act marked him as a prey." But these laws could not
exist in America. The buoyant spirit of the country burst the little
threads of coercion, which petty despots, artfully sought to com-
press it with. The republicanism of the nation rose indignantly at
such efforts, and proscribed from their government, the men
whose acts betrayed, so clearly, the cloven footsteps of their administration.

Of all countries America is the last which should adopt regulations restrictive of naturalization and expatriation. Founded by
emigrants, the pride of her history should make her receive the
stranger with kindness and respect.


### 5.


### RESOLUTIONS AT A WORKING MEN'S MEETING *
[September 26, 1829]

*The* Mechanics' Free Press *was the first labor paper in America. It appeared in Philadelphia on January 2, 1828, and lasted
until October 17, 1835, reaching a circulation of about 1,500,
which, for a labor paper, was very impressive in those days. It
was an important organizing medium of the workers and advocated the election of candidates and the passage of measures
favorable to labor.*


At a meeting of the working men of Philipsburg, Pa. held on
Saturday evening, Sept. 26th, *John Kinnear* was called to the
chair, and *John Dale* appointed Secretary. When on motion, the
following preamble and resolutions were unanimously adopted:—

In a free government, founded upon the authority of the people,
and instituted for their peace, happiness and safety, no artificial
distinctions or inequalities ought to be tolerated by law, inasmuch
as the first principle of nature as well as republicanism, is, that all
men are born equally free and independent.

* *Mechanics' Free Press* (Philadelphia: October 24, 1829).

Natural inequality amongst men do and always will exist to a certain extent; but it is the duty of a wise government to soften and modify them as much as possible and in no case to increase them.

This, we believe to be the spirit and very essence of our excellent Constitution, but yet when we look at the effect which many of our laws have upon the community, and compare the situation of the labouring classes with that of others, it would seem as if our Legislatures were acting upon principles directly the reverse, and were endeavouring to increase these distinctions by throwing all the power and wealth of the country into the hands of the few, and leaving the many wholly unprotected, against the oppressive monopolies which have been established by law.

No system of education, which a freeman can accept, has yet been established, for the poor; whilst thousands of dollars of the public money have been appropriated for building colleges and academies for the rich.

No law has been passed, calculated to raise the price of the poor man's labour; but yet, the whole community has been taxed, by heavy Tariff duties upon foreign importations, in order that rich men may build up manufactories.

Banks and other privileged corporations are increasing without number through the land, all tending by their power to monopolize business and controll [*sic*] the circulating medium, to strengthen the aristocracy, and reduce the power of the farmer, mechanic and labourer.

The effect already is, that one half of society are the slaves of etiquette, and the other of excessive labour.

The hardest labour is made the least productive; and the most useless drones of society are the best paid.

One class is doomed to toil for bread, and another privileged to wanton in luxurious idleness.

The producers of wealth are poor and dependent, whilst the *consumers* are rich and powerful.

Therefore, *Resolved*, That in the opinion of this meeting, it is the duty of working men to unite their efforts, to have the laws made and administered more in conformity with the spirit of republican principles.

*Resolved,* That we form ourselves into a political association, similar to those already formed in other parts of the state, and that we make it a part of our duty, to examine and discuss all the political questions, upon which we are called upon to pass judgment, by our votes at the general elections.

*Resolved,* That the proceedings of this meeting be signed by the Chairman and Secretary, and published in the Penn Banner.

JOHN KINNEAR, *Ch'n.*

JOHN DALE, *Sec'ry.*

## 6.

### Samuel Whitcomb, Jr.:
### ADVANTAGES OF A REPUBLICAN CONDITION OF SOCIETY *
### [1833]

*Samuel Whitcomb, Jr. (1792–1879) was born in Massachusetts, son of a Cohasset blacksmith. He traveled extensively as a bookseller. As an advocate of a public school system, he greatly helped men like Edward Everett and Horace Mann. In 1846–8 he had charge of an agency at Boston for supplying teachers to the South and West. Often identified with Dr. Charles Douglas, editor of the* New England Artisan, *and Seth Luther (Chapter Two, 6), he believed in labor solidarity and wanted workingmen's organizations in every New England town.*

Whether we look back to the times in which the institutions of civilization were *originated,* or contemplate their *progress* amid religious excitement and political revolution,—whether we trace the history of each class, the useful, the fine, the liberal, and the polite, or confine our observation to their concurrent results,—we are brought to the conclusion, that the best method of securing, in any given number of human beings, the highest possible attainments in all those acquisitions which adorn an individual, and render glorious a nation, is to so reward the industry of each, and

---

* Samuel Whitcomb, Jr.: *Two Lectures on the Advantages of a Republican Condition of Society, for the Promotion of the Arts, and the Cultivation of Science* (Boston: 1833), 30–1, 35–6, 39–40, 41.

so to regulate the distribution, as to secure the highest possible degree of EQUALITY in the condition and advantages of every citizen. . . .

It has been sometimes remarked, by professional gentlemen among us, that after spending many years and much money in the acquisition of a *classical education,* they find themselves compelled to serve the community for salaries no larger than are paid to persons of but common literary attainments employed in counting houses and public offices; and I think there is sometimes ground for this complaint. But the error consists not so often, perhaps, in our paying the clerk too much, as in *giving neither enough;* and the remedy is to be sought by the professional public servant in reform of opinion and usage in relation to the *wages of labor.* The mass of a people, under every form of government, must be manual laborers; and on these the clergymen, physician and public officer must depend for his support. If *they* are robbed of the *fruits of their labor,* and compelled to *toil for nought,* HE must submit to a participation of their losses. But make their compensation generous, allow *them* to thrive and prosper, and *he* never fails to obtain a full share of their wealth and enjoyments. *Double the wages of the working man,* and you double his powers of production, and his capacity to remunerate the services of all who contribute to promote his prosperity. . . .

It is not, then, to despotic governments nor wealthy aristocracies that the world is most indebted for the advancement of civilization. It is not to drones or monopolists that we may look with confidence for the patronage of humanizing science, and ameliorating arts. It is not on the laureates of Kings and the partizans of Courts that we can rely for those *reforms,* which from ignorance, poverty, and vice, are to emancipate mankind. If we class the arts by that test which philanthropy and intelligence will soon have applied to whatever asserts a claim to human approbation—*the test of utility*—we cannot fail to perceive that the beneficial and ameliorating, still more than the ornamental, have their lodgement with the INDUSTRIOUS CLASSES, and their home with the FREE. While the work of slaves and vassals is often but the expression of a fantastic imagination and a vitiated taste. . . .

For a model of that dignity which becomes a *citizen* and a *freeman,* we must look to such as Franklin, who could dispense alike the sublimest lessons of science and the humblest maxims of domestic economy, sell ballads and Almanacs to our tradesmen and villagers, or negotiate treaties for us with the proudest monarchs of Europe. We must reject that blighting dogma, that a few only of mankind are susceptible of any other than the grossest animal enjoyments, or entitled to leisure and opportunity for intellectual improvement. We must disenthral our youth from those anti-republican influences which seduce them to prefer the grandeur and splendor pictured in a foreign drama or romance, to the simplicity and purity of their own humble homes; to the eloquence, philosophy and truth,—the moral genius and skill which achieved our independence, laid the foundation of our prosperity, reared our political and literary institutions, and have won for our republic the admiration of the world. We must make moral excellence, intellectual superiority, and the useful efforts, in *manual* as well as mental labor, the test of respectability, and the guarantees of individual prosperity. We must call to the aid of truth, the faculties of every mind, and the energies of every soul. And instead of imitating the despots and aristocrats of the *old* world, by *reducing the prices of labor,* and degrading the honest laborer to the character and condition of a slave, a vassal, a serf, or a menial,—we must *encourage* his industrious efforts, and remunerate his skill with a *pecuniary compensation* which shall enable him to command those intellectual helps, those social inducements to mental cultivation and moral improvement, which shall constitute him the glory, as well as the bulwark of our Republic, and make these United States become to the modern world, what those of Greece and Phenicia [*sic*] were to the nations of antiquity.

7.

*William Leggett:*
THE INEQUALITY OF HUMAN CONDITION *
[December 31, 1836]

*Born and reared in New York City, William Leggett (1801–*
*39) had a brief career in the Navy, where he was court-*
*martialled for dueling with another officer. He next became*
*assistant editor of the New York* Evening Post, *then edited by*
*W. C. Bryant. Seeking more radical outlets, he moved to other*
*papers, where he waged a struggle against slavery, limited*
*suffrage, state banks, and repression of trade unionism. Char-*
*acteristic of his courageous journalism is this plea for social*
*equality.*

A very casual and imperfect survey of society, in regard to the
vast disparity of condition it presents, must satisfy any reflecting
mind that there is some great and pervading error in our system.
If the inequalities of artificial condition bore any relation to those
of nature; if they were determined by the comparative degrees of
men's wisdom and strength, or of their providence and frugality,
there would be no cause to complain. But the direct contrary is,
to a very great extent, the truth. Folly receives the homage which
should belong only to wisdom; prodigality riots in the abundance
which prudence has not been able to accumulate, with all his
pains; and idleness enjoys the fruits which were planted and cultivated by industry. It is not necessary to state these facts in figu-
rative language, in order to render them worthy of serious and
attentive consideration. Look through society, and tell us who and
what are our most affluent men? Did they derive their vast estates
from inheritance? There are scarcely a dozen wealthy families in
this metropolis whose property descended to them by bequest.
Did they accumulate it by patient industry? There are few to
whom an affirmative answer will apply. Was it the reward of
superior wisdom? Alas, that is a quality which has not been asserted as a characteristic of our rich. Whence, then, have so many

* *The Plaindealer* (December 31, 1836) from William Leggett: *A Col-*
*lection of the Political Writings of William Leggett*, 2 v. (New York: 1840),
II, 162–5.

derived the princely fortunes, of which they display the evidences in their spacious and elegant dwellings, in their costly banquets, their glittering equipages, and all the luxurious appliances of wealth? The answer is plain. They owe them to special privileges; to that system of legislation which grants peculiar facilities to the opulent, and forbids the use of them to the poor; to that pernicious code of laws which considers the rights of property as an object of greater moment than the rights of man.

Cast yet another glance on society, in the aspect it presents when surveying those of opposite condition. What is the reason that such vast numbers of men groan and sweat under a weary life, spending their existence in incessant toil, and yet accumulating nothing around them, to give them hope of respite, and a prospect of comfort in old age? Has nature been less prodigal to them, than to those who enjoy such superior fortune? Are their minds guided by less intelligence, or their bodies nerved with less vigour? Are their morals less pure, or their industry less assiduous? In all these respects they are at least the equals of those who are so far above them in prosperity. The disparity of condition, a vast multitude of instances, may be traced directly to the errors of our legislation; to that wretched system, at war with the fundamental maxim of our government, which, instead of regarding the equality of human rights, and leaving all to the full enjoyment of natural liberty in every respect not inconsistent with public order, bestows privileges on one, and denies them to another, and compels the many to pay tribute and render homage to the few. Take a hundred ploughmen promiscuously from their fields, and a hundred merchants from their desks, and what man, regarding the true dignity of his nature, could hesitate to give the award of superior excellence, in every main intellectual, physical, and moral respect, to the band of hardy rustics, over that of the lank and sallow accountants, worn out with the sordid anxieties of traffic and the calculations of gain? Yet the merchant shall grow rich from participation in the unequal privileges which a false system of legislation has created, while the ploughman, unprotected by the laws, and dependent wholly on himself, shall barely earn a frugal livelihood by continued toil.

In as far as inequality of human condition is the result of natural causes it affords no just topic of complaint; but in as far as it is brought about by the intermeddling of legislation, among a people who proclaim, as the foundation maxim of all their political institutions, the equality of the rights of man, it furnishes a merited reprehension. That this is the case with us, to a very great extent, no man of candour and intelligence can look over our statute books and deny. We have not entitled ourselves to be excepted from the condemnation which Sir Thomas More pronounces on other governments. "They are a conspiracy of the rich, who, on pretence of managing the public, only pursue their private ends, and devise all the ways and arts they can find out, first, that they may, without danger, preserve all that they have so acquired, and then that they may engage the poor to toil and labour for them, at as low rates as possible, and oppress them as much as they please."

## 8.

### *Henry E. Riell:*
### AN APPEAL TO THE VOLUNTARY CITIZENS *
### [1840]

*In this pamphlet Henry E. Riell denounced the bigotry of the "Native American" movement and pointed out its incompatibility with the doctrine of social equality affirmed in the Declaration of Independence. The pamphlet was first published in the campaign of 1840 in support of Martin Van Buren and was reprinted in 1844, when the "Know-Nothings" were stirring up violence against the Irish Catholics.*

Fellow citizens: As a native American, and the son of a native American, taught from infancy to revere and love the exalted maxims of equal justice, and the heart expanding breadth of political benevolence upon which our proud system of freedom is founded, I blush with shame at the dishonor which is done to it by those who, from the boasted rights and privileges of their birth, should be the first to do justice to its character, and to protect it

* Henry E. Riell: *An Appeal to the Voluntary Citizens of the U.S. From All Nations, on the Exercise of Their Elective Franchise at the Approaching Presidential Election* (New York: 1840), 3.

from the degrading stigma of inhospitality. I disclaim all fraternity of feeling and connection with such men, and regard them as the worst and the most unnatural of aliens—"aliens in their native land"—aliens in spirit to the institutions which they should proudly cherish as the noblest inheritance of their birthright.

As a native American, I exult in the triumph and truth that the country which gave me birth, is destined, both politically and physically, to be the free asylum for the oppressed and the distressed of the Universal World. As an American, with far more than a million millions of the square acres of my native soil around me, I cannot so far crush my feelings of philanthropy and honest pride as to tell mankind that this wide world affords no asylum for suffering humanity—no refuge for the oppressed. On the contrary, I would tell them that it is here without money and without price, and that we lay claim but to an humble meed of beneficence, even for this gratuity; for never had a people so much to give at so slight a sacrifice. Sacrifice!—the boasted gratuity is a loan at interest, and the whole commonwealth becomes enriched by the labor, the skill, the industry, which it thus procures. Partial evils there may be—local pauperism, and therefore unequal burdens—but these evils like those in the economy of a bounteous Providence, tend to redress themselves, and are but the concomitants of universal good.

As a native American Republican, too, I would protest against that erroneously assumed superiority of hereditary to inherent and natural right; of fortuitous and involuntary to chosen and voluntary citizenship, upon which the false pride, the haughty prejudices, and the arrogant usurpations of the "Native American" faction and its allies are founded. To attach merit or demerit to fortuitous events over which we have no control, is identically the fallacious principle upon which hereditary monarchies, the inequitable laws of primogeniture, and all the aristocratic distinctions which exist from birth are founded; but they are utterly exploded and repudiated in our system of government, which is based alone upon the natural rights of man. Every feature of our republican constitution harmonizes with the fundamental doctrine previously promulgated in the Declaration of Independence as a self-evident truth, namely, "that all men are created equal, and endowed by their creator with certain unalienable rights, among which are life, liberty, and the pursuit of happiness."

If this be the prerogative of human nature by birth, then has no man, nor nation of men, any prerogative that contravenes or invalidates it.—No nation can righteously deny these natural and equal rights to those who seek them, and, accordingly, our equitable form of government offers them freely to all, upon the reasonable condition that the recipients of them shall solemnly promise to uphold and preserve, for the benefit of others, that constitution which has conferred these blessings upon themselves, and abjure allegiance to every other authority. Nor does the constitution permit the government to make any laws of naturalization that would operate partially and unequally—favoring foreigners of one nation more than those of another, or one class of foreigners from the same nation, more than another. In strict accordance with the doctrine of equal rights, it requires equal laws of naturalization, without which those rights would be invaded. Every naturalized citizen, therefore, owes it to himself and to the cause of liberty in general, to remember and duly appreciate the truth, that his political position in the United States is in nowise inferior to that of a citizen by birth, except in his disqualification for the highest office of the government; and even this exception establishes the general rule of his equality.


9.


*Michael Walsh:*
SPEECH AT TAMMANY HALL *
[1841]

*Born in Ireland, Michael Walsh (c. 1815–59) came to America in his childhood. A printer by trade, he proclaimed himself champion of "subterranean" democrats and organized young laborers into a Spartan Association with a view towards destroying Tammany's control. This speech was delivered in one of the rough-and-tumble political battles of the day. In 1843 he founded the* Subterranean *(New York), and his editorials*

* Michael Walsh: *Sketches of Speeches and Writings of Michael Walsh* (New York: 1843), 29–30, 32.

*caused his imprisonment for libel twice and scared off advertising. In 1844 for a short time he merged his paper with Evans's Working Man's Advocate (New York). He joined the Hunkers and denounced the abolitionists, who, he charged, neglected wage slaves for the cause of the Negro. He served three terms in the New York State Assembly and once in Congress. Discredited through growing intemperance, he was found dead after a convivial night under circumstances suggested foul play.*

Yes, my friends, I must candidly acknowledge that I am one of those wild youthful enthusiasts who are just foolish enough to believe that every rule ought to work both ways, and that if the democratic party will but stick to their text—if they will but carry out their principles and creed to the letter, without consulting expediency—if they will oppose all charter monopolies and repeal those in existence—if they will cease to contract the public work out for a bonus to unprincipled favorites, who amass fortunes by driving round in their gigs, abusing, goading and driving almost to death the poor half-starved wretches; the chief part of the proceeds of whose labor they are enabled by this plundering contract process to pocket. If they will wage war against all exclusive privileges and special legislation—set their faces against every thing which is calculated to elevate the rich, and degrade and oppress the poor—if they will do all in their power to break down the hoary-headed errors of ages, errors which have loaded the mass of the human race for centuries upon centuries with sorrow, suffering and chains, for the aggrandizement of the lazy, idle few, and simply practice what they preach—if they will but do all this, they need never apprehend a defeat. . . . Like all the revolutions on the earth, they have been for the elevation of one class and the pulling down of another. But both of those classes are our oppressors, each in their turn as they acquire the power. We are the instruments by which these great revolutions have been always affected, and yet we have been invariably excluded from the benefits of each change. Look at the thousand bloody fields which have been fought in the old world where men have carried desolation and death to each other's doors and families, for the *worthy and noble* purpose of deciding which should wear their crown and be their tyrant. Dick or Tom. If the working classes would only use one tenth of the exertion, and make one tenth of the sacrifice to get rid of masters entirely, that they do in trying to have their own choice of that burdensome article, both slaves and tyrants would soon be compelled to mingle—and a middle and happier class would be formed by blending the two extremes. (Great cheers and crys of "True.") And what have we gained by the numberless political triumphs which we have achieved? Nothing but a change of masters! We have had to bear all the evils of legislation—and its benefits have never reached us. . . . The great and fruitful source of crime and misery on earth is the *inequality of society*—the abject dependence of honest, willing industry upon idle and dishonest capitalists. The more that wealth is concentrated in the hands of the few, the more miserable must be the many. You may do as they bid in England—first make laws to reduce the poor to starvation, and then pass laws to hang them for stealing a loaf of bread to lull to sleep the starvation which by this means is brought upon them; but will this stop the crime—will it benefit mankind in the mass? No! Look at the blood-stained records of law-made and law-murdered poverty in England, and you will see that the laws became more severe as poverty increased, and that crime kept pace with the severity of the laws. There is no tyranny on earth so oppressive as the tyranny of wealth—and no slavery so great as the slavery of poverty! So long as one portion of mankind are wallowing in wealth, idleness and luxury, the rest will never be satisfied with toil, want and degradation! (Tremendous cheering.) If exclusive privileges were granted to the poor instead of the rich—if legislators legislated for our elevation instead of our degradation, without going any farther, it would be but a step towards our regeneration. Legislation may greatly increase our wrongs and wretchedness, but it never can cure them. Unless men carry their democracy into private life, their public acts are of little consequence. . . . [*]

* This abridged report, as now published, was purchased from O. J. Pinckney, who was paid for suppressing it. [Note is in the source.]

10.

*Margaret Fuller:*
THE GREAT LAWSUIT *
[July, 1843]

*Born in Massachusetts of Puritan ancestry, Sarah Margaret
Fuller (1810–50) developed from a precocious child to one of
the foremost literary critics in America. Her friends included
William Henry Channing, Bronson Alcott, and Henry David
Thoreau. Through her famous "conversations" with the
women of Boston society, she derived material for "The Great
Lawsuit," which first appeared in* The Dial, *the transcendentalist organ edited by her, and then, in an extended ver-
sion, as* Woman in the Nineteenth Century (1845). *She was
the first American to present a logical plea for improving the
position of women.*

And, as to men's representing women fairly, at present, while
we hear from men who owe to their wives not only all that is comfortable and graceful, but all that is wise in the arrangement of
their lives, the frequent remark, "You cannot reason with a woman," when from those of delicacy, nobleness, and poetic culture,
the contemptuous phrase, "Women and children," and that in no
light sally of the hour, but in works intended to give a permanent
statement of the best experiences, when not one man in the million, shall I say, no, not in the hundred million, can rise above the
view that woman was made *for man,* when such traits as these are
daily forced upon the attention, can we feel that man will always
do justice to the interests of woman? Can we think that he takes
a sufficiently discerning and religious view of her office and destiny, ever to do her justice, except when prompted by sentiment;
accidentally or transiently, that is, for his sentiment will vary according to the relations in which he is placed. The lover, the poet,
the artist, are likely to view her nobly. The father and the philoso-
pher have some chance of liberality; the man of the world, the
legislator for expediency, none.

Under these circumstances, without attaching importance in

* Margaret Fuller: "The Great Lawsuit" in *The Dial*, IV (1843), no. 1,
pp. 13–14.

themselves to the changes demanded by the champions of woman, we hail them as signs of the times. We would have every arbitrary barrier thrown down. We would have every path laid open to woman as freely as to man. Were this done, and a slight temporary fermentation allowed to subside, we believe that the Divine would ascend into nature to a height unknown in the history of past ages, and nature, thus instructed, would regulate the spheres not only so as to avoid collision, but to bring forth ravishing harmony.

Yet then, and only then, will human beings be ripe for this, when inward and outward freedom for woman, as much as for man, shall be acknowledged as a right, not yielded as a concession. As the friend of the negro assumes that one man cannot, by right, hold another in bondage, so should the friend of woman assume that man cannot, by right, lay even well-meant restrictions on woman. If the negro be a soul, if the woman be a soul, apparelled in flesh, to one master only are they accountable. There is but one law for all souls, and, if there is to be an interpreter of it, he comes not as man, or son of man, but as Son of God.

## 11.

### *George Lippard:*
### THE WHITE BANNER *
### [1851]

*George Lippard (1822–54) was born on his father's farm in Pennsylvania. Renouncing the ministry because of the "contradiction between theory and practice," and abandoning law because of its injustice, he went on to journalism. When his health failed, he turned to writing and lectures. Disgusted with the conventions of his time, he originated a philosophy and religion of his own that was reflected in his many novels. In 1850 he organized the Brotherhood of the Union, constituting himself the "Supreme Washington" to lead the crusade for the brotherhood of man. There were lodges in twenty-three*

* George Lippard (ed.): *The White Banner* (Philadelphia: 1851), 5–8, 141–2.

*states at the time of his death, expressing an anticapitalistic,
pre-Marxian viewpoint. As a writer he appealed to the worker
rather than the literary man.*

## Prologue.

### THE POOR MAN

One day a Rich Man came to a Poor Man, who stood talking by
the roadside.

It was where a fountain gushing from the rocks, and half shad-
owed by vines, sprinkled coolness upon the heated dust and sent
low music upon the evening air.

The Rich Man was clad in fine apparel: a diamond shone above
his young forehead, amid the curls of his chestnut hair. . . . And
this palace, these slaves, these stores of gold and silver—ALL were
his own.

For he was a Rich Man. The jewel that gathered the folds of his
robe across his young breast, was worth the life-long labor of a
hundred slaves.

And the Poor Man who stood talking by the roadside, was clad
in the coarse garments of toil. . . . He knew not where to lay his
head. The coarse garments which covered him, the rude staff in
his hand—these were all his possessions.

He was a wanderer upon the face of the earth.

And he stood in the midst of a throng of men, who listened to
him with earnestness, and hung upon every word, as though every
word was life or death to them. They were all poor men; the very
poorest of the poor; some clad in rags, and not a few crippled by
disease, or pitiful with blindness, or miserable to look upon with
their leper's sores.

And the accents of the Poor Man's voice held every ear, and
those who were not blind, looked earnestly into his eyes, and one,
half-kneeling on a solitary rock, regarded with mute wonder—
a kind of dumb adoration—the white forehead of the Poor Man.

For the face of the Poor Man, with its flowing hair, covered with
dust, and its sunburnt cheeks, touched by the trace of thought,
or time, or hardship, was a face that won you to it, with peculiar

power, and made you wish to look upon it forever, and mark the strange light of its eyes, and note the smile which hung about its lips.

There was, in truth, a strange Power, upon that face.

The Rich Man drew nigh with steps at once languid and eager, with a manner at once impetuous and full of dignity. His fair face, and perfumed hair, and jewelled robes, were terribly contrasted with the rags and lameness, the disease and leprosy, which encircled the Poor Man. . . .

The Rich Man sighed. He pressed his hand to his fair forehead. With all his wealth, his lands and slaves, his harvests and his palaces, he was not at peace with himself. He felt his bosom devoured by a gnawing restlessness. He was unhappy, and yet the darkness of these blind men had not visited him; his rounded limbs were free from leper's sores; the curse of the poor man's poverty was not upon his delicate hands. . . .

Quickening his footsteps, he drew near the Poor Man, brushing his fine linen against the beggar's rags, and with his gaze fixed upon the dilating eyes of the Poor Man, his ear enchained by every sound that fell from the Poor Man's tongue.

A word rose to his lips. He could not choke it down. And yet that word was "MASTER!" . . .

Thrusting himself into the miserable circle, he joined his hands, and said in a tremulous voice—

*"Master! what shall I do to inherit eternal life?"*

It was in these words that the burden of his soul found utterance. It was as if he had said, What shall I do to be at peace with myself, and while I live, and at the hour of my death, to have a hold on Immortality?

The Poor Man raised his eyes. They were touched with a gleam of divine sadness. He looked first upon the face of the Rich Man, then upon the wide harvest fields, and the herds of cattle, and the white palace, with slaves thronging before its portals—and last of all, upon the crowd of miserable men, who were gathered near him.

It was a painful contrast.

For a moment the Poor Man did not reply. He raised his eyes to the sunset sky, and his face was invested as with the blessing of God, embodied in sunset rays.

All the while the Rich Man awaited in the anxiety of undisguised suspense, the words of the Poor Man.

At last he spoke:

"SELL ALL THOU HAST AND GIVE TO THE POOR!"

And at these words the throng of miserable wretches looked up in wonder, and the Rich Man retreated backward and bowed his head, as suddenly as though some one had smote him on the forehead.

"*Sell* ALL *thou hast and give to the Poor?*"

It was as though he had said——

You have a Palace, Rich Man! Let its luxurious chambers be tenanted by the blind, the halt, the famine-striken, who now surround me. . . . Sell all thou hast and give to the Poor, for the Poor are as much the children of the great family of God as you are, as much entitled to his fruits, his air, his lands, as you are; with as holy a right to peace in this world, immortality in the next, as yourself!

And as the Poor Man spoke his face lighted up with a serene glory, and with the sweetness of his accents there was mingled a strange tone of Power.

But the Rich Man recoiling from the light of his eyes—frightened by the very simplicity of these words, which said so much in so brief a compass—turned sadly away, and went down the hillside, now raising his eyes to gaze upon his great possessions, now burying his face in his trembling hands.

But the Poor Man remained near the fountain by the roadside, talking to the blind, and the lame, the slave in rags and the leper clad in sores, who gathered near him, and felt the light of his eyes, while the accents of his voice penetrated their souls.

Thus it is over all the world, in all ages, among all People.

The Rich Man goes down the hill, full of restlessness, yet gazing earnestly upon his great possessions.

The Poor Man remains upon the roadside talking to the outcasts of all the world, and telling them of their right to Peace in this life and Immortality in the next. . . .

### THE BROTHERHOOD

Amid the war of sect and party,—amid the strife of hollow creeds and vindictive antagonisms,—*the* BROTHERHOOD lifts its WHITE BANNER into light.

And what is *the* Brotherhood? Listen——

THE BROTHERHOOD OF THE UNION is a secret organization. . . . It seeks to invest every man with the enjoyment of his Right to Land and Home. It seeks to destroy those social evils, which produce poverty, intemperance and crime. It seeks to inculcate correct views of the relations of Capital and Labor so that Capitalist may no longer be the tyrant, nor the Laborer the victim, but both sharers of the produce of work on the platform of Right and Justice. It seeks to annihilate the oppressions under which Labor has writhed so long and hopelessly; and to give to every Laborer the opportunities of mental as well as physical growth. (By Laborer is meant every one, who by the toil of hand or brain, produces something beneficial to the race.) It seeks, in a word, to band together all true men—to cement them in the bonds of a practical and peaceful association—to enable them to act for the Right, with one heart, one arm and one purse. Regarding the degradation of Labor as the cardinal evil—Land Monopoly, the Banking System and Special Legislation as the three great causes of this evil—the Brotherhood of the Union, has nothing to do with mere *sectional* questions. For it seeks to accomplish a perfect Unity of all the true men—all the men who desire and are willing to work for Human Progress—from Maine to Texas, aye from the Atlantic to the Pacific. While the Brotherhood is a secret society, so far as the means of its organization are concerned—it is public in regard to its principles—open in every respect to the eyes of the world. . . .

Linked with the American Past, in every detail of that glorious history, which commencing with the Landing of the First Pilgrim, traverses the Seven years of Revolution, and extends to the Present,—THE BROTHERHOOD looks forward in fixed Faith, to the dawning future, when this Continent shall become, in every sense of the phrase,—*"The Palestine of Redeemed Labor."* . . .

O, in this day when the wide impulse of a Humanity that loves all the race, is hampered by petty squabbles, and coffined in narrow creeds—when the spirit of sectarism divides mankind into little knots and gangs, setting every man to war with his fellow—when the Worker, despoiled of Home and of the fruits of his Labor, is separated from his Brother Worker, by the poison of some bigot's hatred,—O, is it not a good thing, in this time of party dissension and social war, to see an organization step boldly into light, with no word upon its WHITE BANNER but BROTHERHOOD?

Within its Circles may be found true men of all *creeds* who have agreed to differ in some respects, in order to unite upon the Grand Object. It eschews bigots of all stripes—bigots called by name or title whatsoever—eschews, avoids, and turns away from them, as from the smell of a plague-pit. It welcomes MEN. It is glad to be helped by Men—Men who are in earnest, and who *will work for the cause.*

# CHAPTER FIVE

# TOWARD NEGRO EQUALITY

---

*. . . I will be as harsh as truth, and as uncompromising as justice. On this subject I do not wish to think, or speak, or write, with moderation. No! no! Tell a man whose house is on fire to give a moderate alarm; . . . but urge me not to use moderation in a cause like the present! I am in earnest. I will not equivocate—I will not excuse—I will not retreat a single inch—AND I WILL BE HEARD.*

———WILLIAM LLOYD GARRISON: *First Issue of the Liberator, 1831*

*I do not think there is a mother among us all, who clasps her child to her breast, who could ever be made to feel it right that that child should be a slave; not a mother among us all who would not rather lay that child in its grave.*
*Nor can I believe that there is a woman so unchristian as to think it right to inflict on her neighbor's child what she would think worse than death were it inflicted on her own. . . .*

———HARRIET BEECHER STOWE: *An Appeal to the Women of the Free States of America, February 23, 1854*

Sources of the quotations on the preceding page:

WILLIAM LLOYD GARRISON: Bernard Smith: *The Democratic Spirit* (New York: 1943, 2nd ed.), 252–3.

HARRIET BEECHER STOWE: Harriet Beecher Stowe: "An Appeal to the Women of the Free States of America On the Present Crisis in Our Country," New York *Independent*, VI, no. 273 (February 23, 1854), 57.

THE first indispensable step toward Negro equality was emancipation of the slave. Since the early colonial period, slaves had run away or even rebelled in an attempt to obtain their freedom, and an increasing number of whites were coming to believe that slavery should be abolished. The roster of American colonists opposed to slavery included Samuel Sewall, Benjamin Woolman, Anthony Benezet, James Otis, and the Mennonite settlers of Germantown.

In its insistence on natural rights and social equality the American Revolution stimulated antislavery sentiment. Even many of the slaveholding Revolutionary leaders of the South—Arthur Lee, Thomas Jefferson, George Mason, Charles Carroll and William Pinckney—believed the slave system harmful to society as well as the Negro. Progress against slavery was noticeable wherever economic pressures were insufficient to withstand the humanitarian impulse. Eight states abolished slave trade; three placed difficulties in the way; seven emancipated all imported slaves; eight, including Vermont, gradually or immediately abolished slavery. Slavery remained unchecked only in the planting South, where it later spread with cotton culture.

Between the twilight of tobacco and the dawn of cotton culture, the upper South permitted views on slavery that in the deep South were admitted by a Georgian to be "not a prudent subject of discussion . . . whether proper or improper." * But in the North, where there were fewer interests at stake, the attacks against slavery grew more voluble. In the first Congress, petitions from

* Alice Felt Tyler: *Freedom's Ferment: Phases of American Social History to 1860* (Minneapolis, Minn.: 1944), 468. The Reverend David Rice of Kentucky presented a vigorous antislavery view (1).

Quaker antislavery groups were vainly presented against the slave trade, constitutionally protected until 1808. The *Address of a Convention of Delegates from the Abolition Society of the United States* (1794) (2) at Philadelphia set the antislavery case before the people. Elihu Smith's *Discourse* (1798) (3) before the New York Society was a characteristic denunciation of American legislators who permitted the injustice to survive.

During the Jeffersonian period a surface calm on the slavery issue was undisturbed except by the turbulent fight over the admission of Missouri as a slave state, a fight that, in Jefferson's words, startled the country like a "fire-bell in the night." Yet the growing manufactures of the Northeast and the spreading cotton culture of the South were drawing lines behind which Southerners were building militant defenses for their "peculiar institution." While Northerners like William Hamilton (4), a free Negro, and Elias Hicks (5), a Quaker, were quietly planting antislavery seeds in their small patches, the battle over Missouri aroused John Taylor of Caroline and John Randolph of Roanoke to passionate warnings against the opponents of slavery. Dr. Thomas Cooper of South Carolina College elaborated the earlier biblical and historical arguments for slavery, and Governor Stephen D. Miller of South Carolina insisted that *"slavery is not a national evil; on the contrary, it is a national benefit."* * Thus long before the *Liberator* began its crusade in 1831, Southern leaders were elaborating their defense of slavery as a "positive blessing." By this time antislavery Southerners were finding it expedient to leave the South. The Grimké sisters of South Carolina, James G. Birney of Alabama, Levi Coffin of North Carolina, and Edward Coles of Virginia were on their way North.

In this transition period the American Colonization Society was established in 1817 to free slaves who were willing to go to Africa. Designed for free Negroes as well as slaves, Liberia interested Northern and Border state antislavery leaders. But the Negroes themselves went in insignificant numbers to the Black Utopia. A more important force for their emancipation was the abolition press, which, under Quaker influence, was spreading in the Northern and Border states. Especially important was the *Genius of*

* William Sumner Jenkins: *Pro-Slavery Thought in the Old South* (Chapel Hill, N.C.: 1935), 76.

*Universal Emancipation,* founded by Benjamin Lundy in Ohio in
1821. Many Friends also nourished over a hundred abolition societies, of which the Manumission Society of North Carolina was
a prototype (6). In the South under the growing pressure of King
Cotton these societies lost members steadily until by 1831 they had
virtually disappeared.

Three events hastened the end of Southern tolerance of slavery
discussions. An incendiary call for Negro insurrection was published in 1829 by David Walker, a free Negro of Massachusetts;
the uncompromising cry of the *Liberator* was sent out in 1831 by
William Lloyd Garrison; and Nat Turner's insurrection burst upon
Virginia in August, 1831, reviving memories of Gabriel's revolt in
1800 and Denmark Vesey's conspiracy of 1820. Throughout the
South, slave codes were made harsher, and antislavery sentiment
was more rigorously suppressed than before. After making its internal defenses impregnable, the South advanced beyond to demand that Northern states also limit the expression of opinion,
that Congress deny the right of petition, and that all Northern
authorities assist in the maintenance of slavery.

By this time the antislavery movement was becoming an organized part of a larger humanitarian movement sweeping through
the North, which stressed the individual worth and essential equality of man. With religious fervor the crusaders painted the slaveholders as cruel sinners indulging in the basest human passions.
The bitter cry of the slave throbbed with pathos in Lydia Maria
Child's *Oasis* (1834) (7), in Angelina Grimké Weld's speeches
(8), and in Theodore Weld's *American Slavery As It Is* (1839)
(9), which Harriet Beecher Stowe acknowledged as the inspiration for *Uncle Tom's Cabin.* The American Anti-Slavery Society
was formed at Philadelphia in December, 1833, by Western, New
England, and New York groups. The Western group, inspired by
Rev. George Gale, Charles Finney, and Theodore Weld, operated
at Lane Theological Seminary, Cincinnati, and later at Oberlin.
The New England Anti-Slavery Society, founded by Garrison in
1831, was a more radical and uncompromising group. The New
York group, including the Tappans, a wealthy merchant family,
was concerned with broad publicity of a less radical nature. Under
these divided auspices the American Anti-Slavery Society carried
on for seven years, slowly gaining about two hundred thousand

members. Yet it never attracted the majority of antislavery men, though its lecturers were instructed by men like Theodore Weld and John Greenleaf Whittier, the New England poet.

Even in the North, abolitionism stirred opposition. Moderate antislavery men opposed the "immediatism" of Garrison, whose capture of the American Anti-Slavery Society's organization in 1840 caused its collapse. Mobs fearing free Negro competition for jobs, businessmen disturbed by disrupted trade relations, and wealthy elites sympathetic with their Southern counterparts were often incited to violence against the abolitionists. But brutality like the murder of Elijah Lovejoy or the burning of Pennsylvania Hall opened men's eyes to the civil liberty issues at stake. Gerrit Smith became an abolitionist after witnessing the break-up of a Utica meeting in 1835. The young Brahmin Wendell Phillips became a convert when he stared through his law office window at a well-dressed mob dragging Garrison through the streets of Boston with a rope about his waist. John Quincy Adams sprang to the defense of civil liberty when in 1836 the South invoked a "gag" rule in the House to table all petitions on slavery. Thrusting aside threats and abuse, "Old Man Eloquent" argued: "I hold the resolution to be a violation of the Constitution of the United States, of the right of petition of my constituents, and of the people of the United States and of my rights to freedom of speech as a member of this House." * He finally secured the repeal of the "gag rule" in 1845. Well might William Jay retire from the helm of the New York Anti-Slavery Society with the observation: "We commenced the present struggle to obtain the freedom of the slave; we are compelled to continue it to preserve our own." †

As the planting slavocracy observed the advance of Northern industrial capitalism, it grew increasingly insistent upon safeguards. Southerners like George Fitzhugh the sociologist and Chancellor William Harper of South Carolina rang the changes on the "positive blessing" theme which only a few brave Southerners dared to challenge. Hinton Rowan Helper, though hating the Negro, argued in the *Impending Crisis* ( 1857) that slavery was

* *Letters from John Quincy Adams to His Constituents of the Twelfth Congressional District in Massachusetts* . . . (Boston: 1837), 48.
† Bayard Tuckerman: *William Jay and the Constitutional Movement for the Abolition of Slavery* (New York: 1893), 80.

an economic blight; and Henry Ruffner's *Address to the People of West Virginia* (1847) (10) presented the slaveholder's practical argument against slavery. But these dissident voices went unheeded in the South.

During the two decades before the Civil War the antislavery movement became an inextricable part of the clash between the slave system and the industrial system of free labor. Slavery as a human institution was defended or attacked mostly in so far as it affected the needs of each competing system. Against the slave system, the industrial capitalists, farmers, and workers, expressing the needs of the Nation, found a working alliance in a program of higher tariffs, free soil, and free homesteads. The growing militancy and extension of the antislavery movement was but a part of the gathering forces against the slave system. Nor were all these Northern forces primarily concerned with advancing the rights of the Negro, as Charles T. Russell's *Minority Report of the Boston Grammar School Board* of 1849 attests (11). Though dwindling, violence against the abolitionist persisted.

Among the more direct antislavery activities was the help rendered to fugitive slaves. Intrepid conductors on the "Underground Railroad" spirited these fugitives toward freedom. Midwestern students and professors and Quakers like Isaac T. Hopper of Philadelphia, Thomas Garrett of Delaware, and Levi Coffin of Indiana performed prodigious feats of self-sacrifice in helping the fugitive. When Garrett was brought before Judge Taney in 1848 and ruinously fined, he exclaimed: "Judge, thou hast not left me a dollar, but I wish to say to thee, and to all in this courtroom, that if any knows of a fugitive who wants a shelter and a friend, send him to Thomas Garrett and he will befriend him." * Even more daring were those who conducted their charges through the South—John Fairfield of Virginia, Charles Torrey the New England minister, William Chaplin the Albany editor, and John Brown (13), who led a band of twelve slaves from Missouri in the winter of 1858–9 and six months later paid with his life for his Harper's Ferry raid. Negroes aided their people in this dangerous work—Josiah Henson of Canada and Harriet Tubman, the "Moses" of her people. Important also was the influence of Fred-

* Wilbur H. Siebert: *The Underground Railroad from Slavery to Freedom* (New York: 1898), 110.

erick Douglass, who devoted himself to the abolitionist cause
(12).

The stringent Fugitive Slave law of 1850 provoked widespread
defiance in the North. Theodore Parker, Samuel Gridley Howe,
and Wendell Phillips were conspicuous in defying the law and in
rescuing its victims. Outside of Massachusetts the opposition was
even more successful. The Supreme Court of Wisconsin upheld
the rescuer of a fugitive, Joshua Glover of Racine, and declared
the law unconstitutional.

The succession of events that led to the Civil War are well
known. Significant was the free-soil creed of the Liberty party,
which first entered the presidential lists in 1840. This conception,
not that of immediate abolition, was one of the prime influences
that shaped the Republican party, newly hatched in 1854. This
program and this party finally brought Abraham Lincoln to the
presidency and led to Southern secession and the firing on Fort
Sumter that heralded the military phase of the irrepressible conflict.

---

1.

*Rev. David Rice:*
SLAVERY INCONSISTENT WITH JUSTICE AND GOOD POLICY *
[1792]

*Born in Virginia, David Rice (1733–1816) was known as the
"father" of Presbyterianism in Kentucky. He was steeped in
the antislavery outlook of his parents, poor but highly respected farmers. He helped found Hampden-Sydney College
in Virginia and promoted schools in Kentucky, all the while
busily engaged in writing newspaper articles, pamphlets, and
sermons. Elected as a delegate to the Kentucky constitutional
convention of 1792, he tried to embody his hatred of slavery
in a provision for gradual emancipation, but it was defeated.*

* Rev. David Rice: *Slavery Inconsistent with Justice and Good Policy
Proved by a Speech Delivered in the Convention, Held at Danville, Kentucky*
(Philadelphia: 1792; reprinted London: 1793), 4, 11–12.

*In this speech at the convention, he stressed the danger of slavery to white man's rights. The next convention, in 1799, made sure that he would be kept from politics by a constitutional provision barring all clergymen from high office.*

As creatures of God we are, with respect to liberty, all equal. If one has a right to live among his fellow creatures, and enjoy his freedom, so has another: if one has a right to enjoy that property he acquires by an honest industry, so has another. If I by force take that from another, which he has a just right to according to the law of nature, (which is a divine law) which he has never forfeited, and to which he has never relinquished his claim, I am certainly guilty of injustice and robbery; and when the thing taken is the man's liberty, when it is himself, it is the greatest injustice. I injure him much more, than if I robbed him of his property on the high-way. In this case, it does not belong to him to prove a negative, but to me to prove that such forfeiture has been made; because, if it has not, he is certainly still the proprietor. All he has to do is to show the insufficiency of my proofs.

A slave claims his freedom; he pleads that he is a man, that he was by nature free, that he has not forfeited his freedom, nor relinquished it. Now, unless his master can prove that he is not a man, that he was not born free, or that he has forfeited or relinquished his freedom, he must be judged free; the justice of his claim must be acknowledged. His being long deprived of this right, by force or fraud, does not annihilate it; it remains; it is still his right. When I rob a man of his property, I leave him his liberty, and a capacity of acquiring and possessing more property; but when I deprive him of his liberty, I also deprive him of this capacity; therefore I do him greater injury, when I deprive him of his liberty, than when I rob him of his property. It is in vain for me to plead, that I have the sanction of law; for this makes the injury the greater: it arms the community against him, and makes his case desperate.

If my definition of a slave is true, he is a rational creature reduced by the power of legislation to the state of a brute, and thereby deprived of every privilege of humanity, except as above, that he may minister to the ease, luxury, lust, pride, or avarice of another, no better than himself. . . .

Slavery naturally tends to destroy all sense of justice and equity. It puffs up the mind with pride; teaches youth a habit of looking upon their fellow creatures with contempt, esteeming them as dogs or devils, and imagining themselves beings of superior dignity and importance, to whom all are indebted. This banishes the idea, and unqualifies the mind for the practice, of common justice. If I have, all my days, been accustomed to live at the expence [*sic*] of a black man, without making him any compensation, or considering myself at all in his debt, I cannot think it any great crime to live at the expense of a white man. If I can rob a black man without guilt, I shall contract no great guilt by robbing a white man. If I have been long accustomed to think a black man was made for me, I may easily take it into my head to think so of a white man. If I have no sense of obligation to do justice to a black man, I can have little to do justice to a white man. In this case, the tinge of our skins, or the place of our nativity, can make but little difference. If I am in principle a friend to slavery, I cannot, to be consistent, think it any crime to rob my country of its property and freedom, whenever my interest calls, and I find it in my power. If I make any difference here, it must be owing to a vicious education, the force of prejudice, or pride of heart. If in principle a friend to slavery, I cannot feel myself obliged to pay the debt due to my neighbour. If I can wrong him of all his possessions, and avoid the law, all is well.

2.

### PETITION OF THE AMERICAN CONVENTION AGAINST SLAVERY *
### [January 1, 1794]

*This "Petition" was adopted by the abolition societies at their first convention, held at Philadelphia in January, 1794. The meeting was sponsored by the Pennsylvania and New York antislavery societies, the first two in America, founded in 1775 under Benjamin Franklin and Benjamin Rush and in*

* American Convention for Promoting the Abolition of Slavery and Improving the Condition of the African Race: *Address of a Convention of Delegates from the Abolition Society of the United States* (New York: 1794), 3, 4–6.

*1785 under John Jay, respectively. Others were organized in Delaware (1788), Maryland (1789), Rhode Island (1790), Connecticut (1790), Virginia (1791), New Jersey (1792), and Kentucky. These older societies, which withered and died after the Missouri Compromise of 1820, were succeeded by the more militant Garrisonian New England Anti-Slavery Society, American Anti-Slavery Society, and New York Anti-Slavery Society of the thirties.*

## To the Citizens of the United States

The address of the Delegates from the several Societies, formed in different parts of the United States, for promoting the abolition of slavery, in Convention assembled at Philadelphia, on the first day of January, 1794.

Friends and Fellow Citizens, . . .

Many reasons concur in persuading us to abolish domestic slavery in our country.

It is inconsistent with the safety of the liberties of the United States.

Freedom and slavery cannot long exist together. An unlimited power over the time, labour, and posterity of our fellow-creatures, necessarily unfits men for discharging the public and private duties of citizens of a republic.

It is inconsistent with sound policy; in exposing the states which permit it, to all those evils which insurrections, and the most resentful war have introduced into one of the richest islands in the West-Indies.

It is unfriendly to the present exertions of the inhabitants of Europe, in favour of liberty. What people will advocate freedom, with a seal proportioned to its blessings, while they view the purest republic in the world tolerating in its bosom a body of slaves?

In vain has the tyranny of kings been rejected, while we permit in our country a domestic despotism, which involves, in its nature, most of the vices and miseries that we have endeavored to avoid.

It is degrading to our rank as men in the scale of being. Let us use our reason and social affections for the purposes for which they were given, or cease to boast a pre-eminence over animals, that are unpolluted with our crimes.

But higher motives to justice and humanity towards our fellow-creatures remain yet to be mentioned.

Domestic slavery is repugnant to the principles of Christianity. It prostrates every benevolent and just principle of action in the human heart. It is rebellion against the authority of a common Father. It is a practical denial of the extent and efficacy of the death of a common Saviour. It is an usurpation of the prerogative of the Great Sovereign of the universe, who has solemnly claimed an exclusive property in the souls of men.

But if this view of the enormity of the evil of domestic slavery should not affect us, there is one consideration more which ought to alarm and impress us, especially at the present juncture.

It is a violation of a divine precept of universal justice, which has, in no instance, escaped with impunity.

### 3.

*Elihu Hubbard Smith:*
Discourse before the New York Abolitionist Society *
[April 11, 1798]

> *A descendant of an old Massachusetts family, Elihu Hubbard Smith (1771–98) became a practicing physician. His great interest in literature brought him into intimate contact with Charles Brockden Brown and the Hartford Wits. The detestation of slavery, expressed in the* Discourse, *was one of the many indications of his concern for human progress.*

In the existing circumstances of society, encumbered as we are with this mighty evil, which slavery has cast upon us, we are only free to chuse, amid variety of embarrassments. There is no fear that even this factitious right of property, so much insisted on, will not be sufficiently respected. Alas! there is no hope but that it

* Elihu Hubbard Smith: *Discourse Delivered April 11, 1798 at the Request and before the New York Society for Promoting the Manumission of Slaves* . . . (New York: 1798), 24–8.

long continue triumphantly to oppose all the efforts of benevolence. But, were it justly insisted on, what demons of malignant cruelty paralize the senses and the reason of legislators? Do they not see the ruin which surrounds us? . . . You, yes you, the Legislators of America, you are the real upholders of slavery! You, yes you, Legislators of this Commonwealth, you foster and protect it here! Is it not recognized by your laws? and in the very face of your Constitution? of that instrument which you maintained by your arms, and sealed with your blood? Have not those laws authorized, systematized, and protected, and do they not now protect it? If you fear the clamors of the enslavers of men, or if you acknowledge the justice of their claims to compensation, it is you who sanction, you who uphold the crime. It is you who are deaf to the demands of justice, the sighs of humanity, the representations of policy, the calls of interest, the suggestions of expediency, the warning voice of domestic tranquillity. . . . The opposers of justice do not read, think, reason, feel,—they do not so much as listen. They admit but one idea, that of gain from the labour of their slaves; they are occupied but with one care, that of maintaining their authority. And you nourish that gain, you cherish that care, you defend with double mounds that monstrous authority, at the hazard, if not with the sacrifice, of all the dearest interests of society, of its very existence. These you hazard, when the remedy is obvious, certain, easy to be obtained, and safe to be applied. Mad insensibility! the little interests of the moment, the gratifications of vanity, and the contests of passion, a market, a palace, or a strip of land, engross your thoughts and dissipate your treasures, while the welfare of a nation sleeps unregarded, while thousands of your fellow-beings, children of the same father, and inheritors of the same destiny, eat the bitter bread of slavery, writhe under the lash of cruelty, and sink into the untimely grave amid the taunts of oppression! . . .

The conduct of men conscious of their villainy, is always and every where the same. Accused, they attempt their justification; but, failing here, they strive to overwhelm with censure those who have detected their baseness, and called upon them to repair their injustice. . . . Incapable of vindicating themselves, or of effectually misrepresenting the purity of our motives, the encouragers of slavery have fallen on the miserable Africans; as though their vices

and their follies constituted a reason for subjecting them to bondage, and bending them with reiterated wrong. Shallow subterfuge!
feeble malice! Every motive urged against them ought to interest
us in their behalf. Are they dull and stupid, it is ours to startle
them into thought, and rouze [*sic*] them to inquiry; are they
ignorant, it is ours to cultivate and instruct them; base, ours to
elevate; vicious, ours to reclaim them. The more forlorn and hopeless their condition, the more energetic and persevering should be
our efforts. The measure of our benevolence should be capacious
as their wants; and our zeal commensurate with their insensibility. Stupidity, ignorance, folly, vice, have each its several remedy;
and our security as well as interest, our duty as well as happiness,
demand the application. What must be the texture of his heart
who can find reason in the ignorance, in the vices, and in the sufferings of men, in all that most can render them objects of compassion and of charity, for insuring that ignorance, augmenting
those vices, and adding to these sufferings the yoke of bondage,
and the sting of torture? Call you him man, or demon?

The experience of many years, evidence palpable to the most
hardened and obstinate sense, has demonstrated the capacity of
the Blacks. The very vices of which they stand so bitterly accused, demonstrate it. They, like all men else, are the creatures
of education, of example, of circumstances, of external impressions. Make them outcasts and vagabonds, thrust them into the
society of drunkards and of thieves, shut from them the fair book
and salutary light of knowledge, degrade them into brutes, and
trample them in the dust, and you must expect them to be vile
and wretched, dissolute and lawless, base and stupid. Madmen!
would you "gather grapes of thorns, or figs of thistles?"

## 4.

### William Hamilton:
### AN ADDRESS TO THE NEW YORK AFRICAN SOCIETY *
### [January 2, 1809]

*William Hamilton, evidently a free Negro, is shown by this address to be a cogent defender of his people against the charge that Negroes were racially inferior. Two other extant imprints place him at the African Zion Church, New York, in 1827 and at the fourth annual convention of the Free People of Color of the United States in June, 1834.*

But my Brethren, however this may be, it is for us to rejoice that the cause or source from whence these miseries sprang are removing, it is for us to rejoice not only that the sources of slavery are drying away, but that our condition is fast ameliorating, it is for us to rejoice, that science has begun to bud with our race, and soon shall our tree of arts bear its full burthen of rich and nectarious fruit, soon shall that contumelious assertion of the proud, be proved false, to wit, that Africans do not possess minds as ingenius [*sic*] as other men.

The proposition has been advanced by men who claim a pre-eminence in the learned world, that Africans are inferior to white men in the structure both of body and mind; the first member of this proposition is below our notice; the reasons assigned for the second are, that we have not produced any poets, mathematicians, or any to excel in any science whatever; our being oppressed and held in slavery forms no excuse, because, say they, among the Romans, their most excellent artists and greatest scientific characters were frequently their slaves, and that these on account of their ascendant abilities, arose to superior stations in the state; and they exultingly tell us that these slaves were white men.

My Brethren, it does not require a complete master to solve this problem, nor is it necessary, in order like good logicians to meet this argument, . . .

* William Hamilton: *An Address to the New York African Society for Mutual Relief, Delivered in the Universalist Church, January 2,* 1809 (New York: 1809), 6–7.

Among the Romans it was only necessary for the slave to be manumitted, in order to be eligible to all the offices of state, together with the emoluments belonging thereto; no sooner was he free than there was open before him a wide field of employment for his ambition and learning and abilities with merit, were as sure to meet with their reward in him, as in any other citizen. But what station above the common employment of craftsmen and labourers would we fill, did we possess both learning and abilities; is there aught to enkindle in us one spark of emulation: must not he who makes any considerable advances under present circumstances be almost a prodigy; although it may be true we have not produced any to excel in arts and sciences, yet if our situation be properly considered, and the allowances made which ought to be, it will soon be perceived that we do not fall far behind those who boast of a superior judgment, we have produced some who have claimed attention, and whose works have been admired, yes in despight [*sic*] of all our embarresments [*sic*] our genius does sometimes burst forth from its incumbrance although the productions of Philis Whately may not possess the requisitions necessary to stand the test of nice criticism, and she may be denied a stand in the rank of poets, yet does she possess some original ideas that would not disgrace the pen of the best poets.

5.

*Elias Hicks:*
OBSERVATIONS ON SLAVERY *
[1814]

*Elias Hicks (1748–1830) was a Quaker preacher born in Long Island. His "religious visits" to nearby places impressed Walt Whitman, who heard him frequently and admired him greatly. Possessed of a tender humane spirit, he was a powerful advocate of kindness to animals and a pleader for the underprivileged. This tract on slavery reveals him as a devoted friend*

* E. Hicks: *Observations on the Slavery of the Africans and Their Descendants and on the Use of the Produce of Their Labour* (New York: 1814), iii–iv.

*of the slave. He was often considered a dangerous radical because of his liberal views and his emphasis upon inward light rather than external conformance, which he expressed as founder of the "Hicksite" branch of the Quakers.*

. . . The design . . . was to impress on the minds of my friends and fellow-citizens, and others concerned, as far as might be, by fair reasoning, a full sense of the abhorrent cruelty and unrighteousness of holding our fellow creatures in bondage, and wresting from them, by violence, the produce of their labour; . . .

And as the slave holder can have no moral right whatever to the man he stiles [*sic*] his slave, nor to the produce of his labour; he cannot possibly convey any to a second person by any transfer he can make: for, having nothing but a criminal possession himself, he can convey nothing to a second person but the same possession: and should this possession be continued through a line of transfer to the twentieth person, still it would be nothing more than the same criminal possession that was vested in the first possessor, and would convey no moral right whatever. And should any other person come forward, and, by the same mode of violence and power that was exercised by the first possessor, in reducing the man he stiles [*sic*] his slave to the abject state of slavery, and by which he violently took from him the produce of his labour, forcibly take from such twentieth or more remote possessor, the slave and the produce of his labour, the right of such person, in point of equity, to such slave and the produce of his labour would be just equal to the right of such remote possessor; as neither of them could have had any more than a criminal possession: and whether that possession is obtained by violence or by transfer, (if the person who receives it by transfer is informed of the criminal circumstances,) it can make no possible difference, except that one is protected by the indulgence of a partial law of the country we live in, and the other is not. By which undeniable proposition, it appears, that when any man becomes possessed of a slave, or the produce of his labour, wrested from him without his consent, whether it be by transfer or otherwise, any other person who has power so to do, may, by violence, take from such possessor, such slave and the produce of his labour: and when he has in that way obtained possession thereof, he has as good a right to such slave and to use the produce of his labour as the former; and the former can have no just cause to complain of such usage, as he is only paid in his own coin. For, although the first possessor committed the act of violence, when he took from the man he stiles his slave his liberty, and compelled him to work, and by the same cruel force, took from him the produce of his labour; yet, every purchaser of such slave and the produce of his labour, if he is apprized of the criminal circumstance attending it, is as guilty as the first perpetrator, and should such slave and the produce of his labour pass through the hands of twenty persons, all knowing at the time of transfer the criminal circumstances attending, each would be guilty of the entire crime of the first perpetrator. This being assented to, and I conceive it is incontrovertible, I have a hope that this edition may produce a good effect, and tend to raise up many more faithful advocates in the cause of this deeply oppressed people, who may be willing to suffer every necessary privation, rather than be guilty of the least thing that may, in any degree, possibly strengthen the hands of their oppressors. I therefore recommend this little treatise to the candid and impartial consideration of the reader, and subscribe myself his sincere friend,                              E. HICKS.

## 6.

### *Manumission Society of North Carolina:*
### AN ADDRESS TO THE PEOPLE OF NORTH CAROLINA *
### [1830]

*The General Association of the Manumission Society of North Carolina was organized on July 19, 1816, at the Center Meeting House in Guilford County, North Carolina, by the delegates of several local manumission societies connected with certain Quaker churches. After passing through a controversial period in 1823–4, it declined swiftly in 1828, lapsing into virtual nonexistence in 1834. When this Address was widely publicized in 1830, Southern temper was changing,*

* Manumission Society of North Carolina: *An Address to the People of North Carolina on Evils of Slavery by Friends of Liberty and Equality* (Greensboro, N.C.: 1830), 4–6, 65–8.

*making similar appeals in the South virtually impossible. Thirty years later, when the pamphlet came into Lewis Tappan's hands, the New York abolitionist was so impressed by it that he reprinted and commended it to his contemporaries, who, he felt, fell below the high moral level of these North Carolinians of 1830.*

Whatever the people of this State may be with respect to information on other subjects, on this they are very destitute, owing, we suppose, to the *"awful delicacy"* we hear so much about, and which we would briefly examine. Then what renders this subject so *awfully* delicate? Is it the incapacity of the people to investigate it? Is the discussion of this subject *delicate* because it favors the *innocent* and condemns the *guilty*? Is it *delicate* because it shows republicans their inconsistency? Is it *delicate* because it accuses the professors of the Christian Religion of crimes in which a Mahomedan would blush to commit? Is it *delicate* because it impeaches the right to hold human beings as property? Is it *delicate* because free men are ashamed or afraid for slaves to know that they incline to do them justice? . . .

Under the protection offered by our Constitution in the 18th section of a Declaration of Rights made by the Representatives of the Freemen of this State, we now set out in a calm, and more full investigation of the evils consequent on the existence of absolute slavery. And as we cherish no unkind feelings toward any class of our citizens, but prompted by philanthropy and patriotism, we labour to expose inconsistencies, and to hold up to public gaze, and we hope to public execration, principles that tend to destroy our liberties, our morals, and even our souls; we hope that every man having an opportunity to examine this subject with us, will do it impartially and honestly, in attending to, and investigating the following propositions:

PROPOSITION I. Our slave system is radically evil.

II. It is founded in injustice and cruelty.

III. It is a fruitful source of pride, idleness and tyranny.

IV. It increases depravity in the human heart, while it inflames and nourishes a numerous train of dark and brutal passions and lusts, disgraceful to human nature, and destructive of the general welfare.

V. It is contrary to the plain and simple maxims of the Christian Revelation, or religion of Christ.

After demonstrating these propositions we shall briefly state in conclusion, some of the most prominent features in the plan which we would adopt for the abolition of slavery. . . .

The following principles, most of which are deducible from the foregoing remarks, we give as the primary principles held by us as a Society—together with a brief outline of the plan which we would adopt for the abolition of the evil complained of: and

*First.* We hold, with the venerable founder of our republican institutions, that liberty is the *unalienable birth-right* of every human being; and that God has made no difference in this respect between the *white* and *black.*

*Secondly.* We believe that, in a national and individual point of view, the negro is entitled to the same measure of justice with the white man, and that neither his skin, nor any other material consequence attending him, can afford a reasonable pretext for his oppression.

*Thirdly.* We believe that the evil is one which affects every part of the community, in a greater or less degree; and may therefore be termed a national evil; and that both emancipation and colonization are necessary to its removal.

With regard to emancipation, we hold 1st, that it should be gradual; so conducted as not to interfere with the rights of property;—But 2ndly, that it should be universal. This however, is not enough.—The debt which we owe the negroes is not sufficiently paid by merely suffering the oppressed to go free. We believe it to be the duty of our countrymen, to use all possible means to enlighten and elevate the minds, ennoble the hearts, and improve and elevate the character of the negroes among us, that they may be prepared both to enjoy and appreciate liberty, and to discharge the important duties assigned them by their creator, as well to himself as to their fellow creatures, with honour to God and benefit to mankind.

In order to remove this alarming evil which is threatening in its aspect, and which if continued long enough, must be so destructive in its consequences, we would recommend the following:

*First.* Let a law be enacted, preventing the further introduction of slaves into the State for sale or hire.

*Secondly.* Let a law be enacted, facilitating individual emancipation, by allowing such masters as wish to liberate their slaves,
to do so; provided the liberated slave be capable of earning a
comfortable livelihood.

*Thirdly.* We would recommend a law to facilitate individual
emancipation still further, by authorizing negroes to make contracts with their masters by which they may purchase their own
freedom.

*Fourthly.* We would recommend the passage of laws imposing
still further restraints upon the abuse of slaves, and affording the
unlawfully abused slave, at the same time, easy means of redress.

*Fifthly.* We would recommend a law providing for the instruction of slaves in the elementary principles of language, at least so
far as to enable them to read the Holy Scriptures.

*Sixthly.* We would provide by law that all children in this
State after a certain period, should be free at a certain age; and
from and after the passing of said act, no negroes should be removed from the State in such a way as to lose the benefit of said
act upon their posterity.

7.

*Lydia Maria Child:*
OASIS *
[1834]

*Lydia Maria Child (1802–80) was born in Massachusetts.
She opened a private school in Watertown in 1825 and began
the* Junvenile Miscellany. *Joining the abolitionists, she wrote*
An Appeal in Favor of that Class of Americans Called Africans
*(1833), making many converts and enemies. In 1841–9 she
was coeditor with her husband of the* National Anti-Slavery
Standard. *When John Brown lay wounded, she asked Governor Henry A. Wise for permission to nurse him. But the
abolitionist dissuaded her from coming, urging her to take up
a collection for his impoverished family instead. She was dis-
satisfied with the Civil War because abolition was not made
the prime issue. In the* Oasis, *her plea for the Negro is sugges-*

---

* Lydia Maria Child (ed.): *Oasis* (Boston: 1834), vii–ix.

*tive of Professor Franz Boas's classic disproof of the natural inferiority of the Negro,* The Mind of Primitive Man *(1911).*

In preparing this volume I have not been guided by any romantic desire to idealize the African character. I know very well that, *as a class,* the colored people are what any people would be, who had so long been trampled upon by the iron heel of contemptuous tyranny; but I likewise know that there are many admirable exceptions to this remark.

My purpose is a simple and honest one. I wish to familiarize the public mind with the idea that colored people are *human beings*—elevated or degraded by the same circumstances that elevate or degrade other men. Perhaps there are few who will openly deny this; but many have the latent feeling. If it were otherwise, we could not look upon their wrongs so coldly as we do. . . .

On what is the prejudice founded, which makes us so unwilling that a colored person should have a *chance* to be our equal? It cannot be a natural, instinctive antipathy; for white children have no repugnance to black nurses, and the African schools show infinite shadings of complexion. If you say your dislike is founded upon the vice and ignorance of this unfortunate class, I earnestly conjure you,—in the name of that religion which we all profess to believe,—to consider seriously whether it is not *your* prejudice that makes them so.

The attempt to sanction our illiberality, by assertions of a natural and remediless inferiority of intellect, would be unworthy of a cultivated mind, or a kind heart, even if such assertions had a shadow of truth. The physiological argument adduced is indeed a weak one. We have established a very arbitrary standard with regard to the "African skull" and "African features." The testimony of travellers proves a vast variety of conformation among the tribes which have furnished white nations with slaves. The Fellatahs, Caffrarians, Nubians, Abyssinians, and many other tribes, have skulls and features totally different from those to which we attach ideas of mental degradation. With regard to the colored population of the United States, both slave and free, it is well to remember that great numbers of them are nearly white men.

But even if it could be proved that negro blood inevitably produces stupidity in the brain, who would be absurd enough to say that the civil and social rights of mankind must be regulated according to the measure of genius? *Individuals* of the human species are unquestionably fitted to perform different uses in society, and true freedom consists in giving every man a fair chance to find the place he is qualified to fill; but here a *whole class* is excluded from opportunities for improvement, merely on account of complexion. Americans mistake if they consider this arrangement as more liberal, or just, than the arbitrary and unchanging distinction of *castes* in benighted Hindostan.

On the subject of equality, the principles of abolitionists have been much misrepresented. They have not the slightest wish to do violence to the distinctions of society, by forcing the rude and illiterate into the presence of the learned and refined. The learned and refined have indeed important duties to perform on this subject; but those duties are to be decided between their own consciences and their God. The abolitionists merely wish that colored people should have the same opportunities for instruction, the same civil treatment at public places, the same chance to enlarge their sphere of usefulness, that is enjoyed by the lowest and most ignorant white man in America.

8.

*Angelina E. Grimké Weld:*
SPEECH ON SLAVERY *
[May 16, 1838]

*Angelina Grimké (1805–79) was born in South Carolina of a wealthy slaveholding family. She and her older sister, Sarah, became active speakers for the American Anti-Slavery Society and were also staunch champions of the peace movement and of the rights of women. Angelina married the abolitionist leader Theodore Weld (9). Two days later, while she was speaking to a women's antislavery convention at Pennsylvania*

* *History of Pennsylvania Hall, which Was Destroyed by a Mob, May 17,* 1838 (Philadelphia: 1838), 123–5.

*Hall, a mob gathered, broke windows, and howled derisively, vainly seeking to drown her voice. The next night the mob set fire to the hall, keeping off all comers until it was completely destroyed.*

Men, brethren and fathers—mothers, daughters and sisters, what came ye out for to see? A reed shaken with the wind? Is it curiosity merely, or a deep sympathy with the perishing slave, that has brought this large audience together? (A yell from the mob without the building.) Those voices without ought to awaken and call out our warmest sympathies. Deluded beings! "they know not what they do." They know not that they are undermining their own rights and their own happiness, temporal and eternal. Do you ask, "what has the North to do with slavery?" Hear it—hear it. Those voices without tell us that the spirit of slavery is *here*, and has been roused to wrath by our abolition speeches and conventions: for surely liberty would not foam and tear herself with rage, because her friends are multiplied daily, and meetings are held in quick succession to set forth her virtues and extend her peaceful kingdom. This opposition shows that slavery has done its deadliest work in the hearts of our citizens. Do you ask, then, "what has the North to do?" I answer, cast out first the spirit of slavery from your own hearts, and then lend your aid to convert the South. Each one present has a work to do, be his or her situation what it may, however limited their means, or insignificant their supposed influence. The great men of this country will not do this work; the church will never do it. A desire to please the world, to keep the favor of all parties and of all conditions, makes them dumb on this and every other unpopular subject. They have become worldly-wise, and therefore God, in his wisdom, employs them not to carry on his plans of reformation and salvation. He hath chosen the foolish things of the world to confound the wise, and the weak to overcome the mighty.

As a Southerner I feel that it is my duty to stand up here tonight and bear testimony against slavery. I have seen it—I have seen it. I know it has horrors than can never be described. I was brought up under its wing: I witnessed for many years its demoralizing influences, and its destructiveness to human happiness. It is admitted by some that the slave is not happy under the *worst* forms of slavery. But I have *never* seen a happy slave. I have seen him dance in his chains, it is true; but he was not happy. There is a wide difference between happiness and mirth. Man cannot enjoy the former while his manhood is destroyed, and that part of the being which is necessary to the making, and to the enjoyment of happiness, is completely blotted out. The slaves, however, may be, and sometimes are, mirthful. When hope is extinguished, they say, "let us eat and drink, for to-morrow we die." (Just then stones were thrown at the windows,—a great noise without, and commotion within.) What is a mob? What would the breaking of every window be? What would the levelling of this Hall be? Any evidence that we are wrong, or that slavery is a good and wholesome institution? What if the mob should now burst in upon us, break up our meeting and commit violence upon our persons—would this be any thing compared with what the slaves endure? No, no: and we do not remember them "as bound with them," if we shrink in the time of peril, or feel unwilling to sacrifice ourselves, if need be, for their sake. (Great noise.) I thank the Lord that there is yet life left enough to feel the truth, even though it rages at it—that conscience is not so completely seared as to be unmoved by the truth of the living God.

Many persons go to the South for a season, and are hospitably entertained in the parlor and at the table of the slave-holder. They never enter the huts of the slaves; they know nothing of the dark side of the picture, and they return home with praises on their lips of the generous character of those with whom they had tarried. Or if they have witnessed the cruelties of slavery, by remaining silent spectators they have naturally become callous—an insensibility has ensued which prepares them to apologize even for barbarity. Nothing but the corrupting influence of slavery on the hearts of the Northern people can induce them to apologize for it; and much will have been done for the destruction of Southern slavery when we have so reformed the North that no one here will be willing to risk his reputation by advocating or even excusing the holding of men as property. The South know it, and acknowledge that as fast as our principles prevail, the hold of the master must be relaxed. (Another outbreak of mobocratic spirit, and some confusion in the house.)

How wonderfully constituted is the human mind! How it resists, as long as it can, all efforts made to reclaim from error! I feel that all this disturbance is but an evidence that our efforts are the best that could have been adopted, or else the friends of slavery would not care for what we say and do. The South know what we do. I am thankful that they are reached by our efforts. Many times have I wept in the land of my birth, over the system of slavery. . . . But in the midst of temptation I was preserved, and my sympathy grew warmer, and my hatred of slavery more inveterate, until at last I have exiled myself from my native land because I could no longer endure to hear the wailing of the slave. I fled to the land of Penn; for here, thought I, sympathy for the slave will surely be found. But I found it not. The people were kind and hospitable, but the slave had no place in their thoughts. . . . Animated with hope, nay, with an assurance of the triumph of liberty and good will to man, I will lift up my voice like a trumpet, and show this people their transgression, their sins of omission towards the slave, and what they can do towards affecting Southern mind, and overthrowing Southern oppression.

We may talk of occupying neutral ground, but on this subject, in its present attitude, there is no such thing as neutral ground. He that is not for us is against us, and he that gathereth not with us, scattereth abroad. If you are on what you suppose to be neutral ground, the South look upon you as on the side of the oppressor. . . . (Shoutings, stones thrown against the windows, &c.)

There is nothing to be feared from those who would stop our mouths, but they themselves should fear and tremble. The current is even now setting fast against them. If the arm of the North had not caused the Bastile of slavery to totter to its foundation, you would not hear those cries. A few years ago, and the South felt secure, and with a contemptuous sneer asked, "Who are the abolitionists? The abolitionists are nothing?"—Ay, in one sense they were nothing, and they are nothing still. But in this we rejoice, that "God has chosen things that are not to bring to nought things that are." (Mob again disturbed the meeting.)

We often hear the question asked, "What shall we do?" Here is an opportunity for doing something now. Every man and every woman present may do something by showing that we fear not a mob, and, in the midst of threatenings and revilings, by opening our mouths for the dumb and pleading the cause of those who are ready to perish.

9.

*Theodore Weld:*
AMERICAN SLAVERY AS IT IS *
[1839]

*Theodore Dwight Weld (1803–95) was born in Connecticut, of New England stock. Influenced by the Presbyterian revivalist Charles G. Finney, he prepared for the ministry, laboring for the cause of temperance and antislavery. With the support of Arthur and Lewis Tappan, abolitionist merchants of New York, he spread abolitionism at Western Reserve College and Lane Theological Seminary, Cincinnati, Ohio. Forced out of Lane in 1834, he carried his ablest fellow students to Oberlin College and into the work of the American Anti-Slavery Society. By 1836, Weld was commissioned to give training to a band that included Angelina Grimké, the Carolinian abolitionist who became his wife. Although an almost morbid modesty kept his name from public notice, he served in a Washington post as adviser to John Quincy Adams and others in the campaign against slavery. American Slavery As It Is, compiled largely from Southern newspapers, was acknowledged by Harriet Beecher Stowe to have crystallized Uncle Tom's Cabin.*

*Introduction*

READER, you are empannelled as a juror to try a plain case and bring in an honest verdict. The question at issue is not one of law, but of fact—"What is the actual condition of the slaves in the United States?" A plainer case never went to a jury. Look at it. TWENTY-SEVEN HUNDRED THOUSAND PERSONS in this country, men, women, and children, are in SLAVERY. Is slavery, as a condition for human beings, good, bad, or indifferent? We submit the ques-

* Theodore Weld: *American Slavery As It Is; Testimony of a Thousand Witnesses* (New York: 1839), 7, 8–9.

tion without argument. You have common sense, and conscience, and a human heart;—pronounce upon it. You have a wife, or a husband, a child, a father, a mother, a brother or a sister—make the case your own, make it theirs, and bring in your verdict. The case of Human Rights against Slavery has been adjudicated in the court of conscience times innumerable. The same verdict has always been rendered. . . . There is not a man on earth who does not believe that slavery is a curse. Human beings may be inconsistent, but human *nature* is true to herself. . . . We repeat it, every man knows that slavery is a curse. Whoever denies this, his lips libel his heart. Try him; clank the chains in his ears, and tell him they are for *him.* Give him an hour to prepare his wife and children for a life of slavery. Bid him make haste and get ready their necks for the yoke, and their wrists for the coffle chains, then look at his pale lips and trembling knees, and you have *nature's* testimony against slavery.

Two millions seven hundred thousand persons in these States are in this condition. They were made slaves and are held such by force, and by being put in fear, and this for no crime! Reader, what have you to say of such treatment? Is it right, just, benevolent? Suppose I should seize you, rob you of your liberty, drive you into the field, and make you work without pay as long as you live, would that be justice and kindness, or monstrous injustice and cruelty? Now, every body knows that the slaveholders do these things to the slaves every day, and yet it is stoutly affirmed that they treat them well and kindly, and that their tender regard for their slaves restrains the masters from inflicting cruelties upon them. We shall go into no metaphysics to show the absurdity of this pretence. The man who *robs* you every day, is, forsooth, quite too tenderhearted ever to cuff or kick you! True, he can snatch your money, but he does it gently lest he should hurt you. He can empty your pockets without qualms, but if your *stomach* is empty, it cuts him to the quick. He can make you work a life time without pay, but loves you too well to let you go hungry. He fleeces you of your *rights* with a relish, but is shocked if you work bareheaded in summer, or in winter without warm stockings. He can make you go without your *liberty*, but never without a shirt. He can crush, in you, all hope of bettering your condition, by vowing that you shall die his slave, but though he can coolly torture your feelings, he is too compassionate to lacerate your back—he can break your heart, but he is very tender of your skin. He can strip you of all protection and thus expose you to all outrages, but if you are exposed to the *weather*, half clad and half sheltered, how yearn his tender bowels! What! slaveholders talk of treating men well, and yet not only rob them of all they get, and as fast as they get it, but rob them of *themselves*, also; their very hands and feet, all their muscles, and limbs, and senses, their bodies and minds, their time and liberty and earnings, their free speech and rights of conscience, their right to acquire knowledge, and property, and reputation;—and yet they, who plunder them of all these, would fain make us believe that their soft hearts ooze out so lovingly toward their slaves that they always keep them well housed and well clad, never push them too hard in the field, never make their dear backs smart, nor let their dear stomachs get empty. . . .

As slaveholders and their apologists are volunteer witnesses in their own cause, and are flooding the world with testimony that their slaves are kindly treated; that they are well fed, well clothed, well housed, well lodged, moderately worked, and bountifully provided with all things needful for their comfort, we propose—first, to disprove their assertions by the testimony of a multitude of impartial witnesses, and then to put slaveholders themselves through a course of cross-questioning which shall draw their condemnation out of their own mouths. We will prove that the slaves in the United States are treated with barbarous inhumanity; that they are overworked, underfed, wretchedly clad and lodged, and have insufficient sleep; that they are often made to wear round their necks iron collars armed with prongs, to drag heavy chains and weights at their feet while working in the field, and to wear yokes, and bells, and iron horns; that they are often kept confined in the stocks day and night for weeks together, made to wear gags in their mouths for hours or days, have some of their front teeth torn out or broken off, that they may be easily detected when they run away; that they are frequently flogged with terrible severity, have red pepper rubbed into their lacerated flesh, and hot brine, spirits of turpentine, &c., poured over the gashes to increase the torture; that they are often stripped naked, their backs and limbs cut with knives, bruised and mangled by scores and hundreds of blows with the paddle, and terribly torn by the claws of cats, drawn over them by their tormentors; that they are often hunted with bloodhounds and shot down like beasts, or torn in pieces by dogs; that they are often suspended by the arms and whipped and beaten till they faint, and when revived by restoratives, beaten again till they faint, and sometimes till they die; that their ears are often cut off, their eyes knocked out, their bones broken, their flesh branded with red hot irons; that they are maimed, mutilated and burned to death over slow fires. All these things, and more, and worse, we shall *prove.* Reader, we know whereof we affirm, we have weighed it well; *more and worse* WE WILL PROVE. Mark these words, and read on; we will establish all these facts by the testimony of scores and hundreds of eye witnesses, by the testimony of *slaveholders* in all parts of the slave states, . . . We shall show, not merely that such deeds are committed, but that they are frequent; not done in corners, but before the sun; not in one of the slave states, but in all of them; not perpetrated by brutal overseers and drivers merely, but by magistrates, by legislators, by professors of religion, by preachers of the gospel, by governors of states, by "gentlemen of property and standing," and by delicate females moving in the "highest circles of society." We know, full well, the outcry that will be made by multitudes, at these declarations; the multiform cavils, the flat denials, the charges of "exaggeration" and "falsehood" so often bandied, the sneers of affected contempt at the credulity that can believe such things, and the rage and imprecations against those who give them currency. We know, too, the threadbare sophistries by which slaveholders and their apologists seek to evade such testimony. If they admit that such deeds are committed, they tell us that they are exceedingly rare, and therefore furnish no grounds for judging of the general treatment of slaves; that occasionally a brutal wretch in the *free* states barbarously butchers his wife, but that no one thinks of inferring from that, the general treatment of wives at the North and West.

## 10.

### *Henry Ruffner:*
### ADDRESS ON THE GRADUAL ABOLITION OF SLAVERY
### IN WEST VIRGINIA *
### [1847]

*Henry Ruffner (1790–1861) was born in Virginia, of German-Swiss descent. Licensed to preach, he was associated with Washington College, Lexington, Virginia, as a teacher and president for thirty years. The appended* Address on slavery *grew out of a debate in the Franklin Literary Society of Lexington. Widely known as the "Ruffner pamphlet," it was a remarkable presentation of a slaveholder's practical argument against slavery. Originally it was published anonymously, but another edition was published in Louisville, Kentucky, bearing the author's name. It was read widely and probably helped shape antislavery sentiment in the border states.*

Nowhere, since time began, have the two systems of slave labor and free labor, been subjected to so fair and so decisive a trial of their effects on public prosperity, as in these United States. Here the two systems have worked side by side for ages, under such equal circumstances both political and physical, and with such ample time and opportunity for each to work out its proper effects,—that all must admit the experiment to be now complete, and the result decisive. No man of common sense, who has observed this result, can doubt for a moment, that the system of free labor promotes the growth and prosperity of States, in a much higher degree than the system of slave labor. In the first settlement of a country, when labor is scarce and dear, slavery may give a temporary impulse to improvement: but even this is not the case, except in warm climates, and where free men are scarce and either sickly or lazy: and when we have said this, we have said all that experience in the United States warrants us to say, in favor of the policy of employing slave labor.

* Henry Ruffner: *Address to the People of West Virginia Showing that Slavery Is Injurious to the Public Welfare and that It May Be Gradually Abolished, without Detriment to the Rights and Interests of Slaveholders, by a Slaveholder of West Virginia* (Lexington, Va.: 1847), 11, 12, 14–17, 20, 23, 28–30.

It is the common remark of all who have travelled through the United States, that the free States and the slave States, exhibit a striking contrast in their appearance. In the older free States are seen all the tokens of prosperity:—a dense and increasing population;—thriving villages, towns and cities;—a neat and productive agriculture, growing manufactures and active commerce.

In the older parts of the slave States,—with a few local exceptions,—are seen, on the contrary, too evident signs of stagnation or of positive decay,—a sparse population,—a slovenly cultivation spread over vast fields, that are wearing out, among others already worn out and desolate;—villages and towns, "few and far between," rarely growing, often decaying, sometimes mere remnants of what they were, sometimes deserted ruins, haunted only by owls;—generally no manufactures, nor even trades, except the indispensable few;—commerce and navigation abandoned, as far as possible, to the people of the free States;—and generally, instead of the stir and bustle of industry, a dull and dreamy stillness, broken, if broken at all, only by the wordy brawl of politics. . . .

Density and increase of population are, especially in the United States, both an element of power—not only military power, and political power—but what is of more importance, *productive* power. The labor of men produces wealth, and with it the means of all human comfort and improvement. The more men there are on a square mile, the more power there is on that square mile, to create everything that conduces to the welfare of man. We know that the natural resources of every country are limited; and that whenever there are men enough in a country, to improve all its resources of wealth to the best advantage, increase of population becomes an evil. But no State in this Union has yet approached that point; no slave State has advanced half way to it.

. . . Fellow citizens, we esteem it a sad, a humiliating fact, which should penetrate the heart of every Virginian, that from the year 1790 to this time, Virginia has lost more people by emigration, than all the old free States together. Up to 1840, when the last census was taken, she had lost more by nearly 300,000. She has sent—or we should rather say, she has driven from her soil—at least one third of all the emigrants, who have gone from the old States to the new. More than another third have gone from the other old slave States. Many of these multitudes, who have left the slave States, have shunned the regions of slavery, and settled in the free countries of the West. These were generally industrious and enterprising white men, who found by sad experience, that a country of slaves was not the country for them. It is a truth, a certain truth, that *slavery drives free labourers— farmers, mechanics, and all, and some of the best of them too— out of the country, and fills their places with negroes.*

What is it but slavery that makes Marylanders, Carolinians, and especially old Virginians and new Virginians—fly their country at such a rate? Some go because they dislike slavery and desire to get away from it: others, because they have gloomy forebodings of what is to befall the slave States, and wish to leave their families in a country of happier prospects: others, because they cannot get profitable employment among slaveholders: others, industrious and high-spirited working men, will not stay in a country where slavery degrades the working man: others go because they see that their country, for some reason, does not prosper, and that other countries, not far off, are prospering, and will afford better hopes of prosperity to themselves: others, a numerous class, who are slaveholders and cannot live without slaves, finding that they cannot live longer with them on their worn out soils, go to seek better lands and more profitable crops, where slave labor may yet for a while enable them and their children to live.

## 11.

*Charles T. Russell:*
Minority Report of the Boston Grammar School Board *
[August 29, 1849]

*Charles Theodore Russell (1815–96) was born in Massachusetts. His father was a storekeeper who rose from the office of town clerk to that of state senator. Successful as a lawyer, the son filled many offices of trust, among which was membership*

* Boston (Mass.) Grammar School Board: *Report of a Special Committee of the Grammar School Board, August 29, 1849, adverse to the Petition of Sundry Colored Persons, Praying for the Abolition of the Smith School* (Boston: 1849), second pagination, 4–8, 10–11.

> *on the Grammar School Board of Boston. While thus serving,*
> *he entered this strong minority protest in 1849, when a com-*
> *mittee ruled adversely on the petition of several Negroes to*
> *abolish the "Jim Crow" Smith School. The view expressed by*
> *Russell was eloquently but vainly advocated by Charles Sum-*
> *ner in* Sarah C. Roberts v. The City of Boston *(1849). In*
> *1855, segregation was finally uprooted by statute.*

. . . The Undersigned believes that we have no moral or legal
right to exclude the colored children from the ordinary public
schools of this City. . . .

The Undersigned is led to this conclusion by considerations
founded in the origin, the nature, and the design of our system of
public education. It is believed that the right claimed by those
who would exclude the blacks, cannot be maintained, consistently without eradicating the vital principle, upon which our
*common public* schools rest. . . . Their great distinctive feature
has been and is, that they are supported by, designed for, and
open to the whole public equally. Every citizen must, according
to his means, contribute to their support. Every citizen has an
equal voice in their establishment, maintenance and control.
Every man and woman in the Commonwealth, is equally eligible
to become their teachers. The children of the rich and the poor,
the strong and the weak, the influential and the obscure, after
they pass the wide open door of these schools, stand upon a common level, in the presence of the Great Father of them all. Their
design seems to be, and their whole influence is, practically to
teach the great theoretical principle of our government, that "all
men are born free and equal." Nowhere, out of the church of
God, is this great doctrine more perfectly recognized than in our
common schools. These highways of knowledge, like the highways of communication, are established and maintained by all,
and of course for all, and to be restricted in their use by no regulations, save those that apply to all. Equality is the vital principle
of the system. Destroy this in the free schools, and you not only
destroy these schools, but the government which rests upon them,
as one of its main supports. No matter how few are to be favorably or unfavorably affected by the particular manner in which
you war against this principle of equality in a given case, the

general result must be pernicious, and only pernicious. It is war upon the *common public* school system.

Now what is the result of this principle of equality? Why, that no child in the Commonwealth can have any superior right over any other child to participate in the benefits of the common school. Nor has any class of children the right to different and separate schools, from any other class of similar age and general character. Religious differences may not intrude into the common schools. . . . Political differences are barred out from their doors. Political opinion, though like religious, deeply affected by education, is no ground of division, or exclusion in the school. Social condition and standing create no distinction here. The rich and the poor must sit upon the same form, yield to the same discipline and participate equally in the struggle for the same honors. Birth and origin are as impotent as social condition and standing. The child of the foreigner, and the native citizen, may equally share in this common blessing. Although the unnaturalized foreigner can neither hold office, nor land, among us, and has no voice in our government, still his children are, and should be, entitled to all the privileges of our common schools.

. . . If then the colored child may be excluded from the schools, it must be upon some legal distinction, superior to any of the distinctions here named.

What is this distinctive mark? *Color,* and *color* alone. Passing over the question of the degree of color necessary to create the distinction, and the difficulty of settling this; waiving the consideration of the inquiry whether color creates a moral distinction, affecting the right to be instructed, in children of a common Father, and descended from a common ancestor, it is enough for us to ask whether the laws of this Commonwealth recognize a distinction so founded. We find no warrant for it. There is not a colored citizen of the Commonwealth who is not as eligible to the office of Governor, or any subordinate civil office as the present chief magistrate. There is not a colored citizen in the State, who may not be elected, if the people choose to elect him, to the places we fill at this Board. There is not one who may not be elected, if we choose to elect him, to the mastership of any public school in the City. . . . There is not one who is not as eligible to any civil office in the gift of the appointing power of the State, as any white citizen. In point of fact, two or three colored men have been admitted, and are practising láw at the Suffolk bar. Some or all of them hold commissions as ·Justices of the Peace.

The colored citizen has no exemption from taxation. He is entitled equally with the white to vote at the polls. He is thus called upon to discharge the duties and share in the honors of the citizen. Hence he would seem to be entitled to enjoy equally all the public means provided to qualify him for such duties, and enable him to attain to such distinctions. In all the honors and pursuits of life, in this Commonwealth, in the sovereignty itself, the black man shares equally with the white. With what pretense, then, can it be urged that he may be excluded from the schools, on account of his color? In Massachusetts at least, *in law,* the complexion gives no rights and creates no disabilities. . . .

There is another consideration, which has no little influence with the Undersigned. The exclusion of the colored people from the schools, has undoubtedly proceeded from prejudices, growing out of their oppressed and enslaved condition. Its effect, also, has been to foster the opinion that they are an inferior and degraded race, incapable of any thing, but to do the drudgeries of life, under the instigation of the lash. From this opinion, human slavery draws its most specious argument. And the free and philanthropic North are cited to prove the opinion well founded. Every mode of degradation put upon the blacks here, is cited elsewhere in support of slavery, and contributes to sustain it. And so desireable is it forever to destroy that system of inequity and oppression, that I should deem it some redemption of error, even, if it leaned against it. But when this consideration is combined with those of justice and equity, and all tend to the same conclusion, it becomes irresistibly strong. . . .

CHARLES THEO. RUSSELL
*Boston, August 29th, 1849*

12.

### Frederick Douglass:
### A LECTURE ON AMERICAN SLAVERY *
[December 1, 1850]

*Born in slavery as Frederick Augustus Washington Bailey in Maryland, Douglass (1817?–95) twice sought to escape. The second attempt in 1836 was successful. After an extemporaneous speech at a convention of the Massachusetts Anti-Slavery Society he was immediately employed as agent of the society. He wrote his* Narrative of the Life of Frederick Douglass *(1845) in spite of the danger of re-enslavement. Returning from Great Britain to the United States in 1847 with money to buy his freedom, he founded the* North Star *against Garrison's wishes. He counseled John Brown to desist from his "mission," but had to flee to Canada when Governor Henry A. Wise of Virginia sought his arrest. In the Civil War, he assisted in recruiting Negro regiments and agitated for suffrage and civil rights for the freedman. His advice was sought by Lincoln, and he held many offices, including that of Minister to Haiti. This first of his Corinthian Hall lectures is fairly typical of his many pleas for Negro equality.*

More than twenty years of my life were consumed in a state of slavery. My childhood was environed by the baneful peculiarities of the slave system. I grew up to manhood in the presence of this hydra-headed monster—not as a master—not as an idle spectator—not as the guest of the slaveholder; but as A SLAVE, eating the bread and drinking the cup of slavery with the most degraded of my brother bondmen, and sharing with them all the painful conditions of their wretched lot. In consideration of these facts, I feel that I have a right to speak, and to speak *strongly*. Yet, my friends, I feel bound to speak truly. . . .

First of all, I will state, as well as I can, the legal and social relation of master and slave. A master is one (to speak in the vocabulary of the Southern States) who claims and exercises a right of property in the person of a fellow man. This he does with

* Frederick Douglass: *Lectures on American Slavery, Delivered at Corinthian Hall, Rochester, N.Y.* (Buffalo: 1851), 7–11.

the force of the law and the sanction of Southern religion. The
law gives the master absolute power over the slave. He may work
him, flog him, hire him out, sell him, and in certain contingencies,
*kill* him, with perfect impunity. The slave is a human being,
divested of all rights—reduced to the level of a brute—a mere
"chattel" in the eye of the law—placed beyond the circle of human
brotherhood—cut off from his kind—his name, which the "record-
ing angel" may have enrolled in heaven, among the blest, is im-
piously inserted in a *master's leger* [*sic*], with horses, sheep and
swine. In law, the slave has no wife, no children, no country,
and no home. He can own nothing, possess nothing, acquire nothing, but what must belong to another. To eat the fruit of his own
toil, to clothe his person with the work of his own hands, is considered stealing. He toils that another may reap the fruit; he is
industrious that another may live in idleness; he eats unbolted
meal, that another may eat the bread of fine flour; he labors in
chains at home, under a burning sun and biting lash, that another
may ride in ease and splendor abroad; he lives in ignorance, that
another may be educated; he is abused, that another may be exalted; he rests his toil-worn limbs on the cold, damp ground, that
another may repose on the softest pillow, he is clad in coarse and
tattered raiment, that another may be arrayed in purple and fine
linen; he is sheltered only by the wretched hovel, that a master
may dwell in a magnificent mansion; and to this condition he is
bound down as by an arm of iron.

From this monstrous relation, there springs an unceasing stream
of most revolting cruelties. The very accompaniments of the slave
system, stamp it as the offspring of hell itself. To ensure good be-
havior, the slaveholder relies on *the whip;* to induce proper humility, he relies on *the whip;* to rebuke what he is pleased to term
insolence, he relies on *the whip;* to supply the place of wages, as
an incentive to toil, he relies on *the whip;* to bind down the spirit
of the slave, to imbrute and destroy his manhood, he relies on
*the whip,* the chain, the gag, the thumb-screw, the pillory, the
bowie-knife, the pistol, and the blood-hound. . . . It makes no
difference whether the slaveholder worships the God of the Chris-
tains [*sic*] or is a follower of Mahomet, he is the minister of the
same cruelty, and the author of the same misery. *Slavery* is always

*slavery;* always the same foul, haggard, and damning scourge, whether found in the Eastern or in the Western Hemisphere.

There is a still deeper shade to be given to this picture. The physical cruelties are indeed sufficiently harassing and revolting; but they are as a few grains of sand on the sea shore, or a few drops of water in the great ocean, compared with the stupendous wrongs which it inflicts upon the mental, moral and religious nature of its hapless victims. It is only when we contemplate the slave as a moral and intellectual being, that we can adequately comprehend the unparalleled enormity of slavery, and the intense criminality of the slaveholder. I have said that the slave was a man. "What a piece of work is man? How noble in reason! How infinite in faculties! In form and moving, how express and admirable! In action, how like an angel! In apprehension how like a God! the beauty of the world! the paragon of animals!"

. . . It is *such* a being that is smitten and blasted. The first work of slavery is to mar and deface those characteristics of its victims which distinguish *men* from *things,* and *persons* from *property.* Its first aim is to destroy all sense of high moral and religious responsibility. It reduces man to a mere machine. It cuts him off from his maker, it hides from him the laws of God, and leaves him to grope his way from time to eternity in the dark, under the arbitrary and despotic control of a frail, depraved and sinful fellow-man. . . .

. . . The great mass of slaveholders look upon education among the slaves as utterly subversive of the slave system. I *well* remember when my mistress first announced to my master that she had discovered that I could read. His face colored at once, with surprise and chagrin. He said that "I was ruined, and my value as a slave destroyed; that a slave should know nothing but to obey his master; that to give a negro an inch would lead him to take an ell; that having learned how to read, I would soon want to know how to write; and that, by and by, I would be running away." I think my audience will bear witness to the correctness of this philosophy, and to the literal fulfilment of this prophecy.

13.

### John Brown:
### Last Speech to the Court *
[November 2, 1859]

*John Brown (1800–59) was born in Connecticut of pious, abolitionist parents of New England descent. In Ohio, Pennsylvania, and New York he worked at various jobs and in several businesses, developing the while an increasing preoccupation with the slavery problem. In the cause of abolition, Brown and his five sons went to Kansas, where they waged guerrilla warfare. As a means of establishing a free stronghold for slaves in the`mountains of Virginia he led a band of men in a raid on the United States Armory at Harper's Ferry, Virginia. After being captured by United States Marines under Captain Robert E. Lee, he was found guilty of treason and murder and sentenced to death.*

I have, may it please the Court, a few words to say.

In the first place, I deny everything but what I have all along admitted,—the design on my part to free the slaves. I intended certainly to have made a clean thing of that matter, as I did last winter, when I went into Missouri and there took slaves without the snapping of a gun on either side, moved them through the country, and finally left them in Canada. I designed to have done the same thing again, on a larger scale. That was all I intended. I never did intend murder, or treason, or the destruction of property, or to excite or incite slaves to rebellion, or to make insurrection.

I have another objection; and that is, it is unjust that I should suffer such a penalty. Had I interfered in the manner which I admit, and which I admit has been fairly proved . . . had I so interfered in behalf of the rich, the powerful, the intelligent, the so-called great, or in behalf of any of their friends, . . . and suffered and sacrificed what I have in this interference, it would have been all right; and every man in this court would have deemed it an act worthy of reward rather than punishment.

* *Testimonies of Captain John Brown, at Harper's Ferry, with His Address to the Court* (New York: 1860), 15–16.

This court acknowledges, as I suppose, the validity of the law of God. I see a book kissed here which I suppose to be the Bible, or at least the New Testament. That teaches me that all things whatsoever I would that men should do to me, I should do even so to them. It teaches me, further, to 'remember them that are in bonds, as bound with them.' I endeavored to act up to that instruction. I say, I am yet too young to understand that God is any respecter of persons. I believe that to have interfered as I have done—as I have always freely admitted I have done—in behalf of His despised poor, was not wrong, but right. Now, if it is deemed necessary that I should forfeit my life for the furtherance of the ends of justice, and mingle my blood further with the blood of my children and with the blood of millions in this slave country whose rights are disregarded by wicked, cruel, and unjust enactments,—I submit; so let it be done!

Let me say one word further.

I feel entirely satisfied with the treatment I have received on my trial. Considering all the circumstances, it has been more generous than I expected. But I feel no consciousness of guilt. I have stated from the first what was my intention, and what was not. I never had any design against the life of any person, nor any disposition to commit treason, or excite slaves to rebel, or make any general insurrection. I never encouraged any man to do so, but always discouraged any idea of that kind.

Let me say, also, a word in regard to the statements made by some of those connected with me. I hear it has been stated by some of them that I have induced them to join me. But the contrary is true. I do not say this to injure them, but as regretting their weakness. There is not one of them but joined me of his own accord, and the greater part of them at their own expense. A number of them I never saw, and never had a word of conversation with, till the day they came to me; and that was for the purpose I have stated.

Now I have done.

# CHAPTER SIX

## COMMUNITY HUMANENESS

———◆———

*Kings believe that they possess their crowns by a divine right: no wonder, therefore, they assume the divine power of taking away human life. Kings consider their subjects as their property: no wonder, therefore, they shed their blood with as little emotion as men shed the blood of their sheep or cattle. But the principles of republican governments speak a very different language.*
> ———BENJAMIN RUSH: On Punishing Murder by Death, 1792

*Political society owes perfect protection to all its members in their persons, reputations and property; and it also owes necessary subsistence to those who cannot procure it for themselves. . . . But the preservation of life is the first object, property is only a secondary one; and if a contract is to be supposed, . . . can it be supposed that any just contract could stipulate that one of the contracting parties should die of hunger, in order that the others might enjoy, without deduction, the whole of their property?*
> ———EDWARD LIVINGSTON: Introductory Report to the Code of Reform and Prison Discipline, 1826

Sources of the quotations on the preceding page:

BENJAMIN RUSH: Benjamin Rush: *Considerations on the Injustice and Impolicy of Punishing Murder by Death* . . . (Philadelphia: 1792), 19.

EDWARD LIVINGSTON: Edward Livingston: *Complete Works of Edward Livingston on Criminal Jurisprudence*, 2 v. (New York: 1873), I, 528, 533.

———◄◆►———

THE colonial New England house raising and twentieth-century social-service institutions are testimony of the deep community feelings of America. Between these two milestones in time stretches the long growth of community responsibility for helping victims of adversity—the impoverished, the deaf, the insane, and the derelicts—and for reforming penal codes and prison regimes.

Like Cesare Beccaria, the eighteenth-century Italian rationalist, William Bradford pleaded in 1792 that it "becomes us to extend our compassion" to mankind through narrowly restricting capital punishment ( 1 ). The function of prisons, he argued, was to isolate and to inspire penitence in prisoners, principles embodied in the first penitentiary in America, built in Philadelphia in 1791. This conception was echoed in the work of the Boston Society for Aiding Discharged Convicts (9), founded in 1846, which strove to extend the hand of kindness to the "disintegrated particles" of humanity. The spirit was early abroad that inspired Enoch Cobb Wine's reforms of the 1860's and Zebulon Brockway's reformatory in 1876.

The compassionate regard for humanity is reflected in the appeal for "pity and mercy to the afflicted" made by Thomas Barnard in 1794 before the Massachusetts Humane Society ( 2 ), which was dedicated to saving the victims of shipwrecks. ( Federal assistance in this work came through the efforts of Congressman William Newell in 1848.) Gradually humanitarian activity was more widely extended. The Humane Society of New York (3) aided the generally destitute and the imprisoned as well. Joseph Tuckerman pioneered in social work through his mission to the poor of Boston in 1826 (6), and the destitute children of New York found their champion in Charles Loring Brace, the first agent of the Children's Aid Society (10), whose objective was to save the children of the underprivileged from a life of crime and grinding poverty.

Those afflicted by nature—the deaf and dumb, the blind, and the insane—found their crusaders. After several short-lived schools for the deaf had been established in New York and Virginia, Thomas Hopkins Gallaudet founded the first free American School for the deaf at Hartford in 1817 (5). Similar schools soon appeared in Philadelphia and New York. In 1823, Kentucky established the first such institution under public auspices. The first school for the blind came into being in New York City in 1832. A state institution first appeared in Ohio in 1837. In 1832, Samuel Gridley Howe began his work for the Massachusetts School and Asylum for the Blind, and in 1837 he undertook the education of seven-year-old Laura Bridgman, the blind, deaf, and dumb girl (7). Thomas Eddy, following the trail blazed by Philippe Pinel, the great French psychiatrist, as well as Benjamin Franklin and Dr. Benjamin Rush, urged decent treatment for the insane with the least possible restraint (4). The first state hospital exclusively for mental patients was opened at Williamsburg, Virginia, in 1773, and Dr. Rush started work in the Pennsylvania Hospital in 1783; but it was not until Dorothea Dix's passionate Memorial to the Massachusetts legislature in 1843 that the battle for adequate and publicly supported care got firmly under way (8). The compassionate feeling for man showed by these reformers laid the foundations of the social service institutions of America.

---

## 1.

### *William Bradford:*
### ON THE DEATH PENALTY *
### [1793]

*Named after his father, the patriot-printer, William Bradford*
*(1755–95) was a student of law at the time the Revolution*
*broke out. Leaving his studies he volunteered as a private and*

* William Bradford: *An Enquiry How Far The Punishment of Death Is Necessary in Pennsylvania* . . . (Philadelphia: 1793), 43–6, 105.

*rose to the rank of colonel. This report on Philadelphia prisons in 1792, published the following year, led directly to the revision of the Pennsylvania criminal code eliminating capital punishment for all crimes except first degree murder. The report was very influential in causing other states to bar "cruel and unusual" punishments from their criminal codes. A brilliant lawyer, he was appointed Attorney General by President Washington.*

## Conclusion

It is from the ignorance, wretchedness or corrupted manners of a people that crimes proceed. In a country where these do not prevail moderate punishments, strictly enforced, will be a curb as effectual as the greatest severity.

A mitigation of punishment ought, therefore, to be accompanied, as far as possible, by a *diffusion of knowledge* and a *strict execution of the laws.* The former not only contributes to enlighten, but to meliorate the manners and improve the happiness of a people.

The celebrated *Beccaria* is of opinion, that no government has a right to punish its subjects unless it has previously taken care to instruct them in the knowledge of the laws and the duties of public and private life. The strong mind of *William Penn* grasped at both these objects, and provisions to secure them were interwoven with his system of punishments. The laws enjoined all parents and guardians to instruct the children under their care so as to enable them to write and read the scriptures by the time they attained to twelve years of age: and directed, that a copy of the laws (at that time few, simple and concise) should be used as a school book.* Similar provisions were introduced into the laws of Connecticut, and the Select Men are directed to see that "none suffer so much barbarism in their families as to want such learning and instruction." The children were to be "taught the laws against capital offences," † as those at Rome were accustomed to commit the twelve tables to memory. These were regulations in the pure spirit of a republic, which, considering the youth

---

* Laws 1682, ch, 60. 112 [footnote in original].
† Laws Conn. p. 20 [footnote in original].

as the property of the state, does not permit a parent to bring up his children in ignorance and vice.

The policy of the Eastern states, in the establishment of public schools, aided by the convenient size and *incorporation* of their townships, deserves attention and imitation. . . . Early education prevents more crimes than the severity of the criminal code.

The constitution of Pennsylvania contemplates this great object and directs, That "Schools shall be established, by law, throughout this state." Although there are real difficulties which oppose themselves as to the *perfect* execution of the plan, yet, the advantages of it are so manifest that an enlightened Legislator will, no doubt, cheerfully encounter, and, in the end, be able to surmount them.

*Secondly*—Laws which prescribe hard labor as a punishment should be strictly executed. The criminals ought, as far as possible, to be collected in one place, easily accessible to those who have the inspection of it. When they are together their management will be less expensive, more systematic and beneficial—Their treatment ought to be such as to make their confinement an *actual* punishment, and the rememberance of it a terror in future. The labor, in most cases, should be real *hard* labor—the food, though wholesome, should be *coarse*—the confinement sufficiently long to break down a disposition to vice—and the salutary rigor of *perfect solitude, invariably* inflicted on the greater offenders. Escapes should be industriously guarded against—pardons should be rarely, *very rarely,* granted, and the punishment of those who are guilty of a second offence should be sufficiently severe.

The reformation of offenders is declared to be one of the objects of the legislature in reducing the punishment—But time, and, in some cases, *much time,* must be allowed for this. It is easy to counterfeit contrition; but it is impossible to have faith in the sudden conversion of an old offender. . . .

The conclusion to which we are led, by this enquiry, seems to be, that in all cases (except those of high treason and murder) the punishment of death may be safely abolished, and milder penalties advantageously introduced—Such a system of punishments, aided and enforced in the manner I have mentioned, will not only have an auspi[ci]ous influence on the character, morals, and happiness of the people, but may hasten the period, when, in

the progress of civilization, the punishment of death shall cease
to be necessary; and the Legislature of Pennsylvania, putting the
key-stone to the arch, may triumph in the *completion* of their
benevolent work. . . .

PREAMBLE TO THE CONSTITUTION of the Philadelphia Society,
*for alleviating the Miseries of Public Prisons.* . . .
When we consider that the obligations of benevolence, which
are founded on the precepts and example of the author of Christianity, are not cancelled by the follies or crimes of our fellow-
creatures; and, when we reflect upon the miseries which penury,
hunger, cold, unnecessary severity, unwhol[e]some apartments,
and guilt, (the usual attendants of prisons) involve with them, it
becomes us to extend our compassion to that part of mankind,
who are the subjects of these miseries, by the aids of humanity,
their undue and illegal sufferings may be prevented: the links,
which should bind the whole family of mankind together under
all circumstances, be preserved unbroken: and, such degrees and
modes of punishment may be discovered and suggested, as may,
instead of continuing habits of vice, become the means of restor-
ing our fellow-creatures to virtue and happiness.

## 2.

### Rev. *Thomas Barnard:*
### A DISCOURSE ON HUMANE SENTIMENT *
### [June 10, 1794]

*The Reverend Thomas Barnard (1748–1814), born in Massa-
chusetts, was a minister of liberal and Unitarian persuasion.
He was an advocate of freedom of thought, rejecting the assumption that one can make one's own opinion a standard for
others. The earliest Humane societies, such as those of
Massachusetts and Philadelphia, were devoted to saving the
lives of shipwrecked sailors. The Massachusetts Humane So-*

* Thomas Barnard: A *Discourse, Delivered before the Humane Society
of the Commonwealth of Massachusetts,* . . . *June* 10, 1794 (Boston: 1794),
15–16.

*ciety began erecting huts on dangerous and lonely coasts in
1789. The New York Society went on to aid the destitute and
imprisoned debtors, and later added other humane activities.*

Humanity is a term of very extensive signification. It compre-
hends sympathy, compassion, pity and mercy to the afflicted:
Not only to this individual or class of the miserable, but to the
whole company of every nation, kindred, and tongue, whatever
the form, or particular causes, of their distress: nor only so, but
all those labours and exertions, which increase the accommodation of men, and render their abode here more pleasant and delightful. We live in a period of the world, and a stage of Society,
favourable to every charitable institution, and useful improvement. With respect to the civilized part of Europe, this perhaps,
may with justice be termed the age of humanity. Education and
affluence have united to soften the heart, and render the mind
capable of liberal and elegant views, as well as render easy the
expence of charitable institutions, and works of public convenience and magnificence. Never were the poor and miserable more
generously taken care of. . . . We are fast following in this
course, which most honourably distinguishes man from the lower
creatures on earth, and civilized man from the barbarous of his
species. Gone through with the necessities and hardships of those,
who first settle an uncultivated country, easy in our circumstances,
though not affluent, from the produce of agriculture, mechanic
arts, and commerce, we evidently amend in our buildings, in the
improvement of our lands, and the convenience and elegance of
our furniture. Let foreign writers say what they please, in these
western countries of the earth, we have equal strength and beauty
of body with them; we have as improveable and elegant minds;
and, unless untoward and sad events alter our situation, may exhibit human nature in as favourable a point of view as it has ever
yet appeared. Often, in meditation upon the causes of national
prosperity and happiness, have I forwarded my fervent prayer to
the great arbiter of events, that our country might display a scene
to the world, which has never yet appeared. That, instead of the
expensive ostentation of European courts, instead of wars of ambition, instead of the immense sums expended to gratify the pride
and favourite humours of State Ministers; our revenues might be

consecrated to the more reasonable purpose of rendering our country more productive, a more comfortable and delightful abode; in founding establishments for the increase of knowledge and improvement of the mind; for the encouragement of christian piety and good morals; for the alleviation and relief of every kind of suffering and misery. All the humane must in this supplication, cordially unite. The order of divine providence however, may see fit to disappoint our wishes. Humanity itself may call us to devote all our time and contributions to enlarge the means of defence; to render our bodies firm, and minds vigorous, that we may be prepared for deeds of hardihood and renown in the field. Yet, the conception of this scene is agreeable. An attempt to realize it is noble; and entitles us to the approbation and gratitude of all the wise and good.

## 3.

### *The Humane Society of New York:*
### REPORT ON A VISIT TO BRIDEWELL *
### [December 27, 1809]

*The Humane Society of New York was unique in that it did not confine its attention to saving lives from the sea, but also ministered to the unfortunate and destitute. Thomas Eddy was a leading spirit in the committee that gave this report.*

It is needless for the committee to make many remarks on the foregoing statement of the condition of this prison; and they are convinced that no remedy can be introduced with any effect, while the present system is pursued. We lose sight of the misery these poor objects of our commiseration undergo, when we reflect on the consequences of confining a number of young inexperienced persons, and sometimes innocent, with hardened old offenders. Here every sort of corruption is generated that it is in the power of wickedness and poverty to produce. The old corrupt the young;

---

* Humane Society of New York: *Report of a Committee of the Humane Society of New York . . . Visit to Bridewell, Dec. 27, 1809* (New York: 1810), 13, 14–15.

the lewd inflame the more modest; and the audacious harden the timid. Every one fortifies his mind as far as he is capable against his own remaining sensibility, endeavouring to practise on others the arts that are practised on himself. In this condition, corrupted and corrupting, imprisonment, instead of amending the culprit, serves, by the contagion of bad example, and the exasperation of bad passions, to render him *an hundred fold more vicious and untractable.*

Shall these irregularities, which are the cause of so much misery, disease, and all kinds of crimes and wickedness, be suffered to exist among an enlightened people, celebrated for their humanity, and making a profession of the mild virtues of the Christian religion?

By an act of the Legislature of this State, passed March 30th, 1802, the Corporation were authorized to erect a prison for solitary confinement. The act directs that persons convicted at the Court of Quarter-Sessions of petit larceny, shall be confined in the said prison at the discretion of the Court, not exceeding ninety days.

If the Corporation could be prevailed on to erect this prison, and if the law could be amended so as to allow Justices of the Peace, who are authorized to act under the laws respecting vagrants and for the suppression of vice and immorality, to send petty offenders to this prison to be confined in a solitary cell on a low diet for a short term or not exceeding thirty days, the Committee are decidedly of opinion that it would be of great public utility, and ( as far as small crimes can be prevented in a populous city) that it would more effectually prevent their commission than any other system of punishment that has been devised. It would be more honourable to the city and state, and more economical; and what is of far superior consequence, it would much conduce to the reformation of the offender: left to reflect in solitude and silence, his thoughts will be naturally directed to his present condition, and past conduct, and it is possible he may become sensible of his wickedness and folly, and by feeling the bitter pangs of remorse, be induced when discharged to amend his life.

| THOMAS EDDY, | JOHN H. HOBART, |
| PETER AUGUSTUS JAY, | J. MORTON. |

*12th month (December) 26th, 1809.*

4.

## Thomas Eddy:
### AN IMPROVED MODE OF TREATING THE INSANE *
### [1815]

*Born in Philadelphia of Irish Quakers, Thomas Eddy (1758–1827) devoted himself to philanthropic ventures. After attaining success in the insurance business, he threw himself into most of the progressive projects of the day—the New York Hospital, Bloomingdale Asylum for the Insane, the Free School of New York City, and the House of Refuge. He made noteworthy contributions to prison reform, advocating the single-cell system, especially for hardened criminals. He opposed slavery and imprisonment for debt, sought to improve the treatment of the American Indian, and, as this paper shows, worked for the welfare of the insane.*

Of the numerous topics of discussion, in subjects relating to the cause of humanity, there is none which has stronger claims to our attention, than that which relates to the treatment of the insane. . . .

. . . I beg leave to suggest the following regulations to be adopted, in accomplishing the objects in view:

1ST. No patient shall hereafter be confined by chains.

2ND. In the most violent states of mania, the patient should be confined in a room which the windows, &c. closed, so as nearly to exclude the light, and kept confined, if necessary, in a strait-jacket, so as to walk about the room or lie down on the bed at pleasure; or by straps, &c. he may, particularly if there appears in the patient a strong determination to self-destruction, be confined on the bed, and the apparatus so fixed as to allow him to turn and otherwise change his position.

3D. The power of judicious kindness to be generally exercised, may often be blessed with good effects, and it is not till after other moral remedies are exercised, that recourse should be had to restraint, or the power of fear on the mind of the patient; yet it may

* Thomas Eddy: *Hints for Introducing an Improved Mode of Treating the Insane in the Asylum* (New York: 1815), 3, 12–17.

be proper sometimes, by way of punishment, to use the shower bath.

4TH. The common attendants shall not apply any extraordinary coercion by way of punishment, or change in any degree the mode of treatment prescribed by the physician; on the contrary, it is considered as their indispensable duty, to seek by acts of kindness the good opinion of the patients, so as to govern them by the influence of esteem rather than of severity.

5TH. On the first day of the week, the superintendent, or the principal keeper of the Asylum, shall collect as many of the patients as may appear to them suitable and read some chapters in the Bible.

6TH. When it is deemed necessary to apply the strait-jacket, or any other mode of coercion, by way of punishment or restraint, such an ample force should be employed as will preclude the idea of resistance from entering the mind of the patient.

7TH. It shall be the duty of the deputy keeper, immediately on a patient being admitted, to obtain his name, age, where born, what has been his employment or occupation, his general disposition and habits, when first attacked with mania; if it has been violent or otherwise, the cause of his disease, if occasioned by religious melancholy, or a fondness for ardent spirits, if owing to an injury received on any part of the body, or supposed to arise from any other known cause, hereditary or adventitious, and the name of the physician who may have attended him, and his manner of treating the patient while under his direction.

8TH. Such of the patients as may be selected by the physician, or the committee of the Asylum, shall be occasionally taken out to walk or ride under the care of the deputy keeper: and it shall be also his duty to employ the patients in such manner, and to provide them with such kinds of amusements and books as may be approved and directed by the Committee.

9TH. The female keeper shall endeavour to have the female patients constantly employed at suitable work; to provide proper amusements, books, &c. to take them out to walk as may be directed by the Committee.

10TH. It shall be the indispensable duty of the keepers, to have all the patients as clean as possible in their persons, and to preserve great order and decorum when they sit down to their respective meals.

11TH. It shall be the duty of the physician to keep a book, in which shall be entered an historical account of each patient, stating his situation, and the medical and moral treatment used; which book shall be laid before the Committee, at their weekly meetings.

The sentiments and improvements proposed in the preceding remarks, for the consideration of the governors, are adapted to our present situation and circumstances; but a further and more extensive improvement has occurred to my mind, which I conceive, would very considerably conduce towards effecting the cure, and materially ameliorate the condition and add to the comfort of the insane; at the same time that it would afford an ample opportunity of ascertaining how far that disease may be removed by moral management alone, which it is believed, will, in many instances, be more effectual in controlling the maniac, than medical treatment, especially, in those cases where the disease has proceeded from causes operating directly on the mind.

I would propose, that a lot, not less than ten acres, should be purchased by the governors, conveniently situated, within a few miles of the city, and to erect a substantial building, on a plan calculated for the accommodation of fifty lunatic patients; the ground to be improved in such a manner as to serve for agreeable walks, gardens, &c. for the exercise and amusement of the patients: this establishment might be placed under the care and superintendence of the Asylum Committee, and be visited by them once every week: a particular description of patients to remain at this Rural Retreat; and such others, who might appear as suitable objects, might be occasionally removed there from the Asylum.

The cost, and annual expense of supporting this establishment, is a matter of small consideration, when we duly consider the important advantages it would afford to a portion of our fellow-creatures, who have such strong claims on our sympathy and commiseration.

5.

## Thomas Hopkins Gallaudet:
### A SERMON ON DEAF AND DUMB PERSONS *
[April 20, 1817]

*Thomas Hopkins Gallaudet (1787–1851) was born in Phila-*
*delphia. He declined a ministerial post because of poor health.*
*As a young man he became acquainted with a deaf child, Alice*
*Cogswell, whose father, among others, commissioned him to*
*go to Europe in 1815 to study the methods of instructing the*
*deaf. Returning with Laurent Clerc, he founded in Hartford*
*the first free American school for the deaf, the opening of*
*which was the occasion for the Sermon. He remained in charge*
*of this institute until 1830 and his work profoundly affected*
*the education of the deaf. Gallaudet also encouraged the es-*
*tablishment of normal schools in Connecticut and influenced*
*education for Negroes and women.*

Nor, we trust, will motives be found wanting for *future* exertions in behalf of these children of misfortune. It is always more
blessed to give, than to receive.—Efforts of charity, prudently and
usefully directed, never fail abundantly to repay those by whom
they are made. This is true, not only with regard to individuals,
but also public bodies of men. That town, whose character is one
of benevolence and good-will towards the unhappy, enjoys, in the
opinion of all the wise and good, a reputation more exalted, more
valuable, more noble, than it can possibly gain by the most extensive pursuits of commerce and the arts; by the most elaborate
improvements in trade or manufactures, by the richest displays
of its wealth, or the splendour of its edifices; by the proudest
monuments of its taste or genius. It gains, too, the smiles of
Heaven, whose blessings descend upon it in various forms of
divine munificence. While the hearts of its inhabitants expand in
charity towards others, and the labours of their hands are united
in one common object, they learn *together* the pleasure of doing
good,—they find, at least, one green spot of repose in the desert of

* T. H. Gallaudet: A *Sermon* . . . at the *Opening of the Connecticut*
*Asylum for the Education and Instruction of Deaf and Dumb Persons . . .*
*April 20, 1817* (Hartford, Conn.: 1817), 11.

life, where they may cull some fruits of paradise, and draw refreshment from streams that flow from the river of God. They feel that they are fellow pilgrims in the same wilderness of cares and sorrows, and, while they look to that country to which they are all hastening, while they tread in the footsteps of Him *who went about doing good,* how quickly do their differences of opinion soften; the lines of sectarian division melt away; and even political jealousies and animosities retire into the shades of forgetfulness.

Yes, my hearers, godliness hath the promise of this life, as well as of that which is to come. The spirit of christian benevolence, is the only one which will change, completely, the aspect of human affairs. It has already begun to knit together the affections, not only of towns and villages, but of numerous sects throughout the world, and seems to be preparing to embrace within its influence even states and kingdoms. On its hallowed ground, a respite is given to political and religious warfare;—men lay down the weapons of contention, and cherish, for a season at least, the divine temper of peace on earth, and good will towards men.

### 6.

### *Joseph Tuckerman:*
### REPORT ON A MINISTRY-AT-LARGE IN BOSTON *
### [1831, 1832]

*Joseph Tuckerman (1778–1840) was born in Boston of a New England family and became a Unitarian minister. In 1812 he started the Boston Society for the Religious and Moral Improvement of Seamen, an interest matched by his zeal for "the neglected poor in our cities." In 1826 he began a "ministry-at-large" in Boston that was in effect a city mission to the poor. His influence was felt in England and France, and as late as 1888 the ladies of the "Tuckerman Sewing Circle" of Boston were still sewing, and selling what they made, for the "Poor's Purse." His work led his biographer to call him "Pioneer in American Social work,—Prophet of Organized Charity."*

* Joseph Tuckerman: *Eighth Semi-Annual Report . . . of his Services as Minister at Large in Boston* (Boston, 1831), 41–4 and *Tenth Semi-Annual Report . . .* (Boston: 1832), 11–12.

We live in a very benevolent community. But Christianity requires a far higher benevolence than that of giving money. Its aim is, to unite men as a family of brothers. Whatever may be our property, our intelligence, our office, or our titles, Christianity requires us to recognise the poor beggar and the convicted criminal, as the children of our Father, and possessors of a common nature with ourselves. They have fallen,—at least, tens of thousands of them fallen,—under circumstances, in which if we had ourselves been, we might have sunk as low as they are. And from whence arose those circumstances? From the fault of the individuals suffering under them? Sometimes, without doubt. But I have referred to circumstances, and I might have referred to many more, which, though not within the control of the individuals who are brought by them to abjectness and crime, may be controlled and entirely changed by others; and which, brought under christian influences, would save thousands from degradation and wretchedness. This view of the condition of society, and of christian duties with respect to it, demands an attention which has never yet been given to it. Men have so long been told that poverty and crime are unfathomable gulfs; that their springs, or the causes producing them, are beyond human power; and that, to a great extent, they are alike necessary and irremediable evils; that, even by multitudes of the wise and good, nothing is deemed more chimerical, more a mere dream of enthusiasm, than a proposition to lay open the causes of these evils and the means by which far the largest amount of them may be remedied or prevented. And yet I am quite as sure that Christianity has given us these means, and that they are entirely sufficient for these ends, as I am of the existence of pauperism and crime. And I am quite as sure, too, that the errors of judgment, and the mistakes in conduct, into which not only legislators, but many others, have fallen on these subjects, are attributable wholly to the fact, that losing sight of christian sentiments of human relations, dependencies and obligations, they have looked alike for the causes and the cure of these evils, where neither was to be found. The poor and criminals have generally been regarded only in their civil relations; as members of the body politic, who are to be affected only by political ordinances; and respecting whom the great question has been, how may they most effectually be coerced? or, what is the immediate cost which must be incurred for them? No error can be more vital than this. Sunk and degraded as we see them, even the lowest and the worst of these unhappy beings has a moral nature; and a moral as well as physical powers and wants. Many, too, even of the lowest and the worst, by wise preventive measures, might have been saved from the degradation in which we see them. . . . Is it asked, what provisions are made by Christianity for the accomplishment of this great redemption? I answer that they are to be found, not in the peculiar doctrines of any sect in Christendom; but as I have already said, in a christian sense of human relations,—of the connexion into which Jesus Christ intended to bring man with man,—and of our responsibilities for all our means of usefulness. And is it asked, how is this mighty change to be wrought through means so simple? I answer, let all the intelligent, the affluent and influential among us, who call themselves Christians, bring home to their own souls what Christ has taught upon the topics to which I have here referred, and there would not then be a single poor or vicious family or individual among us, which would not soon be brought within the sympathies of our religion. How many widows, now suffering under the most distressing embarrassments and perplexities, would then be comforted and encouraged, aided in the direction of their industry, and made comparatively happy? How many intemperate men and women, whose greatest excesses arise from the feeling that they are outcasts and uncared for, might be recovered to a sense of character and to virtue? How many children, both of virtuous and of vicious poor parents, under the restraints and encouragements of this new alliance, might be recalled from vagrancy and filial disobedience, placed and kept in our schools, in due time apprenticed at useful employments, and made respectable and happy members of society? How many filthy families might be made cleanly? . . . How would the distresses of sickness among the poor be thus alleviated? From how many moral dangers, from which they know not how to escape, would they thus be rescued? And is there a man who has a disposition for this service, who might not find leisure for it? Or is there a man who has a christian feeling for his suffering brother, who would not soon acquire a tact, if tact be required, for this service? This feeling of relationship, and this connexion of the classes of society, is one of the most obvious of all the dictates of Christianity; and nothing short of Christianity will ever bring about any great and permanent melioration of the condition of the poor, or any great and permanent means for the prevention of pauperism and crime. . . .

. . . I cannot here discuss the question, of the rights of the poor. But I would invite attention to it. There is often great vagueness, and not infrequently great injustice, in the sentiments of men upon this subject. . . . By the poor, as well as by the rich, rights may be forfeited. But how are rights forfeited except by wrong doing? And, in any case in which they are forfeited, the question is of great importance, to what extent? A criminal, who has forfeited his life to the laws, is not considered to have forfeited his right to food, clothing and shelter, while the laws shall permit him to live. Who, indeed, would not cry out against the injustice, as well as against the inhumanity, of refusing food to a hungry criminal? And why, but because his necessity, and his inability to provide for his wants, give him a right to food from the common stock of others? Has not an innocently poor person, then, in proportion to his inability, a right to a comfortable support from others, which is quite as absolute as is the right by which any property is held in society? I would bring these inquiries to the test of the original principles of civil justice; and I am willing, as far as legislation is concerned, here to leave decisions respecting the rights of the poor. Let legislators, and the community, in view of these principles, "render to all their due," and there will be a vast diminution of human suffering, and sin. It is the doctrine of Malthus on this subject, that "we are bound in honor and justice formally to disclaim the right of the poor to support;" that they have "no claim of right on society for the smallest portion of food, beyond that which their own labor would fairly purchase;" and that, "if this system were pursued, we need be under no apprehensions that the number of persons in extreme want would be beyond the power and will of the benevolent to supply."–If Mr. Malthus, or any of his descendants should ever be poor, God grant that their claims may never be left for decision with the receivers of his system of Political Economy!–Malthus' Essay, Vol. iii, pp. 179, and 181, 182.

# 7.

*Samuel Gridley Howe:*
THE CASE OF LAURA DEWEY BRIDGMAN *
[1840]

*Samuel Gridley Howe (1801–76) was born in Massachusetts.
Upon graduation from Harvard Medical School at the age of
twenty-three, he volunteered to serve in the embattled Greek
army, becoming surgeon of the Greek fleet and from 1824–30
organizing relief work. Upon his return to the United States,
he began work for the Massachusetts School and Asylum for
the Blind by taking six blind students into his father's house.
His work was so impressive that the legislature granted funds
for the institution. Thus was launched one of the three pioneer schools for the blind. In 1837 he undertook to teach
Laura Dewey Bridgman, a pathetic girl of seven who had become blind, deaf, and dumb from scarlet fever. This experience he first described in the* Seventh Annual Report *for 1838.
He also became interested in the care of mentally deficient
children and delinquents and in many other philanthropies.*

At the end of the year [1838] a report of her case was made,
from which the following is an extract:

It has been ascertained beyond the possibility of doubt,
that she cannot see a ray of light, cannot hear the least sound,
and never exercises her sense of smell, if she has any. Thus
her mind dwells in darkness and stillness, as profound as that
of a closed tomb at midnight. Of beautiful sights, and sweet
sounds, and pleasant odors, she has no conception; nevertheless, she seems as happy and playful as a bird or a lamb;
and the employment of her intellectual faculties or acquirement of a new idea, gives her a vivid pleasure, which is
plainly marked in her expressive features. She never seems to
repine, but has all the buoyance and gayety of childhood. She
is fond of fun and frolic, and when playing with the rest of the
children, her shrill laugh sounds loudest of the group.

* Perkins Institution and Massachusetts School for the Blind: *Ninth Annual Report of the Trustees* (Boston: 1841), 27–9.

When left alone, she seems very happy if she has her knitting or sewing, and will busy herself for hours: if she has no occupation, she evidently amuses herself by imaginary dialogues, or by recalling past impressions; she counts with her fingers, or spells out names of things which she has recently learned, in the manual alphabet of the deaf mutes. In this lonely self-communion she seems to reason, reflect, and argue: if she spells a word wrong with the fingers of her right hand, she instantly strikes it with her left, as her teacher does, in sign of disapprobation: if right, then she pats herself upon the head, and looks pleased. She sometimes purposely spells a word wrong with the left hand, looks roguish for a moment and laughs, and then with the right hand strikes the left, as if to correct it.

During the year she has attained great dexterity in the use of the manual alphabet of the deaf mutes; and she spells out the words and sentences which she knows, so fast and so deftly, that only those accustomed to this language can follow with the eye the rapid motions of her fingers.

But wonderful as is the rapidity with which she writes her thoughts upon the air, still more so is the ease and accuracy with which she reads the words thus written by another, grasping their hands in hers, and following every movement of their fingers, as letter after letter conveys their meaning to her mind. It is in this way that she converses with her blind playmates; and nothing can more forcibly show the power of mind in forcing matter to its purpose, than a meeting between them. For, if great talent and skill are necessary for two pantomimes to paint their thoughts and feelings by the movements of the body and the expression of the countenance, how much greater the difficulty when darkness shrouds them both, and the one can hear no sound!

When Laura is walking through a passage way, with her hands spread before her, she knows instantly every one she meets, and passes them with a sign of recognition; but if it be a girl of her own age, and especially if one of her favorites, there is instantly a bright smile of recognition—and a twining of arms—a grasping of hands—and a swift telegraphing upon the tiny fingers, whose rapid evolutions convey the thoughts and feelings from the outposts of one mind to those of the other. There are questions and answers—exchanges of joy or sorrow—there are kissings and partings—just as between little children with all their senses.

During this year, and six months after she had left home, her mother came to visit her, and the scene of their meeting was an interesting one.

The mother stood some time, gazing with overflowing eyes upon her unfortunate child, who, all unconscious of her presence, was playing about the room. Presently Laura ran against her, and at once began feeling of her hands, examining her dress, and trying to find out if she knew her; but not succeeding in this, she turned away as from a stranger, and the poor woman could not conceal the pang she felt, at finding that her beloved child did not know her.

She then gave Laura a string of beads which she used to wear at home, which were recognized by the child at once, who, with much joy, put them around her neck, and sought me eagerly, to say she understood the string was from her home.

The mother now tried to caress her, but poor Laura repelled her, preferring to be with her acquaintances.

Another article from home was now given her, and she began to look much interested; she examined the stranger much closer, and gave me to understand that she knew she came from Hanover; she even endured her caresses, but would leave her with indifference at the slightest signal. The distress of the mother was now painful to behold; for, although she had feared that she should not be recognized, the painful reality of being treated with cold indifference by a darling child, was too much for woman's nature to bear.

After a while, on the mother taking hold of her again, a vague idea seemed to flit across Laura's mind, that this could not be a stranger; she therefore felt of her hands very eagerly, while her countenance assumed an expression of intense interest—she became very pale, and then suddenly red—hope seemed struggling with doubt and anxiety, and never were contending emotions more strongly painted upon the human face: at this moment of painful uncertainty, the mother drew her close to her side, and kissed her fondly, when at once the truth flashed upon the child, and all mistrust and anxiety disappeared from her face, as with an expression of exceeding joy she eagerly nestled to the bosom of her parent, and yielded herself to her fond embraces.

After this, the beads were all unheeded; the playthings which were offered to her were utterly disregarded; her playmates, for whom but a moment before she gladly left the stranger, now vainly strove to pull her from her mother; and though she yielded her usual instantaneous obedience to my signal to follow me, it was evidently with painful reluctance. She clung close to me, as if bewildered and fearful; and when, after a moment, I took her to her mother, she sprang to her arms, and clung to her with eager joy.

8.

*Dorothea Dix:*
MEMORIAL TO THE MASSACHUSETTS LEGISLATURE *
[January, 1843]

*Dorothea Lynde Dix (1802–87), a native of Maine, in her youth tutored the children of Rev. William Ellery Channing and later, as a semi-invalid, taught a Sunday-school class in the East Cambridge House of Correction in Massachusetts. Aroused by conditions in the unheated jails, she spent the next two years investigating the condition of the insane in jails, almshouses, and houses of correction throughout Massachusetts. In 1843, through influential men, her Memorial was presented to the state legislature. Five years later she carried to Congress her battle for tax-supported institutions with trained personnel in a petition concerning "more than nine thousand idiots, epileptics, and insane in these United States." Her independent spirit, intense compassion, and belief in the spiritual possibilities of every human being lent strength to her crusade, waged throughout the United States, Canada, England, and the Continent. During the Civil War, she continued her work as "Superintendent of Women Nurses," furthering the cause of hospitals thereafter until her death.*

* Dorothea Dix: *Memorial of Dorothea L. Dix to the Massachusetts Legislature, Jan.* 1843 (Boston: 1843), 3–5, 24–5, 32.

GENTLEMEN,

I RESPECTFULLY ask to present this Memorial, believing that the *cause*, which actuates to and sanctions so unusual a movement, presents no equivocal claim to public consideration and sympathy. Surrendering to calm and deep convictions of duty my habitual views of what is womanly and becoming, I proceed briefly to explain what has conducted me before you unsolicited and unsustained, trusting, while I do so, that the memorialist will be speedily forgotten in the memorial.

About two years since leisure afforded opportunity, and duty prompted me to visit several prisons and alms-houses in the vicinity of this metropolis. I found, near Boston, in the Jails and Asylums for the poor, a numerous class brought into unsuitable connexion with criminals and the general mass of Paupers. I refer to Idiots and Insane persons, dwelling in circumstances not only adverse to their own physical and moral improvement, but productive of extreme disadvantages to all other persons brought into association with them. I applied myself diligently to trace the causes of these evils, and sought to supply remedies. As one obstacle was surmounted, fresh difficulties appeared. Every new investigation has given depth to the conviction that it is only by decided, prompt, and vigorous legislation the evils to which I refer, and which I shall proceed more fully to illustrate, can be remedied. I shall be obliged to speak with great plainness, and to reveal many things revolting to the taste, and from which my woman's nature shrinks with peculiar sensitiveness. But truth is the highest consideration. *I tell what I have seen*—painful and shocking as the details often are—that from them you may feel more deeply the imperative obligation which lies upon you to prevent the possibility of a repetition or continuance of such outrages upon humanity. If I inflict pain upon you, and move you to horror, it is to acquaint you with sufferings which you have the power to alleviate, and make you hasten to the relief of the victims of legalized barbarity.

I come to present the strong claims of suffering humanity. I come to place before the Legislature of Massachusetts the condition of the miserable, the desolate, the outcast. I come as the advocate of helpless, forgotten, insane and idiotic men and women; of beings, sunk to a condition from which the most unconcerned would start with real horror; of beings wretched in our Prisons, and more wretched in our Alms-Houses. And I cannot suppose it needful to employ earnest persuasion, or stubborn argument, in order to arrest and fix attention upon a subject, only the more strongly pressing in its claims, because it is revolting and disgusting in its details.

I must confine myself to few examples, but am ready to furnish other and more complete details, if required. If my pictures are displeasing, coarse, and severe, my subjects, it must be recollected, offer no tranquil, refined, or composing features. The condition of human beings, reduced to the extremest states of degradation and misery, cannot be exhibited in softened language, or adorn a polished page.

I proceed, Gentlemen, briefly to call your attention to the *present* state of Insane Persons confined within this Commonwealth, in *cages, closets, cellars, stalls, pens! Chained, naked, beaten with rods,* and *lashed* into obedience!

As I state cold, severe *facts,* I feel obliged to refer to persons, and definitely to indicate localities. But it is upon my subject, not upon localities or individuals, I desire to fix attention; and I would speak as kindly as possible of all Wardens, Keepers, and other responsible officers, believing that *most* of these have erred not through hardness of heart and wilful cruelty, so much as want of skill and knowledge, and want of consideration. Familiarity with suffering, it is said, blunts the sensibilities, and where neglect once finds a footing other injuries are multiplied. This is not all, for it may justly and strongly be added that, from the deficiency of adequate means to meet the wants of these cases, it has been an absolute impossibility to do justice in this matter. Prisons are not constructed in view of being converted into County Hospitals, and Alms-Houses are not founded as receptacles for the Insane. And yet, in the face of justice and common sense, Wardens are by law compelled to receive, and the Masters of Alms-Houses not to refuse, Insane and Idiotic subjects in all stages of mental disease and privation.

It is the Commonwealth, not its integral parts, that is accountable for most of the abuses which have lately, and do still exist. I repeat it, it is defective legislation which perpetuates and multiplies these abuses. . . .

Men of Massachusetts, I beg, I implore, I demand, pity and protection, for these of my suffering, outraged sex!—Fathers, Husbands, Brothers, I would supplicate you for this boon—but what do I say? I dishonor you, divest you at once of Christianity and humanity—does this appeal imply distrust. If it comes burthened with a doubt of your righteousness in this Legislation, then blot it out; while I declare confidence in your honor, not less than your humanity. Here you will put away the cold, calculating spirit of selfishness and self-seeking; lay off the armor of local strife and political opposition; here and now, for once, forgetful of the earthly and perishable, come up to these halls and consecrate them with one heart and one mind to works of righteousness and just judgement. Become the benefactors of your race, the just guardians of the solemn rights you hold in trust. Raise up the fallen; succour the desolate; restore the outcast; defend the helpless; and for your eternal and great reward, receive the benediction. . . . "Well done, good and faithful servants, become rulers over many things!" . . .

It is not few but many, it is not a part but the whole, who bear unqualified testimony to this evil. A voice strong and deep comes up from every almshouse and prison in Massachusetts where the insane are or have been, protesting against such evils as have been illustrated in the preceding pages.

Gentlemen, I commit to you this sacred cause. Your action upon this subject will affect the present and future condition of hundreds and of thousands.

In this legislation, as in all things, may you exercise that "wisdom which is the breath of the power of God."

*Respectfully submitted,*
D. L. DIX
*85 Mount Vernon St., Boston,
January, 1843*

9.

*Boston Society for Aiding Discharged Convicts:*
REPORT *
[1848]

*The Boston Society for Aiding Discharged Convicts, formed
in April 1848, established an agency, first occupied by Dr.
Augustine C. Taft, to handle the adjustment of released
prisoners to honest work. The agency received the released
convict, placed him in a boarding house safe from evil con-
tacts, and tried to secure work for him. Under the leadership
of its president Walter Channing and its vice-president (president after 1857) Samuel Gridley Howe, the society drew the
support of the public to this work through fund drives.*

The discharged convict is a peculiar estate in civilization. This
class of persons is conscious of a brand, and shrinks from seeking
communion with the reputed good in society, even when the wish
for amendment and return is strongest, regarding itself as outcast
from creditable association, by a palpable and proveable mark.
To look upon crime as a sin, alone, is but a partial sight of this
dreadful matter. Crime is sin—it is also poverty of being, lack of
the riches of life, and the perennial fountain of inward resource—
lack of the tenure of the social bond, and the sustaining loyalty of
kind—a tendency to throw one's self away as worthless for good, the
cause and the result both of crime. Crime breeds distrust of self,
and of kind—crime looks upon reputable society as an enemy.
This class of persons must have the hand of kindness extended
to them voluntarily, freely, by the good, and kept extended, for
they feel themselves lost to the communion of the good in repute.
This poverty of being is the direst need to be supplied in them.
How hard the struggle of an innocent person upward to the
strength which we call character, with all the relations and helps
of the social state safe; then what must it be to the convict, discharged from prison into the crowd of life, again, a world of men,
and not one righteous soul his brother. Was ever solitude like this

* *Second Annual Report of the Boston Society for Aiding Discharged
Convicts* (Boston: 1848), 6–8.

—was ever temptation to throw one's self away to the first offer of evil companionship like this? To the very best and strongest among this class, the way of return to right among men is long and weary, and will have many doubts and despairs, and many stumblings and falls. Never mind. They must be helped into the way, and then helped along the way. The class of criminals demonstrates the intestine barbarism of our Christian civilization. How this class is to be made to cease, is the problem for civilization to solve, that it may justify itself before God and man. It is not the will of God that one of these shall be left to perish; and society shall never be at rest, so long as it is the theory of man that they must be left to perish. Christian civilization is not Christian, while the intestine barbarism of this class remains within it. . . . The discharged convict is a disintegrated particle, that has lost the social attraction, and dropped out of place in the human sphere. It must be restored again, under the providences of God, by the growth of inward personal power. The power of the world is against the discharged convict, now, in the inward consciousness that his integrity with the mass of virtuous human being is gone. This consciousness takes out from him the heart and pulse of hope. He must be held hold of, and not be let to go back faint again, to the bad attraction of his own self abandoned class, whenever his hope of good shall fail him, which must often be. Except brotherly love continue, and hold him in the currents of the great part of humanity, til he is magnetized with good again, how shall he be restored?

## 10.

### *Charles Loring Brace:*
### FIRST CIRCULAR OF THE CHILDREN'S AID SOCIETY *
### [March, 1853]

*Charles Loring Brace (1826–90) was born in Connecticut, of distinguished New England stock. He taught school and studied theology, but his thoughts turned to work among de-*

---

\* *The Life of Charles Loring Brace Chiefly Told in His Own Letters; Edited by His Daughter* (New York: 1894), 489–92.

*linquents. While in Europe he lingered on in Hungary, where his sympathy for Kossuth, the revolutionary leader, brought imprisonment. After his release, he finally went to New York, where he was influential in founding the Chrildren's Aid Society. This organization worked mainly among foreign immigrants, establishing cheap lodging houses, industrial schools, camps, and sanitariums. It also found homes and jobs for more than 100,000 city waifs. Brace won international repute as a pioneer in modern philanthropic methods; he favored self-help rather than charity. He was inspired by the belief that every human soul had worth within it.*

*To the Public:* This society has taken its origin in the deeply settled feeling of our citizens, that something must be done to meet the increasing crime and poverty among the destitute children of New York. Its objects are to help this class, by opening Sunday meetings and industrial schools, and gradually, as means shall be furnished, by forming lodging-houses and reading-rooms for children, and by employing paid agents, whose sole business shall be to care for them.

As Christian men, we cannot look upon this great multitude of unhappy, deserted, and degraded boys and girls without feeling our responsibility to God for them. We remember that they have the same capacities, the same need of kind and good influences, and the same immortality, as the little ones in our own homes. We bear in mind that One died for them, even as for the children of the rich and the happy. Thus far, almshouses and prisons have done little to affect the evil. But a small part of the vagrant population can be shut up in our asylums; and judges and magistrates are reluctant to convict children, so young and ignorant that they hardly seem able to distinguish good and evil. The class increases. Immigration is pouring in its multitudes of poor foreigners, who leave these young outcasts everywhere abandoned in our midst. For the most part, the boys grow up utterly by themselves. No one cares for them, and they care for no one. Some live by begging, by petty pilferings, by bold robbery. Some earn an honest support by peddling matches, or apples, or newspapers. Others gather bones and rags in the street to sell. They sleep on steps, in cellars, in old barns, and in markets; they hire a bed in filthy and low lodging-houses. They cannot read. They do not go to school or attend a church. Many of them have never seen the Bible. Every cunning faculty is intensely stimulated. They are shrewd and old in vice when other children are in leading-strings. Few influences which are kind and good ever reach the vagrant boy. And yet, among themselves, they show generous and honest traits. Kindness can always touch them.

The *girls*, too often, grow up even more pitiable and deserted. Till of late, no one has ever cared for them. They are the cross-walk sweepers, the little apple-peddlers and candy-sellers of our city; or by more questionable means they earn their scanty bread. They traverse the low, vile streets alone, and live without mother or friends, or any share in what we should call *home*. They, also, know little of God or Christ, except by name. They grow up passionate, ungoverned; with no love or kindness ever to soften the heart. We all know their short, wild life, and the sad end. These boys and girls, it should be remembered, will soon form the great lower class of our city. They will influence elections; they may shape the policy of the city; they will, assuredly, if unreclaimed, poison society all around them. They will help to form the great multitude of robbers, thieves, and vagrants who are now such a burden upon the law-respecting community. . . .

In view of these evils, we have formed an association which shall devote itself entirely to this class of vagrant children. We do not propose in any way to conflict with existing asylums and in-stitutions, but to render them a hearty co-operation, and at the same time to fill a gap, which, of necessity, they have all left. A large multitude of children live in the city who cannot be placed in asylums, and yet who are uncared for and ignorant and vagrant. We propose to give to these work, and to bring them under re-ligious influences. A central office has been taken, and an agent, Charles L. Brace, has been engaged to give his whole time to efforts for relieving the wants of this class. As means shall come in, it is designed to district the city, so that hereafter every ward may have its agent, who shall be a friend to the vagrant child. "Boys' Sunday Meetings" have already been formed, which we hope to see extended, until every quarter has its place of preach-ing to boys. With these, we intend to connect "Industrial Schools," where the great temptations to this class, arising from *want of work*, may be removed, and where they can learn an honest trade. Arrangements have been made with manufacturers, by which, if we have the requisite funds to begin, *five hundred boys* in different localities can be supplied with paying work. We hope, too, especially to be the means of draining the city of these children, by communicating with farmers, manufacturers, or families in the country, who may have need of such for employment. When homeless boys are found by our agents, we mean to get them homes in the families of respectable persons in the city, and to put them in the way of an honest living. We design, in a word, to bring humane and kindly influences to bear on this forsaken class—to preach in various modes the Gospel of Christ to the vagrant children of New York.

Numbers of our citizens have long felt the evils we would remedy, but few have the leisure or the means to devote themselves personally to this work, with the thoroughness which it requires. This society, as we propose, shall be a medium through which all can, in their measure, practically help the poor children of the city. We call upon all who recognize that these are the little ones of Christ; all who believe that crime is best averted by sowing good influences in childhood; all who are the friends of the helpless, to aid us in our enterprise. We confidently hope this wide and practical movement will have its share of Christian liberality. And we earnestly ask the contributions of those able to give, to help us in carrying forward the work.

*March, 1853*

# CHAPTER SEVEN

# FREE PUBLIC EDUCATION

———◆◆———

*It is my firm conviction, that the common schools of the state can be made so good, within the range of studies which it is desirable to embrace in them, that wealth cannot purchase better advantages in private schools, and at the same time be so cheap as to be within reach of the poorest child. It will be a bright day for our state, and a pledge of our future progress and harmony as a people, when the children of the rich and the poor are found, more generally than they now are, side by side in the same school and on the same playground, without knowing or caring for any other distinctions than such as industry, capacity, or virtue, may make.*

———HENRY BARNARD: *Third Annual Report on Common Schools of Connecticut, 1841*

*The will of God . . . places the right of every child . . . to such a degree of education as will enable him, and . . . will predispose him, to perform all domestic, social, civil, and moral duties, upon the same clear ground of natural law and equity, as it places a child's right, upon his first coming into the world, to distend his lungs with a portion of the common air . . . or to receive that shelter, protection, and nourishment, which are necessary to the continuance of his bodily existence. And so far is it from being a wrong or a hardship to demand of the possessors of property their respective shares for the prosecution of this divinely-ordained work, that they themselves are guilty of the most far-reaching injustice, when they seek to resist or to evade the contribution.*

———HORACE MANN: *Tenth Annual Report on the Massachusetts Common Schools, 1849*

Sources of the quotations on the preceding page:

HENRY BARNARD: Henry Barnard: *Third Annual Report of the Secretary of the Board of Commissioners of Common Schools of Connecticut* (Hartford, Conn.: 1841), 33.

HORACE MANN: Horace Mann: *The Massachusetts System of the Common Schools, Being an Enlarged and Revised Edition of the Tenth Annual Report of the First Secretary of the Massachusetts Board of Education* (Boston: 1849), 17–18.

FREE public schools, in the broadest meaning, are nonsectarian schools supported and controlled by the public and open and free to all teachable children. The development of a free public-school system was far from complete by 1860, even if the grade schools alone are considered. Yet in time the system came to include secondary schools and, recently, colleges as well.

The first general school law in America was the Massachusetts "Old Deluder" Act of 1647. Its origin was not actually secular, for the authority asserted was essentially that of the Puritan congregation upon which the Massachusetts theocracy rested, but it imposed upon the community the requirement that education be provided for all children. This pattern of community responsibility for establishing schools, followed by all the New England colonies except Rhode Island, was reaffirmed in the Revolutionary era. Indeed, the right to education was deemed inherent in the doctrine of natural rights widely discussed at that time. The early constitutions of Pennsylvania, North Carolina, Georgia, Vermont, Maryland, and New Hampshire made provision for public schools before 1790. But unfortunately, the absence of specific instructions to legislatures and the lack of an aroused popular movement resulted in a long delay before implementation of these provisions followed.

That a "general diffusion of knowledge among the people" (2) was deemed a right and essential to the security of the Republic was voiced in one way or another by Washington, Jefferson, and Madison. Benjamin Rush advanced *A Plan for the Establishment of Public Schools and the Diffusion of Knowledge in Pennsylvania* (1786), and in the following year he issued his *Thoughts* *upon Female Education,* in which he urged that women have educational opportunities equal to those of men.* Many others —Samuel Knox, Robert Coram (1), Robert Howland (2), Nathaniel Chipman, and Noah Webster—offered various plans and programs for a free public system. These early efforts were generally abortive. Although some states passed laws, these were gestures toward, rather than foundations for, an adequate, free, public-school system.

The burgeoning nationalism and democratic agrarianism of the Jeffersonian period encouraged fulfillment. The consciousness of the need for education was quickened by societies for establishing free schools, which were formed primarily in behalf of poor children. Conspicuous was that of New York (1805), which numbered De Witt Clinton among its founders. The westward movement with its expanding frontier of democracy stirred support for free public education (Nathan Guilford, 4). In the Jacksonian era the Western Literary Institute (9) sounded a call to "spread intelligence at every door" and safeguard the Republic through universal knowledge and through the infusion of enlightened patriotism (Chapter Three, 6).

The rise of industrialism brought the growing power of labor to the fight for the free public schools. The Working Men parties, Robert Dale Owen, Frances Wright and Seth Luther (Chapter Two, 6) added their voices to the cause (5). In Pennsylvania in 1835, Thaddeus Stevens battled vigorously to maintain the principle of public-school support affirmed in the report of the Joint Committee of the Two Houses of the Pennsylvania Legislature (7). In New Jersey the committees of correspondence for public schools (8) and in the West the Western Literary Institute (9) called for a free public-school system.

In the two decades before the Civil War public awareness was shaped by the zeal of devoted crusaders: Horace Mann and Henry Barnard in the East, Calvin H. Wiley in the South, and Caleb Mills in the West. Through their educational journals, reports as educators, or appeals to legislatures, they drew attention

---

* The common prejudice against sending girls to schools was not combatted vigorously until later, as in Emma Willard's *Address to the New York Legislature* in 1819 (3). Her main purpose in this speech was to win public appropriations for higher education for women.

to needed reforms. The Lyceum movement, founded by Josiah Holbrook in 1831 (6), made the advancement of education, especially the common schools, its principal business. To its lecture platforms came Edward Everett, Henry Ward Beecher, Wendell Phillips, and Abraham Lincoln. Teachers' institutes, like that of Onondaga County, New York (10) were useful in this respect as well as for the training of teachers.

If fulfillment was incomplete by 1860, much progress had been made. By 1870 responsibility of the state for elementary education had been firmly established. "Rate bill" support for the indigent, through a tuition tax levied upon attending children whose parents were able to pay, was yielding to the principle of tax-supported public schools. In this progress the South lagged behind (11).

---

1.

*Robert Coram:*
A PLAN FOR THE GENERAL ESTABLISHMENT OF SCHOOLS *
[1791]

*A Delaware journalist and school teacher, Robert Coram felt that society, through the establishment of public schools, should teach everyone how to make a living. Each was to be taught the rudiments of the English language, writing, bookkeeping, mathematics, natural history, mechanics, and husbandry. He favored apprenticeship regulations binding youth out to the trades or professions. Literary discussions were a regular feature at his schoolhouse.*

The necessity of a reformation in the country schools, is too obvious to be insisted on; and the first step to such reformation, will be, by turning private schools into public ones. The schools should be public, for several reasons—1st. Because, as has been

* Robert Coram: *Political Inquiries: to Which Is Added a Plan for the General Establishment of Schools throughout the United States* (Wilmington, Del.: 1791), 97–9.

before said, every citizen has an equal right to subsistence, and ought to have an equal opportunity of acquiring knowledge. 2d. Because public schools are easiest maintained, as the burthen falls upon all the citizens. The man who is too squeamish or lazy to get married, contributes to the support of public schools, as well as the man who is burthened with a large family. But private schools are supported only by heads of families, & by those only while they are interested; for as soon as the children are grown up, their support is withdrawn; which makes the employment so precarious, that men of ability and merit will not submit to the trifling salaries allowed in most country schools, and which, by their partial support, cannot afford a better.

Let public schools then be established in every county of the United States, at least as many as are necessary for the present population; and let those schools be supported by a general tax. Let the objects of those schools be to teach the rudiments of the English language, writing, bookkeeping, mathematics, natural history, mechanics and husbandry—and let every scholar be admitted gratis, and kept in a state of subordination, without respect to persons. The other branch of education, I mean, instruction in arts, ought also to be secured to every individual, by laws enacted for that purpose, by which, parents and others having authority over youth, should be compelled to bind them out at certain ages, and for a limited time to persons professing mechanical or other branches, and the treatment of apprentices during their apprenticeship, should be regulated by laws expressly provided, without having recourse to the common or statute law of England. I mention this, because, independent of the difference of circumstances, between these United States and England, I think a more humane and liberal policy might be established, than that now in usage in England, and better adapted to the present circumstances of America; and indeed it is high time to check that blind adherence to trans-atlantic policy, which has so generally prevailed. It would be superfluous to insist on the necessity of trades—their use is obvious. . . . How much then is it to be lamented, that ever the tyranny of fashion, or pride of birth, gave an idea of disgrace to those virtuous and useful occupations.

## 2.

### John Howland:
### MEMORIAL TO THE GENERAL ASSEMBLY OF RHODE ISLAND *
### [February, 1799]

*John Howland (1757–1854), born in Rhode Island of New England stock, went to Providence as an apprentice to a hairdresser. He served in the American Revolutionary army and subsequently became president of the Rhode Island Historical Society. An earnest advocate of free schools, he was a member of the Mechanics Association founded in 1789 and was on its committee to draft the Memorial (1799), which he wrote himself. His interest in education kept him a member of the association's school committee for twenty years.*

To the Hon. the General Assembly of the State of Rhode Island, etc., to be holden at East Greenwich, on the last Monday in February, A.D. 1799. The Memorial and Petition of the Providence Association of Mechanics and Manufacturers, respectfully represents:—

That the means of Education which are enjoyed in this State, are very inadequate to a purpose so highly important: That numbers of the rising generation, whom nature has liberally endowed, are suffered to grow up in ignorance, when a common education would qualify them to act their parts in life with advantage to the public, and reputation to themselves:—That in consequence of there being no legal provision for the establishment of Schools, and for the want of public attention and encouragement, this so essential a part of our social duty is left to the partial patronage of individuals, whose cares cannot extend beyond the limits of their own families, while numbers in every part of the State, are deprived of a privilege which it is the common right of every child to enjoy: That when to that respect, which, as individuals we feel ourselves bound to render to the representatives of the people, we add our public declaration of gratitude for the privileges we enjoy as a corporate body, we at the same time solicit

* Reprinted in Edwin M. Stone: *Life and Recollections of John Howland* (Providence, R.I.: 1857), 329–30, 140–1.

this Honorable Assembly to make legal provision for the establishment of Free Schools, sufficient to educate all the children in the several towns throughout the State. With great confidence, we bring this our earnest solicitation before this Honorable Assembly, from the interest we feel in the public welfare, and from the consideration that our Society is composed of members, not originally of any one particular town, but assembled mostly in our early years from almost every town in the State: That we feel as individuals, the want of that education which we now ask to be bestowed on those who are to succeed us in life, and which is so essential in transacting its common concerns. That we feel a still greater degree of confidence, from the consideration that while we pray this Honorable Assembly to establish Free Schools, we are, at the same time, advocating the cause of the great majority of children throughout the State, and in particular of those who are poor and destitute—the son of the widow and the child of distress: Trusting that our occupations as Mechanics and Manufacturers, ought not to prevent us from adding to these reasons an argument which cannot fail to operate with those, to whom are committed the guardianship of the public welfare, and that is that liberty and security, under a republican form of government, depend on a general diffusion of knowledge among the people.

In confiding this petition and the reasons which have dictated it, to the wisdom of the Legislature, we assure ourselves that their decision will be such, as will reflect on this Honorable Assembly the praise and the gratitude, not only of the youth of the present generation, but of thousands, the date of whose existence is not yet commenced.

[JOHN HOWLAND TELLS ABOUT THE MEMORIAL]

The more we discussed the subject, the greater became its importance in our eyes. After a good deal of consultation and discussion, we got the Mechanics' Association to move in the matter. This was an important point gained, and an encouragement to persevere. A committee was chosen to take up the subject. Of this committee I was a member. They met at my house, and after due deliberation, it was resolved to address the General Assembly. I told them, that as neither of us were qualified to draw up a paper in a manner suited to go before that body, we had each better write a petition embodying our individual views, and bring it to our next meeting. Out of these mutual contributions we could prepare a petition that would do. This was agreed to, and the committee separated. When we next met, it was found that but two had been written according to previous recommendation. Those were by William Richmond and myself. Richmond then read his. It was in the usual *petition* style, ending, 'as in duty bound will ever pray.' I told the committee I did not like the doctrine of that paper. It was too humble in tone. I did not believe in *petitioning* legislators to do their duty. We ought, on the contrary, in addressing that body, to assume a tone of confidence that with the case fairly stated, they would decide wisely and justly for the rising generation. I then took out my memorial and read it. It was not in the shape of an "humble petition." It expressed briefly our destitution, and the great importance of establishing free schools to supply it. It received the approbation of the committee, and was adopted.

3.

*Emma Willard:*
A PLAN FOR IMPROVING FEMALE EDUCATION *
[1819]

*Born in Connecticut, and trained as a teacher, Emma Hart Willard (1787–1870) took charge of the Female Academy at Middlebury, Vermont, for two years until her marriage to Dr. John Willard in 1809. In 1814 she opened the Middlebury Female Seminary where she sought to include a curriculum similar to that for men. Combatting the idea that women were incapable of being educated, she pleaded for state aid in founding schools for girls. She established the Waterford Academy and, finally, the Emma Willard Troy Female Seminary for training female teachers. From 1838 her prime interest in the*

* Emma Willard: *An Address to the Public, particularly to the Members of the Legislature of New York, Proposing a Plan for Improving Female Education* (Middlebury, Vt.: 1819), 19–24.

*improvement of common schools led her to join forces with
Henry Barnard in Connecticut.*

. . . Not even is youth considered in our sex, as in the other,
a season which should be wholly devoted to improvement.
Among families, so rich as to be entirely above labor, the daughters are hurried through the routine of boarding school instruction, and at an early period introduced into the gay world; and,
thenceforth, their only object is amusement. Mark the different
treatment, which the sons of these families receive. While their
sisters are gliding through the mazes of the midnight dance, they
employ the lamp, to treasure up for future use the riches of ancient wisdom; or to gather strength and expansion of mind, in
exploring the wonderful paths of philosophy. When the youth
of these two sexes has been spent so differently, is it strange, or
is nature in fault, if more mature age has brought such a difference of character, that our sex have been considered by the other,
as the pampered, wayward babies of society, who must have
some rattle put into our hands, to keep us from doing mischief
to ourselves or others?

Another difference in the treatment of the sexes is made in our
country, which, though not equally pernicious to society, is more
pathetically unjust to our sex. How often have we seen a student,
who, returning from his literary pursuits, finds a sister, who was
his equal in acquirements, while their advantages were equal, of
whom he is now ashamed. While his youth was devoted to study,
and he was furnished with the means, she, without any object of
improvement, drudged at home, to assist in the support of the
father's family, and perhaps to contribute to her brother's subsistence abroad; and now, a being of a lower order, the rustic innocent wonders and weeps at his neglect.

Not only has there been a want of system concerning female
education, but much of what has been done, has proceeded upon
mistaken principles.

One of these is, that, without a regard to the different periods
of life, proportionate to the importance, the education of females
has been too exclusively directed, to fit them for displaying to
advantage the charms of youth and beauty. Though it may be
proper to adorn this period of life, yet, it is incomparably more

important, to prepare for the serious duties of maturer years.
Though well to decorate the blossom, it is far better to prepare
for the harvest. In the vegetable creation, nature seems but to
sport when she embellishes the flower; while all her serious cares
are directed to perfect the fruit.

Another error is that it has been made the first object in educating our sex to prepare them to please the other. But reason
and religion teach, that we too are primary existences; that it is
for us to move in the orbit of our duty, around the Holy Center of
perfection, the companions not the satellites of men; else, instead
of shedding around us, an influence that may help to keep them
in their proper course, we must accompany them in the wildest
deviations. . . .

Neither would I be understood to mean, that our sex should
not seek to make themselves agreeable to the other. The errour
[sic] complained of, is that the taste of men, whatever it might
happen to be, has been made a standard for the formation of the
female character. In whatever we do, it is of the utmost importance, that the rule, by which we work, be perfect. For if otherwise what is it but to err upon principle? A system of education
which leads one class of human beings to consider the approbation of another, as their highest object, teaches that the rule of
their conduct should be the will of beings, imperfect and erring
like themselves, rather than the will of God, which is the only
standard of perfection.

4.

*Nathan Guilford:*
LETTER TO THE SCHOOL COMMISSIONERS *
[1822]

*Nathan Guilford (1786–1854) was born in Massachusetts.
He conducted a classical school and practiced law eventually
moving to Cincinnati. Here he acquired a publishing house
and edited an educational almanac,* Solomon Thrifty's

* N. Guilford: *Letter Addressed to the Chairman of the Board of School
Commissioners* (Columbus, Ohio: 1822), 5–7.

Almanac. *Appointed a member of a committee to report on a common school plan, he issued this Letter as a dissenting report to the public, winning election to the state senate on this platform. Here he urged a tax for educational purposes and succeeded in getting a free public-school system established in 1829. Withdrawing from law to publish improved school textbooks, he was elected superintendent of public schools for Cincinnati in 1850. Because of his deist outlook he refused to permit the use of the Bible in the schools, which action cost him his position as superintendent.*

It is a dep[l]orable fact, that a great portion of our youth are growing up without the means of acquiring the first rudiments of an education. Almost every state in the Union has taken the lead of us in this all important subject. The laudable example therefore of our sister states—the vital and indispensable importance of education to a free people—the immense number of our children of both sexes, who are growing up in a state of ignorance, idleness and vice, call upon the state to exercise its authority, and provide the means of general instruction.

This cannot be done effectually, without the establishment of free schools. It would be incompatible with the present enlightened state of the world, with the genius of our free institutions, and with the cause of justice and humanity, that the children of the poor, among their other misfortunes should be deprived of the blessing of a common education.

By the establishment of free schools all classes have equal opportunities of receiving the rudiments of knowledge and moral instruction from the same sources. It lessens the distinction, which fortune makes between the children of the rich and the poor, and places their intellects, at least, more upon a footing of equality.

Free schools have been established and supported for a long time in the eastern states, by means of a tax levied and raised as other taxes; and such has been their salutary effects upon both sexes, and all classes of the community, that instead of considering the taxes raised for their support as a burden, the people of those states pay them with the greatest cheerfulness, and consider their free schools not only their greatest pride and ornament, but the most useful and salutary of all their free institutions. And indeed the funds raised for their support are managed with so much care and economy, that they are not in the least burthensome to those who pay them. The sum which would be required to educate every child in the state, upon the system of free schools as practiced in the eastern states, would not exceed the amount required to educate the one fourth part under the present mode of supporting them by subscriptions.

5.

### Six Essays on Public Education—Essay VI *
### [1830]

*The* Six Essays on Public Education *first appeared in the* New York Daily Sentinel *in 1830, a predecessor of* The Man, *edited by George Henry Evans, and were reprinted in the* Free Enquirer, *a radical New York paper edited by Robert Dale Owen and Frances Wright. Thomas Skidmore and his faction denounced the plan advocated in this essay as being destructive of the family, arguing that education could not be equalized until the "condition" of adults were equalized.*

The system of Public Education, then, which we consider capable, and only capable, of regenerating this nation, and of establishing practical virtue and republican equality among us, is one which provides for all children at all times; receiving them at the earliest age their parents choose to entrust them to the national care, feeding, clothing, and educating them, until the age of majority.

We propose that all the children so adopted should receive the same food; should be dressed in the same simple clothing; should experience the same kind treatment; should be taught (until their professional education commences) the same branches; in a word, that nothing savoring of inequality, nothing reminding them of the pride of riches or the contempt of poverty, should be suffered to enter these republican safeguards of a young nation of equals. We propose that the destitute widow's child or the

* *New York Daily Sentinel* (1830), 19–22.

orphan boy should share the public care equally with the heir to a princely estate; so that all may become, not in word but in deed and in feeling, free and equal.

Thus may the spirit of democracy, that spirit which Jefferson labored for half a century to plant in our soil, become universal among us; thus may luxury, may pride, may ignorance, be banished from among us; and we may become, what fellow citizens ought to be, a nation of brothers.

We propose that the food should be of the simplest kind, both for the sake of economy and of temperance. A Spartan simplicity of regimen is becoming a republic, and is best suited to preserve the health and strength unimpaired, even to old age. We suggest the propriety of excluding all distilled or fermented liquors of every description; perhaps, also, foreign luxuries, such as tea and coffee, might be beneficially dispensed with. These, including wine and spirits, cost the nation at present about *fourteen millions* of dollars annually. Are they worth so much?

Thus might the pest of our land, intemperance, be destroyed— not discouraged, not lessened, not partially cured—but *destroyed:* this modern Circe that degrades the human race below the beast of the field, that offers her poison cup at every corner of our streets and at every turn of our highways, that sacrifices her tens of thousands of victims yearly in these states, that loads our country with a tax more than sufficient to pay twice over for the virtuous training of all her children—might thus be deposed from the foul sway she exercises over freemen, too proud to yield to a foreign enemy, but not too proud to bow beneath the iron rod of a domestic curse. Is there *any* other method of tearing up this monstrous evil, the scandal of our republic, root and branch?

We propose that the dress should be some plain, convenient, economical uniform. The silliest of all vanities (and one of the most expensive) is the vanity of dress. Children trained to the age of twenty-one without being exposed to it, could not, in after life, be taught such a folly. But, learnt as it now is, from the earliest infancy, do we find that the most faithful preaching checks or reforms it?

The food and clothing might be chiefly raised and manufactured by the pupils themselves, in the exercise of their several occupations. They would thus acquire a taste for articles produced in their own country, in preference to foreign superfluities.

Under such a system, the poorest parents could afford to pay a moderate tax for each child. They could better afford it than they can now to support their children in ignorance and misery, *provided* the tax were less than the lowest rate at which a child can now be maintained at home. For a day school, thousands of parents can afford to pay nothing.

We do not propose that any one should be compelled to send a child to these public schools, if he or she saw fit to have them educated elsewhere. But we propose that the tax should be payed by all parents, whether they send their children or not.

We are convinced, that under such a system, the pupils of the state schools would obtain the various offices of public trust, those of representatives, &c. in preference of any others. If so, public opinion would soon induce the most rich and the most prejudiced, to send their children thither; however little they might at first relish the idea of giving them *equal* advantages only with those of the poorest class. *Greater real advantages* they could not give them, if the public schools are conducted as they ought to be.

We propose that the teachers should be eligible [*sic*] by the people. There is no office of trust in a republic, more honorable or more important, nor any that more immediately influences its destinies, than the office of a teacher. They ought to be chosen— and, if we read the signs of the times right, they *will* be chosen with as much, nay, with more care than our representatives. The office of General Superintendent of Public Schools will be, in our opinion, an office at least as important as that of president.

At present the best talent of the country is devoted to the study of law; because a lawyer has hitherto had the best chance for political honors and preferment. Let the office of teacher be equally honored and preferred: and men will turn from a trade whose professors live by the quarrels of mankind, to an occupation which should teach men to live without quarrelling.

6.

*American Lyceum:*
ITS NATURE *
[1831]

*The American Lyceum, the precursor of the Chautauqua
movement, was an important influence in adult education. It
was begun by an article in the* American Journal of Education
*by Josiah Holbrook on a "Society for Mutual Education." The
first society was organized by Holbrook at Millbury, Massachusetts, November, 1826. At the time of the New York Convention in 1831, lyceums existed in all New England states
and in northern New York. This meeting in New York was
called to organize a national lyceum that was to reach as far
west as Missouri. By 1835 there were about three thousand
town lyceums, and they continued to grow until the early
twentieth century, some developing into historical and literary
societies.*

1. *It is a voluntary Institution.* It resorts to no law but the
law of motives, and the freedom of choice. . . . It believes that
the essence of a moral being is freedom of choice; that a right to
choose is his privilege—that the power to choose is his dignity
and glory. It believes that every rational being, whether an enlightened citizen of America, a vassal of Russia, or a vagrant of
Africa, has both the power and the right to intellectual and moral
culture; that whenever man is created, he is endowed with capacities for improvement—wherever he is placed he is surrounded
with materials designed for his improvement; that intellectual,
moral, and *social* faculties are confined to no favored few of our
race; that science is confined to no favored spot under heaven;
that intellects and affections are coextensive with the race of
man, and that science is as boundless as the earth and the heavens.

It is upon these principles, that the American Lyceum invites
the citizens of every town, village, and neighborhood in our wide

* *American Lyceum, with the Proceedings of the Convention Held in
N.Y., May 4, 1831, to Organize the National Department of the Institution*
(Boston: 1831), 4–6.

spread [*sic*] and growing republic, to operate and co-operate in the purposes of the institution; to associate for the double purpose of advancing their own improvement and the general improvement of the nation; to unite for mutual instruction and the general diffusion of knowledge. It proposes the organization of a Branch Lyceum in every town in our Union, but requires it in no one. It invites the co-operation of all the friends of *common schools* in the great and dignified cause of *universal education*, but even for that it is unwilling to urge. It would gladly embrace within the circle of its influence, not every town merely, but every individual—every man, woman, and child, in our republic; but it would embrace them by their voluntary consent—by their voluntary, nay, by their *cheerful efforts*.

*It is a social institution.* The Lyceum recognizes the social nature of man as among the most prominent, dignified, and happy features of his character. It believes that our social faculties are among the first developed in the child; that they are multifarious, powerful, and ceaseless in their action; that they are the great source, both of the happiness and the misery of our race, and that they are lamentably neglected and perverted, and constantly lost sight of, in most of our seminaries of learning, from the primary school to the university. It acts upon the principle, that that system of instruction, especially in institutions for common education, is the best, which, other things being equal, exerts the greatest and most happy influence on the daily social intercourse and relations of life. It believes that social intercourse of an intellectual, moral, and elevated character, always has, and always must perform, a more important and certain part in establishing individual and national character, than the school, academy, or university; that if the social party, the family circle, the table and the fire side [*sic*], can become schools for rational improvement, connected, as it must be, with high social enjoyment, the mass of society must be enlightened and happy.

Upon this principle, subjects of instruction in Lyceums are to a considerable extent of a common practical character, and treated in a familiar, conversational way. Things connected with the business and domestic relations in life, are examined in their bearings and applications, no less than in their properties and laws. Natural science is made practical science; precise instruction is rendered familiar instruction; the grandeur of nature is shown in the simplicity of nature; the principles illustrated in the Lyceum Hall are exemplified and amplified in the shop of the mechanic, the farm of the husbandman, and the kitchen of the housekeeper. Those who associate upon this principle, are a town lyceum when together, and several family lyceums when separated.

*The Lyceum is a self-adapting Institution.* Any community, and any class of the community, can form a Lyceum, not only to suit their wishes, but to advance their own purposes and pursuits. A farming community can associate, not only as intellectual, moral, and social beings, but as farmers. . . .

*The Lyceum is a Republican Institution.* This has before been asserted, and few it is believed, will be disposed to doubt it. Its foundation is moral freedom and independence, without which no one can be truly free. It permits, invites, and enables all who unite in its operations to think, judge, and act for themselves. It would liberate them from the slavery of a party, of a demagogue, and of their passions.

It has for its object the universal diffusion of knowledge, which has ever been considered the strongest and surest, if not the only foundation of a republican government. It aims at universal education, by inducing and enabling all whom it embraces to *educate themselves.* . . .

*It is a Benevolent Institution.* It is mutual, or gives, hoping to receive. It also gives, *not hoping to receive;* it recognizes love to our neighbor, or universal and disinterested benevolence, as the dignity and glory of the moral universe; it maintains that teachers are bound, not only to instruct their pupils, but to do good to each other, and to make their improvements in the science and art of teaching *public property;* it holds that every intellectual, social, and moral being, that every man, woman, and child is bound by a law as strong as their love of happiness, and as lasting as their existence, to add all to the *common stock* of human happiness that their talents and opportunities will permit—*to do all the good they can;* it believes that supreme selfishness, or making one's self the centre of the universe, is as mean and inglorious, as it is unchristian and ruinous; that the Christian religion, is at once a system of the purest morals and of the soundest philosophy the world ever saw.

Such is briefly the nature of the American Lyceum.

# 7.

## REPORT OF THE PENNSYLVANIA JOINT COMMITTEE *
### [February 1, 1834]

*In Pennsylvania the principle of a free school, championed by Thaddeus Stevens, was established by law in 1834 as a result of this report. Although there had previously been schools open to the poor and supported wholly by public tax, it was not until then that a permissive free school system was established on a general basis. A long time elapsed between the provision for the permissive system and its actual operation. In 1836 the law was amended to permit a district to vote every third year on the question of whether it wanted school or not. In 1848 the provision for this triennial vote was repealed. Not until 1874 did the last resistant district accept a free school.*

The number of voters in Pennsylvania, unable to read, have been computed, from data in other states, at one hundred thousand; and two thousand five hundred, grow up to be voters annually, who are equally ignorant. In a republican government, no voter should be without the rudiments of learning; for aside from political considerations, education purifies the morals, and lessens crime. Our philanthropists, who visit our jails, have ascertained that more than half the convicts are unable to read. It is better to avert crime, by giving instruction to our youth, than punish them when men, as ignorant convicts.

A radical defect in our laws upon the subject of education, is that the public aid now given, and imperfectly given, is confined *to the poor.* Aware of this, your committee have taken care to exclude the word *poor,* from the bill which will accompany this report, meaning to make the system *general;* that is to say, to form

* *Report of the Joint Committee of the Two Houses of the Pennsylvania Legislature on the Subject of a System of General Education . . . Feb. 1, 1834* (Harrisburg, Pa.: 1834), 3, 4–6.

an educational association between the rich, the comparatively rich, and the destitute. Let them all fare alike in the primary schools; receive the same elementary instruction; imbibe the same republican spirit, and be animated by a feeling of perfect equality. In after life, he who is diligent at school, will take his station accordingly, whether born to wealth or not. Common schools, universally established, will multiply the chances of success, perhaps of brilliant success, among those who else may forever continue ignorant. It is the duty of the State to promote and foster such establishments. That done, the career of each youth will depend upon himself. The State will have given the first impulse; good conduct and suitable application must do the rest.—Among the indigent, "some flashing of a mounting genius" may be found; and among both rich and poor, in the course of nature, many no doubt will sink into mediocrity, or beneath it. Yet let them start with equal advantages, leaving no discrimination then or thereafter, but such as nature and study shall produce. . . .

But the chief preparatory step is, unquestionably, the formation of teachers; and on this highly important subject, the information collected by your committee is ample. Wherever systems of common schools exist, there is but one voice on this head. Seminaries for the instruction of teachers, are as important as medical schools for physicians. Under the proposed system, a large supply of teachers will soon be wanted; and these must be properly formed for that vocation. They must be taught the art of well governing a school: they must acquire the knowledge necessary to be communicated, and the art of communicating that knowledge. For this purpose, a central school, associated with manual labour, has been suggested, and a bill was reported to the House of Representatives, last year, upon that subject. It was a favourite plan of the great De-Witt Clinton. One or two hundred teachers, under the direction of the State, might be thus prepared annually; but the method recommended by the Governor, has been adopted by your committee, who believe that the existing colleges may be able to furnish model schools and a teacher's course. . . .

. . . But how are young men to be induced to take up the business of teaching? To this your committee answer, by giving them a respectable standing in society—by making their salaries large enough to maintain them and their families. The character of a school is formed by the character of the teacher; and the respect and obedience of the pupil, is regulated by the measure of respect which the master receives from the public. A shameful parsimony prevails in the remuneration of teachers of common schools. The male teacher's pay, in New York, is something under twelve dollars a month; in Ohio, it is from twelve to twenty. Females, in New York, average five dollars, and in Connecticut, some women teach for seventy-five cents a week!! Well paid teachers are the cheapest.

8.

### George Washington Doane:
### To the People of New Jersey on Common Schools *
### [1838]

*George Washington Doane (1799–1859) was born in New Jersey, the son of a contractor and builder. He was consecrated bishop of New Jersey in 1832 and was a promoter of Episcopal missions, a hymn writer, and the founder of St. Mary's Hall for girls (1837) and Burlington College for Men (1846). He was author of this Address and chairman of the committees of correspondence for common schools. The Address so aroused people that a new law partially establishing a public school system was secured.*

Circular to the committees of correspondence for common schools. Gentlemen,

. . . It was unfortunate for the cause of public education that the popular movement on the subject did not occur at an earlier period. Had the members of the Legislature enjoyed the opportunity which was afforded to us who remained at home of thus learning the wishes of the people, they would have been better prepared to meet them. As it was, a Bill was reported to the house of Assembly, which, though not all that was desired, contained many excellent features, and was well calculated, especially in its provision of a Superintendent of Common Schools, to secure a

---

* *An Address to the People of New Jersey on the Subject of Common Schools* (Burlington, N. J.: 1838), 15–16.

good beginning of the work. It passed the House by a vote of full two thirds, but was lost as to its main provisions, in the Council. The present result, is that instead of $20,000 as before, $30,000 are to be distributed among the townships for the support of Common Schools; and, inasmuch as the whole subject is left as before, without system, without immediate supervision, and with but little accountability, to be distributed, we fear, with about the same results.

Such is not the state of things contemplated by the Convention, or by their constituents. The subject must go back then to the highest authority in the State, the Sovereign People. It is for them to say what they desire, and what they are resolved to have. The Legislature which shall be elected with a knowledge of their will, may be relied on for its full accomplishment. It is upon you, Gentlemen, as the Committees of Correspondence for the counties, that the Convention relies, for awakening their attention to the subject, and for securing such an expression of their wishes as must be understood and shall be felt.

The best means for attaining this result is indicated in the ninth resolution of the Convention—the appointment of a Committee in every township. To this important measure we respectfully solicit your immediate attention. It is thus that the link is to be formed by which the electric chain will be completed that shall unite the Convention with every citizen of New Jersey, and bring up from every citizen, to the seat of government, and to the Legislature of the State in a way that cannot be mistaken, the expression of his will.

When the Township Committees shall be organized, the charge of collecting the popular will in their respective sphere may safely be reposed in them; and it is the recommendation of the General Committee that as soon as possible after their appointment, they invite the people, in their primary assemblies, to hear the Address, to consider the subject, and to take such measures as to them may seem expedient. To the copies of the Address directed to the several townships in your respective counties, you are respectfully requested to give such direction as will most speedily and most effectually secure the desired results.

It is not necessary to suggest to you the various ways in which the duty assigned by the Convention to you, "to operate with the

General Committee," may best be discharged. The importance of the interest involved calls for the exertion by every lover of his country of all the influence which he possesses. By public meetings, through the press, in your occasional and daily intercourse with your fellow citizens, you will find constant opportunity; and the State can ask no better pledge than your well known intelligence and patriotism, that you will faithfully improve it.

To aid you in the discharge of the other duty assigned to you by the sixth resolution, "to collect information," and to secure a general uniformity in the results, we send with the Circular several interrogatories, to which we respectfully request returns, as full as can be had, to be forwarded to the Secretary, at Burlington, before the third Tuesday in September next. On the completeness of these returns, the excellence of the system to be devised will much depend.

With a full confidence in the goodness of the cause we have in hand, we leave it, with you; well assured that there needs no better motive to your exertion than the recorded sentiment of the Convention, the noble blazon of its radiant and triumphant banner —*the education of the people is indispensable to free institutions!*

GEORGE W. DOANE, *Chairman*

SAMUEL R. GUMMERE, *Secretary*

9.

*Elijah Vance:*
IMPORTANCE OF A UNIFORM COMMON SCHOOL SYSTEM *
[1839]

*Elijah Vance (1801–71) was born in Maryland and came to Ohio in 1816. He held various offices, such as speaker of the state senate, Common Pleas judge and member of the Constitutional Convention of 1850. He was a trustee of Miami*

* Elijah Vance: "An Address on the Importance of Introducing a Uniform System of Common School Education, and Adapting it to the Genius of our Republican Institutions," *Western Literary Institute and College of Professional Teachers: Transactions of the Eighth Annual Meeting . . . 1839* (Cincinnati, Ohio: 1840), 94–5.

*University and was frequently a member of the Hamilton
Board of Education. This speech shows the educational reform
movement at work.*

We are too much disposed to neglect the sacred duty which we
owe to our fathers, to posterity, and to ourselves, in sustaining
unscathed our free institutions. It is not the wealth but the intelligence of our people, which will secure national happiness and the
continued prosperity of the country.

We should seek to spread intelligence at every door. . . . The
importance of a system of popular education which will reach
alike every portion of the people—inspiring all our youth with the
same spirit of emulation, the same feeling of patriotism, the same
love of letters and of knowledge, must be admitted by every
citizen and philanthropist. The good morals—the religion of a
people, draw their chief support from the rich sources of intellectual treasure. The refinements and elegancies of life are but the
chosen fruits of that beautiful garden wherein the seeds of literature are carefully cultured. The safety of the republic depends
upon the universal knowledge and patriotism of the people. Intelligence generally diffused, like the majestic mountain which
throws its summit aloft amidst the clouds, standing calm in security from the danger of the warring elements around, will be
hailed as an impregnable rampart against the ravages of civil
feuds or the thunders of foreign invasion. It has been the primary
care of every people whose career has been marked with celebrity.
It is by a general diffusion of knowledge that we may expect to
sustain the cause of political freedom, and particularly under our
happy form of government does it become necessary in order to
the security and perpetuity of liberty, whether civil, political
or religious, to maintain a system of policy which has for its aim
the general intellectual and moral improvement of its people.
Our constitution guarantees to the high and to the low, to the
rich and to the poor, and to the unlearned as well as to the man of
letters, the same equality of freedom, and the same voice in the
administration of the government. In other words, our government
is emphatically a government of the people. The pathway to distinction lies open alike to every citizen. The same share of duty
in sustaining the government, devolves alike upon each individual

member of the republic. The right of suffrage is universal; at least it is extended to all who are regarded as lawful citizens of the country. All therefore have a voice in the election of public officers—and every citizen has the same undisputed right to share in the honors which the occupancy of office may be thought to confer. The only disqualification which our people acknowledge, is the want of capability or merit. The laws are but the echo of the people's voice—and the great edifice of political freedom must be alone sustained from decay and ruin through the virtue, wisdom and patriotism of the whole people. Recognizing them as our social condition does, the great principles of equal rights—the universal right to knowledge, and the elevation, and pleasures and powers which it gives, is not subject to be doubted or disputed. How shall we maintain this equality of rights from the grasp of despotism or the ravages of time? How shall the glory of our free institutions be perpetuated to coming generations? The answer is, by a general, appropriate, lasting, and uniform system of popular education, which shall be so modeled as to extend its influence alike to every grade and condition of the people composing the nation. By such an influence and such only, can our boasted equality of rights be sustained. A general and well regulated system of common schools can afford the only sure and effectual remedy against geographical divisions and jealousy—it will be the safest barrier to the ravages of internal feuds; the best defence against the evils of lawless and misguided ambition; the only sure protection from the furious and bloody disasters of the outraged and maddened mob, and the most effectual shield against the accumulated thunders of civil commotion and internal strife. A diffusion of knowledge will invite universal obedience to the laws—it will promote industry, and a happy interchange of commerce; and in the place of licentiousness and faction, the fundamental means of the lasting and secure establishment of civil liberty will be deeply rooted in the hearts of our people. Under its influence fanaticism must yield to the religion of the true God, and dissimulation to the revealed obligations of Christianity.

We repeat that the plan should be a national one, or, in other words, general throughout the several States. Such a plan of common schools will serve as a principal agency in nationalizing the citizens of the Union, and would infuse a feeling of enlightened patriotism which would add stability to all our institutions, and secure general harmony throughout the several States. The plan should also be an appropriate one. A system of popular education should be studiously adapted to the peculiar structure of the government, and should conform to the republican simplicity of our free institutions. I do not wish to be understood as saying that a particular system or creed of politics should be taught in our public schools—no such thing. Such a plan of education, so far from remedying existing evils, would be most likely to swell the catalogue of mischiefs which we should be the most desirous to avoid —but we should endeavor to introduce into our schools those important branches of education which are best calculated to infuse the sentiment of patriotism, and which would lead to a familiar knowledge of the leading principles upon which our government is founded and by which it must be sustained.

## 10.

### *Onondaga County Teachers' Institute Committee:* REPORT ON FREE SCHOOLS * [October, 1844]

*This "Report" was drawn up by a committee of three— William Barnes, David Parsons, and N. P. Stanton, Jr.— appointed by the Onondaga County Teachers' Institute of New York. It represents one of the earliest official actions of this character and illustrates the free-school campaign in New York State.*

The committee on Free Schools respectfully report: That they are deeply impressed with the incalculable importance of this subject to the best interests of the American people. We believe that the time has arrived when the discussion and agitation of this question is called for, and when it would be productive of good results. The committee are in favor of the Free School system for the following reasons:

* S. S. Randall: *History of the Common School System of the State of New York* (New York: 1871), 215–17.

1. *We maintain that every human being has a right to intellectual and moral education; and that it is the duty of government to provide the means of such education to every child under its jurisdiction.* Man is not born with the matured mind which education produces. Unlike the brute creation, who receive by nature the knowledge necessary for their future support and happiness, men totally uneducated would die, or live in misery. The intelligence of brutes remains stationary for ages; man has the capacity of continual progression, and seems designed for a state of education and progressive improvement. If man, in a state of total helplessness, and without the natural education of the brute creation, has no right to demand the intellectual and moral culture so essential to his existence and happiness, from his fellow men, then his right to 'life and liberty' is of no consequence. The right to the air we breathe is not more necessary to physical existence than culture to mental health. Who would accept the gift of life, unaccompanied with the cultivation of the intellect and moral faculties?

The community, or government, its representative, is bound to provide the intellectual and moral culture without which the people will be miserable. The presence of uneducated persons in the body politic impairs the happiness of its other members—we feel sorrow for their degradation, and are injured by their actions and crimes. Government conceives it to be its duty to construct 'internal improvements'—how much stronger is the obligation to make improvements on the uncultivated soil of mind? If, for the common benefit, our government is bound to build jails, prisons, lunatic asylums, and canals, the duty to educate the people is as much greater as the results of it would be more beneficial than the construction of those works.

2. As a means for the *prevention of crime,* we approve the Free School system. The cause of crime is a defective moral education. The means which government uses to reform the offender, and prevent the repetition of the offense, have but little influence to effect the objects; they do not reach the *cause* of crime—a defective moral training. Accordingly, we find that convicts often commit crimes as soon as they are at liberty, and even while witnessing the execution of criminals.** [*Sic*] It will be found universally true that the *minimum* of crime exists, where the *maximum* of moral education is found. The prevention of the repetition of

crimes by the offender or others—the great object of human punishment—has never been, and never can be, attained by the present
system. *The diseased moral nature must be cured, or the cause of
crime will ever remain.* In view of these facts, does not a system of
*prevention,* which strikes at the foundation of crime, become the
imperative duty of government?

3. The Free School system is in accordance with the nature of
our democratic institutions. Is it not proper that persons created
with equal rights, and destined to govern our nation—with whose
right action our happiness is intimately connected—should receive
the education so necessary to a correct discharge of their duties?
Why should the child of *accident,* alone, receive that intellectual
and moral culture which *angelizes* man? Let the children of our
nation have equal privileges for ennobling themselves from brute
existence. . . .

Under the Free School system, the Washingtons, the Franklins,
the Henrys, the Jeffersons, who now live and die unknown, would
live to benefit, to purify, and exalt the race. From the immutable
laws of mind, the largest part of the great men of our country
must come from the poorer classes. The children of the rich do
not generally form those habits of energy or perseverance—steady,
unwearied, continuous labor—without which no man can attain
eminence. The Free School sytem would benefit the poorer classes,
and develop talent which is now chilled by the Greenland winds
of poverty; it would benefit the children of the rich, by the lesson,
invaluable to them, that they are just such beings as the children
of the pauper, and that if they would attain greatness they must
work and toil with untiring energy and perseverance. FREE
SCHOOLS ARE TRULY THE AMERICAN SYSTEM OF EDU-
CATION. They are already in successful operation in several of
the cities of our State and Union. The committee indulge the hope
that the State of New York will soon extend her liberality, *and
either by a tax or general fund assume the entire support of our
Common School system.* They report the following resolution:

*Resolved,* That we approve of the Free School system, and
recommend its adoption in this State.

WILLIAM BARNES
DAVID PARSONS
N. P. STANTON, JR.

11.

### Moncure Daniel Conway:
### FREE SCHOOLS IN VIRGINIA *
### [October, 1850]

*Moncure Daniel Conway (1832–1907) was born in Virginia. After serving as a young Methodist circuit rider, he inclined towards Unitarianism and abolitionism. He was dismissed as pastor of the Unitarian Church of Washington in 1856 because of his antislavery views, and he later devoted himself to this cause in an antislavery paper, the* Commonwealth, *and in other publications. After holding a London pastorate from 1863 to 1884, he returned to America. Among his many writings the most scholarly was the* Life of Thomas Paine, *2 v. (1892) and* The Writings of Thomas Paine, *4 v. (1894–6). His* Free Schools in Virginia (1850), *written at the age of eighteen, was addressed to the Constitutional Convention of Virginia of 1850.*

On the recognized principle then, that we should feel ourselves morally concerned to prepare our children for the happiest and most useful sphere of action, to thoroughly educate them is our duty.

It is a community's best policy. Society is a bundle of relations: whatsoever, whether remotely or otherwise, affects one atom of the system disturbs the whole mass. I put my hand in this lamp beside me and it is not only my hand that suffers, every nerve of their system is shocked. Why does society punish the criminal? It is because the security of every other individual is concerned in the crime that has been committed. Society thus in reprobation acknowledging the existence of these relations in its contract must recognize them in whatever is promotive of its welfare. The grand proposition here comes up that has been so often reiterated by human lips from the inculcations of God; THAT IT IS THE INTEREST OF EVERY MEMBER OF A COMMUNITY THAT EVERY OTHER MEMBER THEREOF SHOULD BE EDUCATED! . . .

* Moncure Daniel Conway: *Free Schools in Virginia: A Plea of Education, Virtue and Thrift vs. Ignorance, Vice and Poverty* (Fredericksburg, Va.: 1850), 6, 8, 11, 29, 31–3.

If something more substantial is required in confirming the opinion of [this] policy, we aver that it develops more than anything else the sources of production and wealth in a nation of state. Necessity is the mother of invention; and education creates more wants and larger influences. It raises the standard of expenditure, and this calls for a higher standard of supply. The wealthiest and most industrious communities are the best educated, and from these, if there be confidence in history and daily experience, spring the novel and marvellous discoveries that follow each other so swiftly in this age. . . .

If then intellectual culture is the best minister and physician, the question arises, how may a State best diffuse intelligence? Every thinking man admits that public authority must render some sort of aid to Education. People, as a general proposition, must be instructed [to attain] high or worthy achievement in life. How often to the burning disgrace of humanity do those who would have been shining lights under other auspices, go down to the grave "unwept, unhonored and unsung?" How few are the souls that can overtop these social barriers which hem in those who are born in their pale, as the Indians tie their offspring to boards? Our Rittenhouses and Franklins are few indeed. . . .

To what conclusion can every intelligent mind come, but that the most *infinitely superior mode of Education is the Free School System!* And if there be any faith in the indications of human experience, this is TRUE. It is not only the most superior in that it is the cheapest and justest—but it is the ONLY plan of thorough universal instruction that has been devised. . . .

The people have elected Non-Conservatives to the framing of their Constitution. The Chief Reforms will be a sudden and a large extension of the Right of Suffrage, and an equally sudden and large increase of Elective Power with the People. Here then is a singular growth of popular Responsibility. ARE YOU WILLING AS CONSCIENCIOUS REFLECTING STATESMEN TO AWARD THIS TO THE STATE, WITHOUT EFFORT TO UNDERMINE THAT FEARFUL PROPORTION OF US WHO CANNOT READ NOR WRITE? . . .

Our present Code is not only extremely defective in this, as well as many other respects, but it is also oppressive. . . . Members of the Convention! *It is your duty to overrule this Code in its provisions, and to plant the system in the Constitution.* If you will examine, you will find that not one state has succeeded in establishing and maintaining common schools or any available plan of education, except those who have put it in their Constitutions— NOT ONE! . . .

You need not fear the misrepresenting of the People in this matter. There is a strong feeling availing with them for the Reform. The excitement last winter at Fredericksburgh originated to my personal knowledge in some half dozen illiterate mechanics. I attended the meetings on that subject in that Town, and there can be no issue as to whether the People there desired free schools! We have decided leaning to the doctrine of vox populi vox dei; and we have shown this to be the voice of God that all should be instructed, and that this is the sole way to the persistence of His mandate and will. . . .

We have opportunity here in Virginia to carry on the most perfect system of common schools on earth. We have a chance for dispersing information over the State like the wind. . . . If instead of incurring debts in the digging of canals, the building of monuments, and maintenance of Militia, and the dressing up of Cadets, with tomfoolery of various other sorts, the State would enter earnestly in the work of preparing men to give intelligent votes and verdicts, we would see this State blossoming so as no rose ever blossomed. . . .

You will all live to rue the day that you enacted such a radical Constitution, unless you shall plant in it likewise the germ of its safety and its beneficence. . . . Let then the cause of education, virtue and thrift, rise victorious! We are better prepared for this Reform than for any that has been proposed.

# CHAPTER EIGHT

## PEACE AMONG NATIONS

————◆————

I repeat, therefore, that war is a public armed contest, between nations, in order to establish justice between them.
. . . It is, in short, a temporary adoption, by men, of the
character of wild beasts, emulating their ferocity, rejoicing
like them in blood, and seeking, as with a lion's paw, to
hold an asserted right. This character of war is somewhat
disguised, in more recent days, by the skill and knowledge
which it employs; it is, however, still the same, made more
destructive by the genius and intellect which have been
degraded to its servants.

————CHARLES SUMNER: *The Grandeur of Nations:*
*An Oration, July 4, 1845*

Ez fer war, I call it murder,—
    There you hev it plain an' flat;
I don't want to go no furder
    Than my Testament fer that; . . .

Ef you take a sword an' dror it,
    An' go stick a feller thru,
Guv'ment aint to answer for it,
    God'll send the bill to you.

Wut's the use o' meetin'-goin'
    Every Sabbath, wet or dry,
Ef it's right to go amowin'
    Feller-men like oats an' rye?

————JAMES RUSSELL LOWELL:
*Ez fer War, 1846*

Sources of the quotations on the preceding page:
    CHARLES SUMNER: Charles Sumner: *The Grandeur of Nations: An Oration Delivered before the City of Boston, July 4, 1845* (Boston: 1845), 9.
    JAMES RUSSELL LOWELL: Bernard Smith: *The Democratic Spirit* (New York: 1943, 2nd ed.), 353.

PRIOR to the War of 1812 expressions against war were generally individualistic or derived from the Friends. Yet even these reflected significant latter-day cleavages between the more and the less radical exponents of peace; the non-resistance of Isaac A. Van Hook (1) went far beyond the mere opposition to aggressive war expressed by "Repubesco" in the Charleston *City Gazette* (2). Organization of the peace movement began after the War of 1812. What may have been the first peace society in the world was founded in August, 1815, by David Low Dodge, a New York merchant (3). Four months later the Reverend Noah Worcester, author of a *Solemn Review* (4), and the Reverend William E. Channing instituted the Massachusetts Peace Society, thus establishing the pattern for many local societies, which appeared as far west as Ohio. These united into the American Peace Society, founded by William Ladd in 1828. The American societies corresponded with the London Peace Society.*

In the Jacksonian period advocates of arbitration and the federation of nations increased in number and articulateness. Following Worcester's lead, William Ladd pleaded for a permanent court and a congress of nations (5). In 1842, William Jay called for "stipulated arbitration." The idea won over the Senate Committee on Foreign Relations, which reported favorably in 1851 and 1853 on the inclusion of compulsory arbitration clauses in treaties. Against this moderate tack ran those who opposed all coercion, even when exerted by civil government. William Lloyd Garrison,

---

* The London Peace Society had been founded in 1816 out of a post-Napoleonic revulsion against war, which was regarded as contrary to Christian ethics.

Adin Ballou (6), Henry C. Wright (7) and other such militants tried to commit the American Peace Society to the doctrine of absolute non-resistance. When they failed they withdrew to form the New England Non-Resistance Society in 1838.

After Ladd's death in 1841 the American Peace Society became dominated by the moderate policy of George S. Beckwith. In 1846, dissident militant pacifists followed Elihu Burritt into a newly formed League of Universal Brotherhood, an international organization committed to condemnation of all wars. It represented twenty thousand Americans and a similar number of Britons who had unqualifiedly sworn to support no war. Burritt sponsored ocean penny postage, "friendly addresses," and "assisted emigration" from Europe to America. Such activities, he hoped, would help bind together the brotherhood of man. In 1855, as an alternative to impending war, he advocated a workingmen's strike (8). Indeed, the thought that war was a special threat to the people's progress was growing and was expressed by W. R. Alger's *An American Voice on War* in 1856 (9). Burritt played a great role in the universal peace congresses held abroad from 1848 through 1853. He sought through compensated emancipation to avoid the Civil War, which, unlike most former pacifists, he consistently opposed.

The Mexican War kindled many expressions of protest against war by poets like James Russell Lowell, statesmen like John Quincy Adams, and professional "non-resisters" like Henry C. Wright (7). But the Civil War killed—temporarily, at least—the peace movement in the United States. Nearly all pacifists, even non-resistants like Wright, allowed their opposition to slavery and Southern "imperialism" to dominate their abhorrence of force.

# 1.

*Isaac A. Van Hook:*
AN ORATION ON WAR *
[May 3, 1797]

*When Isaac Van Hook (?–1834), son of Arondt Van Hook,
was graduated from Columbia University in 1797, he delivered this commencement address in which he expressed his abhorrence of war. He probably entered the ministry at a fairly
advanced age, after he had been graduated from the New
Brunswick Theological Seminary in 1819. He served as a
missionary to various places in New Jersey and New York
until his death about 1834.*

. . . Other animals, indeed, destroy one another, according to
their respective superiority in strength, swiftness, or sagacity; but
their own kind they view with complacence and affection. The
human species alone exhibits the shameful spectacle of creatures
of the same kind eagerly bent upon each other's destruction. The
lion seizes upon the wolf; the tyger [*sic*] darts upon the kid. The
whale pursues and devours the smaller tribes of fish; but MAN
*devours* man!

If we look back into the remote ages of the world, we see nothing but battles, seiges [*sic*] and revolutions. Every volume of history is a detail of the terrors of war. Every page is stained with
blood. If we examine the temple of fame, its most numerous
votaries are those who have been distinguished as the desolators
of the world. Its loudest notes are sounded in praise of the greatest
enemies of mankind. Its fairest riches are usurped by murderers
and assassins. Sages, orators, and poets, either carried away by
the general delusion, or, prostituting their talents for the sake of
wealth and distinction, have lavished their encomiums upon
wretches who merited universal execration. . . .

* "An Oration on War, May 3, 1797. Delivered at the Commencement
of Columbia College," in *New York Magazine* (October, 1797), 530–2.

If we review those periods of history which approach nearer to our own times; if we survey them in the ages subsequent to the revival of letters, and the improvement of every department of knowledge, we still discover the same rancorous animosity between nations, the same thirst for conquest, the same invincible propensity to shed each other's blood.

The calculations of numbers, the inductions of the mathematics, the researches of philosophy, at first view, appear adapted to ameliorate the state of society, and, in every respect, to promote the happiness of man; but they have been perverted to the horrid purposes of slaughter and devastation. The discovery of metals and minerals has multiplied and improved the instruments of destruction. The mathematician has regulated their force, and directed their impulse with the most unerring fatality. Every discovery in nature and art has been seized upon with avidity, to point the aggressive arrow, or to blunt the hostile dart.

If we examine the grounds of such frequent repetition of hostilities, they will appear most commonly weak and frivolous; frequently wicked and profligate: how seldom they can, in reality, be attributed to self-defence, the only justifiable, but not always a justifiable cause, of an appeal to arms! The acquisition of territory—the propagation or suppression of opinion—the personal ambition, or revenge of the depositories of natural power—the iniquitous desire of embezzling a part of the funds destined for the support of such contests, have disfigured the fair face of nature, filled the world with broils, and precipitated to an immature grave millions of its inhabitants. . . . Mark the solemn, the awful pause which precedes the contest. The heart of the general is appalled, while he gives the signal to attack. The cannon roars—the thick column of smoke mercifully conceals the deeds of death. The shouts of victory are heard; the orders for pursuit are given. The friendly shade of night arrests the victor's murdering arm. On every side is heard the shriek of terror, and the groans of anguish and expiration. . . .

Let us follow the career of the victorious army—behold it marked with universal desolation; the country is filled with violence and murder. The soldier, enraged by opposition, and hardened by success, degenerates into a savage. He riots in excess; he is familiarized with scenes at which humanity blushes, and which nature disowns. The peasant bewails his luxuriant fields (the produce of his toils and patience) trampled and burnt. His stores are plundered. All his improvements, the pride of his heart, the support of his declining years, are in an hour effaced, in the wantonness of brutal ferocity. His hopes are blasted forever; he sinks into wretchedness and despair! . . .

To what powerful cause must we ascribe this phrenzy of the human mind? . . . Can human society, if left to its native impulse, pursue a conduct so hostile to all it holds dear? Certainly not. Let us inquire then, if there are any individuals detached from *society,* whose interests are repugnant to, and inconsistent with ITS interests, but who, at the same time, possess the means of influencing its determinations and directing its impulses? Yes, such *monsters* exist; behold them lodged in gilded palaces; reposing under canopies of state! surrounded by the ministers of their pleasures, and their oppressions. Behold them *inflamed* with intemperance, or *heated* with *savage* apathy! giving orders for the destruction of thousands, and *exulting* in the diffusion of human misery! The *imperial* palace is the *caverns* of those furies. Hence stalks forth the *fiend* of despotism, the *demon* of ambition, the *grim visaged fury* of war!!! . . .

While the rest of the world is convulsed with the horrors of war, the philanthropist views these happy, these peaceful shores, and is consoled. Here the reign of PEACE, I trust, will have no end. Individuals may endeavour to infuse into the public mind, a portion of their prejudices and their passions, but the attempt will be fruitless. The deliberate voice of this country can never be for *war,* because no object can present itself, the attainment of which can compensate for its evils. Let the revolutions in Europe terminate as they will, the public mind will be enlightened, the public voice will henceforth be respected! Let us hail the auspicious morn of universal peace, whene'er it begins to appear! Let all the friends of human dignity and human happiness raise their voices to welcome its appearance! Let science and philosophy prepare all their charms and elegancies to accelerate its approach, to decorate its empire, and to secure its *eternal* duration!!

J. [*sic*] A. V. H.

New York, Oct. 8, 1797.

2.

*Repubesco:*
LETTER TO THE EDITORS ON PEACE *
[July 4, 1800]

*This paper in 1800 was under the editorship of Peter Freneau
and Seth Paine. Unfortunately little is known about these
editors or the true identity of "Repubesco." This letter was
probably inspired by the war clouds that had been hovering
over Franco-American relations ever since the publication of
the correspondence of the "XYZ" affair. The Federalist war
party under Alexander Hamilton had whipped up a feeling for
war, and an outbreak was narrowly averted by President John
Adams in 1799. But the fear of war lingered on.*

But at all events, (that is, with justice and honor) let peace be
preserved to the people, and not lightly expose them to the fury
of arms. War offers nothing but a frightful spectacle of misery
and ruin. In a time when it is kindled, an infinity of people are
cut off in the flower of their age, either by arms, or by the licence
which reigns in camps, without their giving to the state the citizens which they otherwise would. Husbands being separated for
a time, or forever from their wives, marriages cannot with the
same facility repair the losses which the human species suffers.
Countries ravaged; cities pillaged and sacked; arts and commerce
neglected; excessive exactions burthening the people; fatal mala-
dies, the common consequence of great indigence: all these concur to depopulate the unfortunate countries which are desolated
by the fire of war, and to deprive the inhabitants of the means of
subsisting.

But, under the happy auspices of peace, the face of the scene
is changed. The people live without fear in the shade of their
laws; their harvests fall not the prey of strangers; arts and commerce are exercised with tranquility; and all the necessary resources for nourishing and preserving a great people, multiply
themselves, without care, on all sides. We cannot remove, therefore, too far those frightful tempests, which move one nation

* *City Gazette and Daily Advertiser* (Charleston, S.C.: August 7, 1800), 2.

against another, and cause such horrible disorders. We ought only to make war when it is absolutely necessary for opposing unjust aggressors, stopping their ambitious enterprizes, and maintaining the sacred rights of a people; and the interests of humanity require all the views of mildness, before we have recourse to arms, for terminating the differences which arise among nations.

Such is the true spirit of a genuine republican government. Its dictates, we trust, will ever be followed by that of the United States.

REPUBESCO.

3.

*David Low Dodge:*
WAR INCONSISTENT WITH THE RELIGION OF JESUS CHRIST *
[1812]

*David Low Dodge (1774–1852) was born on a Brooklyn farm. After a boyhood of privations, he became a schoolmaster and subsequently a storekeeper, jobber, and manager of a cotton mill. He became active in philanthropic and religious movements. This was his second pamphlet on pacifism. In 1815 his supporters formed the New York Peace Society, and Dodge became its first president. He seems to have been one of the first to argue that there was little distinction between offensive and defensive wars, since every combatant fought in defense of some territory, principle, or ambition. He was also active in founding the New York Bible Society and the New York Tract Society.*

*War is inhuman as it destroys the youth and cuts off the hope of grey hairs.*

Mankind are speedily hastening into eternity, and it might be supposed sufficiently rapid, without the aid of all the ingenuity and strength of man to hurry them forward; and yet it is a melancholy *truth*, that a great proportion of the *wealth*, *talents* and

---

* David Low Dodge: *War Inconsistent with the Religion of Jesus Christ as It Is Inhuman, Unwise, and Criminal* (New York: 1815), 21–4.

labors of men are actually employed in *inventing and using* means for the premature destruction of their fellow beings.

One generation passes away, and another follows them in quick succession. The young are always the stay and hope of the aged: parents labor and toil for their children to supply their wants, and to educate them to be happy, respectable, and useful; and then depend upon them to be their stay and comfort in their declining years. Alas! how many expectations of fond parents are blasted? their sons are taken away from them, and hurried into the field of slaughter.

I would here wish to caution such parents as desire to keep their sons from voluntarily joining military ranks, to be sparing of their eulogies on heroes in the ears of their children.

One of the most fruitful sources of engendering the spirit of war, is that *unjustifiable practice,* not to say of immortalizing, but *deifying heroes,* or rather man-destroyers. When children daily hear heroes *toasted to heaven,* they thirst to follow the same career of glory.

. . . In times of war, the youths, the flower, strength, and beauty of the country are called from their sober, honest, and useful employments, to the field of battle: and if they do not lose their lives or limbs, they generally lose their habits of morality and industry. Alas! few ever return again to the bosom of their friends.

Though from their mistaken and fascinating views of a soldier's life and honor, they may be *delighted in enlisting, and merry in their departure* from their peaceful homes, yet their joy is soon turned into pain and sorrow. Unthinking youth, like the horse, rushes thoughtlessly into the battle; their repentance is then too late, to shrink back is death, and to go forward is only a faint hope of life. Here on the dreadful field are thousands and hundreds of thousands driven together to slaughter each other by a few ambitious men, perhaps none of whom are present. A large proportion are probably the youth of their country, the delight and comfort of their parents. All these opposing numbers are most likely persons who *never knew or heard of each other,* having no personal ill-will, most of whom, would in any other circumstances not only *not injure each other,* but be ready to aid in any kind office, yet, by the act of war, they are *ranged against each other*, in all the hellish rage of *revenge and slaughter*.

No pen, much less that of the writer's, can describe the inhumanity and horrors of a battle. All is confusion and dismay, dust and smoke rising, horses running, trumpets blasting, cannon roaring, bullets whistling, and the shrieks of the wounded and dying vibrating from every quarter. Column after column of men charge upon each other in *furious onset*, with the awful crash of bayonets and sabres, with *eyes flashing*, and visages *frightfully distorted with rage, rushing* upon each other with *the violence* of brutish monsters, and when these are literally cut to pieces, others march in quick succession only to share the same cruel and bloody tragedy. Hundreds are *parrying* the blows, hundreds more are *thrusting* their bayonets into the bowels of their fellow mortals, and many while extricating them, have their own heads cleft asunder by swords and sabres, and all are hurried together before the tribunal of their judge, with hearts full of rage, and hands dyed in the blood of their brethren.

## 4.

### Rev. Noah Worcester:
### SOLEMN REVIEW OF THE CUSTOM OF WAR *
### [1814]

*Noah Worcester (1758–1837) was born in New Hampshire. After serving as a fifer in the Revolutionary War, he engaged in farming, teaching, and shoemaking. At the same time he studied religious subjects and at a minister's suggestion applied successfully for a license to preach. His gentle and peaceable nature regarded war as totally unjustifiable. Anticipating Gandhi's non-resistance, he believed love was the surest weapon to overcome one's foes. His Solemn Review was translated into many languages and circulated throughout the world. The originality of this work lay in its recom-*

* Rev. N. Worcester: *Solemn Review of the Custom of War Showing That War Is the Effect of Popular Delusion and Proposing a Remedy* (Cambridge, Mass.: 1815), 3–5, 30.

*mendations for a confederacy of nations and a high court of justice for settling international disputes. Worcester gave impetus to the founding of the Massachusetts Peace Society in 1815, of which he became the secretary. From its inception in 1819, he edited* The Friend of Peace *until 1828.*

It will perhaps be pleaded, that mankind are not yet sufficiently enlightened, to apply the principles of the gospel for the abolition of war; and that we must wait for a more improved state of society. *Improved in what?* in the science of blood? Are such improvements to prepare the way for peace? Why not wait a few centuries, until the natives of India become more improved in their idolatrous customs, before we attempt to convert them to christianity? Do we expect that by continuing in the practice of idolatry, their minds will be prepared to receive the gospel? If not, let us be consistent, and while we use means for the conversion of heathens, let means also be used for the conversion of christians. For war is in fact a heathenish and savage custom, of the most malignant, most desolating, and most horrible character. It is the greatest curse, and results from the grossest delusions that ever afflicted a guilty world. . . .

SECTION I.
*"Shall the sword devour forever?"*

We regard with horror the custom of the ancient heathens in offering their children in sacrifice to idols. We are shocked with the customs of the Hindoos, in prostrating themselves before the car of an idol to be crushed to death; in burning women alive on the funeral piles of their husbands; in offering a monthly sacrifice, by casting living children into the Ganges to be drowned. . . . But that which is fashionable and popular in any country is esteemed right and honorable, whatever may be its nature in the views of men better informed.

But while we look back with a mixture of wonder, indignation and pity, on many of the customs of former ages, are we careful to inquire, whether some customs which we deem honorable, are not the effect of popular delusion? and whether they will not be so regarded by future generations? Is it not a fact, that one of the most horrid customs of savage men, is now popular in every nation in Christendom? What custom of the most barbarous nations is more repugnant to the feelings of piety, humanity and justice, than that of deciding controversies between nations by the edge of the sword, by powder and ball, or the point of the bayonet? What other savage custom has occasioned half the desolation and misery to the human race? And what but the grossest infatuation, could render such a custom popular among rational beings?

When we consider how great a part of mankind have perished by the hands of each other, and how large a portion of human calamity has resulted from war; it surely cannot appear indifferent, whether this custom is or is not the effect of delusion. Certainly there is no custom which deserves a more thorough examination, than that which has occasioned more slaughter and misery, than all the other abominable customs of the heathen world.

War has been so long fashionable among all nations, that its enormity is but little regarded; or when thought of at all, it is usually considered as an evil necessary and unavoidable. Perhaps it is really so in the present state of society, and the present views of mankind. But the question to be considered is this; cannot the state of society and the views of civilized men be so changed as to abolish a barbarous custom, and render wars unnecessary and avoidable?

If this question may be answered in the affirmative, then we may hope "the sword will not devour forever."

Some may be ready to exclaim, none but God can produce such an effect as the abolition of war; and we must wait for the millennial day. We admit that God only can produce the necessary change in the state of society, and the views of men; but God works by human agency and human means. . . .

As to waiting for the millennium to put an end to war, without any exertions on our own part; this is like the sinner's waiting God's time for conversion, while he pursues his course of vice and impiety. If ever there shall be a millennium in which the sword will cease to devour, it will probably be effected by the blessing of God on the benevolent exertions of enlightened men. Perhaps no one thing is now a greater obstacle in the way of the wished for state of the church, than the *spirit* and *custom* of war, which is maintained by christians themselves. Is it not then time, that efforts should be made to enlighten the minds of christians on a subject of such infinite importance to the happiness of the human race?

It is not the present object to prove, that a nation may not defend their lives, their liberties and their property against an invading foe; but to inquire whether it is not possible to effect such a change in the views of men, that there shall be no occasion for *defensive* war. That such a state of things is desirable, no enlightened christian can deny. That it can be produced without expensive and persevering efforts is not imagined. But are not such efforts to exclude the miseries of war from the world, as laudable as those which have for their object the support of such a malignant and desolating custom?

The whole amount of property in the United States is probably of far less value, than what has been expended and destroyed within two centuries by wars in Christendom. Suppose then, that one fifth of this amount had been judiciously laid out by peace associations in the different states and nations, in cultivating the spirit and art of peace, and in exciting a just abhorrence of war; would not the other four fifths have been in a great measure saved, besides many millions of lives, and an immense portion of misery? Had the whole value of what has been expended in wars, been appropriated to the purpose of peace, how laudable would have been the appropriation, and how blessed the consequences!

5.

*William Ladd:*
ESSAY ON A CONGRESS OF NATIONS *
[1840]

*William Ladd (1778–1841) was born in New Hampshire of New England descent. Except for the few years when he experimented in Florida with free Negro labor, he followed the sea until 1817, when he retired to a farm. In 1819 he became*

* William Ladd: *Essay on a Congress of Nations for the Adjustment of International Disputes* (Boston: 1840), 6–7, 99–100, 123–6.

*interested in international peace, helping the pitifully weak
societies with a forceful pen and winning voice. In May,
1828, he founded the American Peace Society, and he carried its message everywhere, even bringing the question into
politics. Although a "non-resistant," he desired co-operation
of friends of all shades of opinion. In this essay on a Congress
of Nations he showed himself one of the great architects of
the peace movement, with a plan calling for a congress for
formulating principles of international law and a court of
nations for settling differences.*

But man is also a rational animal, and he soon perceives that
there are enjoyments which can more easily be procured by persuasion, than by force; and that though he may be stronger than
another individual, two other individuals may be stronger than
he—that he cannot always be on the watch to preserve the property he has acquired by robbery, the chase, or agriculture—and
that he also is subject to inconvenience from the theft, or violence, of others; hence he soon finds himself compelled to make
a certain convention, or agreement, with others, both inferiors
and equals, both as an individual and as the head of a tribe. These
compacts are guaranteed by religion, public opinion, and certain
undefined laws of honor dependent on them; but most of all by
a general perception of the truth, that the happiness of the whole
is best promoted by the subservience of the interests of the few
to the interests of the many. . . .

It is an incontrovertible axiom, that *every thing of a moral nature which ought to be done, can be done.* There is no object favorable to the happiness of mankind, and founded on the immutable principles of truth, which zeal, intelligence and perseverance,
with self-sacrifice, will not finally accomplish. I do not say that
so great an enterprise, as a Congress of Nations, can be accomplished in a day. It will probably be of slow growth, like the trial
by jury, and by slow degrees it will ultimately arrive at the same
approximation to perfection, which that has arrived at. There is
the greater need, therefore, that those who favor the object
should begin the work without loss of time. If we wish to eat of
the date, we should plant the seed immediately. If we wish our
children to see the flower of the aloe we must ourselves begin
the cultivation. . . .

1. It is a generally acknowledged principle, that nations have no moral right to go to war, until they have tried to preserve peace by every lawful and honorable means. This, the strongest advocate for war, in these enlightened days, will not deny, whatever might have been the opinion of mankind, on the subject, in darker ages. When a nation has received an injury, if it be of such a magnitude as, in the opinion of the injured party, ought not to be submitted to; the first thing to be done is to seek an explanation from the injuring nation; and it will be often found, that the injury was unintentional, or that it originated in misapprehension and mistake, or that there is no real ground of offence. Even where the ground of offence is undeniable, and, in the opinion of the world, the injured nation has a *right* to declare war, it is now generally believed, that they are not so likely to obtain redress and reparation by war as by forbearance and negotiation; and that it is their bounden duty, both to themselves and to the world at large, to exhaust every means of negotiation, before they plunge themselves and other nations into the horrors and crimes of war. The United States had much ground of complaint against Great Britain, during Washington's administration. Instead of declaring war, Jay was sent to England, and full and complete satisfaction was obtained for all the injuries received, by the influence of moral power alone, for we had not then a single ship of war on the ocean. At a subsequent period, with twice the population, and twenty times the means of offence, impatient of a protracted negotiation, we resorted to war, and got no reparation of injuries, or satisfaction whatever, except revenge, bought at an enormous expense of men and money, and made peace, leaving every cause of complaint in the *statu quo ante bellum.* Had we protracted the negotiation thirty days longer, the war and all its evils, physical and moral, would have been avoided. Sometimes negotiations have failed altogether to obtain redress. Then an offer of arbitration should follow. Now what we are seeking for is, a regular system of arbitration, and the organization of a board of arbitrators, composed of the most able civilians in the world, acting on well-known principles, established and promulgated by a Congress of Nations. If there were such a Court, no civilized nation could refuse to leave a subject of international dispute to its adjudication. Nations have tried war long enough. It has never settled any prin-

ciple, and generally leaves dissensions worse than it found them. It is, therefore, high time for the Christian world to seek a more rational, cheap, and equitable mode of settling international difficulties.

2. When we consider the horrible calamities which war has caused, the millions of lives it has cost, and the unutterable anguish which it produces, not only on the battle-field and in the military hospital, but in the social circle and the retired closet of the widow and orphan, we have reason to conclude, that the inquisition, the slave trade, slavery, and intemperance, all put together, have not caused half so much grief and anguish to mankind as war. It is the duty, therefore, of every *philanthropist*, and every *statesman*, to do what they can to support a measure which will probably prevent many a bloody war, even if the probability were but a faint one.

3. When we consider that war is the hotbed of every crime, and that it is the principal obstacle to the conversion of the heathen, and that it sends millions unprepared suddenly into eternity, every *Christian* ought to do all he can to prevent the evil in every way in his power, not only by declaiming against war, and showing its sin and folly, but by assisting to bring forward a plan which is calculated to lessen the horrors and frequency of war. Should all the endeavors of every philanthropist, statesman and Christian in the world be successful in preventing only one war, it would be a rich reward for their labor. If only once in a century, two nations should be persuaded to leave their disputes to a Court of Nations, and thereby one war be avoided, all the expense of maintaining such a court would be repaid with interest.

4. We therefore conclude, that every man, whether his station be public or private, who refuses to lend his aid in bringing forward this plan of a Congress and Court of Nations, neglects his duty to his country, to the world, and to God, and does not act consistently with the character of a statesman, philanthropist, or Christian.

6.

*Adin Ballou:*
CHRISTIAN  NON-RESISTANCE *
[1846]

*Born in Rhode Island, descended from one of the original
Rhode Island co-proprietors, Adin Ballou (1803–90) received a farmer boy's training in hard work. When eighteen,
he announced his supernatural call to the ministry, and, although he began by attacking Universalism, he ultimately became a Universalist minister. His radical social views led him
to oppose war, intemperance, and slavery. He was the founder
and president of one of the better known ventures in Christian Socialism, the Hopedale Community, near Milford,
Massachusetts, and edited its organ,* The Practical Christian.
*In 1838, he helped form the New England Non-Resistant
Society and he edited its paper for a number of years. His*
Christian Non-Resistance *was a solid intellectual defense of
the non-resistance movement, which generally had less so-
phisticated champions like Henry Clarke Wright (7).*

What is Christian Non-Resistance? It is that original peculiar
kind of non-resistance, which was enjoined and exemplified by
Jesus Christ, according to the Scriptures of the New Testament. . . .
The almost universal opinion and practice of mankind has been
on the side of resistance of injury *with* injury. It has been held
justifiable and *necessary*, for individuals and nations to inflict any
amount of *injury* which would effectually resist a supposed
greater injury. The consequence has been universal suspicion, defiance, armament, violence, torture and bloodshed. The earth has
been rendered a vast slaughter-field—a theatre of reciprocal
cruelty and vengeance—strewn with human skulls, reeking with
human blood, resounding with human groans, and steeped with
human tears. Men have become drunk with mutual revenge; and
they who could inflict the greatest amount of injury, in pretended
defence of life, honor, rights, property, institutions and laws,

* Adin Ballou: *Christian Non-Resistance in All Its Important Bearings*
(Philadelphia: 1846), 2, 12–13, 32–3.

have been idolized as the heroes and rightful sovereigns of the world. Non-resistance explodes this horrible delusion; announces the impossibility of overcoming evil with evil; and, making its appeal directly to all the *injured* of the human race, enjoins on them, in the name of God, never more to *resist injury with injury;* assuring them that by adhering to the law of love under all provocations, and scrupulously suffering wrong, rather than inflicting it, they shall gloriously "overcome evil with good," and exterminate all their enemies by turning them into faithful friends. . . .

## THE CONCLUSION.

But the Son of the Highest, the great self-sacrificing Non-Resistant, is our prophet, priest and king. Though the maddened inhabitants of the earth have so long turned a deaf ear to his voice, he shall yet be heard. He declares that *good* is the only antagonist of *evil,* which can conquer the deadly foe. Therefore he enjoins on his disciples the duty of resisting *evil only* with *good.* This is the sub-principle of Christian non-resistance.

"Evil can be overcome only with *good.*" Faith, then, in the inherent superiority of *good* over *evil,* truth over error, right over wrong, love over hatred, is the immediate moral basis of our doctrine. Accordingly we transfer all the faith we have been taught to cherish in *injury,* to *beneficence, kindness,* and *uninjurious treatment,* as the only all-sufficient enginery of war against *evil doers.* No longer seeking or expecting to put down evil with evil, we lift up the cross for an ensign, and surmounting it with the glorious banner of love, exult in the divine motto displayed on its immaculate folds, "RESIST NOT INJURY WITH INJURY." Let this in all future time be the specific rule of our conduct, the magnetic needle of our pathway across the troubled waters of human reform, till all men, all governments and all social institutions shall have been moulded into moral harmony with the grand comprehensive commandment of the living God—"THOU SHALT LOVE THY NEIGHBOR AS THYSELF." Then shall *Love* (God by his sublimest name) "be all in all."

# 7.

### Henry C. Wright:
## THE ASSASSIN AND THE SOLDIER *
### [January 21, 1848]

*Henry Clarke Wright (1797–1870), born in Connecticut, was for a number of years a conservative Congregational clergyman, but in the early thirties he left his church for a more active life as a lecturer on temperance, abolition, peace, socialism, and (later) spiritualism. He soon became too extreme for the tastes even of most reformers, for he came to believe that all coercion was evil, even when employed by civil government. In 1838, unable to persuade the American Peace Society to take this position, Wright and a small group of radicals, including William Lloyd Garrison and Adin Ballou, formed the New England Non-Resistance Society, of which Wright was for several years the guiding spirit. He was not a profound thinker, but he was an effective speaker and skilled at simplifying moral issues. This example of his technique was inspired by the Mexican War.*

### The Difference.

Now, what is the difference between *Zachary*, the soldier, and *Dick* the assassin? In the following particulars they are exactly alike:

The *assassin* killed a man whom he *knew to be innocent;* the soldier did the same.

The *assassin* killed the innocent at the *instigation of his employers;* so did the soldier.

The *assassin* slew his victim for the *benefit of his employers;* so did the soldier.

The *assassin* entered into a contract with his employers *voluntarily;* so did the soldier.

The *assassin* killed his victim *intentionally* and *deliberately;* so did the soldier.

* Henry C. Wright: *Dick Crowningshield, The Assassin, and Zachary Taylor, The Soldier: The Difference Between Them* (Hopedale, Mass.: 1848), 10–12.

The *assassin* "killed a reasonable creature," and was "of a sound mind and discretion"; so did the soldier and in the same state of mind.

The *assassin* killed an innocent man "with *malice and forethought*," "with a sedate, deliberate mind, and former design"; so did the soldier.

As to the state of their minds towards their victims; as to their motives; as to the character of their victims; as to the nature and character of their acts, there is an exact resemblance between Dick the assassin and Zachary the soldier

In the following particulars they differ:

*Zachary* had *millions* of employers; the assassin had but *two*.

*Zachary* killed *thousands;* the assassin killed *one*.

*Zachary's* sword, balls and bomb-shells, were accounted *Christian* weapons to slay men; the *assassin's* bludgeon and dirk were considered *unchristian*.

*Zachary* broke the limbs and tore the flesh of his victims and left them to die in protracted agony; the *assassin* killed his instantly and without protracted pain.

*Zachary's* deeds are said by the priests and churches to be God-approved and Christ-like; the *assassin's* are denounced by them as evil and only evil.

*Zachary* is hailed as a Christian patriot; *Dick* is shunned by all.

*Zachary*, as he returns from Monterey, his face, his hands and garments dripping with the blood of innocent women and children, is welcomed "by the smiles and kisses of his countrywomen"; they shrink from Dick with horror.

*Zachary* is held up by mothers, by teachers, by priests and politicians, as an example of piety and patriotism; *Dick* is held up by them to execration.

*Zachary* is made a life-member of a Missionary Society; *Dick* is cast out as a heathen.

*Zachary* is counted worthy of all honor by a professedly enlightened, civilized, republican and Christian people, and is by them elevated to the Presidency; *Dick*, by the same people, is elevated to the gallows.

Such are the different results of killing one at the bidding and for the benefit of *two*, and killing *thousands* for the benefit and at the bidding of *millions*.

Such are the points of agreement and difference between the assassin and the soldier. They differ solely in reference to incidental circumstances, that affect not the nature of the acts, nor the position, motives and character of the perpetrators. Zachary Taylor and Dick Crowningshield stand in precisely the same relation to their God, and to their employers. Zachary Taylor and every soldier voluntarily hire themselves out to kill innocent human beings, at the bidding and for the benefit of their employers. Dick Crowningshield did the same; and if he is an assassin, so are they. Does killing *one* innocent man at the bidding and for the benefit of *two* make a man an *assassin,* and killing *thousands* at the bidding and for the benefit of *millions* make him a *saint?* Does an act performed for the pleasure and at the instigation of *two* make a man a *murderer,* and the same act done at the instigation and for the pleasure of *millions,* constitute him an *angel?* Does murder become a pious, Christian act, in proportion to the number who commit it? Does the assassin become respectable, Christian, and worthy of confidence in proportion to the number of his employers and of his victims. If not, then is Zachary Taylor and every soldier as certainly a murderer and an assassin as was Dick Crowningshield.

Not only so, but every *advocate of defensive war* is as truly an instigator and promoter of murder as were the Knapps; and is as accessary to and responsible for the death of the people of Monterey as were they of the death of Joseph White. Zachary Taylor is the agent of all that advocate war, as really as was Crowningshield the agent of the Knapps. The acts of their agents are their acts. When he entered Monterey and violated and murdered the women and children, they did the deeds. Let just and truthful words be used in speaking of all warriors and their advocates. Let all soldiers and all advocates of war be told that they are *murderers,* and let this truth be brought home to them on all occasions, till they feel its force; and then, and not till then, will men learn and advocate war no more.

*Framingham Railway Station,*
*Friday Jan. 21, 1848.*

## 8.

### *Elihu Burritt:*
### WORLD'S WORKINGMEN'S STRIKE AGAINST WAR *
### [1850]

*Born in Connecticut, Elihu Burritt (1810–79) was brought
up as a blacksmith and had little formal training. He became
absorbed in the peace movement in 1841, at the time it lost
its chief, William Ladd, and he rose rapidly to leadership.
Burritt worked out the methods of enlisting public support
against war over Oregon and Texas by sending "Olive Leaf"
pamphlets to hundreds of newspapers and peace groups and
by organizing an exchange of "friendly addresses" of peace
advocate meetings. In co-operation with his British friends
he formed in the autumn of 1846 the League of Universal
Brotherhood, which was eventually absorbed by the London
Peace Society. He was instrumental in organizing four peace
conferences held between 1848 and 1852. Unfortunately the
Crimean War and other wars brought about the collapse of
the peace movement. Only two years after the* Communist
Manifesto, *Burritt's advocacy of a strike of workers against
war appeared in* Olive Leaves *and was printed in the German
press. The American imprint, reproduced here, first appeared
in 1855.*

Nations, like individuals, often come to junctures in their lives
where two if not four roads meet, and one of these they must take
with all the hazards of the choice. The world has seen pretty
clearly the road which all the nations of Europe have been traveling for the last quarter of a century. The world sees now what
their armed-peace system has brought them to. For all this period
they have been running neck and neck in this costly and perilous
race of war armaments. This delusion has grown by that it fed
upon. Every additional regiment on land, or iron-clad put on the
sea by one, has created more suspicion in the other, and that suspicion has reproduced its kind in *defenses* against the increased

* Elihu Burritt: *World's Workingmen's Strike against War* (New Britain,
Conn.: 1855?), 1–4. (Copied from a four-page leaflet among the miscellaneous
papers and manuscripts in the Elihu Burritt collection in the Library of the
New Britain Institute, New Britain, Connecticut.)

danger. Thus, while all these nations have been stoutly protesting against an intention to invade or injure a neighbor *offensively,*
their *defenses* have been steadily growing from year to year until
they have reached that point and peril of magnitude at which
Disraeli has called them "bloated armaments."

This, then, is the juncture at which two roads meet on the high-
way thus far traveled by the nations of Europe. They are now to
determine whether they will go straight forward in the old beaten
track, or diverge into a new path. . . .

There is no time to lose in this decision. The great, honest,
toiling masses of the world have waited for them long to take this
new road. These masses are beginning to feel a strength that their
governments would do well to heed now, before it takes an inconvenient direction for the powers that be. They have been
feeling for some time past the strength of a common sentiment,
interest and experience and inheritance. They are beginning to
get their eyes open to some of the wicked delusions that have vic-
timized them in past generations. They begin to see whither they
have been led, and how they have been cheated, by the syren [*sic*]
lights and syren [*sic*] songs of a false patriotism. And while this
deceptive music was still in their ears, they have shaken hands
with each other across the boundaries that once made them enemies. And the hands they interfolded in friendly grasp felt very
much alike each other, hard and horny with their common lot.
And they have compared the blisters and callous ridges made on
their hands by "foreign policies." They have weighted and compared the burdens put upon them by their governments, and
found and said that the most crushing of them all was the Armed-
Peace System of Christendom. And their governments, at the
junction of the two roads, will do well to heed now, and honestly,
what these workingmen, in congress assembled, feel, and say, and
determine in regard to this system. Their feeling and meaning
grow stronger and louder on the subject every time they meet in
their international assembly; and, doubtless, they will meet every
year, and their annual parliaments will begin soon to legislate
for the great democracy of labor throughout the civilized world.
And "the great Powers," at the junction of the two roads, will do
well to heed this habit of their workingmen of sending their
representatives, chosen at primary meetings, to these annual Par-

liaments. It is a very significant and portentous habit in itself. And their *agenda* and *facienda* are more portentous still to the powers that be. If they work out their programme, it will upset the classic poetry of that malignant patriotism which worships silken rags covered with beastial emblems, and sacrifices to the idolatry more human blood than all the pagan altars of this wide world ever drank this side of the murder of Abel. It is very rude, very unsentimental, and unpatriotic for them to say and purpose these things when they come together in this way. It will doubtless shock the sensibilities of the whole military aristocracy of Christendom, and of all the students, professors and amateurs of the school and history of military glory, to hear what these working-men will say in the next session of their parliament. They have said strong things before about war and its burdens upon them. But this time their representatives will have to pass to their assembly half a million of fresh graves in France and Germany, wherein lie, like buried dogs, half a million of their own fraternity of toil, taken from honest labor to mutual butchery on the field of battle. They will see a million of blackened, blasted homes on their way, and widows and orphans trying to quench the still red ashes of those homes with their own tears. They will see wan, armless, or legless men by the ten thousands begging on crutches, by the roadside, for the bread they once earned and ate by the sweat of the brow. Now these sights and the low, faint voices of woe they will see and hear on their way to their parliament will very sensibly affect their discussions, and give an utterance and a character to their resolutions which their governments, at the junction of the two roads, will do well to heed in advance, anticipate and supercede by their own action. Such action, honest and effective and immediate, is their only alternative, if they would evade or check the rising of a power too strong for their old "foreign policy."

What is asked of the great Powers, at the junction of the two roads, is a very simple, straight-forward matter. It is the step proposed to them, before these late and bloody wars, by Louis Napoleon; to convene a Congress of Nations to agree upon a *ratio* of general and simultaneous disarmament. The idea was not original with him; for it had been developed and propounded by eminent philosophers and philanthropists for two hundred years. . . .

The toiling, patient masses of the great commonwealth of labor
do not ask a great deal of these Powers; they do not say how far
in the new road they shall reach at the first step, but that they
shall make one, however small. They know what a thorny crop of
suspicions the armed-peace system has grown among them.
Therefore they will be contented with a very short step that
brings their faces and feet in the right direction. Even if they
should only venture to reduce their standing armies by sending
home to the plow or hammer, one man in five, they would be
satisfied with the installment, knowing that it would be followed
by larger reductions. Even a reduction of one-fifth of the present
armed-peace expenditure, to begin with, would so lighten the
burden upon the masses of the people of Christendom that they
would feel the relief at every meal and at every hour of their toil.
Just think what that small, tentative reduction would do. In the
first place it would send back to peaceful and reproductive labor,
nearly a million of picked, stalwart men from the armies of
Europe. See what it would do for England, who does not pretend
to be a military power in the French or German sense. One-fifth
taken from the expense of her armed peace establishment for
1870, would be £5,600,000. Think what taxes might be lifted
from the people by that small *ratio* of reduction. But the working-
men and women in France, Germany, Italy, and other continental
countries, would be more relieved still by this reduction, because
their wages do not average, in the gross, more than half what
their English brethren receive for their labor.

Now if the press, the platform, and the pulpit of these Christian countries have any power with their governments, every consideration that should move them, ought to enlist their best influence in behalf of a Congress of Nations for this one object to
begin with, whatever other measures it might subsequently accomplish. The necessity is very pressing for such a Congress to
be convened before the next Parliament of the working-men of
Christendom. Their national organizations, represented in these
Parliaments, are growing more and more powerful. And when
they meet next time, they will see the condition and prospects of
their class in a new light, and feel them with a new sensibility.
They may not strive to alter the past, but they will grasp at their
future with a rough, strength of heart and hand which the great

Powers, at the junction of the two roads, will do well to anticipate and avoid. Poor, patient masses! thousands and tens of thousands of them have fought, bled and died for national territory who could not buy enough in that or their own land to make their graves in. They cannot change this new and horrible past of one year's length. This huge abomination of desolation wrought upon the late peaceful and sunny bosom of Europe, will fall upon their industry and life of toil and trial with a burden they never bore before. As the yoke upon the necks of two working oxen presses upon each with equal weight, so the yoke of this great war's burden will bear with equal weight upon the raw necks of the French and German working-classes. They will have to work out the damages done to each other by this war. The yoke will gall and bend alike victors and vanquished; and the weight will tell on every plow, sickle, and spindle in Europe, and on every meal earned by these honest tools.

This is the new weight that the armed-peace system has just now added to the burdens it had before put upon the working-classes of Europe. Now then if the great Powers, at the junction of the two roads, do not say to this destroying angel, begotten and winged of their madness and folly, "It is enough," its millions of patient victims, even without a Moses, may break the bondage and find on their side and behalf the same God who led an equal number of working-men, more lightly taxed, to a better land and condition. It may appear unnatural and unseemly for an edge-tool to rebel and turn against the hand that wields it. It will doubtless spoil the romance of modern chivalry, and many martial songs of military glory, if the "food for powder" should rebel at the cannon's mouth. It may even disgust the classic predilections of the great class of hero-worshipers and hero-makers if the working-men of Christendom venture to put an end to such pretentious valuations upon their earthly possibilities as to believe they are worth more for producing food for man and beast, than for feeding with their own flesh and blood the hungry maws of mortar and *mitralleuses* on fields of human slaughter. But the great Powers, at the junction of the two roads, must face the alternative before them. These working-men have been practising for several years on "strikes," organized to affect their condition throughout large sections of their country. They have been perfecting the machinery and the forces of these combinations for a wider field of action, and in their last Parliament they decided upon the field for employing their co-operative forces; they proposed a Strike against War, and the whole armed-peace system, when they last met. If they had motive then for this resolution, what a trebled one will they have at their next session to carry out that resolution! This, then, is the alternative: either a Congress of Nations for simultaneous and proportionate disarmament, or an organized strike of the working-men of Christendom against war, root and branch. The great Powers, at the junction of the two roads, must choose without delay which of these two measures they will adopt.

9.

*William Rounceville Alger:*
AN AMERICAN VOICE ON WAR *
[1856]

*Born in Massachusetts, William Rounceville Alger (1822–1905), worked in a grocery, later in a broker's office, then in a cotton mill. Finally, he was ordained a Unitarian clergyman and became a favorite on the Lyceum platform, speaking his mind despite criticism. In 1857 he was chosen to deliver the Fourth of July oration in Boston. But his criticism of the proslavery attitude of the people was so strong that Boston refused to publish it until seven years later. This extract from one of his many publications was occasioned by the Crimean War.*

Seeking to discern and correctly estimate the *cause* of the war, we are forced to the sad conclusion that it did not spring from generous sympathy with the oppressed or sacred fealty to the right, but from mean jealousy and wicked pride. It resulted as most wars ever have and ever will from a shameful mixture of petty squabbling, inflamed arrogance, timid conservatism, contemptible envy, and unbelieving bureaucracy. Of course we must

* W. R. Alger: *An American Voice on the Lessons of War* (Boston: 1856), 7–9, 15–16.

discriminate between the broad currents of conviction and emotion sweeping through the masses of a country, and the plans and motives ruling its king and ministers. The former unquestionably are often just and magnanimous (as I believe they were with the overwhelming majority of Englishmen in the recent conflict), while the latter are base and curdling. This war, it must be remembered, was not made by the spontaneous sentiment of peoples, but by the selfish policy of cabinets. It was not a fair, unmasked struggle between outrageous injustice and crushing oppression on one side, disinterested righteousness and uprising humanity on the other, but it was the league of egotistical tyrannies to weaken another tyrant who threatened to outstrip them in the race and outweigh them in the scale. This is proved, in the first place, by European history for the past hundred years; and, secondly, it is demonstrated afresh by the glaring facts of the present case. If the leading governments of Europe undertake mutually to protect, so far as they can, the just rights, and enhance the best welfare, of nations, to defend the weak against wrongful violence, and to further the interests of morality, freedom, and happiness against all traitorous foes of God and man, then where were they when unhappy Poland was murdered and dismembered?—a deed bad enough, one should think, to turn the sun into blood and fetch on the day of doom. Why did they so meanly coalize and summon forth their servile armies against enthusiastic France, the hour her democratic banner flouted the battlements of antiquated crime? Where were their voices and right arms seven years ago, when Hungary, without a shadow of justification, was trodden down by two fraternizing despotisms? Plainly enough, it is no matter how foully a brutal tyranny tramples on a tributary dependent or a weak neighbor, even if to the utter extinguishment of its national existence; they all look calmly on with never a word or gesture; they keep very quiet while the outrage is perpetrated, the extermination accomplished. The Czar may seat himself in Warsaw, and populate Siberia with Poland's nobles, driven, as wretched beggars, into perpetual banishment, for no crime; the Austrian may serve Hungary in the same way, with inexcusable aid from abroad; the Pope may sprinkle the world, stuff prisons, and cram graves with Italy's bravest and best sons, exiled, immured, executed,—and nought is done. But let any people, goaded to desperation by vexatious bondage and intolerable persecutions, kindled by grand ideas and visions, rise to hurl a titled scoundrel from his seat, and take the reins of power as they have a right divine to do, and the royal minions clasp hands and spread their forces from St. Petersburg to Rome, to suppress the insurrection, smother out its intelligent sparkles, and rescue and fortify yet a while longer their imperilled kinghood and their darling priestcraft. . . .

It will be one fit improvement of the theme we are considering to deepen our abhorrence of all armed strife, and to intensify our desire for the permanent pacification of the nations, by contemplating those devilish scenes of crime, agony, and thronging horror, which necessarily belong to the intrinsic laws of war, as they have been freshly developed before our own eyes in the Crimean campaign. In the lapse of ages and the expansion of civilizing refinement, the immediate encounters of man have lost none of their horrid barbarity, but have gained incomparably in destructiveness. We should baulk [*sic*] the occasion of its just claim and deprive the subject in hand of half its power, did we not receive anew into our docile minds and shuddering sensibilities the old, old lesson of the terrific crimes and cruelties inevitably wrapt up in war. We are apt to think these things belong only to the past; but the ancient tales have just now been re-enacted, with aggravations unknown before. Those horrors which first made a human battle the frightful wonder of the universe remain yet, and men are still convertible into wolves and demons. Such an array of infernal engines, of such tremendous execution, directed with such deadly precision, as that which circled Sebastopol with a blazing coil of volcanoes whose swift eruptions stunned the Chersonese, raining on the devoted city and troops hailstorms of red-hot iron in thousands of tons and showers of exploding death, is without parallel in history. More frenzied conflicts, accompanied by greater fatality, or more intolerable features of disgusting laceration and outrage,—the pillage and stripping of the dead, the deliberate bayonetting and shooting of the wounded as they lay, helpless and supplicating,—than some of those just closed, are nowhere revealed in the savage annals of antiquity. Some of the sights of carnage and mangled corruption afforded by this war, on gory plain, and in fetid hospital, and beside the huge pits filled with indiscriminate heaps of dead men and horses, with layers of lime between, were unquestionably as horrible as any sights ever gazed on by human eyes. O, in the sweet name of mercy, how can such deeds be done by brother men? Why will they not submit their discordant wills to the attuning voice and hand of friendly umpirage, beneath the all-seeing eye of God?

# CHAPTER NINE

## RELIGIOUS FREEDOM

———◆———

*The religion, then, of every man must be left to the conviction and conscience of every man; and it is the right of every man to exercise it as these may dictate. This right is in its nature an unalienable right. It is unalienable because the opinions of men, depending only on the evidence contemplated by their own minds, cannot follow the dictates of other men. . . . We maintain, therefore, that in matters of religion, no man's right is abridged by the institution of civil society, and that religion is wholly exempt from its cognizance.*
　　———JAMES MADISON: *A Memorial and Remonstrance to the Virginia General Assembly, 1785*

*Whoso would be a man, must be a nonconformist. He who would gather immortal palms must not be hindered by the name of goodness, but must explore if it be goodness. Nothing is at last sacred but the integrity of your own mind. Absolve you to yourself, and you shall have the suffrage of the world. . . . No law can be sacred to me but that of my nature. Good and bad are but names very readily transferable to that or this; the only right is what is after my constitution; the only wrong what is against it.*
　　———RALPH WALDO EMERSON: *Self-Reliance, 1841*

Sources of the quotations on the preceding page:

JAMES MADISON: Bernard Smith: *The Democratic Spirit* (New York: 1943, 2nd ed.), 104.

RALPH WALDO EMERSON: R. W. Emerson: *Emerson's Complete Works*, 11 v. (London: 1853–8, Riverside ed.), II, 51–2.

THE ideal of religious freedom or liberty affirms the right of the individual to worship or not worship, as he pleases. It demands the complete separation of the church and state, thus excluding the establishment of a state church sustained by taxation of all. It prohibits any preference shown to any religious sect in exercise of the right to vote or to hold office.

The colony of Rhode Island was the first place in the world where religious liberty was actually affirmed and tried in a political state. If the "soul liberty" of Roger Williams was not completely attained in other colonies, varying conditions of toleration were approached in Pennsylvania, Maryland, and elsewhere.* Such conditions were encouraged by the need for attracting settlers to the vast land space of America, and by the character of settlers, many of whom were refugees in quest of religious peace.

The American Revolution hastened the drift towards freedom of conscience and separation of church and state. The pattern was set by the Virginia Statute of 1786, which enacted "that no man shall be compelled to frequent or support any religious worship, place or ministry whatsoever . . . nor shall otherwise suffer on account of his religious opinions or belief; but that all men shall be free to profess, and by argument to maintain, their opinion in matters of religion, and that the same shall in no wise diminish, enlarge or affect their civil capacities." Penned by Jefferson, this statute on religious liberty was passed through the efforts of James Madison, George Nicholas, and other Virginians.

* Even in Rhode Island the eighteenth-century record was marred by an enactment of uncertain date that limited citizenship and eligibility for public office to Protestant Christians.

Yet the Revolution left much unfinished business, for a distinct Protestant preference was embedded in most state constitutions. Seven states through test oaths confined officeholding exclusively to Protestants, and others had additional handicaps for Catholics and others. Congregationalism reigned supreme as the established church in all New England except for Rhode Island. Even in New England, however, John Leland raised a powerful cry for religious liberty in *The Rights of Conscience Inalienable* (1791) (1). More important, the national arrangements in the Northwest Ordinance of 1787 and in the Federal Constitution (Article VI and Amendment 1) were remarkably liberal. In the decade that followed the writing of the Constitution the separatists received new support from Thomas Paine's *Age of Reason* (1794–6); and the separatist spirit reflected in this document eradicated test laws from many state constitutions.

In the Jeffersonian era complete separation of church and state gathered momentum. John Leland struck at the Connecticut test acts in 1801 in *A Blow at the Root,* which contributed to the disestablishment of the Congregational Church in 1818. Baptists, Presbyterians, Catholics, and Jews found allies in a common cause to which William Plumer lent his great influence and Abraham Bishop his sharp pen (2). Jacob Henry fought the exclusion of Jews from the North Carolina legislature in 1809 (3). Thomas Kennedy's plea in 1818 and thereafter that the Maryland "Jew bill" ought to be passed not only "to do justice to the long oppressed Hebrews" but also to establish a general principle long overdue, reflects a militant temper. Yielding to its force in 1822, New York removed the test oath that barred Catholics.

The Jacksonian period witnessed the violence and bigotry of militant Protestantism. The "No Popery" crusade was stimulated by the influx of Irish Catholics and other immigrants and by the Western revivalists like the Reverend Charles G. Finney, who in the thirties were fanning the fires of crusading Protestantism. The latent animus flared into open violence in Boston in 1829. It reached a climax in the burning of the Ursuline Convent in Charlestown, Massachusetts, August 11, 1834. What was most appalling was the general acquiescence in such mob action in the face of the warnings of preachers and statesmen (6). Amid rising religious hysteria, Richard M. Johnson's refusal to discontinue Sunday mails (4) reaffirmed his faith in separation of church and state. The Rochester Friends of Liberal Principles and Equal Rights, following the argument on separation presented by Zelotes Fuller of Philadelphia, *The Tree of Liberty* . . . (1830), added their voices in 1831, approving Johnson's stand for complete separation (5). The saintly Abner Kneeland in 1834–8 waged his lost cause in Massachusetts "to protect all of every belief and unbelief respecting religion." (7)

Before merging with the greater conflagration of the Mexican War and the slavery question, the spreading flames of anti-Catholicism proved very destructive. Virulent anti-Catholicism was nurtured by the American Protestant Union, headed in 1841 by Samuel F. B. Morse, the inventor of the telegraph. It entered national politics as American Nativism in 1840–4, with antiforeign as well as anti-Catholic biases, and reached a climax of mob violence in Philadelphia in the summer of 1844, when lives were lost and a church burned. The Protestant crusade poured into the Know-Nothing movement, which came into being in 1849 and reached an apogee in 1854–5 before it was absorbed by the passions of the approaching Civil War. This flood of bigotry was denounced by statesmen like Governor William Henry Seward of New York and Governor Henry A. Wise of Virginia.

Transcendentalism proved a stalwart bulwark of freedom. It was rooted in the belief in the divinity of human nature, and its flowering was prepared by Unitarianism and Universalism. Ralph Waldo Emerson pleaded the cause of nonconformance and individual liberty. Theodore Parker struck blows against all that shackled man's nature and bred social inequality (8). The freethinkers found their Massachusetts champion in John W. Le Barnes (9), who in 1853 continued the struggle for complete separation along battle lines marked out by Abner Kneeland.

Horace Mann fought the advocates of sectarian education in the public schools. "If, then," he argued, in his *Twelfth Annual Report for 1848,* "a government would recognize and project the rights of religious freedom, it must abstain from subjugating the capacities of its children to any legal standard of religious faith with as great fidelity as it abstains from controlling the opinions of men." * In similar vein Jeremiah S. Black, a distinguished jurist wrote:

> The manifest object of the men who framed the constitu-
> tion of this country, was to have a *State without religion* and
> a *Church without politics*—That is to say, they meant that
> one should never be used as an engine for any purpose of
> the other. . . . Our fathers seem to have been perfectly sin-
> cere in their belief that the members of the Church would
> be more patriotic, and the citizens of the State more re-
> ligious, by keeping their respective functions entirely sep-
> arate. For that reason they built up a wall of complete and
> perfect partition between the two.†

---

1.

### *John Leland:*
### THE RIGHTS OF CONSCIENCE INALIENABLE ‡
### [1791]

*A Baptist clergyman, John Leland (1754–1841) was born in
Massachusetts. He moved to Virginia, where he became a
fervent exponent of religious liberty, advocating the repeal of
discriminatory legislation. Although nominated to the Virginia Constitutional Convention as an opponent of the Federal Constitution, he campaigned for his rival when he
became convinced that the Federal Constitution would not
interfere with religious freedom. At a Baptist General Convention he proposed the abolition of slavery. Returning to
Massachusetts, he championed disestablishment in New England in pamphlets such as* The Rights of Conscience In-

* Horace Mann: *Life and Works of Horace Mann,* 5 v. (Boston: 1891),
IV, 334.
† From an address, September 17, 1856 on "Religious Liberty" in J. S.
Black: *Essays and Speeches* (New York: 1885), 53.
‡ John Leland: *Writings of the Late Elder John Leland* (New York:
1845), 184, 184–5, 187, 191–2.

*alienable. His advocacy of Jeffersonian Republicanism and
Jacksonian Democracy was the political correlative of his religious liberalism, which he reaffirmed in* A Blow at the Root
(1801).

"Does a man, upon entering into social compact, surrender his
conscience to that society, to be controlled by the laws thereof;
or can he, in justice, assist in making laws to bind his children's
consciences before they are born?" I judge not, for the following
reasons:

*First.* Every man must give an account of himself to God, and
therefore every man ought to be at liberty to serve God in a way
that he can best reconcile to his conscience. If government can
answer for individuals at the day of judgment, let men be controlled by it in religious matters; otherwise, let men be free.

*Second.* It would be sinful for a man to surrender that to man,
which is to be kept sacred for God. A man's mind should be always open to conviction, and an honest man will receive that doctrine which appears the best demonstrated: and what is more
common than for the best of men to change their minds? Such are
the prejudices of the mind, and such the force of tradition, that
a man who never alters his mind, is either very weak or very
stubborn. How painful then must it be to an honest heart, to be
bound to observe the principles of his former belief, after he is
convinced of their imbecility? And this ever has, and ever will
be the case, while the rights of conscience are considered alienable.

*Third.* But supposing it was right for a man to bind his *own*
conscience, yet surely it is very iniquitous to bind the consciences
of his children—to make fetters for them before they are born, is
very cruel. And yet such has been the conduct of men in almost
all ages, that their children have been bound to believe and worship as their fathers did, or suffer shame, loss, and sometimes life,
and at best to be called dissenters, because they dissent from that
which they never joined voluntarily. . . .

*Fourth.* Finally, religion is a matter between God and individuals: the religious opinions of men not being the objects of civil
government, nor in any way under its control. . . .

Is uniformity of sentiments, in matter of religion, essential to
the happiness of civil government? Not at all. Government has no

more to do with the religious opinions of men, than it has with the principles of mathematics. Let every man speak freely without fear, maintain the principles that he believes, worship according to his own faith, either one God, three Gods, no God or twenty Gods; and let government protect him in so doing, i.e., see that he meets with no personal abuse, or loss of property, for his religious opinions. Instead of discouraging him with proscriptions, fines, confiscations or death, let him be encouraged, as a free man, to bring forth his arguments and maintain his points with all boldness; then, if his doctrine is false, it will be confuted, and if it is true, (though ever so novel,) let others credit it. . . .

The duty of magistrates is, not to judge of the divinity or tendency of doctrines; but when those principles break out into overt acts of violence, then to use the civil sword and punish the vagrant for what he has done, and not for the religious phrenzy that he acted from.

It is not supposable that any established creed contains the whole truth, and nothing but the truth; but supposing it did, which established church in the world has got it? All bigots contend for it, each society cries out, "the temple of the Lord are we." . . . So when one creed or church prevails over another, being armed with a coat of mail, law and sword, truth gets no honor by the victory. Whereas if all stand upon one footing, being equally protected by law, as citizens, (not as saints,) and one prevails over another by cool investigation and fair argument, then truth gains honor; and men more firmly believe it, than if it was made an essential article of salvation by law.

Truth disdains the aid of law for its defence—it will stand upon its own merit. The heathen worshipped a goddess, called truth, stark naked, and all human decorations of truth, serve only to destroy her virgin beauty. It is error, and error alone, that needs human support; and whenever men fly to the law or sword to protect their system of religion, and force it upon others, it is evident that they have something in their system that will not bear the light, and stand upon the basis of truth. . . .

This certificate law is founded on this principle, "that it is the duty of all persons to support the gospel and the worship of God." Is this principle founded in justice? Is it the duty of a deist to support that which he believes to be a cheat and imposition?

Is it the duty of a Jew to support the religion of Jesus Christ, when he really believes that he was an imposter? Must the Papists be forced to pay men for preaching down the supremacy of the pope, who they are sure is the head of the church? . . . If we suppose that it is the duty of all these to support the Protestant Christian religion, as being the best religion in the world; yet how comes it to pass, that human legislatures have a right to force them so to do? I now call for an instance, where Jesus Christ, the author of his religion, or the apostles, who were divinely inspired ever gave orders to, or intimated that the civil powers on earth, ought to force people to observe the rules and doctrine of the gospel. . . .

It is the duty of men to love God with all their hearts, and their neighbors as themselves; but have legislatures authority to punish men if they do not; so there are many things that Jesus and the apostles taught, that men ought to obey, which yet the civil law has no concern in. . . .

How mortifying must it be to foreigners, and how far from conciliatory is it to citizens of the American states, that when they come into Connecticut to reside, they must either conform to the religion of Connecticut, or produce a certificate? Does this look like religious liberty, or human friendship? Suppose that man,* whose name need not be mentioned, but which fills every American heart with pleasure and awe, should remove to Connecticut for his health, or any other cause, what a scandal would it be to the state, to tax him to support a Presbyterian minister, unless he produced a certificate, informing them that he was an Episcopalian.

. . . The federal constitution certainly had the advantage of any of the state constitutions, in being made by the wisest men in the whole nation, and after an experiment of a number of years trial upon republican principles; and that constitution forbids Congress ever to establish any kind of religion, or require any religious test to qualify any officer in any department of federal government. Let a man be Pagan, Turk, Jew or Christian, he is eligible to any post in that government. So that if the principles of religious liberty, contended for in the foregoing pages, are supposed to be fraught with Deism, fourteen states in the Union are now fraught with the same. But the separate states have not

* George Washington.

surrendered that supposed right of establishing religion to Congress. Each state retains all its power, saving what is given to the general government, by the federal constitution. The assembly of Connecticut, therefore, still undertake to guide the helm of religion; and if Congress were disposed, yet they could not prevent it, by any power vested in them by the states. Therefore, if any of the people of Connecticut feel oppressed by the certificate law, or any other of the like nature, their proper mode of procedure will be to remonstrate against the oppression, and petition the assembly for a redress of the grievance.

2.

*Abraham Bishop:*
PROOFS OF A CONSPIRACY AGAINST CHRISTIANITY *
[1802]

> *Abraham Bishop (1763–1844) was born in New Haven of a respected and well-to-do family. After gaining admittance to the bar, he went off to Europe, where, like his classmate Joel Barlow, he was profoundly influenced by the French Revolution. He returned to teach school, lecture, and engage in various jobs. In a rock-ribbed Federalist community, he was an ardent supporter of Jefferson and was appointed collector of the port in 1803. In a series of pamphlets similar to this one he attacked the alliance of the church and state and the arch-conservatism of the Federalists.*

But mere personal freedom was not the only object [of the American Revolution]: the mind of man had been enslaved for centuries, and its strongest fetters had been put on by the clergy. Toleration became a favorite theme and the people resolved that religion was a connection between God and man; that as every man was to render account for himself he ought to think and decide for himself, and that the mind ought always to be balanced by the greatest weight of evidence.—This was a point of resolu-

* Abraham Bishop: *Proofs of a Conspiracy against Christianity and the Government of the United States; Exhibited in Several Views of the Union of Church and State in New England* (Hartford, Conn.: 1802), 106–7, 124–5, 166.

tion, which church and state could not endure. An experiment of this would have destroyed all dignities in the church, have exploded all establishments, and have reduced even the most powerful of the clergy to the simple elements of sense and usefulness. Hard lot indeed that a dominion over the conscience, which had been gained by the labor of a century, should be wholly lost, and that common people should read and expound their bibles! This would be lowering the ambassadors at once and destroying a kind of influence, which our American nobles would need for the re-establishment of the old order of things: for amidst all the ardors of the revolution every subtle unionist kept sight of the doctrines of the old school, and resolved that when a proper season should arrive, the people of this country should be as the people of other countries, the nation should be as great as other nations, and our leaders in church and state like those of other countries.

The people have seen that religion and liberty had always been in danger, and that this danger *arose wholly* from the fact that those, who excited alarms about them, had their exclusive management, and that neither could exist within the region of their examples and power—and to the doctrines of passive obedience and non-resistance they opposed the manly sentiment, "THAT RE-BELLION AGAINST TYRANTS IS OBEDIENCE TO GOD."

Such revolutionary sentiments appeared rational in the days of the revolution: they were well understood by the people: they were all susceptible of practice; but the application of them would have been ruin to our unionists, the champions of the throne and the altar. They hated such sentiments with a cordial hatred, and from this hatred they were led to those measures, which have degraded the people more rapidly than their most sanguine hopes could have calculated, and these measures have assumed the form of a conspiracy in that very union of church and state, where the passions of the country have concentered their strength. . . .

Church and state are subtle: they will pretend that they are gaining strength even in the midst of debility: but their strength will be that of convulsions. They will precede your elections with false reports of forced loans and augmented salaries or some others equally false and to their purpose—they will abuse republican candidates—they will intimidate the weak—they may reduce us for a season: but we begin to work with solid capital—the republicans, who act with us openly, will be constant—those, who are opposed to us, must be knowingly opposed to the government of a majority and to every general principle, which their leaders formerly taught.

Their cause, their past means, their certain duplicity are so many arguments that they must fail. THE POLITICAL CLERGY ARE THE WORST ENEMIES OF THE CHURCH. THE FEDERAL LEADERS ARE THE WORST ENEMIES OF OUR REVOLUTION, AND BOTH ARE ENEMIES TO THE COMMON PEOPLE.

This declaration is not the *sentiment* of one man only, but of many thousands in New-England, whose united force and responsibility will be competent to its defence.

## 3.

### *Jacob Henry:*
### SPEECH IN THE NORTH CAROLINA LEGISLATURE *
### [1809]

*Jacob Henry was elected to the North Carolina lower House in 1808. When he was re-elected in 1809, his right to remain seated was challenged because he was a Jew. He stood his ground, and Roman Catholics, similarly excluded, rallied to his support. His speech was included in* The American Orator *and was cited in the Maryland Assembly in 1818 by the Hon. H. M. Brackenridge as "part of our education as Americans." Although Henry retained his seat, he won only a partial victory, for the discriminatory clause remained in the state constitution. Not until 1868 did North Carolina adopt a constitution that granted full religious liberty and equality.*

I certainly, Mr. Speaker, know not the design of the Declaration of Rights made by the people of this State in the year 1776, if it was not to consecrate certain great and fundamental rights and

* From J. H. Wheeler: *Historical Sketches in North Carolina from 1584 to 1851* (Philadelphia: 1851), II, 74–6. (In the interest of readability we have used this text, which is substantially the same as the original manuscript in the State Legislative Records, State Department of Archives and History, Raleigh, North Carolina.)

principles, which even the Constitution cannot impair; . . . If, then, a belief in the Protestant religion is required by the Constitution to qualify a man for a seat in this house, and such qualification is dispensed with by the Declaration of Rights, the provision of the Constitution must be altogether inoperative; as the language of the Bill of Rights is, "that all men have a natural and inalienable right to worship Almighty God according to the dictates of their own consciences." It is undoubtedly a natural right, and when it is declared to be an inalienable one by the people in their sovereign and original capacity, any attempt to alienate [it] either by the Constitution or by law, must be vain and fruitless.

It is difficult to conceive how such a provision crept into the Constitution, unless it is from the difficulty the human mind feels in suddenly emancipating itself from fetters by which it has long been enchained; and how adverse it is to the feelings and manners of the people of the present day every gentleman may satisfy himself by glancing at the religious belief of the persons who fill the various offices in this State: there are Presbyterians, Lutherans, Calvinists, Mennonists, Baptists, Trinitarians, and Unitarians. But, as far as my observation extends, there are fewer Protestants, in the strict sense of the word, used by the Constitution, than of any other persuasion; for I suppose that they meant by it, the Protestant religion as established by the law in England. . . .

If a man should hold religious principles incompatible with the freedom and safety of the State, I do not hesitate to pronounce that he should be excluded from the public councils of the same; and I trust if I know myself, no one would be more ready to aid and assist than myself. But I should really be at a loss to specify any known religious principles which are thus dangerous. It is surely a question between a man and his maker, and requires more than human attributes to pronounce which of the numerous sects prevailing in the world is most acceptable to the Deity. If a man fulfills the duties of that religion, which his education or his conscience has pointed to him as the true one, no person, I hold, in this, our land of liberty, has a right to arraign him at the bar of any inquisition; and the day, I trust, has long passed, when principles merely speculative were propagated by force; when the sincere and pious were made victims, and light-minded bribed into hypocrites.

The purest homage man could render the Almighty was in the sacrifice of his passions and the performance of his duties. That the ruler of the universe would receive with equal benignity the various offerings of man's adoration, if they proceeded from the heart. Governments only concern the action and conduct of man, and not his speculative notions.

Who among us feels himself so exalted above his fellows as to have a right to dictate to them any mode of belief? Shall this free country set an example of persecution, which even the returning reason of enslaved Europe would not submit to? Will you bind the conscience in chains, and fasten conviction upon the mind in spite of the conclusions of reason and of those ties and habitudes which are blended with every pulsation of the heart? Are you prepared to plunge at once from the sublime heights of moral legislation into the dark and gloomy caverns of superstitious ignorance? Will you drive from your shores and from the shelter of your Constitution, all who do not lay their oblations on the same altar, observe the same ritual, and subscribe to the same dogmas? If so, which, among the various sects into which we are divided, shall be the favored one?

I should insult the understanding of this House, to suppose it possible that they could ever assent to such absurdities; for all know that persecution in all its shapes and modifications, is contrary to the genius of our government, and the spirit of our laws, and that it can never produce any other effect than to render men hypocrites or martyrs. . . .

Nothing is more easily demonstrated than that the conduct alone is the subject of human laws, and that man ought to suffer civil disqualification for what he does, and not for what he thinks. The mind can receive laws only from Him, of whose Divine essence it is a portion; He alone can punish disobedience; for who else can know its movements, or estimate their merits? The religion I profess, inculcates every duty which man owes to his fellow-men; it enjoins upon its votaries the practice of every virtue, and the detestation of every vice; it teaches them to hope for the favor of heaven exactly in proportion as their lives have been directed by just, honorable, and beneficent maxims. . . . At any rate, Mr. Speaker, I am sure that you cannot see anything in this religion, to deprive me of my seat in this house. So far as relates

to my life and conduct, the examination of these I submit with
cheerfulness to your candid and liberal construction. What may
be the religion of him who made this objection against me, or
whether he has any religion or not I am unable to say. I have
never considered it my duty to pry into the belief of other members of this house. If their actions are upright and conduct just,
the rest is for their own consideration, not for mine. I do not seek
to make converts to my faith, whatever it may be esteemed in the
eyes of my officious friend, nor do I exclude anyone from my
esteem or friendship, because he and I differ in that respect. The
same charity, therefore, it is not unreasonable to expect, will be
extended to myself, because in all things that relate to the State
and to the duties of civil life, I am bound by the same obligations
with my fellow-citizens, nor does any man subscribe more sincerely than myself to the maxim, "Whatever ye would that men
should do unto you, do ye so even unto them, for such is the law
and the prophets."

## 4.

### Richard M. Johnson:
### ON THE SABBATH MAILS *
### [January 19, 1829]

*Richard Mentor Johnson (1780–1850) was born in Ken-*
*tucky. As a Congressman, he vigorously supported Jefferson's*
*embargo and later favored the war with England, in which*
*he was wounded. As Senator he strove to persuade Congress*
*to enact a Federal law, such as he had sponsored in Ken-*
*tucky, abolishing imprisonment for debt. While chairman of*
*the Senate Committee of Post Offices and Railroads, he is-*
*sued this Report on the Sabbath Mails. President Andrew*
*Jackson picked him as vice-presidential running mate of Mar-*
*tin Van Buren. He was popular with labor because of his po-*
*sition on debts, Sunday mail, and education. The New York*
*Journeymen Bookbinders Association hailed him as the "fear-*
*less and uncompromising champion of religious freedom."*

* *American State Papers*, 38 v. (Washington, D.C.: 1832–61), Class
VII, pp. 211, 212.

It should, however, be kept in mind that the proper object of government is to protect all persons in the enjoyment of their religious as well as civil rights, and not to determine for any whether they shall esteem one day above another, or esteem all days alike holy.

We are aware that a variety of sentiment exists among the good citizens of this nation on the subject of the Sabbath day; and our Government is designed for the protection of one, as much as for another. The Jews, who in this country are as free as Christians, and entitled to the same protection from the laws, derive their obligation to keep the Sabbath day from the fourth commandment of their decalogue, and, in conformity with that injunction, pay religious homage to the seventh day of the week, which we call Saturday. One denomination of Christians among us, justly celebrated for their piety, and certainly as good citizens as any other class, agree with the Jews in the moral obligation of the Sabbath, and observe the same day. There are also many Christians among us who derive not their obligation to observe the Sabbath from the decalogue, but regard the Jewish Sabbath as abrogated. . . .

With these different religious views the committee are of opinion that Congress cannot interfere. It is not the legitimate province of the Legislature to determine what religion is true, or what is false. Our Government is a civil and not a religious institution. Our constitution recognises in every person the right to choose his own religion, and to enjoy it freely, without molestation. Whatever may be the religious sentiments of citizens, and however variant, they are alike entitled to protection from the Government, so long as they do not invade the rights of others.

The transportation of the mail on the first day of the week, it is believed, does not interfere with the rights of conscience. The petitioners for its discontinuance appear to be actuated from a religious zeal, which may be commendable if confined to its proper sphere; but they assume a position better suited to an ecclesiastical than to a civil institution. They appear, in many instances, to lay it down as an axiom, that the practice is a violation of the law of God. Should Congress, in their legislative capacity, adopt the sentiment, it would establish the principle that the Legislature is a proper tribunal to determine what are the laws of God. It would involve a legislative decision in a religious controversy, and on a point in which good citizens may honestly differ in opinion, without disturbing the peace of society, or endangering its liberties. If this principle is once introduced, it will be impossible to define its bounds. Among all the religious persecutions with which almost every page of modern history is stained, no victim ever suffered but for the violation of what Government denominated the law of God. To prevent a similar train of evils in this country, the constitution has wisely withheld from our Government the power of defining the divine law. It is a right reserved to each citizen; and while he respects the equal rights of others, he cannot be held amenable to any human tribunal for his conclusions.

Extensive religious combinations to effect a political object are, in the opinion of the committee, always dangerous. This first effort of the kind calls for the establishment of a principle, which, in the opinion of the committee, would lay the foundation for dangerous innovations upon the spirit of the constitution, and upon the religious rights of the citizens. If admitted, it may be justly apprehended that the future measures of Government will be strongly marked if not eventually controlled, by the same influence. All religious despotism commences by combination and influences; and when that influence begins to operate upon the political institutions of a country, the civil power soon bends under it; and the catastrophe of other nations furnishes an awful warning of the consequence.

Under the present regulations of the Post Office Department, the rights of conscience are not invaded. Every agent enters voluntarily, and, it is presumed, conscientiously, into the discharge of his duties, without intermeddling with the conscience of another. Post offices are so regulated as that but a small proportion of the first day of the week is required to be occupied in official business. In the transportation of the mail on that day, no one agent is employed many hours. Religious persons enter into the business without violating their own consciences, or imposing any restraints upon others. Passengers in the mail stages are free to rest during the first day of the week, or to pursue their journeys, at their own pleasure. While the mail is transported on Saturday, the Jew and the Sabbatarian may abstain from any agency in carrying it, from conscientious scruples. While it is transported on the first day of the week, another class may abstain, from the same religious scruples. The obligation of Government is the same to both of these classes; and the committee can discover no principle on which the claims of one should be more respected than those of the other, unless it should be admitted that the consciences of the minority are less sacred than those of the majority. . . .

If the principle is once established that religion, or religious observances, shall be interwoven with our legislative acts, we must pursue it to its ultimatum. We shall, if consistent, provide for the erection of edifices for the worship of the Creator, and for the support of Christian ministers, if we believe such measures will promote the interests of Christianity. It is the settled conviction of the committee that the only method of avoiding these consequences, with their attendant train of evils, is to adhere strictly to the spirit of the constitution, which regards the General Government in no other light than that of a civil institution, wholly destitute of religious authority.

What other nations call religious toleration, we call religious rights. They are not exercised in virtue of governmental indulgence, but as rights, of which Government cannot deprive any portion of citizens, however small. Despotic power may invade those rights, but justice still confirms them. Let the National Legislature once perform an act which involves the decision of a religious controversy, and it will have passed its legitimate bounds. The precedent will then be established, and the foundation laid for that usurpation of the divine prerogative in this country, which has been the desolating scourge to the fairest portions of the old world. Our constitution recognises no other power than that of persuasion for enforcing religious observances.

### 5.

*The Friends of Liberal Principles and Equal Rights in Rochester:*
RESOLUTIONS *
[January, 1831]

*The appearance in the* Free Enquirer *of the resolutions of this organization indicate its spiritual affinity with the Working Men's Party of New York and Philadelphia. The Friends*

* New York *Free Enquirer* (February 12, 19, 1831), III, 122, 131.

*of Liberal Principles and Equal Rights opposed ecclesiastical influence and the attempt to stop Sunday mails. It favored equality of education and the abolition of imprisonment for debt, and sympathized with the contemporaneous revolutions in Europe.*

. . . The law of this state as it now stands on the statute book and is expounded by our courts, it is believed infringes upon this provision of the Constitution, and discriminates and creates a preference in religious sentiment. . . . A *preference* is given when an individual professing the required belief is admitted to take an oath, and when one not possessed of this belief is excluded. And when we consider how many of our civil rights depend upon the oath of the individual interested . . . we cannot but be struck with the dangerous and fatal tendency of the required qualification, and also alarmed at its palpable violation of our natural and constitutional rights. A clearer case of religious *preference* and discrimination cannot well be supposed.

In accordance with the above views the following Resolution is recommended:

*Resolved,* That while we regard the belief in a Supreme Being as essential to the good order of society, and lament the want of such belief in any individual, yet that we view that the requirement of it, a violation of that part of the Constitution, which guarantees the free enjoyment of religious profession without preference or discrimination. . . .

Let our motto be,—Equal Rights—Equal, practical, moral (but *not* sectarian) Education—Perfect freedom of opinion—No legislation for or against Religion. Then shall we be indeed LIBERAL; and our only opponents, the crafty, the designing, the *illiberal.*

*Resolved,* That perfect freedom of opinion upon religious subjects, is the birth-right of every man—is guaranteed to us by the Constitution, and cannot be resigned without an abandonment of the sacred principles for which our patriot fathers bled.

*Resolved,* That the history of the past teaches us that encroachments upon the religious liberties of mankind are the work of crafty men, brought about gradually and by almost imperceptible means, disguised under a pretence for improving the condition of man—and that it behooves us to watch narrowly the movements of a hireling clergy, when their chief object seems to be the accumulation of wealth and political power.

*Resolved,* That the amassing of immense wealth by the American Bible Society, and the investing the same in permanent securities, affords reason to believe that its managers have some ulterior objects in view, incompatible with the spirit of our free institutions.

*Resolved,* That the simultaneous presentation of petitions to Congress from all parts of the Union last winter, praying Congress to stop the transportation of the United States mail on the first day of the week commonly called Sunday, on the ground that said day is holy time, is alarming, inasmuch as it exhibits a singular concert of action in an attempt to induce Congress to sanction by law, the sanctity of the first day of the week.

*Resolved,* That the pertinacity with which these men adhere to their plan of sanctifying Sunday by a law of the land—both by petitions for stopping the mail and closing the post offices on Sunday, furnishes to us conclusive evidence that there is an organized party in this country, striving to procure an union of church and state, by inducing Congress to recognise their creed as the only true one. . . .

*Resolved,* That we believe ignorance to be, too often, the true cause of superstition, crime, and misery, and that we consider the latter evils can only be eradicated by an equal system of *moral, liberal* and *practical education,* giving the children of the poor equal opportunity for instruction with the children of the rich.

*Resolved,* That we consider imprisonment for debt as odious, and unjust—wrong in principle, and unequal in its operation—and confounding the poor but honest debtor with the rich rogue—and that we recommend to the legisature of this state, the entire abolition of this relic of barbarism.

*Resolved,* That as Liberals, we will strive to promulgate the sentiments contained in the foregoing Address and Resolutions. . . .

H. BISSELL, *Chairman*
D. PERRIN,
T. ANDREWS, *Secretaries.*

# 6.

## Report on the Destruction of the Ursiline Convent *
## [1834]

*A Miss Rebecca Reed had fled from the Ursiline Convent bearing tales of cruelty. The flight and disappearance of Sister Mary John led to wild rumours of murder. The latent fury of anti-Catholic feeling exploded on the night of August 11, and a mob drove the inmates of the convent from their beds, sacked the building, and set it on fire. News of the outrage caused a public meeting to be called at Faneuil Hall. A committee to investigate was appointed, including Charles G. Loring as chairman, Horace Mann, and others. After three weeks of investigation, they issued this report. Unfortunately, more anti-Catholic violence followed, and still more would have occurred had not Bishop Fenwick ordered aroused Irish laborers to refrain from reprisals.*

The fact that the dwelling of inoffensive females and children, guiltless of wrong to the persons, property, or reputation of others, and reposing in fancied security under the protection of the law, has been thus assaulted by a riotous mob, and ransacked, plundered, and burnt to the ground, and its terrified inmates, in the dead hour of night, driven from their beds into the fields; and that this should be done within the limits of one of the most populous towns of the commonwealth, and in the midst of an assembled multitude of spectators; that the perpetrators should have been engaged for seven hours or more in the work of destruction, with hardly an effort to prevent or arrest them; that many of them should afterwards be so far sheltered or protected by public sympathy or opinion, as to render the ordinary means of detection ineffectual; and that the sufferers are entitled to no legal redress from the public, for this outrage against their persons and destruction of their property, is an event of fearful import as well as of the profoundest shame and humiliation.

It has come upon us like the shock of the earthquake, and has

---

* *Documents Relating to the Ursiline Convent in Charleston, Massachusetts* (Boston: 1842), 16–17.

disclosed a state of society and public sentiment of which we believe no man was before aware.

If for the purpose of destroying a person, or family, or institution, it be only necessary to excite a public prejudice, by the dissemination of falsehoods and criminal accusations, and under its sanction to array a mob; and there be neither an efficient magistracy nor a sense of public duty or justice sufficient for its prevention, and if property may be thus sacrificed without the possibility of redress, who among us is safe?

The cry may be of bigotry to-day, and heresy to-morrow; of public usurpation at one time, and private oppression at another; or any other of those methods by which the ignorant, the factious, and the desperate, may be excited; and the victim may be sacrificed without protection or relief.

It is hoped that the fearful warning thus suddenly given, enforced as it is by similar occurrences in other states, will arrest the public attention; check the prevailing disposition to give credence to injurious and calumnious reports; will produce throughout the country a higher sense of the qualifications requisite for magisterial office; and lead to amendments and improvements of our laws, which are thus found so sadly defective.

And above all, may it rebuke the spirit of intolerance thus unexpectedly developed, so fatal to the genius of our institutions, and unrestrained, so fatal to their continuance. If there be one feeling which more than any other should pervade this country, composing, as it were, the atmosphere of social life, it is that of enlightened toleration, comprehending all within the sphere of its benevolence, and extending over all the shield of mutual protection.

## 7.

### *Abner Kneeland:*
### SPEECH BEFORE THE SUPREME COURT OF MASSACHUSETTS *
### [March, 1836]

*Abner Kneeland (1774–1844), born in Massachusetts, began editing in 1827 the Olive Branch, a paper devoted to "free inquiry, pure morality and rational Christianity." Founding the First Society of Free Enquirers, he began in 1831 to expound pantheistic views in the Boston Investigator, probably the first rationalist journal in America. The magazine attacked churches, opposed Whigs, and supported Andrew Jackson. In the issue of December 20, 1833, he used words that led to his indictment for a "certain scandalous, impious, obscene, blasphemous, and profane libel of and concerning God." He was convicted after a fourth trial in November, 1835. Acting as his own counsel, the old man appealed to the Supreme Court of Massachusetts, where in 1836 he vainly presented his plea. A petition bearing 170 illustrious names and a remonstrance of 230 citizens were unsuccessful in sparing him from a sixty-day jail sentence. Upon emerging, he emigrated to a Free Enquirer colony in Iowa, where he played a part in Democratic politics.*

If none are to enjoy protection from being hurt, molested or restrained in person, liberty or estate, except those, whom the Legislature and the Courts, may consider to be of "religious profession or sentiments," the provision in the [Massachusetts] Bill of Rights is altogether superfluous, for those who are of "religious profession or sentiments," according to the opinion of the Legislature and the Courts, never can be in danger of being hurt, molested or restrained, in person, liberty or estate, for their "religious profession or sentiments," and therefore need no protection. They need no shield against religious persecution, for they are already guarded by the shield of the Government. They do not punish, even in Spain, those who hold to the "religious profession or sentiments" of the Government and people. They only burn, in the

---

* *Speech of Abner Kneeland, Delivered Before the Full Bench of Judges of the Supreme Court, in His Own Defence for the Alleged Crime of Blasphemy* (Boston: 1836), 31–2.

Inquisition, the heretics, those who were not of the "religious profession or sentiments," which the Government approved. . . . It is for those, who hold a profession and sentiments which are not considered by the Government and people as religious, for those alone are in danger of persecution. This Bill of Rights is a shield for the weak, not a weapon of persecution for the hand of the strong. It is intended for those who alone need protection— those who profess unpopular sentiments respecting religion.

The [Massachusetts] Constitution intended to protect all of every belief and unbelief respecting religion. The framers of the Constitution did not intend to have any Inquisition here. They did not intend their Legislature and Courts should have any power to interfere, in what they have no right to interfere, in matters of belief or unbelief respecting religion. They intended to have no heresy laws, and no heresy persecutions, and therefore abolished and prohibited all penal laws and penal persecutions on the subject of religion in this Commonwealth. Who shall say what are religious profession or sentiments? . . . One Court will set up one standard of faith, and another Court a different standard,— thus our Constitution will be subverted, and the rights of conscience forever prostrated. To this construction an Inquisition would be far preferable. An Inquisition would have many advantages that would not be found in our Courts, if they are to say what are and what are not religious sentiments. The rule of faith and mode of worship with us would be subject to continual fluctuations and changes, as different religious sects were dominant in power, and no man would know what to believe to exempt him from persecution. What are religious sentiments to day [*sic*] may be irreligious sentiments to-morrow, and vice versa. An Inquisition would at least preserve uniformity in their persecutions.

Here I wish to enter my most solemn protest against this Court, or any other undertaking to decide between a man and his God; to undertake to say, for any one but themselves, what are or what are not religious sentiments. I deny the right, I deny the authority of any human tribunal to interfere, or to undertake to decide in this matter. My religion is my own. . . . Hence I do not hold myself amenable to any human authority on account of my religion. It is an inalienable right; and can only be parted with with life. If any man or any human authority ever had the power to

establish a uniformity of faith, it was Constantine the Great. But
he failed in the attempt, and so has every attempt failed since.
Men would not conform, neither would they abstain from avowing
contrary sentiments to the established creed, although banishment and death were the dreadful consequences.


8.


*Theodore Parker:*
THE STATE OF THE NATION *
[November 28, 1850]

*Theodore Parker (1810–60) was born in Massachusetts, the
son of a poor New England farmer and mechanic. After being
ordained as a minister, he was denounced by the orthodox
for his insistence on man's direct communion with God. But
his friends offered him the ministry of the new Twenty-
Eighth Congregational Society of Boston. In this Thanks-
giving Day sermon of November 28, 1850, Parker shows his
love of individual liberty and of social equality. In him religious, political, and social theory and action were integrally
fused. He was a transcendentalist crusader in the cause of
nonconformance and of human freedom on all fronts. His
fervent abolitionism led him to give active aid to fugitive
slaves and he was one of the secret committee that abetted
John Brown's project. His defiance of unconscionable laws
drew inspiration from the American Revolutionary tradition,
of which he said: "We are a rebellious nation: our whole
history is treason."*


Now in public opinion and in the laws of the United States, there
are two distinct political ideas. I shall call one the Democratic
and the other the Despotic idea. Neither is wholly sectional; both
chiefly so. Each is composed of several simpler ideas. Each has
enacted laws and established institutions. This is the democratic
idea: that all men are endowed by their Creator with certain
natural rights which only the possessor can alienate; that all men

* Francis Power Cobbe (ed.): *The Collected Works of Theodore Parker,*
14 v. (London: 1863–72), III, 244–5, 248–9.

are equal in these rights; that amongst them is the right to life, liberty, and the pursuit of happiness; that the business of the government is to preserve for every man all of these rights until he alienates them.

This democratic idea is founded in human nature, and comes from the nature of God, who made human nature. To carry it out politically is to execute justice, which is the will of God. This idea, in its realization, leads to a democracy, a government of all, for all, by all. Such a government aims to give every man all his natural rights; it desires to have political power in all hands, property in all hands, wisdom in all heads, goodness in all hearts, religion in all souls. I mean the religion that makes a man self-respectful, earnest, and faithful to the infinite God, that disposes him to give all men their rights, and to claim his own rights at all times; the religion which is piety within you, and goodness in the manifestation. Such a government has laws, and the aim thereof is to give justice to all men; it has officers to execute these laws, for the sake of justice. Such a government founds schools for all; looks after those most who are most in need; defends and protects the feeblest as well as the richest and most powerful. The state is for the individual, and for all the individuals, and so it reverences justice, where the rights of all, and the interests of all, exactly balance. It demands free speech; everything is open to examination, discussion, "agitation," if you will. Thought is to be free, speech to be free, work to be free, and worship to be free. Such is the democratic idea, and such the State which it attempts to found.

The despotic idea is just the opposite:—That all men are *not* endowed by the Creator with certain natural rights which only the possessor can alienate, but that one man has a natural right to overcome and make use of some other men for his advantage and their hurt; that all men are *not* equal in their rights; that all men have *not* a natural right to life, liberty, and the pursuit of happiness; that government is *not* instituted to preserve these natural rights for all. . . .

This leads to aristocracy in various forms, to the government of all by means of a part and for the sake of a part. In this state of things political power must be in few hands; property in few hands; wisdom in few heads; goodness in few hearts, and religion in few souls. I mean the religion which leads a man to respect himself and his fellow-men; to be earnest, and to trust in the infinite God; to demand his rights of other men and to give their rights to them. . . .

Each idea has its allies, and it is worth while to run our eye over the armies and see what they amount to. The idea of despotism has for its allies:—

1. The slaveholders of the South with their dependents; and the servile class who take their ideas from the prominent men about them. This servile class is more numerous at the South than even at the North.

2. It has almost all the distinguished politicians of the North and South; the distinguished great politicians in the Congress of the nation, and the distinguished little politicians in the Congress of the several states.

3. It has likewise the greater portion of the wealthy and educated men in many large towns of the North; with their dependents and the servile men who take their opinions from the prominent class about them. And here, I am sorry to say, I must reckon to greater portion of the prominent and wealthy clergy, the clergy in the large cities. . . .

Then on the side of the democratic idea there are:—

1. The great mass of the people at the North; farmers, mechanics, and the humbler clergy. This does not appear so at first sight, because these men have not much confidence in themselves, and require to be shaken many times before they are thoroughly waked up.

2. Besides that, there are a few politicians at the North who are on this side; some distinguished ones in Congress, some less distinguished ones in the various legislatures of the North.

3. Next there are men, North and South, who look at the great causes of the welfare of nations, and make up their minds historically, from the facts of human history, against despotism. Then there are such as study the great principles of justice and truth, and judge from human nature, and decide against despotism. And then such as look at the law of God, and believe Christianity is sense and not nonsense; that Christianity is the ideal for earnest men, not a pretence for a frivolous hypocrite. Some of these men are at the South; the greater number are in the North;

and here again you see the difference between the son of the
Planter and the son of the Puritan. . . .


9.


*John W. Le Barnes:*
MEMORIAL TO THE MASSACHUSETTS CONSTITUTIONAL CONVENTION *
[May 12, 1853]

> *On May 12, 1853, Mr. Schouler, a delegate from Boston to
> the Massachusetts Constitutional Convention of 1853, pre-
> sented a petition for John W. Le Barnes and four hundred
> other Bostonians. Their Memorial vainly strove to delete
> Article Two of the Declaration of Rights on the duty "to
> worship the Supreme Being." Two years later, however, the
> Eighteenth Amendment to the Massachusetts Constitution
> did prohibit the use of school funds for any sectarian school.*


MEMORIAL

*To the Convention assembled to revise the Constitution of
Massachusetts:*

The Undersigned, in behalf of the petition of himself and others,
citizens of Massachusetts, asking *"that the Constitution be so
amended, that the doctrines of no Religion shall be established* or
recommended therein, and that no religious or ecclesiastical *interference with the Laws of the State, its Official Institutions, or its
Public Schools, shall be hereafter possible in this Commonwealth,"*
begs leave respectfully to submit, that this amendment is desired,
for these, among other reasons:—

1ST. Because government is justly ordained for the protection
of the rights of its people, and not for the propagation of religion,
and, therefore, its constitutional power and its legislative functions
should be civil, not ecclesiastical.

2D. Because, whenever the doctrines or interests of any religion
are particularly patronized by State, or in anywise incorporated in
its official institutions, then Church and State connection becomes

---

* John W. Le Barnes: *Memorial to the Massachusetts Constitutional
Convention, Presented May 12, 1853* (n.p.; n.d.) 3–5, 8–10.

established, exclusiveness is generated, and that democracy of religion, which affirms that all systems should bear a legal equality to each other and to the government, essentially abrogated.

3D. Because Church influence in matters of government is vitally antagonistic to the existence of a democratic state,—it being a truth, attested by the sad and universal experience of the human race, that whenever and wherever Church interests and governmental power have been consolidated, their union has proved the most prolific source of tyranny, outrage and manifold wrong, which the world has ever known. And the startling facts to which history points mankind may well be a warning to us, to make sure, whenever the people's remodeling hand may touch their Constitution of government, that no point therein shall be left unguarded against that sleepless foe of Liberty, *Religious interference with Civil Law.*

4TH. Because the Public Schools are established for the immediate benefit of all the children of the State, or whatever religious or irreligious antecedents, and not for the benefit of any particular class, nor for the inculcation of any theological bias; and therefore, the interference of any religious sect or system therewith, is a perversion of the educational design, and an imposition upon the rights of the people.

5TH. Because there now obtains in this Commonwealth, a positive union of the State government thereof with the dominant Church, manifest in certain statutes and legal customs authorized and sustained by the present Constitution, and by force whereof a portion of your people are deprived of their just rights, and subjected to certain onerous evils, of which we ask briefly to speak.

The first clause of the second article of the Declaration of Rights in the Constitution affirms that *"it is the right as well as the duty of all men in Society, publicly and at stated seasons to worship the Supreme Being, the great Creator and Preserver of the Universe."* That all men, who choose to do so, have a right to worship whatsoever they think proper, your Memorialists by no means dispute. But when a government declares it to be the DUTY of its people to worship *any thing,* either God or the Christ of the Christians, the Allah of the Mussulmen, the Bramah of the Indians, or the Deities of any faith whatsoever, then, in the opinion of your Memorialists, government oversteps its just province and interferes with individual liberties; and we therefore protest against such provisions in the Constitution, believing that to worship or not to worship, is an optional right with all men, and wholly outside of any legislative control. . . .

We hold that the right to doubt underlies the right to believe; that a man has the same right to be an Infidel or an Atheist, that he has to be a Christian; that the State, having to take cognizance of men's acts and not of their opinions, has no authority whatever to make any religious faith a test of citizenship; that it has nothing to do with the belief or the unbelief of any individual, nor with any publication of sentiments; but that it is held, by the first principles of republicanism, to conserve the entire freedom of all its people, to know citizens, not sects, and to guarantee to all men an absolute equality before the law. . . .

Again, you are aware that the public funds are now often applied to the support of sectarian colleges. The injustice of this we desire to bring particularly to your notice. We hold, that the treasury of the State is the property of the whole people of the State, and belongs no more to any party in religion than it does to any party in politics, or to any commercial interest. And we hold, that the government of the State has no more right to give the people's money to sustain an ecclesiastical school, than it has to open the treasury to any ordinary manufacturing corporation. . . .

We submit, that all laws for enforcing the observance of the Sunday are projected upon a religious creed; that Constitutional authority, therefore, is a direct Constitutional establishment of religion; and we hold that such establishment is contrary to every principle of a free government; that the State can only enforce the creeds of any church, or the observance of any religious ceremonial, but by sacrificing its democracy, and becoming *"an engine of combined clerical and political usurpation."* And we believe that not only is Constitutional authority for enacting and enforcing Sunday laws most undemocratic in theory, but that such laws, organizing into political power the theologic idea of the sacredness of Sunday, help deny to that day some of its most wholesome advantages, by making penal many uses of it which would contribute to the social comfort, the happiness and the enlightenment of the people. Moreover, it is the benefit of the working classes that these laws particularly strike down.

# CHAPTER TEN

## SHARE THE LAND

———◄◆►———

*Thus Speculation is perpetually operating to scatter, to retard and barbarize our pioneer settlements, compelling each settler to wander off into the untrodden wilderness unless he is able and willing to pay five times what he should pay for his location. Banish the speculator or break up his pestilent calling, and our new lands will be settled far more compactly than they now are, since almost every one would prefer to have neighbors if he were not required to pay too much for the privilege. Then Schools, Mills, Churches and all the incidents of civilized society would spring up where they are now precluded by the sparseness of population, and we should cease to hunt the poor Aborigines from Lands which they need and we do not.*

———HORACE GREELEY: *On the Land Question, January 24, 1852*

*For if a man has a right on earth, he has a right to land enough to rear a habitation on. If he has a right to live, he has a right to the free use of whatever nature has provided for his sustenance—air to breathe, water to drink, and land enough to cultivate for his subsistence. For these are the necessary and indispensable means for the enjoyment of his inalienable rights, of life, liberty, and the pursuit of happiness. And is it for a Government that claims to dispense equal and exact justice to all classes of men, and that has laid down correct principles in its great chart of human rights, to violate those principles, and its solemn declarations in its legislative enactments?*

———GALUSHA A. GROW *of Pennsylvania: Speech in Congress, March 30, 1852*

Sources of the quotations on the preceding page:

HORACE GREELEY: *The New York Tribune* (January 24, 1852).

GALUSHA A. GROW: *Congressional Globe*, 32nd Cong., 1 sess., 1852, Appendix, p. 427.

———◆———

THE earliest emigrants to the Atlantic frontier beheld the vision of a homestead and a farm. This hope for a share in the land persisted and was transmuted through the years into a right to the soil. The early belief in the "natural right" to land was vigorously expressed by the Reverend John Higginson of Salem to Governor Andros about 1687: ". . . The right to Land Soil we had received from God according to his Grand Charter to the Sons of Adam and Noah, and with the consent of the Native Inhabitants." * Similarly, a Jersey yeoman in 1746 claimed: "No Man is naturally intitled [sic] to a greater Proportion of the Earth, than another. . . ." † The recurring waves of westward moving settlers came to regard the vast public domain of the United States as the common property of the nation. They had equitable claims springing not only from the toil of the occupant but also from the expenditure of money and blood.

In a common sacrifice the original states ceded to the nation their western lands; and little more than a half-century later, the United States had acquired the Louisiana Territory, Florida, Oregon, the Mexican Cession, and the Gadsden Purchase. The disposal of this great empire was thus a problem for the Federal government. From the founding of the Republic, the Hamilton-Jefferson cleavage affected Federal land policy. Hamilton believed in securing quick returns in cash, by selling land in large blocks to speculators, who could make large profit at the expense of the actual settlers. Jefferson favored selling land in small parcels at low prices, a policy that would be primarily in the interest

* *The Andros Tracts*, 3 v. (Boston: 1868–74), I, 124.
† *New York Weekly Post-Boy*, June 9, 1746.

of the real farmer. The imprint of Hamilton's policy was dominant at least until the Pre-emption Act of 1841, but the persistent demand for land grew with swelling force. It was expressed by the settlers in Illinois in their "Petition to Arthur St. Clair, Governor of the Northwestern Territory" in 1790 (1), in which the squatters asked for land and a prior claim to their improved lands. The provisions of the Land Act of 1796 for public auctions of 640-acre blocks at a minimum of $2.00 per acre provoked angry objections in the Fourth Congress from William Findley, James Holland, and Jeremiah Crabb. These men were "for encouraging farmers, and against engrossing." John Evert Van Alen of New York in 1796 vainly strove to reduce the size of allotments in behalf of the small holder (2). From the settlers along the Ohio in 1797 came the request for free land after three years of occupancy. Although Congress bent to the extent of allowing 320-acre blocks to be sold on four-year credit west of the Muskingum River, it did not yield.

In the Jeffersonian era agitation for free homesteads continued. John Parrish's *Remarks on Slavery* (1801) and Thomas Brannagan's *Serious Remonstrance* (1805) argued for land grants to poor Negroes. Petitions for free land continued to reach Congress from Mississippi (1804) and also from Indiana (1806, 1814). In 1812, Representative Jeremiah Morrow of Ohio presented a similar request from "the True American Society," whose members held "every man entitled by nature to a portion of the soil of the country." The Irish Emigrant Societies of New York (3) and Baltimore memorialized Congress in 1818, requesting land for newcomers on easy credit terms. Such pressures led to the Land Act of 1820, which reduced the minimum price to $1.25 per acre and the allotment to 80 acres. There followed more petitions for a fair share of land from Maryland (4), Illinois, and Missouri (5).

In the Jacksonian period small farmers and mechanics pushed their demands more relentlessly. Thomas Hart Benton called for an inquiry into the expediency of donating lands to settlers, and in 1828 a House committee on public lands reported favorably on such a policy. Langdon Byllesby (6) argued the natural right of the occupier and toiler on the land to own it. *The Mechanics'*

*Free Press,* October 25, 1828 (7), published a memorial to Congress asserting that the "birth-right in the soil" belonged to those who tilled it. Radical mechanics of New York, through the *Report of the Committee of Fifty* . . . (1829), insisted upon equal distribution of the land. Small wonder that President Jackson in his message of December 4, 1832, declared that "the public lands should cease as soon as practicable to be a source of revenue." Labor supported this policy in the National Trades' Union's resolutions in 1834, which favored the granting of land to settlers (8); so did Paul Brown's *The Radical: and Advocate of Equality* in 1835 (9).

The added weight of organized labor brought the Western farmer's cause to fulfillment. The demands of the frontiersmen had at last wrested from Congress the Pre-emption Act of 1841, under which each settler had a right to the first chance to buy unsold land upon which he had "squatted." George Henry Evans championed the homestead cause through his columns in *The Working Men's Advocate.* The National Reform Association (10), supported not only by Evans but Thomas A. Devyr, John Commerford, and Lewis Masquerier (11), agitated for "the right of the people to the soil." Horace Greeley's *New York Tribune* in 1852 presented lengthy statements on the "land reformers." Augustine J. H. Duganné plucked from his *Iron Harp* (13) the cry that "God gave equal earth to mortals."

The inexorable pressure of this public agitation forced political recognition. In 1842, land was donated to a special category of settlers in Florida; in 1850 a similar policy was applied to Oregon. In 1846, Felix G. McConnell of Alabama and Andrew Johnson of Tennessee introduced homestead bills. Despite the persistent support of Johnson of Tennessee, George W. Julian of Ohio (12), and Galusha A. Grow of Pennsylvania, no general bill for free land actually came to a vote in Congress until 1852, and then it was defeated in the Senate. The Free-Soil party declared its support for such a measure in 1848 and again in 1852. The Pittsburgh platform of the Free-Soil Democrats, August 11, 1852, ran: *

. . . 11. That all men have a natural right to a portion of

* E. Stanwood: *A History of Presidential Elections* (Boston: 1892, 3rd ed.), 188.

the soil; and that, as the use of the soil is indispensable to life, the right of all men to the soil is as sacred as their right to life itself.

12. That all the public lands of the United States belong to the people, and should not be sold to individuals nor granted to corporations, but should be held as a sacred trust for the benefit of the people, and should be granted in limited quantities, free of cost, to landless settlers.

But no major party took up the cause until 1860. The opposition was strong. The Southerners feared the spread of free-soil settlements. Eastern manufacturers and land speculators were disturbed by the economic impact of westward emigration. The former feared the loss of labor supply; the latter, the competitive acquisition of land. The Know-Nothing party disliked expending the national heritage upon foreign immigrants.

In 1860, Galusha A. Grow of Pennsylvania pushed through Congress a land-reform measure, albeit amended to include a charge of twenty-five cents an acre. President James Buchanan vetoed this bill. But the Republican Party included the homestead plank in its platform. Its victory and Southern secession opened the way. On May 20, 1862, Abraham Lincoln's signature sealed the passage of the Homestead Act. It was the fulfillment of a dream—but a dream clouded by the prior claims of railroads and speculators and by the financial burdens of beginning afresh.

---

1.

*James Piggott and Others:*
PETITION FOR LAND FROM ILLINOIS SETTLERS *
[May 23, 1790]

*The "Petition to Arthur St. Clair, Governor of the North-western Territory, from Settlers in Illinois," May 23, 1790, accurately reflects the attitude of "squatters" who knew that*

* *American State Papers*, 38 v. (Washington, D.C.: 1832–61), Class VIII, Vol. I, p. 20.

*they were on land that legally belonged to "absentee land-
lords." Quite naturally they felt that the actual occupiers of
the wilderness ought to have some equitable claim to the
land that they improved. Hence they banded together and
addressed their request to General Arthur St. Clair, under
whom James Piggott (c. 1739–99), one of their leaders, had
served in the Revolution. Piggott became a resident of Illinois county and rose to be a justice of the quarter sessions.
In 1797 he established a ferry service that earned him an
honorary citizenship to St. Louis.*

*Great Run, May 23, 1790*

We, your petitioners, beg leave to represent to your excellency
the state and circumstances of a number of distressed but faithful
subjects of the United States of America, wherein we wish to continue, and that, under your immediate government; but, unless
our principal grievance can be removed by your excellency's encouragement, we shall despair of holding a residence in the State
we love. The Indians, who have not failed one year in four
past to kill our people, steal our horses, and at times have killed
and drove off numbers of our horned cattle, render it impossible
for us to live in the country any way but in forts or villages, which
we find very sickly in the Mississippi bottom; neither can we cultivate our land, but with a guard of our inhabitants equipped
with arms; nor have we more tillable land, for the support of
seventeen families, than what might be easily tilled by four of us:
and as those lands whereon we live are the property of two individuals, it is uncertain how long we may enjoy the scanty privileges we have here; nor do we find by your excellency's proclama-
tion that those of us which are the major part, who came to the
country since the year 1783, are entitled to the land we improved,
at the risk of our lives, with a design to live on. Those, with many
other difficulties which your excellency may be better informed
of by our reverend friend Mr. James Smith, hath very much
gloomed the aspect of a number of the free and loyal subjects of
the United States. In consideration of which your petitioners
humbly request, that, by your excellency's command, there may
be a village, with in-lots and out-lots sufficient for families to subsist on, laid out and established in or near the Prairie de Morivay.
We know the other American settlers near the Mississippi to be

in equal deplorable circumstances with ourselves, and, consequently, would be equally benefited by the privileges we ask; and that those of us that came to the country and improved land since the year 1783, may be confirmed in a right of pre-emption to their improvements, is the humble request of your petitioners; and we, as in duty bound, shall ever pray.

JAMES PIGGOT, *and forty-five others.*

To His Excellency ARTHUR ST. CLAIR, Esq.
*Gov. and Commander-in-Chief of the territory of the U. S. Northwest of the River Ohio.*

2.

*John Evert Van Alen:*
REMARKS ON LAND ALLOTMENTS *
[March 4 and April 5, 1796]

*John Evert Van Alen (1749–1807) was born in New York. He engaged in extensive farming operations, conducted a general store, and practiced civil engineering. He held office as assistant county-court justice, as United States Congressman from 1793 to 1799, and as New York State Assemblyman in 1800 and 1801. While in Congress he vainly strove to amend the Land Act of 1796 so as to reduce the size of allotments in favor of the small holder.*

Mr. Van Allen observed, that the selling one half the land in lots of three miles square, or 5,760 acres, as contemplated by the bill, appeared to him to be a measure replete with such evident advantages to that part of the wealthy class of citizens whom they had been in the habit of styling speculators, that he conceived it his duty to state his objections to it, and, if in his power, to obtain an alteration. He moved an amendment which went to selling no larger lots than 640 acres.

He considered the land now about to be sold as the joint and common property of every citizen in the United States, and that

* *Annals of Congress*, 4th Cong., 1 sess., 1796, pp. 422, 865, 866, 867.

therefore it ought to be disposed of in such manner as would best promote the general interest of the whole community: that, if this idea was a correct one, it would naturally lead to an inquiry what would be such disposition: the result of which he believed would be, first, to accommodate actual settlers; and secondly, to bring money into the Treasury; and added, that, as he conceived the first to be the greatest object, it ought to be attended to, even if it would in some degree require a sacrifice of the other. But he hoped it would not be opposed, if it could be shown that it might be accomplished without any additional expense or loss to the public. . . .

He then adverted to the sales, and observed, that actual settlers might become purchasers from the Government of lots of 160 and of 640 acres; that none would be prohibited from purchasing; that of course the competition would be increased, and he believed, the land sell best; that as the large lots would, at the minimum price, amount to 11,520 dollars, settlers were by no means likely to become purchasers, as it was presumable few could command such a sum, and therefore they were as effectually prohibited as if a clause to that effect had been inserted in the bill; that the competition would of course be lessened, and the land purchased chiefly, if not altogether, by speculators, and consequently sell for a less price. One reason which had been assigned for this measure was, that all purchasers might be accommodated. He was willing to accommodate all such as were to be settlers, but no others. No one man, he thought, wanted to purchase so large a lot for his own actual improvement.

It had been said, the price fixed upon the land would prevent speculation. He believed that might be the case if the fixed price was the full value, or so nearly so, as not to afford a profit. But these gentlemen understood figures, and considered more the per centage they could make than the high or low price they paid for an article.

It had been frequently said, and he believed, this was an excellent tract of land; that some of it would sell at from three to eight dollars per acre; and if so, would it not, he asked, afford a handsome profit?

He said, it was fair to presume no land would be purchased to sell again, which could not afford a reasonable prospect of at least

25 per cent. profit. This, at the lowest stated price, would be half a dollar per acre; that about five millions of acres were contemplated to be sold in large lots, which, at this rate, would eventually be a loss of two millions five hundred thousand dollars, besides the difference of the granting fees, (which he made no doubt would net a profit,) and answer no other purpose than that of enriching individuals; that to sell the land when it was not wanted for actual settlement, or in a manner which would preclude settlers from becoming purchasers, would be making a sacrifice: that, he thought, could only be justifiable under peculiar circumstances, such as did not now exist; that it was but another way of paying a high rate of interest, and establishing a bad precedent; that, to sell the land in such large lots would, he thought, operate as an indirect tax upon the cultivator—of so much at least as the small lots would sell per acre more than the large—not to say anything about the rise of the land, which would be increased in proportion to the settlements they made, without benefiting the Government. In short, he considered it as an act of favoritism towards that class of citizens, for which he could see no reason, unless it was their having paid a considerable proportion of the Domestic Debt to the original holders. But he never heard they had been sufferers by it, and he presumed this would not be assigned as the reason.

Mr. V. A. concluded by observing that he did not, from anything he had said, wish to be considered as an advocate for an Agrarian law. He disavowed any such principle, but did not hesitate to acknowledge himself a friend to equality—at least so far as it respects the rights of individuals—and hoped, that if ever any discrimination between different classes of citizens should be thought proper, the poorer and middle class would not be considered the least deserving the care and attention of Government.

3.

## The Memorial of the New York Irish Emigrant Association *
[1818]

*Irish Emigrant Societies were formed in Philadelphia, New York, Boston, and elsewhere. Their primary purpose was to combat the frauds perpetrated on newcomers. But their sustained interest in the immigrant is indicated in this Memorial to Congress. The New York Society was headed by Thomas Addis Emmet, an Irish-born lawyer and director of the Society of United Irishmen. In 1804 he came to New York, where his eloquence rapidly brought him to prominence.*

*The memorial of the New York Irish emigrant association, to the honorable the senate and house of representatives, in congress assembled,*

RESPECTFULLY SHEWETH,

That your memorialists, while they presume most respectfully to solicit your attention to the helpless and suffering condition of the numerous foreigners, who, flying from a complicated mass of want and misery, daily seek an asylum in the bosom of the United States, are emboldened by the recollection that a liberal encouragement to the settlement of meritorious strangers, has always characterized the government and constituted authorities of this union. The wise and brave fathers and founders of its independence, held out to the oppressed and suffering of every nation the consoling assurance, that in this country, at least, they should find a refuge and a home. The successors of these illustrious men have continued to redeem, in calmer and happier times, the pledge made to philosophy and benevolence amidst perilous scenes of distress and difficulty. From this humane and beneficent policy, America has reaped a rich and happy harvest. She has added to the national resources, the moral and physical strength to be derived from so many thousands and tens of thousands, who, actuated by attachment to her free constitution, have

* *Niles' Register,* XIV (1818), 211–12.

adopted the nation where liberty has made, and is making, her most glorious stand, as the country of their choice.

. . . In the extended territory and scattered population of the United States, however, and under their free and blessed institutions, it is an unquestionable and important truth, that every increase of inhabitants, when wisely and judiciously distributed and settled, adds to the social comforts and productive industry of the whole, and that the excess of population which cannot be considered as giving stability to the various governments of Europe, if suffered or encouraged to settle here, would incalculably increase our wealth and strength; but that accession is doubly valuable which also brings to the common fund, with a mass of laborious industry, unalterable attachment to the laws and constitution of the country. And surely to give a wise direction to that industry, and to secure by well placed kindness that attachment, are amongst the noblest exercises of legislative authority.

Your memorialists beg leave respectfully to represent, that at no period since the establishment of American independence, have the people of Europe, particularly the laboring classes, discovered so great a disposition as at present to emigrate to the United States. But the people of Ireland, from the peculiar pressure under which that country has so long been placed, have flocked hither in the greatest numbers, and perhaps under the most trying and necessitous circumstances. . . .

A serious consideration of these circumstances induces your memorialists to hope and most earnestly but respectfully to request on behalf of those, whose interests they urge, that a portion of unsold lands may be set apart, or granted to trustees, for the purpose of being settled by emigrants from Ireland on an extended term of credit. The conditions of this grant your memorialists wish to be such as may give to the settlers its entire benefit, and may exclude all private speculation in others.

They also beg leave to suggest, after contemplating the various uncultivated tracts which invite the labor of man, that a situation peculiarly adapted for a settlement of that description, might be found amongst the lands lately purchased in the Illinois territory.

Your memorialists are fully sensible that many of their most persuasive arguments in favor of their application, must be addressed, and will not be addressed in vain, to the benevolence and sympathies of the legislature, but they also confidently appeal to its wisdom and patriotism. The lands to which they have alluded being frontier and remote, are neither likely to be speedily exposed to sale, to be rendered by cultivation subservient to the general prosperity, nor by settlement, conducive to the general strength. The portion which might be granted on an extended credit, would probably be paid for almost as soon as if it had not been brought into the market before its regular turn. During that time, in which it would otherwise remain unproductive, (and therefore unprofitable) thousands of families would have acquired opulence, would have benefitted the country by its cultivation, by the establishing of schools, the opening of roads, and the other improvements of social and civilized life. They would form a nucleus, round which a more abundant population would rapidly accumulate, and all the contiguous lands would be largely increased in value. The small loss which might appear to be sustained by the suspension of interest on the credit, if it should have any existence, will be abundantly compensated by the money and labor that must be almost immediately expended on works of general utility, which the convenience and necessity of the settlers will naturally induce them to accomplish.

But who can calculate the physical or moral, or even the pecuniary advantages in time of war, of having such a strong and embattled frontier; the Irish emigrant, cherished and protected by the government of the U[nited] States, will find his attachments to their interests increase in proportion to the benefits he has acquired; he will, with enthusiasm, love the country that affords him the means of honorable and successful enterprize, and permits him to enjoy unmolested and undiminished the fruits of his honest industry. Ingratitude is not the vice of Irishmen;—fully appreciating his comparative comforts, and the source from whence they flow, the Irish emigrant will himself cherish, and will inculcate on his children, an unalterable devotion to his adopted and their native country. Should hostilities approach him in that quarter, whether in the savage form of the tomahawk, and scalping knife, or with the deadlier weapons of civilized warfare,

—the Irish settlers and their hardy sons will promptly repel the invasion, drive back the war upon the enemy, and give to our extended frontier security and repose.

Your memorialists therefore humbly pray your honorable body to receive and listen favorably to their application.

*For President—*THOMAS ADDIS EMMET,
*First Vice-President—*DANIEL M'CORMICK,
*Second Vice-President—*JAMES M'BRIDE,
*Secretaries,* { JOHN W. MULLIGAN,
                 WILLIAM SAMPSON,
*Treasurer—*ANDREW MORRIS.

*Standing Committee.*

| | |
|---|---|
| *John Chambers,* | *William Edgar, jun.* |
| *Matthew Carroll,* | *Robert Fox,* |
| *Thomas Kirk,* | *John Meyher,* |
| *Dennis M'Carthy,* | *James R. Mullany,* |
| *John R. Skiddy,* | *Matthew L. Davis,* |
| *Robert Swanton,* | *Wm. James M'Neven,* |
| *John Heffernan,* | *Dennis H. Doyle,* |
| *James Sterling,* | |

[DELEGATE—MR. JOHN CHAMBERS.]

## 4.

## REPORT ON PUBLIC LANDS FOR EDUCATION IN THE MARYLAND SENATE *
[January 30, 1821]

*This Report was submitted to the Maryland Senate by Mr. Virgil Maxcy, chairman of a committee on education and public instruction. The committee was aware of the need for a "general diffusion of knowledge" and "the present embarrassed state of our pecuniary concerns" of providing for this.*

* *Report with Sundry Resolutions Relative to Appropriations of Public Land for the Purposes of Education, to the Senate of Maryland, January 30, 1821* (Concord, N.H.: 1821), 4, 9–10.

*One thousand copies were directed to be printed for distribution.*

. . . The object of those Resolutions was to call the attention of congress, and the legislatures of the several states, to the Public Lands, as a fund, from which appropriations for the purposes of education may with justice be claimed, not only by Maryland, but all the original states, and three of the new ones. . . .

In whatever point of view therefore the public lands are considered, whether as acquired by purchase, conquest or cession, they are emphatically the *common property of the Union.* They ought to enure, therefore, to the common use and benefit of *all* the states, in just proportions, and cannot be appropriated to the use and benefit of any *particular* state or states, to the exclusion of the others, without an infringement of the principles, upon which cessions from states were expressly made, and a violation of the spirit of our national compact, as well as the principles of justice and sound policy.

So far as these lands have been sold, and the proceeds been received into the national treasury, all the states have derived a justly proportionate benefit from them:—So far as they have been appropriated for purposes of defence, there is no ground for complaint; for the defence of every part of the country is a common concern:—So far, in a word, as the proceeds have been applied to NATIONAL, and not to STATE purposes, although the expenditure may have been local, the course of the general government has been consonant to the principles and spirit of the Federal Constitution. But so far as appropriations have been made, in favour of any state or states, to the exclusion of the rest, where the appropriations would have been beneficial, and might have been extended to all alike, your committee conceive there has been a departure from that line of policy, which impartial justice, so essential to the peace, harmony, and stability of the union, imperiously prescribes.

## 5.

### MEMORIAL OF THE MISSOURI LEGISLATURE ON FEDERAL LAND POLICY *
#### [January 4, 1825]

*This memorial was an application of the Missouri legislature
to the United States Congress for a reduction in the price of
public lands and for a donation to actual settlers. It was communicated to the Senate on December 27, 1827 and represents a milestone in the development of Federal land policy
in the direction of the Homestead Act. Similar pleas came
from Illinois, Louisiana, and other Western states.*

*To the honorable the Senate and House of Representatives
of the United States of America in Congress assembled:*

The memorial of the general assembly of the State of Missouri
respectfully represents: That the interest and welfare of this State
are intimately connected with the measures which may be pursued by your honorable bodies in relation to the sale and settlement of the public lands of the United States.

This general assembly believe that it is a paramount desire
with your honorable bodies to appropriate these vast and fertile
regions of the west, the property of the nation, for supplying the
wants and promoting the happiness of its citizens. Our country
is peculiarly the asylum of the oppressed, and emphatically the
poor man's home. Every law, then, which opens before the poor
man the way to independence, which lifts him above the grade
of a tenant, which gives to him and his children a permanent rest-
ing and abiding place on the soil, not only subserves the cause of
humanity, but advances and maintains the fundamental principles of our government.

This general assembly also represent that the richest bodies of
land lay detached from each other in different parts of the State;
and the intermediate lands being of a poorer quality, must long,
and perhaps forever, remain unsold at the present price, to the
great injury as well of the United States as of this State. This gen-

* *American State Papers*, 38 v. (Washington, D.C.: 1832–61), Class
VIII, Vol. V, p. 36.

eral assembly therefore respectfully request of your honorable
bodies that provision may be made by law for the offering to sale
of the public lands at a minimum price of fifty cents per acre
where they shall have remained unsold at the present price for a
certain number of years. That where any of the public lands shall
remain unsold at the minimum price of fifty cents per acre, the
same may be granted in small fractions of a section to citizens
who will actually settle on and cultivate the same for a certain
length of time. This general assembly assure your honorable
bodies that the passage of such a law would, in their opinion, not
only promote the strength and prosperity of this frontier State,
but the happiness of thousands who, from the want of pecuniary
means, are compelled to remain in an anti-republican state of dependence on rich landlords. And your memorialists, &c.

    H. S. GEYER, *Speaker of the House of Representatives.*
    B. H. REEVES, *President of the Senate.*
*Approved January 4, 1825.*

                                 FREDERICK BATES.

## 6.

### Langdon Byllesby:
### THE SOURCES AND EFFECTS OF UNEQUAL WEALTH *
### [1826]

*Langdon Byllesby was a Philadelphia printer, inventor, and
journalist. Indebted to William Thompson, the "Ricardian
Socialist," he saw in producer co-operatives the salvation of
labor. The labor force as he saw it consisted of independent
artisans who were being strangled by the capitalist's control
of the machine. Harking back to Jefferson, he demanded that
labor no longer be deprived of its due share of the products
of its efforts. Land inheritance, he asserted, violated the "natural equality of rights" to acquire subsistence and property,
while technological improvements increased the power of
wealth over labor. To offset this power, he advocated the voluntary associations of mechanics.*

  * L. Byllesby: *Observations on the Sources and Effects of Unequal
Wealth; with Propositions toward Remedying the Disparity of Profit in Pur-
suing the Arts of Life, and Establishing Security in Individual Prospects and
Resources* (New York: 1826), 20–4.

"All men are born free and equal." The agency and offices of nature are equal and the same, in the production and endowment with life and sensation both one and the other. They are each invested with precisely the same mediums of pleasure and pain; with the same sources of want, and capacity for its relief; the same desire of enjoyment, and disposition to administer to its gratification; the same horror of misery, and inclination to pursue happiness. They are all alike placed on the earth, and provided with those physical powers that will enable them, either directly or by compensation, to derive their sustenance from its bosom; and an intuitive intimation given them, that so far as they exert those powers, they are entitled to the products. But, when arrived at maturity, and prepared to execute the functions to which nature and his necessities point, if one inquire, "Where is my portion of the earth, from whence to supply my wants?" the answer of civilized society, in its present state, is, "You can have none: it is all pre-occupied, and in possession of others." Should it be remarked, "Here is one who claims far more than is necessary for him, double what he can or doth use, and has been endowed by his Creator with no qualities or wants different from myself," the challenged defends it by saying, "True; but I have obtained the ownership of it according to the customs of society, and they protect me in continuing it. You must not, therefore, presume to infringe my right. However, if you are disposed to expend the labour of which you are capable in the cultivation of these lands, you shall therefor have so much of the products of your labour as will support life; but the excess must go to enrich and maintain me in ease, indolence, and luxurious enjoyment."

In palliation of this manifest injustice, and violation of natural equality of rights, it may be urged, that "to every one, there is no *positive* hindrance against his acquiring property, and enjoying the same immunities;" yet, when this plea is fairly examined, it will be found only a specious gilding, no way tending to avert or mollify the wretchedness inseparable from the system, but rather, on the contrary, to the promotion of dishonesty and crime. . . .

The late President of these states, whose wisdom and philosophy it is not yet time to question, has said, "The earth was given to mankind, to support the greatest number of which it is capable; and no tribe or people have a right to withhold from the wants of others more than is necessary for their own support and comfort;" * and if so, the congregation of vast portions of its surface under the power of an individual, beyond what is necessary to afford him ample means of subsistence and enjoyment, must be at war with this doctrine, especially when it is withheld from the general benefit on pretexts involving exclusive pleasure, or, as is common, for the purpose of speculation, in order to deprive those to whom it may be finally conveyed of half the profits of their labour for a long series of years. Under such countenance, there will, therefore, be but little audacity in asserting, that no one has a just *natural* right to occupy more of the soil than will, with a due portion of the physical labour of which he is capable bestowed thereon, afford him a fair share of the comforts of life and means of happiness; and whatever more he claims, or takes, must, in some shape or other, be unjustly withheld or taken from those who lack it, wherever talents and industry are equal in one and the other.

## 7.

### MEMORIAL TO CONGRESS ON THE LAND QUESTION †
### [1828]

*This* Memorial *to Congress was reproduced in the* Mechanics' Free Press *with a notation by the editor reading: "The following is a copy of a Memorial which will be presented to Congress at its next session."*

To the Honourable the Senate and the House of Representatives of the United States, in Congress assembled.

The undersigned citizens of the United States, respectfully suggest to Congress the propriety of placing all the Public Lands, without the delay of sales, within the reach of the people at large, by the right of a title of occupancy only.

Their reasonings on the case, to be brief, are as follows:

1ST. That until the Public Lands shall have been actually put under cultivation, it is clear they will be entirely useless.

* Mr. Monroe's Message to Congress, Dec. 2nd, 1817. [Note in original source.]

† *Mechanics' Free Press* (Philadelphia: October 25, 1828).

2DLY. That they are fully satisfied that the present state of affairs, must lead to the wealth of a few, and thus place within their reach the means of controlling all the lands of our country.

3DLY. That as all men must occupy a portion of the earth, they have, naturally, a birth-right in the soil: And that while this right shall be subject to the control of others, they may be deprived of life, liberty, and the pursuit of happiness.

4THLY. That hence, it is perceived by them, that a true spirit of independence can not be enjoyed, by the great body of the People, nor the exercise of freedom secured to them, so long as the use of the soil is withheld.

5THLY. That the General Government can be under no necessity of holding these Lands as an indemnity for existing appropriations nor for future expenditures. The National Debt, within a very few years, will have been liquidated: And the necessary tendency of the Revenue to the Treasury will then demand more legislation in order to keep its surplus judiciously diffused for the purposes of an efficient Circulating Medium, than for those of any future constitutional disbursements.

6THLY. That the mere sale of these Lands can give little ability to the people in sustaining national expenditures. As the relief thus to be derived, could only arise from resources at that time extant, it is clear that this would be but the shifting of existing resources, however insufficient, from the People to the Government. But by the widely extensive improvements of an Agricultural nature, which the general cultivation of these Lands would induce, the people would, against the hour of emergency, by large additions to the ordinary Revenue, have absolutely created the means of meeting all the prospective expenditures of the most generous administration of the General Government.

And, finally, that they deprecate every species of monopoly and exclusive privileges, and more especially all those which produce unnatural exclusions with relation to the Public Lands. But that it is further respectfully suggested to the Representatives of the People, that should any of the purchasers of these Lands for the purpose of speculation, conceive that they are to be injured by the operation of the proposed measure, for which, however, there can be but a remote apprehension entertained, your Memorialists recommend that the purchase money, with interest if necessary, be refunded to them: and that those Lands be thus suffered to revert again to the Government for the use of the People.

That it is the opinion of your Petitioners that, (the People themselves being, *de facto,* the Government) were the Public Lands thus perpetually held only to their use, it would be, perhaps, the only effectual prevention of future monopoly and the best safeguard of the American Republic.

That your Memorialists recommend to Congress that the Public Lands be reserved as a donation to the citizens of the United States in the character of perpetual leases, free from rent, and subject to revert to the Government when the lessee or his heirs fail to cultivate or occupy it in proper person, for—years together; providing that, in the future location of towns, &c. for general or public purposes, the incidental possessor of the soil, besides a reasonable compensation for it, shall only share and share alike, in the lots and other advantages thus to be derived.

That your Petitioners, therefore pray your Honourable Body to enact a law authorizing a Grant to any individual who shall apply for it, of the free use of so much of the Public Lands (not less, perhaps, than twenty nor more than forty acres) as they in their wisdom shall deem sufficient, and limiting its conditions to the principles above suggested.

8.

*Trades' Union National Convention:*
RESOLUTION ON LAND *
[August 29, 1834]

*In 1834 the General Trades' Union issued a call for a national convention, which met in New York City to form the loosely organized National Trades' Union that held conventions nationally until its disappearance in 1837. Mr. John Ferral, a Philadelphia delegate and chairman of the committee on resolutions, introduced the appended resolutions, which were unanimously adopted. These resolutions also concerned equal and universal education, long hours for women and children, illegal combination laws, and the theory that labor was the sole legitimate source of wealth.*

* *The Man* (New York: August 30, 1834).

The Committee to whom was referred the duty of drafting resolutions expressive of the views of the National Trades' Union Convention on the social, civil, and intellectual condition of the laboring classes, beg leave to report,

That whereas all the actions and pursuits of man have for their object the possession of happiness, . . .

And whereas the social, civil, and intellectual condition of the laboring classes of these United States, and the like classes in all countries, exhibit the most unequal and unjustifiable distribution of the produce of labor, thus operating to produce a humiliating, servile dependency, incompatible with the inherent natural equality of man.

And whereas each and every man is by nature compelled to consume the produce of labor in the supply to his necessary wants, moral justice would exact from every individual, when not incapacitated by natural imbecility or accident, a fair and full equivalent to society for that which he consumes, and also that he should contribute his due portion of labor towards the contingencies of society, for the protection and security he derives therefrom;

And whereas the accumulation of the wealth of society in the hands of a few individuals (which has been abstracted from the producers thereof by means of the erroneous customs, usages, and laws of society) is subversive of the rights of man, seeing that wealth or property only can be justly acquired in three ways, viz. 1st, by producing, 2d, by exchanging labor for labor in equal quantities, and 3d, by donation; it therefore becomes a duty imperative on every productive laborer, who values the liberties of his country, the welfare of the human family, and his own social happiness, to keep the evils that exist in society steadily in view, that knowing them, he may the more effectually direct his energies to destroy the causes from whence they arise, and by a well concerted union with his fellow laborers, concoct and carry out into practice such measures as will secure, at least to the present generation, the gratitude of their descendants, for their having barked the tree of Corruption, and nourished that of LIBERTY AND EQUALITY, without which life itself is a burden to its possessor;

Therefore, be it resolved, that this Convention, deeply impressed with the conviction, that the primary causes of all the evils and difficulties with which the laboring classes are environed, can be traced to the want of a correct knowledge of their own value as producers, and the just estimate of their resources, would recommend, that such of the working classes of these United States as have not already formed themselves into societies for the protection of their industry, do so forthwith, that they may by these means be enabled effectively to make common cause with their oppressed brethren, and the more speedily disseminate such knowledge as may be most conducive to their interests in their respective trades and arts, as well as their general interests as productive laborers. . . .

RESOLVED, that this Convention deprecate the system now practised in the disposal of the Public Lands, because of its violating the inherent rights of the citizen, seeing that the whole of the unseated lands belong unto the people, and should not be disposed of to the prejudice of any class of society each and every citizen having a just claim to an equitable portion thereof, a location upon which being the only just title thereunto.

RESOLVED, that this Convention would the more especially reprobate the sale of the Public Lands, because of its injurious tendency as it affects the interests and independence of the laboring classes, inasmuch as it debars them from the occupation of any portion of the same, unless provided with an amount of capital which the greater portion of them, who would avail themselves of this aid to arrive at personal independence, cannot hope to attain, owing to the many encroachments made upon them through the reduction in the wages of labor consequent upon its surplus quantity in the market, which surplus would be drained off, and a demand for the produce of mechanical labor increased, if these public lands were left open to actual settlers.

9.

*Paul Brown:*
THE RADICAL AND ADVOCATE OF EQUALITY *
[1835]

*Paul Brown was the author of several other books and pam-*
*phlets, including* Twelve Months in New-Harmony *(1827)*
*and (probably)* A Dialogue on Commonwealths *(1828). He*
*was a forceful exponent of equal landholdings as a basis for*
*social equality.*

We want an equalization of the property of lands and the main
resources of subsistence, so that we can have secured to us equal
opportunities of access to a comfortable livelihood, both as it respects employment and other means necessary to preserve health
and life. And we want assurance of the same access to all useful
knowledge that others have; that no set of men may in future
have the advantage of superior knowledge to cheat us out of any
of our rights. . . .

Another scandalous regulation they have which proceeds from
the same aristocratical spirit, is their wholesale disposal of the
public lands; by which no man can purchase less than one hundred dollars worth of the regular surveys, and he who is unfortunately too poor to be able to produce this sum, how much soever
he needs ground to cultivate, is barred from purchasing any at
all; while the purse-proud capitalist who never cultivates land,
wallowing in the luxury of a commercial city, is allowed to purchase thousands and thousands of acres which at his ease he
guards from the possession of the poor, or at every emergency
husbands their exigencies to his own account by accommodating
them with small quantities on the terms of three hundred per cent
profit. What a tantalizing delusion is the report so current abroad
among us, that the government lands (or United States lands)
are to be had for one dollar and a quarter per acre, when in fact
they are not sold by the acre at all!

If a poor man who has been barely able to lay by fifteen dollars

* Paul Brown: *The Radical: and Advocate of Equality* . . . (Albany,
N.Y.: 1835), 10, 71–2, 74–5.

with which to buy him a foothold upon earth, cannot have the worth of it in land on the public territory while millions of acres belonging to the government are offered for sale, for the reason or pretext that it is too small a sum to be received, it is because he does not live in a free country nor under a republican government, but under a tyrannically oppressive aristocracy. I shall insist, if we have public land for sale to individuals, it is tyranny for the United States to refuse to sell to a poor man fifteen dollars worth of land. . . .

But there can be no equality of condition, when one man is rich and another is poor. Equality of property, then, is necessary to equality of condition. An equal division of property cannot make it *remain* in an even state of equal distribution, while the trading-system exists, while a value is set on pre-eminence in individual wealth, while means are available for one to make himself richer than another. Here would be a continual struggle among the people to make themselves unequal. This, however, would find a powerful check in the institution of frequent periodical divisions of the whole property, and the abolition of the testamentary prerogative. It would at least correct the asperities of our inequality even if trade should be allowed to continue, with exception of the sales of land, which last were to be wholly interdicted. Still the state of things would be liable to be more or less disturbed and vacillating, from time to time; and we cannot expect perfect equality till the notion of individual wealth or gain, and the respectability of power attached to it, shall be done away. Nothing, therefore, is able to secure permanent equality of condition, but *common property;* i.e. the annihilating of individual property and trade, and making all property *common.* This can have its beginning only in small societies. (It has been said, and will be said again, that experiments of this have been fairly tried; that fair experiments of it have been made in this country. I deny it. And if I am contested I shall undertake to *prove* that not one fair and full experiment has ever yet been made in the United States to found a community of equality and common property, decisive of the question whether such establishment can exist or not.) It cannot be brought about at *once*, upon a general scale. It may be *approximated* by an equal division of property. But *this* cannot be effected of a sudden through these States. At present we can only expect it to be approximated by such acts of the National Legislature as a law prohibiting monopolies of the public lands, and limiting the sales in every instance to such quantity as is sufficient for one family, or so much as one family would probably be entitled to were all the land in the States equally divided; and a law granting an equal distribution of some part of this public land to individuals in lots never to be transferred. To divide all the *improved* lands, must be a work of more time and force. Howsoever; with rich men for lawmakers, men of the world, men who admire our beautiful structure of "free institutions," such as we now have and hitherto usually have had in our Halls of legislation, we cannot so much as *approximate* such an order of things— (I fear we are on the contrary course:)—we can neither have our bad laws repealed, nor better ones enacted.

## 10.

### REPORT OF THE NATIONAL REFORM UNION *
### [1844]

*In 1844 the National Reform Union of the City of New York set up headquarters at Chatham and Mulberry Streets, where meetings were held weekly. On March 13, at a public meeting of workingmen, a committee was appointed to inquire into "a depression of labor, and a social degradation of the laborer." At the next public meeting the committee submitted its "report," which was unanimously adopted and which was publicized by the* Working Man's Advocate *over the signatures of the most militant land reformers of the times.*

But in this Republic, all that the Creator designed for man's use, is ours—belongs, not to the Aristocracy, but to the People. The deep and interminable forest; the fertile and boundless prairie; the rich and inexhaustible mine—all—all belong to the People, or are held by the Government in trust for them. Here, indeed, is the natural and healthful field for man's labor. Let him apply to his

* *Working Man's Advocate* (New York: July 6, 1844).

Mother Earth, and she will not refuse to give him employment—neither will she withhold from him in due season the fulness of his reward.

We are the inhabitants of a country which for boundless extent of territory, fertility of soil, and exhaustless resources of mineral wealth, stands unequalled by any nation, either of ancient or modern times.

We live under a Constitution, so just and so equal, that it may well lay claim to a divine origin.

As a People we are second to none, in enterprize, industry, and skill.

Thus it is clear, that we are in possession of all the elements of individual and national prosperity. And, yet, we allow those elements to lie dormant, that labor which ought to be employed in calling forth the fruitfulness of Nature, is to be found seeking employment in the barren lanes of a city, of course, seeking it in vain.

Have we not boundless territories of unsettled, almost unexplored, lands? Were not those lands created for the express purpose of furnishing us with food, and clothing, and happy homesteads? Have not those lands been redeemed from the British Crown by the priceless blood that flowed in our Revolution? Have they not been redeemed from the aboriginal tribes by monies paid into the Treasury by the productive classes of the whole United States?

Are they not ours, therefore, by every just right, natural and acquired? And if so, on what principle should they be withheld from us, their rightful owners? Already have we paid for them twice over; wherefore should we be required to pay for them again? . . .

Your Committee does not recognize the authority of Congress to shut out from those lands such citizens as may not have money to pay another ransom for them. Still less do we admit their authority to sell the Public Domain, to men who require it only as an engine to lay *our children* under tribute to *their children* to all succeeding time. We regard the Public Lands as a Capital Stock, which belongs, not to us only, but also to posterity. The *profits* of that stock are ours, and the profits only. The moment congress, or any other power, attempts to alienate the *stock itself* to speculators, that moment do they attempt a cruel, and cowardly, fraud upon posterity, against which, as citizens and as honest men, we enter our most solemn protest. It is enough for us to eat our own bread—what right have we to sit down and consume the bread of our children? . . .

The first great object, then, is to assert and establish the right of the people to the soil; to be used by them in their own day, and transmitted—an inalienable heritage—to their posterity. The principles of justice, and the voice of expediency, or rather of *necessity,* demand that this fundamental principle shall be established as the paramount law, with the least possible delay.

That once effected, let an outlet be formed that will carry off our superabundant labor to the salubrious and fertile West. In those regions thousands, and tens of thousands, who are now languishing in hopeless poverty, will find a certain and a speedy independence. The labor market will be thus eased of the present distressing competition; and those who remain, as well as those who emigrate, will have the opportunity of realizing a comfortable living. . . .

The labor of your committee ends here, but we cannot close without expressing our belief, that, if the working men lead the way, manfully, in this reform, they will be immediately joined by a great majority of the non-producing classes. Various motives of a personal nature will induce them to join us—not to say a word about that patriotism and love of justice which, we trust, belong alike to every class in this Republican Community. *Signed:*

> THOMAS A. DEVYR, GEORGE H. EVANS, JOHN COMMERFORD, CHARLES P. GARDNER, DANIEL FOSTER, E. S. MANNING, JOHN WINDT, ROBERT BEATTIE, JR., JAMES MAXWELL, MIKE WALSH, D. WITTER, W. L. MACKENZIE, JAMES A. PYNE, LEWIS MASQUERIER.

11.

*Lewis Masquerier:*
MONOPOLY OF LAND THE GREAT EVIL *
[July 19, 1845]

*Lewis Masquerier (1802–?) was born in Kentucky of French
Huguenot parents. Schooled on the frontier, he worked in a
printing shop and, as a lawyer in Illinois, speculated in land.
While in New York to improve his phonetic spelling system,
he became attracted to George H. Evans and to anarchism.
He lectured on agrarian utopianism and abolition of the
landlord system, the wage system, and organized religion. In
this succinct editorial for* Young America, *the organ of the
National Reform Association, he presented a forceful argument for equal distribution of the land.*

Society may be classed into three divisions—the rich, the competent, and the poor. The very fact of the existence of the extremes of rich and poor is a proof that there is not much more
than a competence for all. Man's natural labor, when alternated
with due recreation, can produce no more over what his natural
wants require than what is needful to guard against emergencies.
As, therefore, his natural wants and powers of production are so
nearly equal, it is evident that he should have an equal share of
all the natural elements and enjoy the whole product of his labor.
Whoever, therefore, claims more than his just proportion could
not have acquired it by his own labor, and must have usurped that
of others. As nothing but labor, bestowed upon the natural elements, can produce property, nothing else can give a righteous
title to it.

It is self evident, then, that the very act of man's existence on
earth entitles him with the same exertion to an equal share in all
the goods of life. The earth is the common inheritance of man as
tenants in common, and nothing but the occupation of as much
as he can cultivate can give a separate title to it. His existence is so
inseparably interwoven with an equal share of the soil that he
has no more right to alienate it than he has that of his life or per-

---

* *Young America* (New York: July 19, 1845).

sonal liberty. Land, therefore, should be so restricted to each that all can be freeholders. It should not be alienated any more than life and liberty. As it is only our services and skill that should be exchanged for that of another; it is only the improvements, the houses, the fields, and the orchards that should be transferred. The soil itself should never be valued in money any more than life and liberty. It is the unrestricted sale and transfer of land that has occasioned its monopoly and in its train all evils.

By putting a price upon the land as well as its improvements, the tenants are made to pay double the rent to what the improvements would come to. And the landlord even contrives, more or less, to make his tenants pay even the interest on that part of his property he occupies himself. Every price, every valuation, every profit, and every duty ultimately settles down upon the laboring class. Thus the monopoly of the land seems to give the usurpers the control of every thing else. The monopolizers of the land, in the first place, extort from the tenant that improves and cultivates it, an enormous rent—with the surplus of this they buy other lands and buildings. These are also tenanted. For the use of other money they extort an interest—the borrower buys and sells the products of the laborer at a profit, and thus the whole settles down upon the poor producing tenant. The poor laborer, in short, is the pedestal of society—the whole burthen rests upon him. As his labor is a glut in the market, all the rent, interest, and profit settle down upon him. There is none that he can shift the burthen upon.

It is through the ignorance of man that this enormous system of monopoly has been suffered to develope [*sic*] itself. But as nature could not have brought other causes into existence, it could not have been otherwise. Though evil has accumulated, yet materials for a better organization have also been amassed, and time will change the system. The fact of the evil being discovered and discussed, is a proof that the change is commencing towards a better institution of things.

The monopoly of land has produced such a glaring destitution among the laborers, that it would seem that the evil would be remedied forthwith; and that the two-thirds of the earth yet unoccupied, except by the savage, would be occupied upon more equitable principles.

As, then, the unlimited accumulation of property has resulted from the usurpation of the soil, and by compelling others to pay rent for the use of it, there seems to be no mode so effectual to counteract as to limit each man's power of accumulation to his own natural labor and equal share of the soil.

L. MASQUERIER.

12.

*George Washington Julian:*
SPEECH ON THE HOMESTEAD BILL *
[January 29, 1851]

*George Washington Julian (1817–99), born in a log cabin in Indiana, was of French-German descent. Though poor, he became a lawyer and was elected to the state legislature as a Whig in 1845. He began to attack slavery and joined the Free-Soil party shortly thereafter. In Congress as a Free-Soiler from 1849 through 1851 and as a Republican in 1861 and for four terms thereafter, he urged the emancipation of slaves. As chairman of the committee on public lands he advocated the Homestead Act, which he had urged upon the House in 1851. He also favored punishing the Confederate leaders by giving their lands and the vote to the freedmen. He stood with the Radicals against President Andrew Johnson and proposed an amendment conferring suffrage upon women.*

I advocate the freedom of our public domain, in the first place, on the broad ground of natural right. I go back to first principles; and holding it to be wrong for governments to make merchandise of the earth, I would have this fundamental truth recognized by Congress in devising measures for the settlement and improvement of our vacant territory. I am no believer in the doctrines of Agrarianism, or Socialism, as these terms are generally understood. The friends of land reform claim no right to interfere with the laws of property of the several States, or the vested rights of their citizens. They advocate no *leveling* policy, designed to strip the rich of their possessions by any sudden act of legislation. They simply

---

   * G. W. Julian: *Speeches on Political Questions* (Albany, N.Y.: 1872), 51–4.

demand that, in laying the foundations of empire in the yet un-peopled regions of the great West, Congress shall give its sanc-tion to the natural right of the landless citizen of the country to a home upon its soil. The earth was designed by its Maker for the nourishment and support of man. The free and unbought occu-pancy of it belonged, originally, to the people, and the cultivation of it was the legitimate price of its fruits. This is the doctrine of nature, confirmed by the teachings of the Bible. In the first peopling of the earth, it was as free to all its inhabitants as the sunlight and the air; and every man has, by nature, as perfect a right to a reasonable portion of it, upon which to subsist, as he has to inflate his lungs with the atmosphere which surrounds it, or to drink of the waters which pass over its surface. This right is as inalienable, as emphatically *God-given*, as the right to liberty or life; and government, when it deprives him of it, independent of his own act, is guilty of a wanton usurpation of power, a flagrant abuse of its trust. In founding States, and rearing the social fabric, these principles should always have been recognized. Every man, indeed, on entering into a state of society, and partaking of its advantages, must necessarily submit the natural right of which I speak (as he must every other) to such regulations as may be established for the general good; yet it can never be understood that he has renounced it altogether, save by his own alienation or forfeiture. It attaches to him, and inheres in him, in virtue of his *humanity*, and should be sacredly guarded as one of those funda-mental rights to secure which "governments are instituted among men."

The justness of this reasoning must be manifest to any one who will give the subject his attention. Man, we say, has a natural right to life. What are we to understand by this? Surely, it will not be contended that it must be construed strictly, as a mere right to breathe, looking no farther, and keeping out of view the great purpose of existence. The right to life implies what the law books call a "right of way" to its enjoyment. It carries necessarily with it the right to the *means* of living, including not only the elements of light, air, fire, and water, but *land* also. Without this man could have no habitation to shelter him from the elements, nor raiment to cover and protect his body, nor food to sustain life. These means of living are not only necessary, but absolutely indispensable.

Without them life is impossible; and yet without land they are unattainable, except through the charity of others. They are at the mercy of the landholder. Does government then fulfill its mission when it encourages or permits the monopoly of the soil, and thus puts millions in its power, shorn of every right except the right to beg? The right to life is an empty mockery, if man is to be denied a place on the earth on which to establish a home for the shelter and nurture of his family, and employ his hands in obtaining the food and clothing necessary to his comfort. To say that God has given him the right to life, and at the same time that government may rightfully withhold the means of its enjoyment, except by the permission of others, is not simply an absurdity, but a libel on his Providence. It is true there are multitudes of landless poor in this country, and in all countries, utterly without the power to acquire homes upon the soil, who, nevertheless, are not altogether destitute of the essential blessings I have named; but they are dependent for them upon the saving grace of the few who have the monopoly of the soil. They are helpless pensioners upon the calculating bounty of those by whom they have been disinherited of their birthright. Was it ever designed that men should become vagrants and beggars by reason of unjust legislation, stripped of their right to the soil, robbed of the joys of home, and of those virtues and affections which ripen only in the family circle? Reason and justice revolt at such a conclusion. The gift of life, I repeat, is inseparable from the resources by which alone it can be made a blessing, and fulfill its great end. And this truth is beginning to dawn upon the world. The sentiment is becoming rooted in the great heart of humanity, that the right to a *home* attaches of necessity to the right to live, inasmuch as the physical, moral, and intellectual well-being of each individual cannot be secured without it; and that government is bound to guarantee it to the fullest practicable extent. This is one of the most cheering signs of the times. "The grand doctrine, that every human being should have the means of self-culture, of progress in knowledge and virtue, of health, comfort, and happiness, of exercising the powers and affections of a man,—this is slowly taking its place as the highest social truth."

. . . More than one half the land already sold at the different land-offices, if I am not mistaken, has fallen into the cold grasp of the speculator, who has held it in large quantities for years without improvement, thus excluding actual settlers who would have made it a source of wealth to themselves and to the public revenue. This is not only a legalized robbery of the landless, but an exceedingly shortsighted policy. It does not, as I shall presently show, give employment to labor, nor productiveness to the soil, nor add to the treasury by increased returns in the shape of taxation. It is legislative profligacy. The true interest of agriculture is to widen the field of its operations as far as practicable, and then, by a judicious tillage, to make it yield the very largest resources compatible with the population of the country. The measure now before us will secure this object by giving independent homesteads to the greatest number of cultivators, thus imparting dignity to labor, and stimulating its activity. It may be taken for granted as a general truth, that a nation will be powerful, prosperous, and happy, in proportion to the number of independent cultivators of its soil.

13.

*Augustine J. H. Duganné:*
IRON HARP *
[1855]

*Augustine Joseph Hickey Duganné (1823–84) was born in Boston and first came to public notice through his patriotic poems. He migrated to Philadelphia, and while writing novels and books on philosophy, economics, and government, he found time to agitate before fraternal and workingmen's organizations in prose and verse for free land in the West. In 1855 he was elected to the New York Assembly for one term. His "Iron Harp" resounded with his sturdy love of the people and their rights. He fought in the Civil War, was captured, and was imprisoned until pardoned. Serving as chief of the bureau of military statistics for a while, he later was connected with the* New York Tribune *and the* Sunday Dispatch, *a sensational Masonic sheet.*

* Augustine J. H. Duganne: *Poetical Works* (Philadelphia: 1855), 136–7, 148–9.

### EARTH-SHARING.

*LISTEN*, workers! listen!
Ye who all your lives are toiling,
In the field and workshop moiling,—
Lo! your serpent-wrongs are coiling
    Closer round you.  Listen!

Ponder, workers! ponder!
While ye poise your iron sledges,
While ye fix your rending wedges,—
Lo! your strength and skill are pledges
    Of your manhood.  Ponder!

Listen, workers! listen!
Sledges may crush else than matter:
Wedges may your curses scatter,—
Toilers once again may batter
    Moral Bastiles.  Listen!

Ponder, workers! ponder!
God gave equal earth to mortals,
Ere they crossed fair Eden's portals:—
Where's the ancient law that foretells
    Mortal slavery?  Ponder!

Answer, workers! answer!
Have the woes which ye are bearing,
Have the chains your limbs are wearing,
Palsied all the hope and daring
    Of your spirits?  Answer!

Listen, workers! listen!
Earth is yours—the broad, wide guerdon
Given to man with life's first burden;—
God hath set his seal and word on
    Man's true title.  Listen!

Ponder, workers! ponder!
Hold this truth within your keeping,
Till the harvest you are reaping:—
God is landlord, and unsleeping
    Watches o'er you.  Ponder!

### KEEP IT BEFORE THE PEOPLE.

*KEEP* IT BEFORE THE PEOPLE—
That the earth was made for man!
That flowers were strown,
And fruits were grown,
To bless and never to ban;
That sun and rain,
And corn and grain,
Are yours and mine, my brother!—
Free gifts from heaven,
And freely given,
To one as well as another!

KEEP IT BEFORE THE PEOPLE—
That man is the image of God!
His limbs or soul
Ye may not control
With shackle, or shame, or rod!
We may not be sold,
For silver or gold:
Neither you nor I, my brother!
For Freedom was given,
By God from heaven,
To one as well as another!

KEEP IT BEFORE THE PEOPLE—
That famine, and crime, and wo,
Forever abide,
Still side by side,
With luxury's dazzling show;
That LAZARUS crawls
From DIVES' halls,
And starves at his gate, my brother!—
Yet Life was given,
By GOD from heaven,
To one as well as another!

KEEP IT BEFORE THE PEOPLE—
That the laborer claims his meed:

    The right of SOIL,
    And the right to toil,
From spur and bridle freed;
    The right to bear,
    And the right to share,
With you and me, my brother!—
    Whatever is given,
    By GOD from heaven,
To one as well as another!

# CHAPTER ELEVEN

# RIGHT TO EARN A LIVING

━━━━◆◆━━━━

*So then it has come to this, that in a land of equal rights
the laborer cannot fix the amount of his wages in connection with his fellow laborers, without being charged as a
criminal before our courts of law. The merchants may agree
upon their prices; the lawyers upon their fees; the physicians upon their charges; the manufacturers upon the wages
given to their operatives, but the* LABORERS *shall not consult his interest and fix the prices of his toil and skill. If
this be* LAW, *it is unjust, oppressive and wicked.*

    ——JOHN GREENLEAF WHITTIER: *On the Journeymen
Tailors Case, July 23, 1836*

*They were condemned because they had determined not
to work for the wages that were offered them! Can anything be imagined more abhorrent to every sentiment of
generosity or justice than the law which arms the rich with
the legal right to fix, by assize, the wages of the poor? If
this is not* SLAVERY, *we have forgotten its definition.*

    ——WILLIAM CULLEN BRYANT: *The Right
of Workmen to Strike, 1836*

Sources of the quotations on the preceding page:

JOHN GREENLEAF WHITTIER: *Essex Gazette* (Haverhill, Mass.: July 23, 1836).

WILLIAM CULLEN BRYANT: Bernard Smith: *The Democratic Spirit* (New York: 1943, 2nd ed.), 210.

———◆———

WHAT homesteads were to the aspiring farmer, job security meant to the mechanic and workingman. Until a predominantly agrarian society had definitely evolved into an industrialized one, the mechanic tended to regard his labor power as a species of property right that he, as any other property owner, was free to utilize towards earning a living. Hence the mechanic and worker sought to legalize collective associations and strike action for the improvement of their pay and hours. In these respects they were but striving to attain a measure of the economic security that Carolina Regulators, New York Antirenters, Shays's men, and the Whisky rebels had tried to achieve in land ownership and debt and tax relief.

In the early years of the Republic, American mechanics and workers were groping towards unionization. Their early efforts were sporadic and resulted in only temporary arrangements to secure more pay. For example, in 1778 the journeymen printers of New York combined temporarily to demand higher wages. Journeymen printers of Philadelphia struck for more pay in 1786. From 1790 to 1800, similar strikes were conducted by Philadelphia carpenters (1) and cordwainers, and Baltimore tailors; and New York carpenters, masons, and printers formed unions. In 1798, William Manning, a keen-minded farmer, proposed a "labouring society" (Chapter Twelve, 1). In the Jeffersonian period such organizations were developed on a more durable basis. Industrial advance, stimulated by the Embargo and the War of 1812, provided the basis for more significant and militant labor organizations. The Philadelphia Typographical Society was founded in 1802. The Philadelphia cordwainers's organizing efforts brought on the first of the conspiracy trials in 1805–06 (2). The journey-men cordwainers of New York City organized in 1805. The New York Typographical Society, in existence in 1800, struck for a better wage scale in 1809 (3). Labor lost in the conspiracy trials of the New York tailors in 1809, and of the Baltimore and Pitts-burgh shoemakers in 1809, 1814, and 1815, but light fines attested to the strength of popular support.

In the Jacksonian era, the tempo of industrialization increased and with it the pace of the labor movement. The depression of 1819–22 temporarily slowed down activity, but from 1827–35 the labor movement undertook vigorous organizing and political ac-tivities. In 1827 the Mechanics' Union of Trade Associations arose out of a ten-hour movement to avert "the desolating evils which must inevitably arise from a depreciation of the intrinsic value of human labour." * One year later it inspired the first labor paper in America, the *Mechanics' Free Press.* But the Mechanics' Union lasted only until 1831, when its place was taken by the newly cre-ated New England Association of Farmers, Mechanics, and Other Workingmen, sponsored by vigorous leaders like Dr. Charles Douglas, editor of the *New England Artisan* of Rhode Island, Seth Luther (Chapter Two, 6), and Samuel Whitcomb, Jr. (Chap-ter Four, 6).

Meanwhile, encouraged by the power of those newly enfran-chised by the revision of state constitutions, labor turned to political action. Working Men's parties first sprouted in Phila-delphia in 1828 and spread to New York in the following year and throughout New England, Delaware, and New Jersey. Their programs called for mechanics' lien laws, free public schools, debt relief, abolition of chartered monopolies, equal taxation, a revised militia system, direct election of public officials and other "Jacobin" reforms. "The objects we have in view," ran one of them, "are hallowed by the sympathy of patriotism—it is the finish of the glorious work of the revolution." † The New York Working Men's party attracted figures distinguished in the labor and in-tellectual world: Frances Wright and Robert Dale Owen of the *Free Enquirer;* George Henry Evans, editor of the *Working Man's Advocate;* Thomas Skidmore, radical machinist and author of

* *Mechanics' Free Press* (Philadelphia: October 25, 1828).
† Ibid. (October 31, 1829).

*The Rights of Man to Property* (Chapter Two, 4); and Ebenezer Ford, president of the Carpenters' Union. In absence of a stable basis in the working class, and for other reasons, these labor parties declined and passed into the Democratic party in the campaign of 1832. They left their mark, however, in the reforming statutes that fulfilled their program and in the strong antimonopolistic bent of the Jacksonian program.

The thirties witnessed a return to militant trade unionism. City General Trades' Unions appeared in New York, Baltimore, Philadelphia, and Washington in 1833 and a National Trades' Union in 1834. The call for action against the enemy "silently encroaching upon our rights" was resoundingly uttered in Frederick Robinson's *Oration* at Boston (4). William Leggett lent support to labor's cause (Chapter Four, 7). The *Ten-Hour Circular* of Boston, May 8, 1835, (5) touched off strikes for the ten-hour day in Boston, Philadelphia, and elsewhere. Meanwhile, Ely Moore, president of the New York General Trades' Union, was elected to Congress on the Democratic ticket, and in 1836, in the face of an adverse judicial opinion in the trials of the Geneva shoemakers (1835) and of the Journeymen Tailors (1836), he made speeches on the floor of the House defending the right to organize. William Cullen Bryant and John Greenleaf Whittier also denounced these court decisions. The Equal Rights movement, or Loco Focoism, which funneled into the Democratic party under Martin Van Buren, expressed labor's resentment. The call for labor solidarity was re-echoed by the Journeymen Printers of New York City (6) in the depression of 1837.

The 1840–60 period was marked by strong currents of utopianism as well as of trade unionism. The crisis of 1837 had dealt labor a severe body blow. Temporarily, trade unionism declined, and in the gloom the Utopians won followers. Owenite community experiments had already waxed and waned in New York, Ohio, and Indiana in 1826–7. But Fourierism was now vigorously publicized in America by Albert Brisbane's *Social Destiny of Man* in 1840 (7). Horace Greeley opened his *New York Tribune* columns to Brisbane. Soon phalanxes were established at Sylvania, Pennsylvania, in 1843 and elsewhere. Brook Farm, Massachusetts, noted for its cluster of intellectuals—William E. Channing, Theodore Parker, John Greenleaf Whittier, Margaret Fuller, among others—

fell under Fourier influence. But these phalanxes proved no more lasting than Owenism, although they left their harvest of co-operatives and land reform in the American scene.

Recovering from the panic of 1837, the trade union movement revived slowly. Vigorous labor newspapers voiced labor's demands. A permanent working class was emerging in the factories. Its numbers were increased by farmers who had lost their farms and by a swelling tide of immigrants, among whom were German labor leaders like Herman Kriege, Wilhelm Weitling, and Joseph Weydemeyer.

The labor cause was sparked by the Ten-Hour movement. A significant advance was made when President Van Buren established a ten-hour day for Federal employees on public works on March 31, 1840. Chief Justice Lemuel Shaw of the Massachusetts Supreme Court recognized the legality of trade unionism and strike action in the Boston Journeymen Bootmakers' Society Case, *Commonwealth* v. *Hunt* (1842), and although this view was by no means prevalent, many strikes in the forties and fifties aimed at the ten-hour goal. Despite the progress of the labor movement, however, the ten-hour day was not established before the Civil War.

During the fifties skilled workers in factories and building trades in their local unions laid the basis for a powerful permanent trade-union movement. A sharper awareness of an "antagonism between labor and capital" appeared in their publications—for example, in the National Typographical Society Address issued by the Convention of 1850 to the Journeymen Printers of the United States (8, and Chapter Twelve, 11). Several national unions were formed, although only three—the typographical, the hat finishers, and the stonecutters—survived the panic of 1857. Thus did the workers assert their right to earn a living. If this right was nowhere inscribed in the constitutions of states, it was everywhere graven in the hearts of the people.

1.

*The Journeymen Carpenters of Philadelphia:*
AN ADDRESS *
[May 11, 1791]

*The strike of the Journeymen Carpenters of Philadelphia in*
*1791 was, so far as we know, the first strike in the building*
*trades. Although the carpenters were concerned with higher*
*wages, their demands for a shorter workday precipitated the*
*strike. Significantly, the strikers offered to work in compe-*
*tition with their former master-employers. Apparently they*
*viewed themselves as middle-class craftsmen rather than as*
*mere wage-earning workers.*

'Tis one of the invaluable privileges of our nature, that when
we conceive ourselves aggrieved, there is an inherent right in us to
complain: it is also a consolatory idea, to know that there is a
principle wisely implanted in the breast of every man, which is
capable of receiving a gratification, even from imparting the grievances under which he labours, to the notice of his fellow-men.
But this privilege of human nature, and that satisfaction arising
from the communication of our sufferings, are both rendered ineffectual, when those to whom we complain, wantonly turn a deaf
ear to the relation of those accumulated injuries, which they themselves have inflicted. . . .

The repeated insults and inconveniences which we, the Journeymen Carpenters of the City and Liberties of Philadelphia, have
in frequent instances, sustained, have become too heavy to be patiently borne by us any longer.

We have not long since, attempted, in a decent manner, to
remove some of the hardships which oppose themselves to the
advancement of our common interests, by endeavouring, on our
part, to reconcile those differences which have too long subsisted
betwixt us and those men by whom we are employed.

* Dunlap's *American Daily Advertiser* (Philadelphia: May 11, 1791).

As a means of accomplishing so desirable an end, and that we might in future be governed by some established rules, mutually agreed to, we appointed, on our part, three of our number, to confer with an equal (or any) number, which the Society of Master-Carpenters might think proper to deputise for the like purpose: The men, thus authorised by us to negociate in our name, instead of meeting with an amicable attention to the claims they were requested to make, were treated with contumelious contempt, by those who stile themselves Master-Carpenters.

Our aggravated distresses have been encreased in a direct proportion to the encrease of the quantum of self-interest contained in the callous bosoms of our infurious employers. Our wages (which are, and have been for a long time too low) are meanly attempted to be reduced to a still lower ebb, by every means within the power of avarice to invent. We have heretofore been obliged to toil through the whole course of the longest summer's day, and that too, in many instances, without even the consolation of having our labour sweetened, by the reviving hope of an immediate reward.

Such being our unhappy situation, we were under the very disagreeable necessity of obeying the powerful dictates of the most active principle which ever influenced the conduct of men, by seeking to redress ourselves by a friendly reciprocated assistance. Self-preservation has induced us to enter into an indissoluble union with each other, in order to ward off the blows which are threatened us, by the insolent hand of pampered affluence:—We mean hereafter, by a firm, independent mode of conduct, to protect each other.

The following then, are the fixed, permanent, and invariable resolutions, which we have mutually and solemnly pledged ourselves to adhere to; and which, for the purpose of exciting public commiseration, protection and patronage, we now submit to the view of our fellow-citizens of the community. We, at the same time, convinced that the public mind, which is generally divested of that bias which arise from the baneful effects of prejudice, will take the extreme hardship of our case into serious consideration, and grant or withhold their assistance, according as they may judge us to deserve.

The resolutions which we have bound ourselves by the sacred ties of honor to abide by, are,

1st. That, in future, a Day's Work, amongst us, shall be deemed to commence at six o'clock in the morning, and terminate at six in the Evening of each day.

2dly. We will undertake buildings, or give designs, of any work in the line of our occupation, for any one who may think advisable to give us employment, at 25 per cent. below the current rate established by the Master-Carpenters; and that we will give any reasonable security for the faithful execution of the work so entrusted to us to perform.

With respect to the first of those resolutions, we shall remark, that we have the universally prevailing custom of Great-Britain, together with the general usage of the other parts of Europe, in favour of the innovation which we are not only anxious but determined to bring about.

In such manual exercises as require the exertion of so much bodily strength as is requisite at our business, we imagine that every disinterested person must be of our opinion, that there is sufficient time between the hours we have mentioned, to fatigue the body so much, as for it to stand in need of a relaxation.

We are, however, by no means averse to labouring hereafter, as we have done heretofore, that is, through the whole day, unless in instances where our domestic concerns, or some other cause, may render it inconvenient or impracticable.

The main object we wish to attain by the first of our resolutions, in future to have it a matter entirely at our option, whether we will begin our work before, or continue at it after, six in the morning, and the same hour in the evening. If we labour early and late, as has been the case heretofore, we shall expect compensation extraordinary for the time each day's work exceeds the hours before mentioned.

Respecting the second resolution, nothing further need be observed, than that the advantages accruing to such as employ us (in the place of those who are called masters, and who are now almost without assistance) will be as many and as great, as that work which is done by men who have served a long and regular apprenticeship, is superior to that which is executed by boys and pretended masters.

THE JOURNEYMEN CARPENTERS.

N. B. Any Gentlemen wanting Carpenter-Work done, by leaving their names at Mr. Alexander Power's, No. 132, South Market-street, will be immediately waited upon.

2.

### The Working Shoemakers of Philadelphia:
ADDRESS TO THE PUBLIC *
[1805]

*When eight shoemakers of Philadelphia were indicted in November 1805 for "conspiracy" to raise wages, the workers before the trial issued this appeal invoking public support. "The Address of the Working Shoemakers of the City of Philadelphia, To the Public" was publicized widely through- out Philadelphia. Despite the defense of Caesar Rodney, a leading Jeffersonian attorney, the jury found them guilty, and they were fined eight dollars.*

Under circumstances unexampled in a free country, we are in- duced to lay a statement of our case before our fellow citizens. . . . For fifteen years and upwards we have assembled together in a peaceable manner and for our common good, and to guard against the accidents to which industrious men are exposed to promote the happiness of the individuals of which our little com- munity is composed, and to render service to those whom age or infirmity may have rendered incapable of labor. . . .

Every citizen must know that in this city, and the other capital cities which are so often exposed to the ravages of yellow fever, the man who acquires his bread and the bread of his family by the labor of his hands, does not labor upon equal terms of advantage with those who live in towns where disease does not so often prevail, and where the necessaries of life and house rent are so much cheaper. The master shoemakers, as they are called after the

* *Aurora* (Philadelphia: November 28, 1805).

slavish style of Europe, but who are only the retailers of our labor, and who in truth live upon the work of our hands, are generally men of large property, to whom the suspension of business, though it is a loss, is not so great a loss as the total suspension of the means of subsistence, is to us who obtain our income from week to week. These masters as they are called, and who would be masters and tyrants if they could, or the law would allow them, have their associations, their meetings, and they pass their resolutions; but as they are rich and we are poor—they seem to think that we are not protected by the constitution in meeting peaceably together and pursuing our own happiness— They suppose that they have a right to limit us at all times, and whatever may be the misfortune of society, the changes in the value of necessaries, the encrease or the decrease of trade, they think they have a right to determine for us the value of our labor; but that we have no right to determine for ourselves, what we will or what we will not take in exchange for our labor.

In this spirit they have within a few days past, caused to be arrested by written warrants, and committed to prison certain members of the association of working shoemakers; and under oath made in the mayor's court of a dangerous conspiracy against their interests and that of the community in general.

It is notorious that for many years back the working shoemakers have been associated and peaceably assembled together, and that they have regulated the wages which they ought to accept for their labor.

It is notorious that the retailing or shop-keeping shoemakers, have also had and now have a similar association, in which they have regulated the prices for which they sell goods to the public.

In both these cases we think the parties are justified and correct; because every man being the sole owner and master of his labor and of his property, has the right to affix the price of his own labor or his own property; leaving to those who are to employ or to purchase, the right to accept of the labor or the goods, or to reject them or either, if they appear too exorbitant. These are the only principles consistent with equal rights and justice between man and man in sight of heaven. . . .

As our claim was founded in right and justice, we have adhered to it, and shall abandon life before we depart from it, unless the circumstances of society itself should so change, as to render a reduction equally proper and just, as the encrease is now reasonable— The employers, however, have endeavored to accomplish by artifices, objects which they now vainly expect to succeed in, by means of terror, by dungeons and prosecutions. Oaths may be sported with, but they must rack the consciences of those who make them; though bodies of innocent men may be torn from their wives and their children and plunged into a prison, where criminals only should be consigned; but though these evil doings may be exhibited in noon day, those who are the authors of it cannot sleep with the same quiet or the same consolation, as those who are the victims of it—and what an example and a warning does the transaction hold up to the industrious men of every art, trade, and manufacture—what avails the constitution which professes to secure to every man equal rights and the power of pursuing his own happiness—what avails it, if the price of any man's labor is to be regulated by the will of another.

If the association of men to regulate the price of their own labor, is to be converted into a crime, and libelled with the same reproachful terms as a design against the freedom of the nation; the prospect is a very sad one for Pennsylvania.

But this is not all—if it is against the law and the constitution for us to associate to regulate the value of our own labor, must it not be at least equally criminal for others to associate to regulate the prices of our labour, without at the same time diminishing their profits in dealing with their customers; such however has been their conduct, and they have gone so far as to depute certain members of their association, to prevent our being employed by men who are more just than themselves, and who do not belong to their association; nay they have gone so far as to proscribe certain boarding houses, and to declare they would never give employment to any person who ate their meals in those houses; thereby proscribing families who subsist by boarding, only because they provided food for payment, for a number of industrious workmen. We shall add only one more fact; the working shoemakers, in order to encourage the export trade, have constantly executed work, declared to be for exportation, at the rate of 25 cents per pair, less than customer's work; during the last eight months it appears, that they have deceived the workmen, by giving work under the denomination of *"orders"* or *"exports,"* and after we have executed them, they have placed them in their shops, and served them on their customers.

To these we might add many other causes of complaint and vindication of ourselves—what we have here said, will inform the public, of our conduct, and will shew that under whatever pretences the thing is done, the name of freedom is but a shadow, if for doing, what the laws of God and the laws of our country authorize, we are to have taskmasters to measure out our pittance of subsistence—if we are to be torn from our firesides for endeavoring to obtain a fair and just support for our families, and if we are to be treated as felons and murderers only for asserting the right to take or refuse what we deem an adequate reward for our labor.

All these considerations we submit to our fellow citizens, and are prepared to meet the oppression to which we are exposed with constancy and the temper that befits men actuated only by justice and the spirit of freemen.

Signed by order and on behalf of the society.

JAMES GHEGAN, *President.*

GEORGE KEAMER, *Secr'y.*

## 3.

### The New York Typographical Society:
### TO THE MASTER PRINTERS OF THE CITY OF NEW YORK *
### [December 30, 1809]

*The New York Typographical Society, a forerunner of which was in existence in 1800, adopted a constitution in 1809. Under its president, S. W. Andrews, and its secretary, David Reins, it undertook the organization of the journeymen. Samuel Woodworth, author of "The Old Oaken Bucket," was an active member. On October 30, 1809 the Society struck to get their wage scale adopted. Two months later, to clarify the matter of the "half-way journeymen" and the laxity of apprenticeship regulations, this circular letter was issued.*

* Ethelbert Stewart: *A Documentary History of the Early Organizations of Printers* (Washington, D.C.: 1905), 874–5.

GENTLEMEN: Viewing with deep concern the improper practices in many of the printing offices in this city, the journeymen composing the New York Typographical Society have appointed the undersigned committee to address you on the subject, and represent the many evil effects they have on the art of printing in general and its demoralizing effects on its professors.

The practice of employing what is termed "halfway journeymen" in preference to those who have served their time, while it holds out encouragement to boys to elope from their masters, as soon as they acquire a sufficient knowledge of the art to be enabled to earn their bread, is a great grievance to journeymen, and almost certain ruin to the boys themselves. Becoming masters of their own conduct at a period of life when they are incapable of governing their passions and propensities, they plunge headlong into every species of dissipation, and are often debilitated by debauchery and disease before they arrive at the state of manhood. And it also tends to an unnecessary multiplication of apprentices, inasmuch as the place of every boy who elopes from his master is usually supplied by another, while at the same time the runaway supplies, after a manner, the place of a regular journeyman, and one who, probably has a family dependent on his labor for support.

We would also beg leave to call your attention to a practice as illiberal and unjust as the former, and attended, perhaps, with evils of a more aggravating nature. We mean that of taking grown men (foreigners) as apprentices to some twelve or fifteen months, when they are to be turned into the situations of men who are masters of their business; which men are to be turned out of their places by miserable botches, because they will work for what they can get. By these means numbers of excellent workmen, who ought to be ornaments to the profession, are driven by necessity to some other means of support. When a parent puts out a child to learn an art, it is with the pleasing idea that a knowledge of that art will enable him, when he becomes a man, to provide for himself a comfortable subsistence. Did he know that after laboring from his youth to manhood to acquire our art he would be compelled to abandon it and resort to some business with which he was totally unacquainted to enable him to live, he would certainly prefer that he should in the first instance seek a livelihood on the sea, or by some other precarious calling, than trust to the equally precarious success of a trade overstocked by its professors. Of the number that have completed their apprenticeship to the printing business within the last five years, but few have been enabled to hold a situation for any length of time. And it is an incontrovertible fact, that nearly one-half who learn the trade are obliged to relinquish it and follow some other calling for support.

Under the direful influence of the unwarrantable practices, the professors of the noblest art with which the world is blessed, have become "birds of passage," seeking a livelihood from Georgia to Maine. It is owing to such practices that to acknowledge yourself a printer is to awaken suspicion and cause distrust. It is owing to such practices that the professors of the noble art are sinking in the estimation of the community. And it will be owing to such practices, if persisted in, that to see a book correctly printed will, in a few years, be received as a phenomenon. . . .

D. H. REINS.

W. BURBRIDGE.

S. JOHNSON.

## 4.

### *Frederick Robinson:*
### AN ORATION DELIVERED BEFORE THE TRADES UNION OF BOSTON *
### [1834]

*Frederick Robinson was a fiery radical from Marblehead who became a weigher and gauger at the Boston Custom House. Thanks to labor support he became a Democratic member of the Massachusetts legislature. Here he fought for abolition of imprisonment for debt. Stressing the silent encroachment on the rights of workers, this* Oration *defended unions and opposed the monopolistic power of the Bank of the United States.*

. . . For although it cannot be denied, that in this country there can be no advantages, powers or privileges, which every one has not an equal right to enjoy, yet do we not see every where around

* Frederick Robinson: *An Oration Delivered before the Trades Union of Boston* (Boston: 1834), 4–5, 14–15.

us, privileges, advantages, monopolies enjoyed by the few, which are denied to the many; indeed do we not see all the same machinery in operation among us, which has crowded the great mass of the people of other countries down into the grossest ignorance, degradation and slavery. While we have been comparing our condition with the miserable slavery of other nations, and boasting of our advantages, and glorying in the achievements of our fathers, ignorantly supposing that we were already in the possession of the highest degree of liberty, and in the enjoyment of the most perfect equality, the enemy have been silently encroaching upon our rights. But this delusion has passed,—the enchantment is broken. The people are beginning to awake. Every day brings to our ears the pleasing intelligence, that the industrious classes, which always constitute the democracy of the country, are beginning to bestir themselves, and are enquiring what they shall do to be saved, not from the threatened evil of another world, but from the evils which they begin to see impending over them and their children here. . . .

Who are they who complain of Trades Unions? Are they not those whose combinations cover the land, and who have even contrived to invest some of their combinations with the sanctity of law? Are they not those, who are the owners of all kinds of monopolies, who pass their lives in perpetual caucuses, on 'change, in halls connected with banks, composing insurance companies, manufacturing companies, turnpike, bridge, canal, rail-road, and all other legalized combinations? Do not each of the learned professions constitute unions among themselves to control their own business? And have they not fortified their unions, by alliance with each other and with the rich, and thus established a proud, haughty, overbearing, fourfold aristocracy in our country? Well may the capitalists, monopolists, judges, lawyers, doctors, and priests complain of Trades Unions. They know that the secret of their own power and wealth consists in the strictest concert of action,—and they know that when the great mass of the people become equally wise with themselves, and unite their power of numbers for the possession and enjoyment of equal rights, they will be shorn of their consequence, be humbled of their pride, and brought to personal labor for their own subsistence. They know from experience that unions among themselves, have al-

ways enabled the few to rule and ride the people; and that, when
the people shall discover the secret of their power, and learn to
use it for their own good, the sceptre will fall from their hands,
and they themselves will become merged in the great 'vulgar' mass
of the people.

The Judge knows this. He knows that he is a member of a combination of lawyers, better organized, and more strict and tyrannical in the enforcement of their rules, than even masonry itself.
He knows that when the dispositions in the community to investigate and destroy secret societies turns itself upon the bar, abuses
will be discovered so enormous as completely to eclipse those of
every other combination. We shall then discover that we have
been 'fishing for minnows and let slip the leviathan.' We shall discover that by means of this regularly organized combination of
lawyers throughout the land, the whole government of the nation
has always been in their hands, that the laws have always been
moulded to suit their purposes, and what are called Courts of Justice, are only engines to promote their interests, and secure their
ascendency in the community. The Judges know, that this combination has enabled them to usurp one entire branch of our government, and to turn all the rest of the citizens out of doors. For
who dares to go into our public courts, and attend to his own concerns, or to perform the business of his neighbor? We all know,
that this preposterous state of things could only have been
brought about by union among lawyers, and by their combination
to involve the laws and the practice of the law in inexplicable ob-
scurity and formality, by the adoption of all the cumbrous learning of British courts.

## 5.

### *The Boston Committee:*
### Ten-Hour Circular *
### [May 8, 1835]

*In 1825 and 1832 the Boston carpenters struck for the ten-
hour day. Both strikes failed. Yet in 1835 the carpenters,
masons, and stonecutters struck again under their leaders A.*

* *The Man* (New York: May 13, 1835).

*H. Wood, Seth Luther (Chapter Two, 6), and Levi Abell. They were defeated. But they issued this widely read Ten-Hour Circular, which led to the successful Philadelphia general strike on the Schuylkill River coal wharves. William Thompson, president of the Carpenters' Society of Philadelphia, acknowledged the influence of the Boston circular.*

At a very large and respectable Meeting of House Carpenters, Masons and Stone Cutters, assembled in Julien Hall, Boston, May 4, 1835, to consider the subject of the hours of labor in order that Ten Hours should at all times constitute a day's work, the Undersigned were appointed a Committee to address a Circular to our brethren in all branches of Mechanical labor in the City, the Commonwealth and elsewhere, to inform them of the state of things in this City, relative to the subject under consideration. In performing the duties assigned to them, the Committee, by the authority in them vested for that purpose, and in the name of the Carpenters, Masons, and Stone Cutters, do respectfully represent—

That we are now engaged in a cause, which is not only of vital importance to ourselves, our families, and our children, but is equally interesting and equally important to every Mechanic in the United States and the whole world. We are contending for the recognition of the Natural Right to dispose of our own time in such quantities as we deem and believe to be most conducive to our own happiness, and the welfare of all those engaged in Manual Labor.

The work in which we are now engaged is neither more nor less than a contest between Money and Labor: Capital, which can only be made productive by labor, is endeavoring to crush labor, the only source of all wealth.

We have been too long subjected to the odious, cruel, unjust, and tyrannical system which compels the operative Mechanic to exhaust his physical and mental powers by excessive toil, until he has no desire but to eat and sleep, and in many cases he has no power to do either from extreme debility.

We contend that no man or body of men, have a right to require of us that we should toil as we have hitherto done under the old system of labor.

We go further. No man or body of men who require such excessive labor can be friends to the country or the Rights of Man. We also say, that we have rights, and we have duties to perform as American Citizens and members of society, which forbids us to dispose of more than Ten Hours for a day's work. We cannot, we will not, longer be mere slaves to inhuman, insatiable and unpitying avarice. We have taken a firm and decided stand, to obtain the acknowledgement of those rights to enable us to perform those duties to God, our Country and ourselves. . . .

When you understand that we are contending for your rights, for the rights of your families and your children as well as our own, we feel full confidence that you will make no movement to retard the accomplishment of the glorious and holy enterprise, both yours and ours. It is for the rights of humanity we contend. Our cause is the cause of philanthropy. Our opposers resort to the most degrading obloquy to injure us. Not degrading to us, but to the authors of such unmerited opprobrium which they attempt to cast upon us. They tell us "We shall spend all our hours of leisure in Drunkenness and Debauchery if the hours of labor are reduced."

We hurl from us the base, ungenerous, ungrateful, detestable, cruel, malicious slander, with scorn and indignation. . . .

To show the utter fallacy of their idiotic reasoning, if reasoning it may be called, we have only to say, they employ us about eight months in the year during the longest and the hottest days, and in short days hundreds of us remain idle for want of work, for three or four months when our expenses must of course be the heaviest during winter. When the long days again appear, our guardians set us to work, as they say, "to keep us from getting drunk." No fear has ever been expressed by these benevolent employers respecting our morals while we are idle in short days, through their avarice . . . Further, they threaten to starve us into submission to their will. Starve us to prevent us from getting drunk!! Wonderful Wisdom!! Refined Benevolence!! Exalted Philanthropy!! . . .

Mechanics of Boston—STAND FIRM—Be true to yourselves. Now is the time to enroll your names on the scroll of history as the undaunted enemies of oppression, as the enemies of mental, moral and physical degradation, as the friends of the human race.

The God of the Universe has given us time, health and strength.

We utterly deny the right of any man to dictate to us how much of it we shall sell. Brethren in the City, Towns and Country, our cause is yours, the cause of Liberty, the cause of God. Respectfully yours, A. H. Wood, Seth Luther, Levi Abell—Committee.

Editors of newspapers in the United States who are in favor of equal rights, are respectfully requested to publish this Circular. the committee. *(Boston, May 8, 1835)*

### 6.

### *The Typographical Association of New York City:* To the Journeymen Printers *
[June 29, 1837]

*In order to hold fast in the face of the depression of 1837, the Typographical Association of New York City sent out this appeal to the journeymen printers of the vicinity. From time to time the association issued "rat offices" and "rat lists," which served to prevent the employment of non-union printers. This broadside was issued to induce the journeymen printers to join the union during the depression.*

To the journeymen printers of New York City and vicinity:

fellow-craftsmen: At an adjourned meeting of the Typographical Association of New York City held at the association rooms on Saturday evening June 24, 1837, information having been given of a regularly organized "combination" on the part of certain of our employers to take advantage of the present depressed state of our trade, and business in general, in order to reduce our present prices, and to render us, if possible, obedient vassals to the nod of the oppressor, a committee was appointed to address you in this particular, and urge you to a prompt and resolute resistance.

That committee is of opinion, that the time has now arrived when you are to prove to the world one of two things—either that you are freemen and capable of understanding and maintaining your rights; or that you are base and servile sycophants, ready and

* Ethelbert Stewart: *Documentary History of the Early Organization of Printers* (Washington, D.C.: 1905), 900–2.

willing to receive whatever compensation and terms your employers may choose to allow.

You are now to show whether, in your judgment, your employers or yourselves possess the right of fixing a value on your labor. If there yet remains one spark of the courage, manhood and determination which sustained you when forming the present scale of prices, let the employing printers of New York and the United States, see that it still exists, and can be easily fanned to a flame; let them see that the insignificant and paltry pittance which you now obtain for your support shall not be reduced at their pleasure—that for them to grow richer you will not consent to become poorer.

That a pressure exists, and that it is more difficult for all employers to procure money with which to meet expenses, we are all aware, but why should your wages be reduced on that account?

The prices for printing advertisements and for newspapers have not been reduced.

The prices that are now paid to printers are no more than will barely support them, and the common necessaries of life are even higher than when your present scale was formed. Then why should you submit to a reduction? Why be the passive minion of the will of tyrants?

The committee can discover no reason why you should, and it is their opinion that if true to yourselves you will not be.

Depend upon it, that if, in obedience to the mandate of grasping avarice—if because your employers say you must, you determine to yield, and go to work for less than the scale demands, you will not only cover yourselves with the consequent odium but you will necessarily involve yourselves in debt from week to week; for it is folly to suppose that if your wages are once reduced your employers will of their own accord advance them again, even though business should resume its accustomed course. No, having accomplished their purposes, and brought you in submission to their feet, they will keep you there, and the iron hand of oppression will be laid more heavily than ever.

Your employer knows well, that without constant employment, your wages are not sufficient for your support, and those of the unholy alliance which is now raising its hydra head against you, are no doubt impressed with the belief, that by seizing upon the present period of depression in the trade, they may compel you to work for whatever they may please to pay. . . .

The truth is your employers are much more able to pay the existing prices than you are to have your wages reduced, the pressure operates in a much greater degree to your disadvantage than to theirs, the depreciated "shinplasters" of the banks, which are bought up, no doubt, with considerable profit to the purchasers, are palmed off upon you in requital for your toil, as though each rag was worth its face in gold, these rags you must take, though on every dollar you get for your labor you suffer a heavy loss. Patiently you have borne all this, and would continue still to bear it; but in the name of evenhanded justice, and for the sake of Heaven, your wives and your children, let the line of demarcation be here drawn—say to the overreaching oppressor, Thus far shalt thou come, but no farther.

The committee are well convinced that the chief reason the unprincipled combination of your employers have thus dared to invade your rights, and attempt the reduction of your wages, is because of a rumored want of the union spirit among yourselves. Without union nothing can be effected—with it, everything. Come forward, then, you who are not members of the association; and join in putting a shoulder to the wheel. Support the association, and the association will support you. There are some of you now in the city who are not members, why is this? You all receive the benefits which result from it. Why, then, do you not join it, and thereby extend its benefits?

The committee would also respectfully impress on the minds of the members the necessity of a strict attention at all meetings of the association and a firm support of its principles. Let each and all of us determined upon union, strong and effectual union; and let the watchword be, the prices of the association must and shall be sustained.

CHAS. A. ADAMS,
H. D. BRISTOL,
W. H. MC CARTENAY,
GEO. HATTEN,
W. N. ROSE,
*Committee*

## 7.

### Albert Brisbane:
### SOCIAL DESTINY OF MAN *
### [1840]

*Albert Brisbane (1809–90) was born in New York of Scotch and English descent. He studied with his mother and various tutors whose social teachings left a profound impression. Influenced while abroad by Cousin, Guizot, Hegel, and others, Brisbane was drawn to the ideas of Saint Simon and most deeply impressed by those of Charles Fourier. After returning to America, he organized a society devoted to Fourierism. His lectures and publications on social reform, particularly Social Destiny of Man, had a wide influence throughout the forties and fifties, although the efforts of his followers to build communities based on his ideas failed.*

Slavery is not an isolated fact, a single blot upon our social order; *it is a symptom, a part of a vast social malady, which is much deeper than is supposed; and which must be cured to eradicate the numberless evils, (one of which Slavery is), which are the disgrace and scourge of human societies. That malady is* REPUGNANT INDUSTRY. *If labor be repulsive, degrading and but poorly rewarded how are the mass to be forced to it otherwise than by* CONSTRAINT? *Constraint is the hideous means which society has made use of to insure production, and the creation of riches; it acts with a two-fold power, one of which is the whip and punishments, the other want and privations. . . .*

*If labor be repulsive, repugnant, man will not undergo it, unless he be forced to it; society, therefore,* TO GUARANTEE *the persistance of the mass in labor, must reduce them to want, force them to it by their own necessities, and by those of their families. Thus, the very foundation of our societies is injustice and oppression; and if we disguise this false basis with a little political liberty, social evils and social servitude are not the less its results. The changes which have taken place in the condition of the laboring classes since the commencement of societies, have only been*

---

* Albert Brisbane: *Social Destiny of Man: or Association and the Reorganization of Industry* (Philadelphia: 1840), 103–05, 111–12.

*so many varieties of one general tyranny; at one epoch we see them Pariahs, at another Slaves, at another Serfs, and now they are the working classes. Individual slavery, as it universally existed in antiquity, has been changed and replaced by the collective servitude of the mass in modern times. . . .*

All these coercive measures, destructive of individual independence, are the means made use of to force the mass to labor; and politicians talk of liberty, when industry, from which the vast majority draw their existence and in which they spend their lives, is based on a system so compulsory and indirectly tyrannical!

This system of industrial servitude is the lot of the laboring classes of the fourth society, called Civilization. But its falseness does not end here; to it is added the violation of the fundamental right of man, THE RIGHT TO LABOR. As we have observed in a former chapter, if man were created to go through a course of existence, which is dependent on labor, if its right be not guaranteed him, his right to existence even is not acknowledged.

If we look at the cities of civilized Europe—and some times at our own—we see the laboring classes wandering from manufactory to manufactory, or shop to shop, inquiring for work and refused it. Without any means of existence while out of employ, pressed by want, often by starvation, they reduce the price of their day's labor, selling fourteen and more hours of monotonous drudgery out of each twenty-four for a miserable pittance. If they manage to avoid actual famine, slow starvation, unhealthy and excessive labor and anxiety, sow the seeds of disease, undermine the constitution, and counteract the healthy influence, which labor should have on the human frame.

To creatures thus situated, what mockery to offer them the right to vote, or the guarantee of not being thrown into prison without a writ of habeas-corpus! Are they free, because they possess these illusory guarantees, when they are at the same time the slaves of labor, the serfs of capitalists? It is true, the whip does not force them to labor, like the real slave; but does not the alternative of want or famine do it as effectually? If their bodies cannot be sold, they have to bargain their liberty and their time, without being able to dispose scarcely of an hour. No: *Civil* liberty is perfectly illusory without *Industrial* liberty; it is a step-stone, a mere means of enabling man to attain to his destiny.

8.

*National Convention of Journeymen Printers:*
ADDRESS TO THE JOURNEYMEN PRINTERS OF THE UNITED STATES *
[December 7, 1850]

*On September 28, 1850, the New York union of Journeymen*
*Printers, joined by those of Boston and Philadelphia, issued*
*a call for a national convention to be held in New York City.*
*Delegates from five states met and discussed chiefly the limi-*
*tation of apprenticeship and the basis of union organization.*
*Eventually, the convention adopted this "Address" and urged*
*the circulation of its official proceedings, published in pam-*
*phlet form by the Philadelphia union. At its second national*
*convention at Baltimore, September 12, 1851, a constitution*
*was adopted for a new and permanent organization, called*
*the National Typographical Union.*

It is useless for us to disguise from ourselves the fact that, under
the present arrangement of things, there exists a perpetual antagonism between labor and capital. The toilers are involuntarily
pitted against the employers: one side striving to sell their labor
for as much, and the other striving to buy it for as little, as they
can. In this war of interests, labor, of itself, stands no chance. The
power is all on the other side. Every addition to the number of
laborers in the market decreases their power: while the power of
capital grows in a ratio commensurate with the increase of the
capital itself. On the one side, the greater the number of dollars,
the greater the ability to succeed in the conflict: on the other the
greater the number of laborers, the less the ability to succeed.
Add to this the fact that wealth accumulates, on the one side,
much faster as the laborers accumulate on the other, and the utter
impotency of unorganized labor in a warfare against capital becomes manifest.

To remedy the many disastrous grievances arising from this
disparity of power, combination, for mutual agreement in determining rates of wages, and for concert of action in maintaining
them, has been resorted to in many trades, and principally in our

* E. Stewart: *Documentary History of the Early Organization of Printers*
(Washington, D.C.: 1905), 981–4.

own. Its success has abundantly demonstrated its utility. Indeed, while the present wages system continues in operation, as an immediate protection from pressing calamities, it is clearly the only effective means which labor can adopt. So far as it extends, it destroys competition in the labor market; unites the working people, and produces a sort of equilibrium in the power of the conflicting parties.

This being the case, it appears evident that an extensive organization, embracing the whole country, would secure to our own, or any other trade, a power which could be derived from no other source. The delegates here assembled have come together deeply impressed with this conviction. They regard such an organization not only as an agent of immediate relief, but also as essential to the ultimate destruction of those unnatural relations at present subsisting between the interests of the employing and employed classes. All their activities have accordingly been regulated with a view to the establishing of such an organization. They have recommended the formation of societies in all the cities and towns throughout the country. They have rendered it obligatory upon all members of the profession traveling to any point embraced in the representation here, for work, to have with them certificates of membership from the society located in the place from which they come. They have established a national executive committee, to urge the enforcement of their recommendations and requirements. They have also instructed that committee to use their utmost exertions to have a full representation of the whole country in the next national convention, which they have ordered to be held in Baltimore, Md., on the 12th of next September.

. . . The principles, therefore, recommended by the convention, upon which it urges the formation of societies throughout the country, are such as can not fail to enlist in their favor the most potent considerations of self-interest. Among them are—

*First.* An understanding in the regulation of scales of prices in different localities, so that those in one place may not be permitted to become so comparatively high as to induce work to be sent elsewhere.

*Second.* The enforcement of the principle of limiting the number of apprentices; by which measure a too rapid increase in the number of workmen, too little care in the selection of boys for the business, and the employment of herds of half men at half wages, to the detriment of good workmen, will be effectively prevented.

*Third.* The issuing of traveling certificates, by which the distresses of brother craftsmen, incurred in journeying from one place to another, in search of work, may be relieved. In this we have one of those means of attracting and attaching to our societies men who, not troubled largely with abstract principles of strict duty, are nevertheless willing to become "repentant prodigals" for the sake of the "fatted calf." Besides, it is eminently calculated to produce a warmer attachment on the part of superior men, inasmuch as it will bind them in ties of gratitude, and in the luxurious fellowship of good deeds.

*Fourth.* Measures to prevent disgraced members of the profession enjoying anywhere in the United States, those privileges which belong exclusively to honorable printers. They consist in keeping a registry of "rats," to be sent by the executive committee to every union in the country, for reference; and admitting to membership no stranger, who does not produce evidence of his having been a member in good standing of the society, if any existed, in the place from which he comes.

*Fifth.* The gradual collection of a sum of money by each union sufficient to enable it to hold out successfully against the employers, in the event of a contention for higher wages.

*Sixth.* The recognition of the right of a union to borrow from any other, when necessary, a sum of money to the amount of $1 for each member thereof, to be repaid in a manner prescribed. This is intended, in conjunction with other matters proposed, to strengthen each individual society in the struggles which it may be called on to make, from time to time, against unjust employers. Its efficacy needs no explanation. . . .

Combination merely to fix and sustain a scale of prices, is of minor importance, compared to that combination which looks to an ultimate redemption of labor. Scales of prices, to keep up the value of labor, are only necessary under a system which, in its uninterrupted operation, gives to that value a continued downward tendency. But when labor determines no longer to sell itself to speculators, but to become its own employer; to own and enjoy itself and the fruit thereof, the necessity for scales of prices will have passed away, and labor will be forever rescued from the control of the capitalist. It will then be free, fruitful, honorable. . . .

The journeymen printers of the United States are earnestly invoked, by their brethren here, to employ their most effective endeavors in the prosecution of this work. . . . And we beg them finally to send a full representation to the next convention, from every section of the country. . . . Let something be evolved, during its deliberations, which will redound to the benefit of our own trade, and, by way of example, to the benefit of all others.

Respectfully,

M. F. CONWAY,

GEO. E. GREENE,

AND. J. ATKINSON,

J. T. NAFEW,

CHAS. BECHTEL,

*Committee.*

*By order of the convention:*

JOHN W. PEREGOY,

*President.*

GEO. E. GREENE,

M. C. BROWN,

*Vice-Presidents.*

F. J. OTTARSON,

JOHN HARTMAN,

*Secretaries.*

*New York, December 7, 1850.*

# CHAPTER TWELVE

## EQUITABLE RETURN FOR
## WORK DONE

———◆———

*We ask, then, what better means can be devised for pro-
moting a more equal distribution of wealth, than for the
producing classes to* claim, *and by virtue of union and concert, secure their claims to their respective portions? And
why should not those who have the toil, have the enjoyment also? Or why should the sweat that flows from the
brow of the labourer, be converted into a source of revenue
for the support of the crafty or indolent?*
———ELY MOORE: *Address to the General Trades' Union
of New York City, December 2, 1833*

*The labor of an industrious man is in my judgment only
adequately rewarded when his wages, together with the
assistance of those members of his family, from whom assistance may reasonably be required, will enable him to provide comfortably for himself and them, to educate his
children and lay up sufficient for the casualties of life and
the wants of advanced age.*

*To accomplish these objects it is necessary that the pay
of the laborer should bear a just proportion to the prices
and necessaries and comforts of life; and all attempts to
depress them below this equitable standard, are in my
opinion at war as well with the dictates of humanity as
with a sound and rational policy.*
———MARTIN VAN BUREN: *On Labor, March 31, 1840*

Sources of the quotations on the preceding page:

ELY MOORE: Ely Moore: *Address Delivered before the General Trades'*
*Union . . . December 2, 1833* (New York: [1833]), 9–10.

MARTIN VAN BUREN: Quoted in Philip S. Foner: *History of the Labor*
*Movement in the United States* (New York: 1947), 163. Reprinted by permission of the author.

———◀◆▶———

AN equitable return for work done is the third prop for assuring equality of economic opportunity. The assumption that a fair minimum share of the nation's wealth is due each citizen is what gives the American standard of living its distinctive meaning. While the fulfillment of this ideal is naturally a special objective of industrial labor, all the common people share it, for upon it is based the dignity of free labor as against slave labor.

Most early Americans visualized this credo within the framework of a "free enterprise" system based upon private property. In fact, working folk of the antebellum period were generally not anticapitalist-minded. In demanding more pay, they were inclined to insist that labor power was a species of "property right." Holding labor as "their actual property," the Journeymen Curriers of Newark in 1835 considered it their "province to put a fair and just value on their own articles." * But free enterprise was not regarded as compatible with monopolistic privilege. Nor was it considered an end in itself, but rather a means towards securing a fair return for one's labor. And when this end seemed unattainable under capitalism, a radical fringe was prepared to scrap the system. In its radicalism, however, it was animated by indigenous humanitarian movements, not by foreign, class-conscious groups such as were creating the socialist and communist parties of Europe. "The preservation of life," said Edward Livingston to the Louisiana legislature, "is the first object, property is only a secondary one. . . . Can it be supposed that any just contract could stipulate that one of the contracting parties should die of hunger,

* Ibid, 119, citing *Newark Daily Advertiser* (August 10, 1835) and others to the same effect.

in order that the others might enjoy, without deduction, the whole of their property?" *

The Federalist era evoked popular pressure for a division of the "fishes and loaves." This demand was put forward by the Democratic Societies, the Whisky Rebels, and by people like William Manning, whose *Key of Libberty* (1) asserted that "Labour is the sole parent of all property" and should assure its fair treatment through a "labouring society." In defense of the Journeymen Cordwainers of New York in 1809, their attorney, William Sampson, asked: "Shall all others, except only the industrious mechanic be allowed to meet and plot?" † More radical was *An Essay on Common Wealths* by the New York Society for Promoting Communities in 1822, wherein an equitable property basis was considered a prerequisite for the attainment of social equality (2).

With the quickening of the labor movement in the Jacksonian period the cry for a fair share of the nation's wealth became more frequent and insistent. The labor spokesmen generally voiced the hope of securing a "just price for our labor," as did the New York Association of Tailoresses in 1831 (3). Some, like Stephen Simpson in his *Working Man's Manual* (1831) (4) and Theophilus Fisk in his *Labor the Only True Source of Wealth* (1837) (7), went further and propounded the idea that labor, as the source of capital, had the sole right to property and that the redistribution of property was essential to "secure the happiness of all." Some few, showing the influence of Robert Dale Owen, Frances Wright, and Thomas Skidmore, were ready to support the dispossession of men of property; such were the members of the New York Association for Gratuitous Distribution of Discussions on Political Economy in 1831 (5) and the "Philanthropist" in his *Address to Farmers, Mechanics, and Laborers* in 1834 (6).

The utopianism and militant trade unionism of the years from 1840 to 1860 swelled the clamor for an equitable return. The Rochester Fourier Society in *Labor's Wrongs and Labor's Remedy*

---

* Edward Livingston: *Complete Works of Edward Livingston on Criminal Jurisprudence*, 2 v. (New York: 1873), I, 533.

† *Trial of the Journeymen Cordwainers of the City of New York for a Conspiracy to Raise Their Wages with the Arguments of Counsel* . . . (New York: 1810), 46–7.

(1843), following the lead of Albert Brisbane (Chapter Eleven, 7) exclaimed: "What are the working classes of every nation considered by the non-producers, the idlers, but beasts of burden: without heart and without souls whose doom it is to labour and to die?" * Their solution was a Fourierist phalanx. The New England Social Reform Society devoted itself to socialism, universal brotherhood, pacifism, and vegetarianism. The American anarchist, Josiah Warren sought a legitimate reward for labor in his *Equitable Commerce* (1846) (8) through his exchange notes of equivalent labor cost; so, to, did his disciple John Pickering, who in the *Working Men's Political Economy* (1847) (9) compared the capitalist to a highwayman, somewhat to the advantage of the highwayman. Less radical was Edward Kellogg, whose *Labor and Capital* (1849) (10) argued for a fair "equivalent" for labor, but with the preservation of the rights of property.

By far the most significant and durable current, however, was the demand of labor for the right to organize for higher pay and fewer hours. The advertisement of the Journeymen Printers of Philadelphia, October 8, 1850, characteristically demanded a higher pay scale and denounced the strikebreakers as "rats" (11). If they did not want the destruction of the capitalistic system, they nevertheless demanded that it be shaped to yield a fair return for their labor. Abraham Lincoln expressed their aspirations when he wrote in 1847: "To secure to each laborer the whole product of his labor, or as nearly as possible, is a worthy object of any good government." †

* As quoted in Foner: *History of Labor Movement,* 176. A copy of the pamphlet is in the Columbia University Library.

† From "Notes for a Tariff Discussion," December 1, 1847 (?), John G. Nicolay and John Hay: *Complete Works of Abraham Lincoln,* 12 v. (New York: 1905), I, 307.

1.

*William Manning:*
THE KEY OF LIBBERTY *
[1798]

*William Manning (1747–1814), a New England farmer, was*
*born in Massachusetts of Puritan stock. He served as a Rev-*
*olutionary minuteman and officer and ten years later was*
*chosen selectman for two terms. He was a Jeffersonian Re-*
*publican, glorying in the French Revolution and distrustful*
*of Federalism. He believed that the remedy for the reaction-*
*ary drift was correct information and a union of the plain*
*people. On the assumption that labor gave to property its*
*value, he favored a more equitable return for "laborers." In*
*1798 he sent his Key of Libberty to the editor of the Boston*
*Independent Chronicle, then under indictment for seditious*
*libel under the Sedition Law. Manning's manuscript was re-*
*jected since his "remidy" would have put the editor out of*
*business.*

To all the Republicans, Farmers, Mecanicks, and Labourers In
Amarica your Canded attention is Requested to the Sentiments
of a Labourer

INTRODUCTION

*Learning & Knowledg is assential to the preservation of Lib-*
*berty & unless we have more of it amongue us we Cannot Seporte*
*our Libertyes Long.*

I am not a Man of Larning my selfe for I neaver had the advantage of six months schooling in my life. I am no travelor for I
neaver was 50 Miles from whare I was born in no direction, & I

---

* William Manning: *The Key of Libberty, Shewing the Causes Why a*
*Free Government Has Always Failed, and a Remedy against It,* Edited by
S. E. Morison (Billerica, Mass.: 1922), 3–4, 14–15, 60, 61–2. (The original
spelling is reproduced here without the customary insertion of *"sic."*) Reprinted
by permission of W. Harold Manning, executor of the Warren H. Manning
estate.

am no grate reader of antiant history for I always followed hard labour for a living. But I always thought it My duty to search into & see for my selfe in all maters that consansed me as a member of society, & when the war began betwen Brittan & Amarica I was in the prime of Life & highly taken up with Liberty & a free Government. I See almost the first blood that was shed in Concord fite & scores of men dead, dying & wounded in the Cause of Libberty, which caused serious sencations in my mind.

But I beleived then & still believ it is a good cause which we aught to defend to the very last, & I have bin a Constant Reader of publick Newspapers & closely attended to men & measures ever sence, through the war, through the operation of paper money, framing Constitutions, makeing & constructing Laws, & seeing what selfish & contracted ideayes of interests would influence the best picked men & bodyes of men.

I have often thought it was imposable ever to seport a free Government, but firmly believing it to be the best sort & the ondly one approved off by heaven it was my unweryed study & prayers to the almighty for many years to find out the real cause & a remidy and I have for many years bin satisfyed in my own mind what the causes are & what would in a grate measure prove a reamidy provided it was carried into efect.

But I had no thoughts of publishing my sentiments on it untill the adoption of the Brittish trety * in the manner it has bin done. But seeing the unweryed pains & the unjustifyable masures taken by large numbers of all ordirs of men who git a living without labour in Elections & many other things to ingure the interests of the Labourer & deprive us of the priviledges of a free government, I came to a resolution (although I have nither larning nor lasure for the purpose) to improve on my Constitutional Right & give you my sentiments on what the causes are & a remidy. . . .

In the swet of thy face shall thou git thy bread untill thou return to the ground, is the erivarsable sentance of Heaven on Man for his rebellion. To be sentanced to hard Labour dureing life is very unplesent to humane Nature. Their is a grate avartion to it purceivable in all men—yet it is absolutely nesecary that a large majority of the world should labour, or we could not subsist. For

---

* Jay's Treaty of 1794 with Great Britain. [Ed. note.]

Labour is the soul parrant of all property—the land yealdeth nothing without it, & their is no food, clothing, shelter, vessel, or any nesecary of life but what costs Labour & is generally esteemed valuable according to the Labour it costs. Therefore no person can posess property without labouring, unless he git it by force or craft, fraud or fortun out of the earnings of others.

But from the grate veriety of capacietyes strength & abilityes of men, their always was, & always will be, a very unequel distribution of property in the world. Many are so rich that they can live without Labour. Also the marchent, phisition, lawyer & divine, the philosipher and school master, the Juditial & Executive Officers, & many others who could honestly git a living without bodily labours. As all these professions require a considerable expence of time & property to qualify themselves therefor, & as no person after this qualifying himselfe & making a pick on a profession by which he meens to live, can desire to have it dishonourable or unproductive, so all these professions naturally unite in their skems to make their callings as honourable & lucrative as possable. Also as ease & rest from Labour are reaconed amongue the gratest pleasures of Li:, pursued by all with the gratest avidity & when attained at once creates a sense of superiority & as pride & ostentation are natural to the humain harte, these ordirs of men generally asotiate together and look down with two much contempt on those that labour.

On the other hand the Labourer being contious that it is Labour that seports the hole, & that the more there is that live without Labour & the higher they live or the grater their salleryes & fees are, so much the harder he must work, or the shorter he must live, this makes the Labourer watch the other with a jelous eye & often has reason to complain of real impositions. . . .

### REAMIDY AGAINST IT

The ondly Remidy against these evils is by improveing our Rights as freemen in elections, nor do we need any other if we ware posesed of knowledge anough to act rationally in them. For as I have before shewed, the duty of a Representitive or any person chosen into office is to act as all his Constitutiants would if they ware all present & all knew what was for their own interests.

And as men being elected into neavour so high offices, remain
men still and are moved by the same prinsaples & passions as
other men are, so that the temtation & emolument of 25 thousand
dollors a year or any other some & to be worshiped into the bargain hath ten thousand charme with it, so that the love of office
will compel them to aim at pleasing their Constituants. Consi-
quently if elections are closely attended to by all the peopel &
they look well ever after their Representitives, their is no dainger
but that they will do their duty. Therefore the ondly Remidi is
knowledge. . . .

As this knowledge cant be obtained without the expence of a
continued sereies of publications that can be red with confidence
as to their truth, and as newspaper knowledg is ruened by the
few, & as the ordir of Cincinaty have purformed such wonders by
their Asociations, I propose a Sociaty of Labourers to be formed
as near after the ordir of Cincinati as the largeness of their numbers will admit of.

The Society to be composed of all the Republicans & Labourers
in the United States who will be at the expense of obtaining the
above described Knowledg.

2.

*New York Society for Promoting Communities:*
AN ESSAY ON COMMON WEALTHS *
[1822]

*This pamphlet, published by the New York Society for Pro-
moting Communities, is a remarkable specimen of early radical literature in the United States. Referring frequently to
Joel Barlow, it anticipated ideas that were advanced and ex-
panded in the late twenties by Thomas Skidmore, Frances
Wright, and Robert Dale Owen.*

Where *human* justice is, there is *political* freedom; and where
*divine* justice is in dominion, there is *religious* freedom. *Love to
our neighbours* as much as to our selves, should attach us to *hu-*

* *An Essay on Common Wealths* (New York: 1822), 24–6, 36–8.

*man justice;* and *love to God,* with all our hearts and minds should unite us to *divine justice.* Is it *right,* that men in a *social* state should possess an *equality of rights, privileges,* and *property,* in an *inconclusive* way? We answer in the affirmative; and that in no systems of government can such an *equality* be produced, unless it be in a community of wealth and interest; and *there,* only can *liberty* and *equality* exist in perfection. For *social equality,* and *social liberty,* cannot flourish in any society, country, or nation, where *exclusive rights* and *property* exist. Indeed, *how* can social equality, liberty, and love flourish, where *exclusive* property generates that *root of all evil,* self-hood, or the *spirit* of self-ishness and *"love of money?" Exclusive* rights to wealth is the origin of *greedy* avarice, and lustful covetousness. To obtain *exclusive wealth* and *advantages,* men and women are daily tempted to cheat, counterfeit, swindle, extort, oppress, steal, lie, deceive, rob, and murder. By usury, rents, and interest, they feed like drones on the labours of the industrious. To enjoy exclusive advantages, they have *annually* enslaved, and caused the death of 80,000 blacks from Africa. For these *exclusive* uses, men litigate, declare war, encourage piratical privateering, pillage, massacre and destruction.

We sincerely believe, we dare assert a paradox, that no man has *a just right,* (though the laws of all governments have granted a *legal right*) to *exclusive* property. To prove this assertion, we must consider *whence* social beings derive *all* they claim *exclusively.* That men would have remained in their *natural* state, unless *civilized* society had been instituted, is a self evident proposition. In a *state of nature,* man would be in a *worse* condition than the *savages;* and could claim an *exclusive* title to nothing. His state would resemble the beasts of the forest. Hence the inference clearly arises, that all the property which men now possess *exclusively,* has been bestowed on them through the favor of *social laws, privileges, customs,* and *advantages.* In other words, that real and personal wealth is derived from, and is the *gift* of society. Joel Barlow says, "Society is the first proprietor, and original cause, of the appropriation of wealth." The *gifts* which society bestows belonged to her and before she *gave* them; and she is religiously obligated to use and bestow her blessings and donations in the most wise, just, equal and social manner;—In other words, the productions and wealth produced by society, should not be *individual, selfish,* and *exclusive property,* but *social* and *common* benefit and wealth. We will illustrate this farther. Man in a natural, solitary and unsocial state has no exclusive right, though a common right, to every natural thing the woods and waters afford him in his poor, weak, ignorant and timorous condition. And, as the wild beasts would claim, and *share* dominion over the forests with such men in a state of nature, we conclude that men in an unsocial state would suffer, and often perish for the necessaries of life. As soon as men become *social* beings, they acquire *wealth* and *power,* and increase in *wisdom;* so that, in the *most civilized society,* they have become very opulent, potent and erudite. If men live in pure perfect communities, where all things were as they should be, man's social rights would not *destroy* as they now do, the *natural rights* he possessed in his wild and unassociated state; but would *increase, exalt* and *perfect all* his *natural* into *social* rights. And, as men claimed a right in their *natural* and *unassociated* state to *every thing around them;* so they should claim, in a pure community, a right to *all around them.* No man by entering into civil government should be abridged of an equitable right of nature. Civil government should extend and enlarge every one of them. Life, liberty, and advantages should be inviolate, extended and exalted. This is *true,* and paradoxical. Joel Barlow confirms these sentiments in his advice to the privileged orders, ch. 4, p. 76, &c.

A *pure common wealth* would put an end to the vast riches of a *few,* and the miserable indigence of *many. All* would have what Agur prayed for when he said, *"Give me neither poverty nor riches." Great wealth,* as well as *great penury,* is a *great evil,* and produces luxury, sensuality, dissipation, vanity, pride, cruelty, oppression, hatred and ruin. A pure common wealth would put an end to the evils and oppressions of craft rulers; and of lords temporal and of lords spiritual; and of all aristocrats, brokers, bankers, userers, shavers, and knaves. It would terminate their numerous mischiefs framed into laws by crafty, ambitious and selfish men and legislatures; such as tythes, taxes, imposts, (absurdly called *duties,*) excise, and stamp acts; things, which unjustly operate so as to make the poorer class of society pay the same price, for the same things, as the opulent, who are a hundred times

more able to bear it. The rich and poor, agreeable to Deut. xvi.
17. ought to pay in *proportion* to their *income* and *wealth.* It
would put an end to litigation, imprisonment for debt, and
debtor's jails; and to pensioners, office-hunters, war and a hireling
ministry. Indeed, what present *evils* of association would not
cease to scourge us? *Evils,* by which men of opulence, office,
learning and power now oppress the poor, weak, ignorant, servile
and labourious parts of society; whose industry would, if society
did them justice in her institutions and laws, produce them
abundance. The monied and governing part of society have done,
and still do, all they can to maintain and exalt themselves in affluence and dominion, and in indolence, luxury and grandeur.
Their great instruments of effecting these objects are arms and
exclusive rights of fealties;—interests, rents and banks; monopolies, imposts miscalled *duties,* &c. These enhance their *exclusive*
opulence; by these they grind the poor to powder. . . .

. . . In the present governments which support the principle
of *selfishness,* by encouraging *exclusive* titles to honor, profit and
wealth, a *few* are very rich, and *many* are very poor. For many
poor and suffering persons are necessary in society, to maintain
one opulent man, surfeiting himself in the pleasures of this life.
. . . Those who are rich, are *generally* the *drones* of the national
*hive.* Were we like *bees,* what would become of them? Twelve
millions or three fourths of the population of Great Britain and
Ireland are censused poor and working folks. The industrious
and poor part of the society are *really,* though not nominally, in
municipal slavery and degradation to the honoured opulent. The
poor labour too much; they are contemned; they cannot study the
sciences; they mourn under their grievances; they perish under
their hardships. What is their stimulus to labour? It is not for the
accumulation of wealth, nor honour, nor the comforts of life.
*Three fourths* of mankind are *compelled,* by dire necessity to
drudge and slave for an uncomfortable subsistence. But in a
pious and pure community, such *servitude, misery* and oppression could not exist; neither would dronish lordlings. Men and
women would labour *diligently,* but not *continually.* They would
do so for health, happiness, competence, and a good conscience
towards God and man. Part of their daily time would be occupied
in the study of useful arts, sciences and literature. Every person

should alternately strengthen the *body* by labour, and the *mind* by study. But in governments of *exclusive* property, most of the rich live without healthy bodily labour; and most of the poor and needy live without literary exercise. These views concerning the stimuli to exertion, are sufficient to prove, that men in pure communities, have both *greater* and *better* excitements to be usefully employed in bodily and mental pursuits, than those who live in nations where property is held exclusively, and where the poor have only the lash of necessity to drive them. Besides these things, other stimuli or motives to good conduct might be enumerated, favourable to wise, just and pious associations with common stock. No militant and contending *interests*, for example, existing therein, as must necessarily exist in all governments, where wealth is held *exclusively* by individuals, they would enjoy in a community the loving sympathy and counsel of their brethren.

3.

*The New York Association of Tailoresses:*
RESOLUTIONS *
[February 28, 1831]

> *The first sign of women participating in labor struggle came in Pawtucket, Rhode Island, in 1824, when the "female weavers," together with male weavers, struck in an attempt to resist a reduction of wages and an increase in hours. The following year, women alone struck for the first time when the tailoresses of New York issued a call for higher wages. The New York Association of Tailoresses was probably an outgrowth of these beginnings.*

The following Resolutions were unanimously adopted by some hundred females, on the 28th of February, 1831, as an amendment to the resolution read at a previous meeting.

1. *Resolved,* That in the opinion of this Society, the prices of Tailoresses ought to be advanced at least one third, and in some

* *The Constitution, &c. of the New York Association of Tailoresses* (New York: 1831), 1–2, 8.

cases doubled. And that we believe it can be effected and made for the following reasons:—Because it is possible to provide a fund sufficient to relieve the necessities of the few who would require it, for the short time that might be necessary to compel employers to give the prices demanded. Because when such a fund is raised in this city, it will excite the oppressed of our sex in other places to similar salutary exertions. Because when these objects are once obtained, self interest, if no higher motive, will prevent any from violating their engagements, and stimulate them to greater exertions.

2. *Resolved,* Therefore, in view of these reasons, and in the opinion of this Society, that we have a well founded hope of obtaining and securing a just price for our labor, and rendering our condition in socity [*sic*] such that our necessities will not compel us to sell our labor for much less than it is worth.

3. *Resolved,* That as soon as shall be thought expedient, a moderate bill of prices be made out, and measures taken to have them presented to every employer in the city, and the names of all such as refuse to give the prices therein mentioned shall be published—that those who wish to protect our interests may know who to regard as our enemies and avoid giving them custom.

4. *Resolved,* That in consideration of the justice of our cause, we pledge ourselves to conform to the rules of the Society, and that as soon as it shall become sufficiently strong, we will work for no person refusing to give the prices adopted.

5. *Resolved,* That as a means of forwarding our cause, a committee of this Society and of other persons friendly thereto, be appointed to receive and solicit donations in aid of the funds of this Society.

6. *Resolved,* That although we obtain our prices, we will not relax in our efforts to support and increase this Society.

7. *Resolved,* That the foregoing resolutions, together with the names of the committee to receive and solicit donations, be published in the papers friendly to our cause. And, that those of our sex and situation in life, in other places, be requested to take them into serious consideration.

NOTICE

All Tailoresses are respectfully and pressingly invited to attend a meeting . . . which meeting shall appoint, if thought best, a Committee of one from each Ward Meeting, to make out a moderate bill of Prices, and report to a future Meeting as mentioned in the Resolutions. It is confidently believed that the present is the time for the Tailoresses to free themselves from the burdens under which they now labour. And further, we entreat every Tailoress into whose hand this comes, to seriously and carefully enquire, while perusing and reperusing and pondering this Constitution, whether it is not, in so extensive a city and so numerous a population, well calculated and well adopted to bring into action the whole united energies of the Tailoresses—*"Union is Strength,"* combine the united exertions of Tailoresses and they can invariably affect any just and reasonable object they choose. This Society will prevent in future, the like depression we now labour under.

4.

*Stephen Simpson:*
WORKING MAN'S MANUAL *
[1831]

*Born in Philadelphia, Stephen Simpson (1789–1854) followed his father's occupation of bank official and note clerk. At the battle of New Orleans he became an admirer of Andrew Jackson. He was the first, though unsuccessful, candidate for Congress of the Working Men's Party of Philadelphia. He wrote several biographies, but the chief expression of his views is the* Working Man's Manual, *where the influence of Robert Owen is seen. In developing Adam Smith's labor theory of value, he gave to it a pre-Marxian twist. He wanted the workers to form a party of producers to struggle politically for improvement, as the Chartists of England were doing. He also wanted a free system of education.*

* Stephen Simpson: *Working Man's Manual* (Philadelphia: 1831), 8–9, 86–9.

The slightest observation will satisfy the most prejudiced and sceptical mind, that nature has superabundantly supplied the industry of man with the means of universal comfort. We behold a demonstration of the fact in every form of luxury—every object of magnificence—every refinement of pleasure—every waste of riot and sensuality—every monument of pride—every display of vanity—every gorgeous decoration of wealth, power, and ambition. We behold the proof in the lord of ten thousand acres, tortured on his sick couch by the agonies of repletion, whilst the labourer famishes at his gate: we behold it in the luxurious capitalist, swelling with the overweening pride of overpampered opulence, whilst the hearts that *laboured* to produce his wealth, shiver and faint with misery and want, or drag out a protracted life of endless toil, blasting existence by the despair even of a bare competence.—But unfortunately for the human family, this abundance of nature, and this industry of man, are alike unavailing to his happiness. What God has spread before us as the reward and the property of him whose *labour* shall bring it into use, government, unjust, despotic, proud, all-grasping government, has ordained shall belong to those who never labour; and for whose exclusive benefit, the labourer shall toil for ever. Thus do human institutions, founded on tyranny, or perverted from their original principles of justice, destroy and circumvent the beneficence of heaven: or, where those institutions are congenial to equity, customs and usages devolved from a prior age and a different government, wrest the fruit of industry from the mouth of labour, and heap it in the overflowing storehouse of the patron, or land proprietary of the monarch whose royal charter superseded the decrees of justice and the laws of nature. . . .

What but a principle of slavery could have made it a felony, for a working man to demand the true and just wages of his labour? If mechanics combine to raise their wages, the laws punish them as conspirators against the good of society, and the dungeon awaits them as it does the robber. But the laws have made it a just and meritorious act, that *capitalists shall combine* to strip the man of labour of his earnings, and reduce him to a dry crust, and a gourd of water. Thus does power invert justice, and derange the order of nature. . . .

There is, there can be, but one rule for estimating the value of labour—on principles of equity—benevolence, and social harmony —that rule is, HUMAN HAPPINESS; general competence and as nearly as possible, an equality of the enjoyments of life. The end of labour being happiness,—it is self-evident, that happiness must regulate the *just* value of labour. If notwithstanding the industry of the working people, they still remain poor and wretched— whilst those for whom they toil are swollen with countless wealth; it demonstrates that the wages of labour are too small, and that capital has continued to absorb that portion of the wages of the son of industry, which of right belongs to him. This is the true mode of estimating the value of labour—that the industrious may enjoy comfort, competence, and happiness. True, this is not the *legal* mode, nor the rule of civil authority; but it is not, on that account, the less true, the less just, nor the less sacred. The faculties of man were bestowed to ensure his comfort; for that he labours— and that he would always accomplish, when industrious, but for the intervention of injustice—the power, fraud, and oppression of CAPITAL, in its various forms, and attitudes.

An idea has been entertained by some, that equality is the condition of man, as designed by nature—and that all have an equal right to the earth, the elements of life, and all the productions so bountifully scattered over its face. The fallacy of this assumption exposes itself—for all men have not equal faculties of mind, or of body; nor equal inclinations to apply them to use; some being indolent, some quick, some slow, some industrious. It is not the equality of faculties, but the *equality of rights,* for which we ought to contend. If I possess industry, or ingenuity, I have a right to their product, in defiance of *capital,* monopoly, or combination— labour constituting the sole right to property, land, produce, and all sort of wealth. It is true, that capital is power, the symbol, or representative of labour accumulated—but this very accumulation stamps it with a coercive power fatal to general happiness; for it extorts its own terms, and unless resisted by the political combination of labour, it is arbitrary and omnipotent, partial, selfish, and exclusively accumulative, without regard to humanity, suffering, penury, wretchedness, and perpetual toil.

Labour in the form of capital is the MASTER—labour in the individual, is the SERVANT. We desire to divest the master of some of his power, in order to add to the comfort of the servant.

It is a fallacy to imagine, that we are aiming to controvert the established legitimate doctrines of political economy: as it respects the principles of supply and demand and other contingencies that regulate the market, or subject labour and property to the vicissitudes of times, seasons and accidents. Our object reaches higher—is more rational—and more laudable. It strikes at a FUNDAMENTAL PRINCIPLE in the distribution of wealth— that LABOUR shall share, with CAPITAL, in the profits of trade, in a more equitable ratio. And as capital is vested in the FEW, and labour resides in the MANY—it only requires that the latter combine to bring government into their own hands, to secure all they desire. At first, the struggle will be great and arduous; but perseverance and concord, *on expansive grounds,* must finally lead to a signal triumph.

**5.**

*New York Association for Gratuitous Distribution of Discussions on Political Economy:*
POLITICAL ESSAYS *
[October 1, 1831]

> *The New York Association for the Gratuitous Distribution of Discussions on Political Economy was promoted by Thomas Skidmore, initiator of the short-lived newspaper the* Friend of Equal Rights. *The propaganda technique of this radical organization, whose chairman was Joel P. White and secretary, William Forbes, is seen by the inscription at the end of tract Number One:*

> Read and lend
> Read and lend again.

Government then we think, and by government we mean in this instance, the whole people at the polls, ordering by their votes the special enactment of such a law; the whole people, we say, should declare all property to be the property of the state; thus dispos-

* New York Association for Gratuitous Distribution of Discussions on Political Economy: *Political Essays*, No. 1 (New York: October 1, 1831), 7, 21–4.

sessing every man. They should order the state to be divided into a great number of small districts; the property in each to be appraised, and its adults and minor citizens registered and numbered, with their name, age, sex, color, occupation and parentage. A copy of the appraisements and census of each district should be taken to the capital of the state; the amount of the value of the property and of the number of citizens who should be of, and over the age of maturity, ascertained, and by dividing this amount by this number should be ascertained also the sum it would amount to for each individual. They should order report of this sum to be sent back to every district; and so soon as this was done, the auctions (one kind of property only being sold at a time, tho' in any number of different places) to commence. Each person is ordered and authorized to bid for what he likes best to an amount not exceeding nor falling short, say 5 or 10 percent under or over the dividend made for each individual at the centre of the state, he being considered as having a debt due to him from the State for that amount. They should order, so soon as the sales are done with, that each district should send a return of the amount of its sales to the Capital. This being done, the whole amount is ascertained; it is divided as before among all people of full age, and the actual amount is made known which is due to each individual. If he have purchased to an amount greater than this, he owes to the state something and his property remains mortgaged till paid; if he have bought less, the State owes him and will make it good. Till the sales are all done, no property to be delivered to the purchaser. In the meantime, while all this is going on, all people may be supplied by the State, with all the necessaries of life, and this, we think, need not be longer than some three or four weeks.

They, the people, should order the property of those who die in any one year to be divided equally among the native born children of the state, who, during the same year come of age, without distinction of sex or color, and this forever after the General Division has once taken place. This patrimony to be all that each individual is ever to receive from the State, except it be insurance for property lost and destroyed, for services rendered, or for relief from distress arising from accident, infirmity or disease. All burials at the public expense. It should be added that at the General Division of all property, foreigners who have previously become citizens, should, with their children, be on the same footing with the native-born—but those coming afterwards cannot expect it. The children only which may be·born to them after they do come, can alone be considered as citizens entitled to support and patrimonies as herein recommended to be ordered.

They should order all children to be fed, clothed, instructed and taught some useful pursuit at the public expense; but in doing this, there is no occasion to separate children from parents till they are of an age to commence the acquisition of the knowledge of some useful occupation; and often not then. All family ties it will be seen, under this system will remain then as they are now; and there will be no exception unless it be in cases where parents do not take proper care of their children. Taxation on property is that which is to enable the State to furnish all these supplies to the rising generations.

Were government modified on principles like these, it is apparent the condition of every man's children would be exactly the same as it might be if every parent had been able to give his offspring the same education and property as another could give his. There is this difference, however, in the two cases; that in the system we recommend, the property of the *dying* only, and of course, *of those who have no further use for it,* is annually divided among those annually coming of age. Nothing would be taken from the living, whereas in the other case parents would be obliged to part with that which is or may be of the utmost importance to their welfare. Admitting every other circumstance in human society as now constituted to be right, one thing must evidently be acknowledged to be wrong; and this is, that parents must part with property which they cannot spare without inconvenience and injury to themselves, as often as their children arrive at maturity, or their *children* must spend the best part of *their* lives surrounded with all the distresses and difficulties which a want of property is sure to inflict upon them. How very desireable then, even in this respect, would be a better system for the transmission of property from one generation to another! . . .

We appeal then

To the Poor!—to come and join their efforts with ours; to assist us to place the means of happiness as much within their own reach as it is or can be within the reach of others; to situate their children not where they may be able to live without labor, but where they shall not be compelled to be the servants of men and of women no better than themselves; where, below the temptations of power and above the necessities of want, they know neither misery nor vice; and where they neither feel fear nor sustain reproach. We ask them to consider that all have right to be happy; that no man has right to *desire*, much less to *possess* property for the purpose of exempting himself from his equal share of labor, and if there be any who does, such person cannot, therefore, have any just claims to be considered by you, by others, or himself, as any thing but a bad man. We beg you to consider that you are free men; that as such you have the right for example, to leave your country; that if you were all to do it, those who now live on your, and of course not on their own, labor, allowing them to be equally rich, and allowing, also, that no more poor men came among them, would then find themselves obliged to support themselves on their own individual labor exactly as they would be required to do if a division of property had taken place; and that if it be right in one way to require all to labor for their living; so is it right in another. We beg you to consider that those who now address you can have no interest in the proposed new modification of society beyond that which will be possessed by every other person, that of having the full value of their labor, if they labor at all and otherwise nothing; that you have the power to bring about even this great change; and that as we have already shown, you have *no right* to give your labor to others without an equal return from them, as must be the case if you suffer society to remain unchanged—nor to allow your children to be doomed to the same unhappy condition. We ask you to reflect, that, in this country, nineteen out of twenty read and are able to understand subjects so plain as this; that every man votes; that the number of your own description of people is probably six or seven out of every ten; and that therefore you command the moral and physical power of every community. Unite then your exertions with ours; spare of the wages of your servitude the trifle you can, if you approve our sentiments, to give them a still more extended circulation, knowing full well that many of your brethren have prejudices, as is natural, against the boldness of our views, and, therefore, in the first instance cannot be willing to pay for what they consider erroneous imprac-

ticable, or unjust. Send abroad our pamphlets to distant friends
and let these in turn either correspond with us for more at cost
price, or republish in their own places. Come also with us for more
at the ensuing election and support a ticket on these principles,
if for no other purpose as to any immediate benefit, than that it
will tend to make our system more correctly and more widely
known. Be not despairing of the accomplishment of so great an
object. Hitherto revolutions have been brought about slowly; but
hitherto men could not read; hitherto men could not write; nor
print; nor vote; and there were few of course to study the science
of government. Now, a thousand men, poor men for example, (so
cheap is printing,) in five or ten years, could easily themselves
furnish to every human being in the United States who can read,
all that is *necessary* for him to read of *any* system, this or any other,
which may be found adequate to make all equally happy. Why
then should we despair? . . .

To the Middling Class!—You who have acquired, either by inheritance or industry, a competence for yourselves and your children. But though your condition is comfortable, you have no
guarantee that it shall remain so. Human life is full of vicissitudes
which each individual for himself can only modify, but can never
control or counteract. It is for *your* interest then to come into a
system, where, happen what will to *you*, your children can never
be situated in a condition inferior to the children of any other
man. Consider well whether you have any just, moral and parental
right, by holding fast to the present order of things, to jeopardize
the happiness of those you have brought into the world! Think
whether you can be a loser even in a pecuniary point of view. . . .
How many are not sinking down into the class of the poor who
have nothing, devoured by the monopolizing operations of still
mightier capitalists? We conjure this Middle Class then to save
themselves and the class below them by making common cause
with us in our effort entirely to re-model the present state of
society.

To the Wealthy!—To you we say that even *your* true interests
are with ours. They cannot be separated. Organized as we wish
to see society, all that you enjoy now, you could enjoy then. . . .
Would you that a man, your equal, your superior perhaps should
fan you while you are hot, bathe your feet at night, stand behind

your chair at your meals, &c, &c? . . . Better, far better, that you be equal with your fellows; that, then, your country insure your property from loss by storm, by shipwreck, by fire, by sickness; that there be no debt; no wars abroad or at home; no thieves, robbers, murderers, no difference of rank, arising from difference of condition; that your children and children's children enjoy the advantage of the same perpetual system to the latest generation and thus be exempted from the possibility of what happens often enough now—of dying in the alms house. These are your true interests—and though many of you will not listen to them now, the time is fast coming when an all powerful public opinion will demand it at your own hands. The time is fast coming when this same omnipotent opinion will consign to an infamy deeper than that which now stains the character of the vilest malefactor, the man who would dare to wish through his wealth to make others support his existence. We pray that among your own class, in America at least, there may be found none so unreasonable as to oppose themselves to a system so holy, benignant and just. . . .

JOEL P. WHITE, *Chairman*
WM. FORBES, *Secretary.*

*Read and lend*
 *Read and lend again.*

**6.**

AN ADDRESS TO FARMERS, MECHANICS AND LABORERS *
[1834]

*This pamphlet, written anonymously by a "Philanthropist," deplored the lack of an "equivalent" return to the farmers, mechanics, and laborers, the real producers of wealth. It advocated the formation of "companies for the mutual exchange of wealth for wealth upon the principles of equivalents," thus anticipating Josiah Warren's "time-store" idea.*

*Fellow Workmen and Fellow Citizens:* . . .

The privations we are subjected to, are, the privation of property, of plenty, of recreation and rest, and the cultivation of mind.

* A Philanthropist: *An Address to Farmers, Mechanics and Laborers* (Philadelphia: 1834), 3–5, 7–8.

If these are denied, the practice of this system will prove them to be facts in the result of its operations on the members. But we have the evidence at hand.

Whose are those dwellings we inhabit? They belong to the rich! Who built them? The working poor! What did we get for those stately mansions now inhabited by the idle rich? Nothing! We, as a body of producers of wealth, lived upon our own and each other's wealth!—Then what has became [*sic*] of that which we received of them as an equivalent for our labor? We had to give it up to them again for house rent and profit added to goods for that purpose, and to make up the losses they met with from honest as well as dishonest men—swindlers, counterfeiters, and other knaves, caused by the madness of speculation! And what has become of the surplus, exclusive of the houses? Oh! they issued an extra quantity of paper from the *bank*, sufficient to cover the whole, and so bought it all up? And did we ever get any thing for our paper money from them? Oh, yes!—They raised our rents by way of a reward, and the profits on the goods we used, and so drew it all back again. Well, what became of it then? They gave it to the workmen who built the house for them! What did they do with it? They gave it to the store-keepers and lumber-men, in order to furnish themselves with food and raiment, and materials to build more houses for the rich! Did they give a profit on these goods? Yes, and a large profit too, to enable these middle men to pay their rent, and other extra expenses? Then all of these middle men cannot get rich, at least very soon: no, but very few of them get rich. They are the veriest dupes of the whole lot of working men; they fight with their workmen, scratch and claw every body, for money to give the rich, or for the inexpressible pleasure of counting change—generally frightened almost out of their wits, for fear the whole of it will finally slip through their fingers, without leaving a mark or a vestige of it behind. By this, we may perceive that nearly all our surplus labor regularly and systematically falls into the possession of the idle rich.

But, why should we not stop off this copious stream from their basket and their store, and fill our own, seeing it is ours by right of production, as they have no right to it, except they can give us as much for it as will confer as many benefits on us, as our labor productions did upon them. If this was done the trade would be fair and equal: then the house we lived in might be ours.

Why should we not own the house we occupy, in preference to him who never produced the value of an apple in his life, or did as much good to society as the value of a pound of coffee. Do you think such a distribution of property among the frugal industrious could harm society? If it could I should like to know how?

It could not take a thing from any one which was properly his, nor prevent any one from obtaining that which he or they were properly entitled to. But we are frequently prevented from working, however justly we may be entitled to it, and the benefits arising therefrom.

We who produce every thing which is of indispensable utility, ought to enjoy as much as they who produce none of these things. They enjoy all the pleasures of literature, without loss on their part, when we eat of the crumbs which fall from their lips. This is not all; we have to pay them richly for every morsel of literary honey that drops from their comb. Why should we not be equal with them? Surely they could find no fault. . . .

### PRODUCERS MUTUAL EXCHANGE
### DEPOT OF WEALTH

Whereas, manufactures and trade are involved in mystery, and only made profitable to the few by chicanery and oppression.

Whereas, the working people have to supply all the wants of society by productive labour; and fill every store of the wealthy to overflowing, for less than what nature requires to restore its exhausted energies, besides the disagreeable necessity of being at the bidding of capricious mortals, seldom governed by any other motive than sordid avarice.

Whereas, banking has extended the credit system to its utmost stretch, overwhelming workmen with high rents and high prices, bringing in a flood of competitors now and then to the great disadvantage of all kinds of workmen, and reducing wages to a bare minimum of a subsistence.

Whereas, our common and statute laws, which direct us to our destiny, are highly colored with f[e]udalism, two-thirds of mankind being fated by them to perpetual hard labor and untold of privations for a scanty subsistence.

Whereas, every scheme of monopoly got up by the rich is sanctioned by legislation, however opposed to the rights and liberties of the people, which seems to threaten the independence of the republic.

Whereas, past and present experience bear testimony against the insatiability of avarice, and that so long as things remained in a situation to be coveted, or to excite the propensity to suppose that any property could be obtained for less than equivalent, and that the effort would not be made, would be absurb [*sic*] in the extreme.

Whereas, it is an ascertained fact, that a change for the better or worse must soon take place, and that if for the worse, the condition of the working people will be hopeless at no distant period. Therefore it has become extremely unsafe for working people longer to trust their welfare under the control of those fatal circumstances, especially when it is in their power otherwise to direct their own destiny to prosperity or mendicity.

Therefore, *Resolved,* that the producers and distributors of wealth form themselves into companies for the mutual exchange of wealth for wealth, upon the principles of equivalents, demonstrated by the new and just standard of value, measured by the unerring rule of time for time in each quantity for exchange. And, at the same time, to sell to the public for cash, upon the well known principles of trade—for cash down upon delivery.

7.

*Theophilus Fisk:*
### LABOR THE ONLY TRUE SOURCE OF WEALTH *
[July 4, 1837]

*Theophilus Fisk (1801–67) was a Jacksonian radical and a workingman leader who attracted attention by his Trade Union lectures in Boston in the winter of 1834–5. He had*

* Theophilus Fisk: *Labor the Only True Source of Wealth, July 4, 1837* (Charleston, S.C.: 1837), 3; inside wrapper, 2.

*turned from a Universalist pulpit to an editor's desk on the*
New Haven Examiner *and the* Boston Reformer. *An anti-clerical turned anticapitalist, he was influenced by Samuel Clesson Allen, Frederick Robinson, A. H. Everett, and William Leggett. Four days after delivering this July Fourth address, Fisk was howled down and slugged by the solid citizens of Charleston, who had packed the hall for his address on the financial situation. Although he defended the South, contending that "the real slaves in the United States have pale faces," Fisk abhorred secession. In 1860 he revived the* Washington Democratic Expositor, *in which he backed Stephen A. Douglas, the Union, and the war.*

The poorer classes are every where [sic] the most numerous, and the greatest good of the greatest number should claim our first attention. But so far from this that the poor, the laboring classes, are the very last who are thought of, or cared for, by our legislative bodies. Their whole time is consumed in granting monopolies and exclusive privileges for the "public good" of a few favored individuals.—Session after session is worse than wasted in legislating against labor, and in favor of capital, for the exclusive benefit of a few rich men. Instead of being as they ought, the inflexible guardians of equal rights, and dispensing like the dews of heaven, their favors upon all, they devote themselves to the building up of privileged orders, and creating artificial distinctions in society, exalting a few and debasing the many; making a small number enormously rich, and reducing the mass to penury and degradation. Suppose the world were a perfect plain—is it not evident that there could be no mountains without making excavations—the valley would deepen in the same proportion as the mountain increased in height. So with the people under the operation of partial legislation; that which is given to the few, is taken from the many; if the few are made rich, the many are robbed, and become poor in the same proportion as the nobility increase in wealth by an act of the legislature, instead of industry. If there were no rich men, there would be equally as much wealth and infinitely more happiness and virtue in the world, than there is at present.—Riches would then be diffused like the other blessings of heaven, the air, the light, and the rain, and the many would be contented and happy. We are greatly deceived by the phrase *poor nations;* it is there where the people are in the enjoyment of ease, and the blessings of comfort; the *rich nations* is where the mass of the people are reduced to poverty, and the wealth is in the hands of a few. This artificial and unequal distribution of property, is at the foundation, is the fruitful source, of all the evils and vice of which society complains. Every inequality of means, and of facilities, is at bottom an inequality of power. Inequality of wealth brings with it that of instruction in knowledge, capacity and influence, producing poverty and its consequent vice. This tends to re-produce or re-establish the inequality of power, and consequently to subvert society. The more there are of great fortunes, the more there are who are idle and pay for no labor but for their pleasure, and the more riches tend to decay, and population to diminish. Wherever you see exaggerated fortunes, you there see the greatest misery and the greatest stagnation of industry. . . .

The laborer seldom possesses this capital; he is willing to give a portion of the proceeds of his labor for the use of it; and the owner of the capital is thus enabled to enjoy a portion of the poor man's labor. Such must ever be the course of things where any inequalities of wealth exist; and inequalities of wealth must exist while inequalities of natural talents, of virtue and intelligence, pervade a community. But it is the policy of political systems which aim to secure the happiness of all, in equal degrees, to diminish these inequalities, as far as possible, by preventing the individual aggregation of capital and securing its entire fruits.

8.

*Josiah Warren:*
EQUITABLE COMMERCE *
[1846]

*Josiah Warren (c.1798–1874) was born in Boston. He be-*
*came a musician and music teacher, settling in Cincinnati*
*where he invented a lard-burning lamp, a speed press, and*
*a self-inking cylinder press. After hearing Robert Owen, he*

* Josiah Warren: *Equitable Commerce: a New Development of Principles* . . . (New Harmony, Indiana: 1846), 11–14, 37–9.

*sold his lard-burning lamp factory and moved his family to
New Harmony, Indiana. He developed an extremely individualistic philosophy that favored "the sovereignty of the individual" in a society where goods and services should be based
solely on cost. He tested these anarchistic theories in "equity
stores," in Cincinnati and elsewhere, which were the basis
for his first book,* Equitable Commerce. *In New York he
teamed up with Stephen Pearl Andrews, his disciple and
chief exponent, and established the eccentric town of Modern Times on Long Island.*

( 1. )  THE PROPER, LEGITIMATE, JUST REWARD OF LABOR.

With regard to the first proposition, (marked 1,) the reward of
labor, it is perhaps, scarcely necessary to add anything to what
has been said within the last twenty years on this subject: it is
now evident to all eyes, that labor does not obtain its legitimate
reward; but on the contrary, that those who work the hardest, fare
the worst. The most elegant and costly houses, coaches, clothing,
food, and luxuries of all kinds are in the hands of those who never
made either of them, nor ever did any useful thing for themselves
or for society; while those who made all, and maintained themselves at the same time, are shiver[ing] in miserable homes, or
pining in prisons or poor-houses, or starving in the streets.

Machinery has thrown workmen out of their tenth-paid employment, and this machinery is also owned by those who never
made it, nor gave any equivalent in their own labor for it. These
starving workmen have no resource but upon the soil; but they
find that this also, is under the control of those who never made it,
nor ever did any thing as an equivalent for it. At this point of
starvation, we *must* have remedy, or, confusion.

At this point, society must attend to the rights of labor, and
settle, once for all, the great problem of its just reward. This appears to demand a discrimination, a *disconnection,* a DISUNION
between COST and *Value.*

If a traveller, in a hot day, stop at a farm house, and ask for a
drink of water, he generally gets it without any thought of price.
Why?—Because it *costs* nothing, or its cost is immaterial. If the
traveller was so thirsty that he would give a dollar for the water,
rather than not have it, this would be the *value* of the water to
him; and if the farmer were to charge this price, he would be act-

ing upon the principle that *"The price of a thing should be what it will bring"*, which is the motto and spirit of all the principal commerce of the world; and if he were to stop up all the neighboring springs, and cut off all supplies of water from other sources, and compel travellers to depend solely on him for water and then should charge them a hundred dollars for a drink, he would be acting precisely upon the principle on which all the main business of the world has been conducted from time immemorial. . . .

The *value* of a loaf of bread to a starving man, is equivalent to the value of his life, and if the "price of a thing" should be "what it will bring," then one might properly demand of the starving man, his whole future life in servitude as the price of the loaf! But, any one who should make such a demand, would be looked upon as insane, a cannibal, and one simultaneous voice would denounce the outrageous injustice, and cry aloud for retribution! Why? What is it that constitutes the cannibalism in this case? Is it not setting a price upon the bread according to its VALUE instead of its COST. If the producers and venders of the bread had bestowed one hour's labor upon its production and in passing it to the starving man, then some other articles which *cost* its producer and vender an hour's *equivalent* labor, would be a natural and just compensation for the loaf. I have placed emphasis on the idea of *equivalent* labor, because it appears that we must *discriminate* between different kinds of labor, some being more disagreeable, more repugnant, require a more COSTLY draft upon our ease or health than others. The idea of *cost* extends to and embraces this difference. The most repugnant labor being considered the most COSTLY. The idea of cost is also extended to all contingent expenses in production or vending.

A *watch* has a *cost* and a value. The COST consists of the amount of labor bestowed, on the mineral or natural wealth, in converting into metal, the labor bestowed by the workmen in constructing the watch, the wear of tools, the rent, firewood, insurance, taxes, clerkship, and various other contingent expenses of its manufacturer, together with the labor expended in its transmission from him to its vender; and the labor and contingent expenses of the vender in passing it to the one who uses it. . . . The *value* of a well made watch, depends upon the natural qualities of the metals or minerals employed, upon the natural qualities or principles of its mechanism, upon the uses to which it is applied, and upon the fancy or wants of the purchaser. It would be different with every different watch, with every purchaser, and its value would change every day in the hands of the same purchaser, and with every different use to which he applied it.

Now, among this multitude of *values*, which one should be selected to set a price upon? or, should the price be made to vary and fluctuate according to these fluctuating *values!* and never be completely sold, but only from hour to hour! Common sense, answers NEITHER. But, that these *values* like those of sunshine and air, are of right, the equal property of all; no one has a right to set any price whatever upon them. COST, then, is the only rational ground of price, even in the most complicated transactions; yet, *value* is made almost entirely the governing principle in almost all the commerce of *what is called civilised society!* . . .

We want a circulating medium that is a definite *representative* of a definite quantity of property, and *nothing but a representative:* so that when we cannot make direct equivalent exchanges of property, we can supply the deficiency with its definite representative, which will stand in its place. And this should not have any reference to the value of property, but only to its COST, so that if I get a bushel of wheat of you, I give you the representative of shoe-making, with which you should be able to obtain from the shoe-maker as much labor as you bestowed on the wheat—cost for cost in equivalent quantities; and to effect these exchanges with facility, each one must always have a plenty of this representative on hand, or be able to make it on the occasion, and so adapt the supply of the circulating medium to the demand for it—a problem that never has yet been solved by any financiers in the world, nor ever will be while *value* is taken into the account of price. The remark is common, that "if money was plenty we would purchase many things that we cannot for want of it." Here, no exchange takes place that otherwise would and division will always be in proportion to exchange or sales. Where there is no circulating medium, there cannot be much exchange or division. On the other hand, where every one has a plenty of the circulating medium, always at hand, exchanges and division of labor would not be limited for want of money. A note given by each individual for his own labor estimated by its cost, is perfectly legitimate and competent for all the purposes of a circulating medium. It is based upon the bone and muscle, the manual powers, the talents and resources, the property, and property producing powers of the *whole people*—the soundest of all foundations, and a circulating medium of the only kind that ever ought to have been issued. The only objection to it is, that it would immediately abolish all the great money transactions of the world—all banks and banking operations—all stock-jobbing, money corporations and money movements—all systems of finance, all systems of national policy and commercial corruption—abolish all distinctions of rich and poor—compel everyone to live and enjoy at his own cost, and would contribute largely to restore the world to order, peace, and harmony.

9.

## *John Pickering:*
## THE WORKINGMAN'S POLITICAL ECONOMY *
## [1847]

*John Pickering was a member of one of Josiah Warren's "anarchist" communities and presented a most systematic defense of the movement in* The Working Man's Political Economy, *which is a severe attack upon the capitalist. He grounded his criticism upon a labor theory of value, holding that the quantity of labor determined the cost of production and was thus the regulator of the exchange value of all products, including specie. He conceived of governments as nothing more than combinations of idle capitalists, landlords, and money lords invented for the purpose of stifling free competition. Free homesteads would solve all social problems by giving labor its full product. He called upon his readers to support National Reform newspapers, especially the New York* Young America.

The reasoning of the robber is similar to that of the capitalist: the difference, which is slight, will be shown presently.

Suppose A should meet B in a solitary place; A has a pistol, but

* John Pickering: *The Workingman's Political Economy* (Cincinnati, Ohio: 1847), 41–2, 48, 95–6, 183–4.

destitute of money or bread; B has three dollars in his pocket; A says, deliver your money, presenting the pistol, and thereby putting B in fear of a sudden death, but who, rather than suffer, is *willing* to part with his purse. In common language, we would call this compulsion; yet, in reality, it is only choosing between two evils. Let us suppose, further, that B remonstrates, and says, do not rob me entirely, or I shall be ruined; I shall want for bread. A then sympathizes with B, and finally takes but two dollars, leaving him one to sustain him on his journey. This kind of transaction A performs each day in succession, but every day finds a new victim. Again suppose: C, having all the comforts of life in abundance much more than he can consume, finds D in a ditch, unable to get out, in fear of starvation, and begs C to help him out. What will you pay me? says C. I have nothing to pay with, which is the reason that I am lying here, answers D. Can you spin out dollars? and how many can you spin out in a day? D answers, I can spin out three dollars a day; but I have nothing to buy fuel with, to set me in motion. Well, my good fellow, says C, if you will set yourself to work, and spin out three dollars a day, (but mind, all the dollars are mine, except the cost of the fuel which is necessary to keep you in motion,) I will have the generosity to help you out. Well, the poor fellow, after considering the matter over, and being in fear of a painful, lingering death by starvation, rather than suffer which, is willing to accept C's terms. In this case, there is as much compulsory action as there is in the case of A and B, with but this difference: A runs some risk in challenging B, because he does not know whether he is armed or not, until he tries the experiment. Again he runs a great risk in regard to the law: he also well knows that B has a remedy, in law, against him. To meet these dangers, it is necessary to evince a spirit of enterprize and courage: in fact, it requires some bravery. In both cases, the victims suffer the loss of the same amount of property; but A's victim goes on his way rejoicing, while, on the other hand, C's victim is consigned to everlasting slavery, without hope of redemption. In both cases, they are conquered by the fear of death: in B's case, the fear of death is produced, at the time, by the courage and bravery of his conquerer; but in D's case, the fear of death has been produced as certainly by his conquerer, as in the case of B, but in a different manner, to wit: by C's influence in contriving those paradoxical and unnatural institutions, which were intended to consign him to the ditch. Our paradoxical and unnatural institutions of society consign A to a dungeon, and to C they award riches, honor, dignity and respect. Why these decisions? we ask. Is A condemned for his courage and bravery, and for risking his life to get bread; and C rewarded for his cowardly treason, in laying secret and unseen contrivances to bring his victim to the fear of death, though he is himself in want of nothing? for this appears to be all the real difference in the two cases. If these be the true grounds of the decisions, Mr. Paley may well call such institutions *"paradoxical and unnatural."*

. . . It may now be asked, what is property? We answer, the products of labor; nothing else can be. . . .

### FUNDAMENTAL ERRORS OF GOVERNMENTS.

The fundamental errors of governments may be all classed under three heads.

The first grand error has been the establishment of the principle, that property rightly belongs not to him that makes it, but to him that has power to take it from him that does make it. From this error, springs almost all the wars and contentions between tribes, nations, kings and individuals. The robber justifies himself on the ground of the admission of this error, somewhat consistently too.

The second is in confirming the usurpations of kingly despots in seizing the elements of Nature; making them their own private property, and dictating the terms upon which the rest of mankind might enjoy them. This error is the grand lever by which the king and the capitalist are enabled to deprive the producers of wealth of the fruits of their industry; reduce them to beggary, starvation and death, just as it may suit their pleasure.

The third, is the right claimed by kings and governments of interfering with the products of labor, by causing them to represent more labor than it has cost to produce them; and by making them cost more labor than is required to produce them. From the prevalence of this error, arises the right of kings and governments to debase the currency of a country, either by the means of base metal, or paper money; thereby swindling the producers of wealth out of the fruits of their industry: also, all the cheating, swindling tricks of commerce, banking, shaving, &c.

In lieu of the above errors, we propose some fundamental curative truths; by the universal understanding of which, most of the moral and social evils, which at present afflict and destroy the peace of mankind, will be destroyed.

First. Let the producers of property be the rightful owners of what they produce; and, when given in exchange for other property, let it be for an equivalent; that is, of equal cost. This, we contend, every man has an unequivocal right to, or a weak or poor man has no right to live. Has a man a right to his own limbs? Surely, no man will deny this. But we deny that he has any better right to his own limbs, than he has to whatever is produced by them. If any man has a right to take from another any portion of what he makes, what portion is it? If it is in proportion to his power, then it follows, as a matter of course, that if A be strong enough, or rich enough, he may take from B every thing he makes; and, finally, starve him to death. But this right we deny. The only just and rightful first owner to a piece of property, is he who makes it.

Second. Let all laws and customs be abolished which confound the natural or intrinsic value of the elements of nature with the products of man's labor. The custom of man in assuming exclusive ownership of the elements of nature, with the right to make another pay him for the use of them, is too glaring an absurdity to require a serious argument. What would you think of a man who should undertake to require other men to pay him daily a certain sum of money; say half as much as he could earn, or half a day's labor, because he enjoyed the sunshine, or because he breathed the atmosphere? Would you not think this a very strange requirement? Surely, you would. But, strange as it may appear, this very thing is effected, virtually, to an immense extent, in the form of *rent for the use of land.* There is just as much propriety and honesty in exacting pay for the use of either, because no man ever did or can make either; therefore, has no right to sell or exact pay for the use of either. All this, and much more tyranny and injustice arises from the error of confounding the value of the elements of nature with that of human labor, and has perplexed and bewildered almost all writers on Political Economy, and has rendered their works so unintelligible, so "unnatural and paradoxical. . . ."

Third. For a remedy for the third grand error, we propose that the gold and silver coins correspond with the standard weights of the country, by which all other commodities are weighed. . . .

Thus, then, is the grand problem of man's misery, and his moral, social, and political relations, solved, and our task is nearly done. Let but the down-trodden millions understand these principles, and, in proportion as they do, so does the day of their redemption draw nigh. And, ere long, Justice, who has been banished from the earth ever since governments began, will find an abiding place among men, and we shall see her as she really is—a being most lovely to behold. Not with a terrible, dark and frightful withering frown, and eyes bandaged; but with a countenance brightly beaming with a benevolent and cheerful smile, and eyes wide open. . . . Then may every man sit peaceably under his own vine and fig tree, and there shall be none in the land to make him afraid.

Producers of wealth, wake up; organize yourselves into societies, associations, and reading clubs; discuss the subject of your wrongs; circulate and encourage "National Reform" newspapers, especially "Young America," the great pioneer of Reform. Institute courts of Humanity, for the purpose of testing the validity of governmental acts, whether they be in accordance with the law of immutable justice, and the common rights of Humanity, or not. Make known the results of your decisions to your suffering fellow men, in order that they may learn how to cast off those chains which so grievously bind, degrade and enslave them.

## 10.

### *Edward Kellogg:*
### LABOR AND OTHER CAPITAL *
### [1849]

*Edward Kellogg (1790–1858), a native of Connecticut, became a wholesale dry-goods merchant. Struck by the panic of 1837, he began to contemplate the evils of the monetary*

\* Edward Kellogg: *Labor and Other Capital* (New York: 1849), xi–xii, xv–xvi, xxxi, xxxiv.

*system, which he believed was controlled by Wall Street
money jobbers. He became convinced that money should be
issued by the government. His real-estate activities in Brooklyn enabled him to retire in 1843 and devote himself to the
study of finance. In 1843 his book* Currency, the Evil and
the Remedy *appeared in newspaper form and was circulated
with Horace Greeley's aid.* Labor and Other Capital *was
published six years later without attracting much notice. But
after his death reprints of this book earned him the title
"father of Greenbackism."*

The laboring classes of all civilized nations have been, and are,
as a body, poor. Nearly all wealth is the production of labor; therefore, laborers would have possessed it, had not something inter-
vened to prevent this natural result. Even in our own country,
where the reward of labor is greater than in most others, some
cause is operating with continual and growing effect to separate
production from the producer. The wrong is evident, but neither
statesmen nor philanthropists have traced it to its true source;
and hence they have not been able to project any plan sufficient
for its removal.

The design of the present volume is to show the true cause; and
to illustrate its operation so plainly and variously, that any ordinary mind may easily perceive how it has produced and continued
this unnatural oppression of laborers. It will also be shown, with
equal clearness, that a simple and effectual remedy can be applied
to the removal of the evil. A good government must have some
system by which it can secure the distribution of property according to the earnings of labor, and at the same time strictly preserve
the rights of property: and no government, whether republican
or not, that fails in these particulars, can ensure the freedom and
happiness of the people and become permanent. . . .

To obtain *labor* without rendering a fair equivalent, is also a
violation of the rights of property.

(*Property, value, or capital,* is anything which, either by combination, or inherently, possesses the means of affording support,
comforts, or luxuries to man. *Labor* is a species of capital, and a
most important one—without which, all other kinds of capital
would be nearly if not wholly useless; for even food of spontaneous growth could not be gathered without labor. Labor is not,

however, generally considered as capital, but as something very inferior to property and products. I have, therefore, found it convenient, in compliance with popular usage, to speak of labor and capital as distinct from each other. *Capital, throughout the treatise, signifies all property but labor, or ability to labor.*)

*Property* is almost entirely the product of labor. Labor has effected every improvement in our country; it has built our cities; cleared, fenced, and improved our farms; constructed our ships, railroads and canals. In short, every comfort of life is the fruit of past or present labor. To appreciate more fully the value of labor, suppose the laborers in this or in any other civilized nation to remain idle for the brief term of five years, and subsist upon the spontaneous productions of the earth. Let the manufacturer cease to toil, commerce be suspended, and gold and silver, however abundant, and however pure and malleable, would cease to be precious to a starving people, compared with food, and with the labor of man, which produces it.

A moderate amount of labor readily produces an abundant supply of necessaries and comforts for man; but the present distribution of these products is such, that a large number of those who labor much more than their share in the production, receive a very small proportion of the products, while the larger proportion accumulates in the possession of those who are employed neither in producing, nor in distributing them. The greater portion of the human family toil day by day for a scanty subsistence, and are destitute of the time and means for social and intellectual culture. The industrious poor, as a class, do not obtain even a competence. Their destitution often induces them to trespass against existing laws, to obtain a small proportion of that, which, under just laws, would be abundantly awarded to them as a fair compensation for their labor. All candid men will acknowledge this truth, that wealth is not distributed in accordance with either the physical or the mental usefulness of those who obtain it. Opposed to the masses who live in toil and poverty, is a small proportion of the human race, surrounded by all the appliances of luxury, and living in comparative idleness; while their abundant means of social and intellectual culture are too often neglected, or rendered useless by indolence and self-indulgence. These extremes of wealth and poverty, of luxury and want, of idleness and labor, are great, somewhat in proportion to the antiquity of the nation, or the length of time that a certain law, or system, has been in operation. . . .

The unfair distribution of wealth is not caused by over-production, but by an unjust *standard of distribution.* Distribution is regulated and effected by the standard of value, which is money. Money, as will be hereafter shown, exercises astonishing power throughout every department of business and industrial occupation. *Unjust distribution originates in wrong legislation.* When monetary laws shall be made equitable, present labor will naturally receive a just proportion of present products, and capital will likewise receive a just reward for its use. . . .

Governments should understand the nature and uses of money, and realize that the currency of a nation, instead of being a standard according to which, and a power by which, a few capitalists may monopolize the greater part of the earnings of labor, should be a standard and power which *should distribute products to producers,* according to their labor expended in the production.

## 11.

### The Journeymen Printers of Philadelphia:
#### AN ADVERTISEMENT *
#### [October 8, 1850]

*This advertisement appeared on the flyleaf of a special edition of Daniel De Foe's* Robinson Crusoe, *published by the Journeymen Printers' Union of Philadelphia. Three editions of this work were published to make up a strike fund. After several meetings, beginning on June 27, 1850, an organization of Journeymen Printers was formed to effectuate a scale of "prices" that was adopted on July 20. A constitution limiting apprentices was approved August 10. The refusal of the employers to accept the scale on September 2 caused a lockout of nearly one hundred workers. The ensuing strike continued until December, when the union gave way on its bylaws limiting apprentices.*

* Daniel De Foe: *The Life and Adventures of Robinson Crusoe* . . . (Philadelphia: 1850), iii–iv.

On the 2d of September, the time fixed for carrying into effect the new scale of prices, some of the employers refused to accede thereto, in consequence of which nearly 100 members of the Union were thrown out of work. To enable these to maintain themselves in their effort to secure what a majority of the employers conceded to be a just remuneration for their labour, the Union resolved to publish this work, thereby to give partial employment to its members, during the period when they might be under the necessity of remaining *on a strike.* The public have so well supported the Union in this work, that two editions (the first of 1000 and the second of 2000 copies) were subscribed for immediately on the appearance of the first number. A third and enlarged edition is now called for, and the Union is greatly encouraged by the prospect of a still more rapid and extensive sale.

The *strike* has now continued five weeks; and only five individuals have left the cause to which they had solemnly pledged themselves and subscribed their names. These, in printers' language, are denominated *rats,* and as such, no doubt, they will find snares set by themselves at every opening to their lurking places.

This movement of the Journeymen Printers' Union must also be looked upon as one of the highest importance, not only with reference to the pecuniary interests of its members, but in regard to its influence upon every branch of industry and trade. It now proposes (forced thereto by necessity) a practical test of the question, whether the wants of the public in its line of business cannot be better supplied, and at *cheaper rates,* by the journeymen assuming the direction of their own labour, than these wants are now supplied by employers and publishers, and at the same time secure for themselves a *higher remuneration.* Further, it is an effort to redeem men from the virtual slavery into which they have been reduced by the unrighteous ascendency of capital. The truth cannot be denied, that capital is the result or product of man's intellectual and physical exertion, that its *virtue* altogether depends upon the *life it receives* from a right application of the mind and sweat of its present victims. But it has reversed both the natural and revealed law. The creature usurps the position of its creator, and demands for itself that subjection and service which it is always beholden to give. God gave life and reason to man, wherefore reverence and obedience to his Creator are his eternal duty.

Such is the doctrine of Christianity, of all religious and moral codes, and of our beloved *American institutions.*

Should the Union be compelled to continue in its present position, it may, therefore, confidently reckon upon the continued favour of the American people; and, if it succeeds in establishing the great principles for which its members are contending, it will occupy a brilliant page in the history of progress and trade.

PHILADELPHIA, *October 8th, 1850.*

As THE MEMBER of an infant empire, as a Philanthropist by character, and (if I may be allowed the expression) as a Citizen of the great republic of humanity at large; I cannot help turning my attention sometimes to this subject. I would be understood to mean, I cannot avoid reflecting with pleasure on the probable influence that commerce may hereafter have on human manners and society in general. On these occasions I consider how mankind may be connected like one great family in fraternal ties. I indulge a fond, perhaps an enthusiastic idea, that as the world is evidently much less barbarous than it has been, its melioration must still be progressive; that nations are becoming more humanized in their policy, that the subjects of ambition and causes for hostility are daily diminishing, and, in fine, that the period is not very remote, when the benefits of a liberal and free commerce will, pretty generally, succeed to the devastations and horrors of war.

—— GEORGE WASHINGTON:

LETTER TO MARQUIS DE LAFAYETTE, AUGUST 15, 1786 *

* W. C. Ford (ed.): *The Writings of George Washington,* 14 v. (New York: 1889–93), XI, 58–9.